THE MERLEAU-PONTY AESTHETICS READER

Northwestern University
Studies in Phenomenology
and
Existential Philosophy

Edited with an Introduction by

Galen A. Johnson

Michael B. Smith,
Translation Editor

THE MERLEAU-PONTY AESTHETICS READER: PHILOSOPHY AND PAINTING

Northwestern University Press
Evanston, Illinois

1993

Northwestern University Press
Evanston, Illinois 60208-4210

Library of Congress Cataloging-in-Publication Data

Merleau-Ponty, Maurice, 1908–1961.
    The Merleau-Ponty aesthetics reader : philosophy and painting /
edited with an introduction by Galen A. Johnson ; Michael B. Smith,
translation editor.
        p.   cm. — (Northwestern University studies in phenomenology
and existential philosophy)
    Includes bibliographical references.
    ISBN 0-8101-1073-3 (cloth : alk. paper). — ISBN 0-8101-1074-1
(pbk. : alk. paper)
    1. Aesthetics, French—20th century.   I. Johnson, Galen A., 1948–
. II. Smith, Michael B. (Michael Bradley), 1940–   . III. Title.
IV. Series: Northwestern University studies in phenomenology &
existential philosophy.
B2430.M3762E5   1993
111′.85—dc20   93-33902
                                                                    CIP

The paper used in this publication meets the minimum requirements of the American
National Standard for Information Sciences—Permanence of Paper for Printed Library
Materials, ANSI Z39.48-1984.

Contents

Acknowledgments

The editors wish to acknowledge gratefully the generous assistance of the staff of the Archives at Collège de France in Paris, France, and the support of this project by the editorial staff of the Northwestern University Press, in particular, Susan Harris, managing editor. We also thank Kathy Gann of Berry College's Research Department for her exemplary professional assistance with final manuscript preparation. Forrest Williams and Richard McCleary made suggestions for the translation revisions of the three Merleau-Ponty essays, and we express our thanks. Hugh Silverman, Patrick Burke, Stephen Watson, and Véronique Fóti, experienced Merleau-Ponty scholars and aestheticians, helped shape the early stages of this project. We thank Katia Stieglitz of the Artists Rights Society in New York City and Linda Mugica, curator of the University of Rhode Island Fine Arts slide collection, for their help with locating and securing permissions for the art work reproduced in the book. Judith Haughton, photographer at University of Rhode Island, provided help with the illustrations. Finally, a word of sincere thanks is expressed to the Office of the Provost of the University of Rhode Island for travel grants in support of this project.

The essays listed below and reprinted here in part 3 originally appeared in other places. The editors express their thanks to the following sources for permission to reprint these works:

Forrest Williams, "Cézanne and French Phenomenology," *Journal of Aesthetics and Art Criticism* 12 (June 1954), 481–92.

Alphonse de Waelhens, "Merleau-Ponty philosophe de

la peinture," *Revue de Métaphysique et de Morale* 67, no. 4 (Oct.–Dec. 1962), 431–49.

Michael B. Smith, "L'ésthétique de Merleau-Ponty," *Les Etudes Philosophiques* 1 (1988), 73–98.

Marjorie Grene, "The Aesthetic Dialogue of Sartre and Merleau-Ponty," *Journal of the British Society for Phenomenology* 1 (May 1970), 59–72.

Linda Singer, "Merleau-Ponty on the Concept of Style," *Man and World* 14 (1981), 153–63.

Olivier Mongin, "Depuis Lascaux," *Esprit* 66 (June 1982), 67–76.

Mikel Dufrenne, "Eye and Mind," in *In the Presence of the Sensuous*, ed. Mark Roberts and Dennis Gallagher (Atlantic Highlands: Humanities Press, 1987), 69–74.

Hugh J. Silverman, "Cézanne's Mirror Stage," *Journal of Aesthetics and Art Criticism* 40, no. 4 (Summer 1982), 369–79.

Jacques Taminiaux, "The Thinker and the Painter," in *Merleau-Ponty Vivant*, ed. M. C. Dillon (New York: SUNY Press, 1991), 195–212.

Véronique M. Fóti, "The Dimension of Color," *International Studies in Philosophy* 22, no. 3 (1990), 13–28.

Jean-François Lyotard, excerpts from *Discours, figure*, 4th ed. (Paris: Klincksieck, 1985), 18–23, 53–59.

Jean-François Lyotard, "Philosophy and Painting in the Age of Experimentation," trans. M. Brewer and D. Brewer, in *Camera Obscura* (Baltimore: The Johns Hopkins University Press, 1984), 110–25.

Rene Magritte, "Letter to Alphonse de Waelhens (28 April 1962)," in *Magritte: Signs and Images*, ed. Harry Torczyner, trans. Richard Miller (New York: Harry N. Abrams, Inc., 1977), 55. © 1992 C. Hersovici/ARS, New York.

Wayne J. Froman, "Action Painting and the World as Picture," *Journal of Aesthetics and Art Criticism* 46 (Summer 1988), 469–75.

Abbreviations

Abbreviations of titles of Merleau-Ponty's works in English translation are given in Roman print; abbreviations of the original French editions are italicized. References to the three essays included in this volume cite both earlier publications and their pagination here.

AD   *Adventures of the Dialectic*, trans. Joseph Bien (Evanston: Northwestern University Press, 1973).

AD   *Les aventures de la dialectique* (Paris: Gallimard, 1955).

CD   "Cézanne's Doubt" (pp. 59–75 in this volume).

EM   "Eye and Mind" (pp. 121–49).

EP   *Eloge de la philosophie* (Paris: Gallimard, 1953).

OE   "L'oeil et l'esprit" (Paris: Gallimard, 1964).

HT   *Humanism and Terror*, trans. John O'Neill (Boston: Beacon Press, 1969).

HT   *Humanisme et terreur* (Paris: Gallimard, 1947).

ILVS   "Indirect Language and the Voices of Silence" (pp. 76–120).

IPP   *In Praise of Philosophy*, trans. John Wild and James Edie (Evanston: Northwestern University Press, 1963).

PhP   *Phenomenology of Perception*, trans. Colin Smith (London: Routledge and Kegan Paul, 1962).

PP   *Phénoménologie de la perception* (Paris: Gallimard, 1945).

PrP   *The Primacy of Perception and Other Essays*, ed.

	James Edie (Evanston: Northwestern University Press, 1964).
PW	*The Prose of the World*, trans. John O'Neill (Evanston: Northwestern University Press, 1973).
PM	*La prose du monde* (Paris: Gallimard, 1969).
RMM	"Un inédit de Maurice Merleau-Ponty," *Revue de Métaphysique et de Morale* 67, no. 4 (1962), 400–409.
S	*Signs*, trans. Richard C. McCleary (Evanston: Northwestern University Press, 1964).
S	*Signes* (Paris: Gallimard, 1960).
SB	*The Structure of Behavior*, trans. Alden L. Fisher (Boston: Beacon Press, 1963).
SC	*La structure du comportement* (Paris: Presses Universitaires de France, 1945; 3d ed., 1963).
SNS	*Sense and Non-Sense*, trans. Hubert L. Dreyfus and Patricia Allen Dreyfus (Evanston: Northwestern University Press, 1964).
SNS	*Sens et non-sens* (Paris: Nagel, 1948; 4th ed., 1963).
TLCF	*Themes from the Lectures at the Collège de France, 1952–60*, trans. John O'Neill (Evanston: Northwestern University Press, 1970).
RCCF	*Résumés de cours: Collège de France, 1952–60* (Paris: Gallimard, 1968).
VI	*The Visible and the Invisible*, trans. Alphonso Lingis (Evanston: Northwestern University Press, 1968).
VI	*Le visible et l'invisible* (Paris: Gallimard, 1964).

Preface

Though it is no longer necessary to introduce Maurice Merleau-Ponty to readers in English, his writings on the arts, especially modern painting, are less well-known than many of his other works. His writings have now all appeared in English translation, and *Phenomenology of Perception* (1945) and *The Visible and the Invisible* (1964) have been incorporated into the celebrated philosophical works of our century. His essays on painting have been scattered in three different sources.[1] By assembling them together and undertaking a detailed, linear study of them, it is possible to watch unfold a philosophy of painting that offers a unique conceptualization of the aesthetic experience of the artist, of perception and imagination, of the artwork as a sign, and of the ontology of the work of art. To this study this book is devoted.

Merleau-Ponty wrote three essays on painting: "Cézanne's Doubt" (1945), "Indirect Language and the Voices of Silence" (1952), and "Eye and Mind" (1960). These essays are among the most original of his works, the most beautiful, and the only area of his thought that he completed before his sudden death in 1961 at the age of fifty-three. In addition to their contribution to contemporary aesthetics, they provide an excellent introduction to the development of Merleau-Ponty's philosophy across his career (1945, 1952, 1960) from the existential phenomenology of "Cézanne's Doubt" influenced by Edmund Husserl, to structuralism in "Indirect Language and the Voices of Silence" in dispute with Jean-Paul Sartre and André Malraux, and then to the formulation of an original ontology in "Eye and Mind" in implicit dialogue with Martin Heidegger. With this development, Merleau-Ponty became a crucial transitional figure in the change from a modern to a postmodern philosophy of art.

The Merleau-Ponty Aesthetics Reader gathers together into one volume all three of Merleau-Ponty's essays on painting in improved English translations by Michael B. Smith. The essays are ordered chronologically and introduced by the editor with respect to text and context, painters and sources, and philosophic themes. It is hoped that these introductions will provide context, scholarly information, and sufficient enumeration and elaboration of the philosophy of painting in each of the essays both to aid first-time readers and to interest long-time Merleau-Ponty scholars.

Included here are reproductions of seven photographs of artworks that Merleau-Ponty selected for inclusion in the original *Art de France* and Gallimard editions of "L'oeil et l'esprit," two oil paintings by Paul Klee and Nicholas de Stael, two drawings by Albert Giacometti and Henri Matisse, a watercolor by Cézanne, and two sculptures by Auguste Rodin and Germaine Richier. These illustrate Merleau-Ponty's philosophic interest in color, line, and movement in the plastic arts, as well as the progress of his own philosophy of painting toward deepened appreciation of modern abstract painting. Also included is a reproduction of the original drawing that Albert Giacometti did as the frontispiece for Merleau-Ponty's 1956 history of philosophy entitled *Les philosophes célèbres*. Since this work has not been translated in an English edition, this is the first time this drawing has been reproduced in an English language edition of Merleau-Ponty's works.

The final part of the book publishes some of the best interpretive and critical essays that have been written regarding Merleau-Ponty's philosophy of painting. These begin from early essays by two Merleau-Ponty scholars who were Merleau-Ponty's students, Forrest Williams and Alphonse de Waehlens. Forrest Williams has revised his essay for this volume. In the middle are important essays on Merleau-Ponty's philosophy of painting by many of the best-known interpreters of his aesthetic ideas since Merleau-Ponty's death in 1961. The harshest critical voice comes from the postmodern aesthetic theorist, Jean-François Lyotard. We have also included a letter from

René Magritte, well-known Belgian surrealist, addressed to Alphonse de Waehlens regarding "Eye and Mind." The interpretive essays conclude with an original work by Robert Burch regarding Merleau-Ponty and Heidegger.

The Merleau-Ponty Aesthetics Reader is focused almost entirely on Merleau-Ponty's engagement with the meaning of modern painting: the artist's phenomenological work with color, the institutions of the museum and offical art, style and the history of painting, imagination and perception, the artwork as sign and the possibility of truth in painting, and the ontology of the visible and invisible world as shown forth in the painter's work. Modern sculpture is treated only briefly in "Eye and Mind," film, photography and music even more briefly, and dance not at all. We have chosen not to enlarge the scope of this volume to include Merleau-Ponty's philosophy of literature, except as it appears in his evaluation of Sartre's "What is Literature?" in the context of his essay "Indirect Language and the Voices of Silence." Merleau-Ponty's interest in literature was extensive and his teaching and writing on this aspect of aesthetic theory substantial, including his 1947 course on modern poetry at the University at Lyon, "The Novel and Metaphysics" (1945) in *Sense and Non-Sense*, and *The Prose of the World* (1953). A detailed and systematic study of these works and the philosophical questions of literary meaning would be a welcome complement to this philosophy of painting for rounding out the complete picture of Merleau-Ponty's aesthetic theory.

PART   1

INTRODUCTIONS TO MERLEAU-PONTY'S PHILOSOPHY OF PAINTING

Galen A. Johnson

1

Phenomenology and Painting: "Cézanne's Doubt"

Galen A. Johnson

Merleau-Ponty's first essay on painting is linked to the philosopher's study of Husserl and phenomenology, and to the philosophic themes of *Phenomenology of Perception*. "Cézanne's Doubt" articulates the topography of a phenomenology of painting, the main features of which we will outline below. Before we turn to that topic, though, we should make a few essential points regarding the context that surrounds the essay in Merleau-Ponty's itinerary and his reasons for singling out Paul Cézanne for philosophic attention.

Text and Context

"Cézanne's Doubt" was published in 1945. It appeared in December of that year in *Fontaine*, a monthly review of poetry and French letters.[1] Merleau-Ponty also published the essay subsequently without changes in 1948 as the leading chapter in *Sense and Non-Sense*, a collection of his essays from the years 1945 to 1948. In the preface to *Sense and Non-Sense*, he situated the significance of "Cézanne's Doubt" within the context of the philosophic problem of the boundary between reason and unreason. "We must form a new idea of reason," he wrote, one not restricted to logic and mathematics, but wide enough to comprehend the meanings expressed in novels, poems and paintings, even in political actions. "Cézanne is an example of how precariously expression and communication are achieved. Expression is like a step taken in the fog—no one can say where, if anywhere, it will lead" (SNS, 3; *SNS*, 8). The preface concludes by raising Cézanne's life and achievement to the level of an exemplary and inspirational power. In spite of rejection by contemporaries and critics, in spite of Cézanne's own self-doubts whether his work had any meaning or would be understood, Merleau-Ponty wrote that Cézanne had "won out against chance, and men, too, can win provided they will measure the dangers and the task" (SNS, 5; *SNS*, 10).

By the year 1945, Merleau-Ponty had been appointed a Professor of Philosophy at the University of Lyon (1945–48), where he would teach courses in modern philosophy (Malebranche, Leibniz), the history of psychology, and language and communication. In 1946 and 1947, he taught a course in aesthetics and modern painting, and the subsequent year a course in aesthetics and modern poetry. By the year 1945, he had also published two books, *The Structure of Behavior* (1942) and *Phenomenology of Perception* (1945). *The Structure of Behavior* is a work in philosophy of psychology, particularly on Pavlov's theory of classical reflex conditioning and on Gestalt psychology, and it contains few references to painting.[2] *Phenomenology of Perception*, on the other hand, is a work laced throughout with references to Cézanne and modern painting in relation to philosophical questions of space, depth, lighting, color, and color perception.

Between his completion of *The Structure of Behavior* in 1938[3] and 1945 when he published "Cézanne's Doubt" and *Phenomenology of Perception*, Merleau-Ponty had discovered and studied the phenomenology of Edmund Husserl, including many of Husserl's unpublished manuscripts housed at the University of Louvain, Belgium.[4] In the preface to *Phenomenology of Perception*, Merleau-Ponty linked the task of phenomenological description of human experience to the painstaking work of modern writers and painters such as Balzac, Proust, Valery, and Cézanne. Both phenomenology and painting exhibit "the same kind of attentiveness and wonder, the same demand for awareness," and in this way, phenomenology "merges into the general effort of modern thought" (PhP, xxi; *PP*, xvi).

Painters and Sources

"Cézanne's Doubt" concentrates attention on two painters, Paul Cézanne (1839–1906) and Leonardo da Vinci (1452–1519). With respect to Leonardo, the discussion is centered less on his paintings than on his life, and Merleau-Ponty attempts to make a response both to Freud's *Leonardo da Vinci: A Study in Psychosexuality* (1910) and to Paul Valery's essay on Leonardo entitled "Introduction to the Method of Leonardo da Vinci" (1895, 1924).[5] There is passing mention of additional painters in "Cézanne's Doubt"—Monet, Emile Bernard, El Greco, Tintoretto, Delacroix, Courbet, and Pissarro—but the work of these painters is not analyzed. In his later essays on painting, Merleau-Ponty would widen his range of interest to include the works of additional painters such as Matisse and Klee, but in 1945 his attention centered almost exclusively on Cézanne.

There seem to be a number of reasons for Merleau-Ponty's singular interest in Cézanne at this time in his philosophical career. For one thing, Merleau-Ponty obviously loved Cézanne's canvases. He said that if one looks at the work of other painters after seeing Cézanne's paintings, one feels somehow relaxed. Another reason for singling out Cézanne is a more philosophical one, what Merleau-Ponty took to be the phenomenological work with paint done by this artist. Merleau-Ponty uses the phenomenological language he learned from Husserl to describe Cézanne's realistic efforts to "paint from nature" but without using the Renaissance techniques of linear perspective and outline. We will say more about what this means below in outlining the themes of Merleau-Ponty's phenomenology of painting.

A third reason should also be noted, namely Merleau-Ponty's titular theme indicating his interest in Cézanne's self-questioning and his struggle to exist as an artist. The discordance between Cézanne's posthumously recognized achievement and its critical reception during his lifetime is well documented. In 1889, J. K. Huysmans referred to the painter as "an artist with diseased eyes who, in the exasperated apperception of his sight, discovered the preambles of a new art."[6] As late in Cézanne's career as two years before his death and following his 1904 exhibit at the Salon d'Automne in Paris, Marcel Fouquier wrote in *Le Journal* that Cézanne's pictures were awkward, "brutal in handling and dull in effect." In 1899, Georges Lecomte had written in *Revue d'Art*: "Because Cézanne has no other guide than his instincts, he gropes, he hesitates. He evidences the awkwardness and imperfection of a true primitive. Can he really paint landscapes? . . . he runs aground in the art of separating his planes, and in giving the illusion of distance. His meagre knowledge betrays him."[7] Under such withering attack, Cézanne had remained true to his solitary work and the desire for a new artistic expression. About this Merleau-Ponty wrote with admiration, "the artist launches his work just as a man once launched the first word, not knowing whether it will be anything more than a shout" (SNS, 19; *SNS*, 32; CD, 69).

In developing his theory of Cézanne's painting, Merleau-Ponty relied upon several scholarly sources. He studied the letters and conversations between Cézanne and Emile Bernard as they are recorded in Bernard's *Souvenirs de Paul Cézanne* (1912). These are cited throughout "Cézanne's Doubt." Emile Bernard (1868–1941) was himself a painter and art theorist, and a member of Paul Gauguin's symbolist circle at Pont-Aven in Brittany. He published several works on Cézanne's art, and met Cézanne in 1904. It was his conversations and letters with Cézanne between 1904 and Cézanne's death in 1906 that Bernard published in *Souvenirs de Paul Cézanne*. Although filtered by Bernard, these gave Merleau-Ponty access to the thoughts and ideas of Cézanne in his own words.

The *Phenomenology of Perception* rounds out the picture of Merleau-Ponty's sources on Cézanne. The chapter of that work titled "The Thing and the Natural World" contains an extended discussion of Cézanne's use of color and color relationships to create an object, to define space and generate depth. In these pages, Merleau-Ponty cites an additional work by Emile Bernard entitled *La methode de Cézanne* (1920), as well as Joachim Gasquet's biography entitled *Cézanne* (1921, 1926). Gasquet was a young poet and essayist also from Aix-en-Provence who met Cézanne in Paris in 1896. Though more than thirty years Cézanne's junior, he spent considerable time with the painter between 1896 and 1902, when there was a rupture in their relationship, most likely due to Cézanne's customary fear that those close to him were trying to "get their hooks into him."[8] Cézanne painted an unfinished portrait of Gasquet, and in Gasquet's biography, the poet published selections from their conversations and correspondence. In addition to Bernard and Gasquet, Merleau-Ponty also relied upon the analyses of the Austrian art historian, Fritz Novotny, whose 1932 German work analyzes spatial structure and the eclipse of scientific perspective in Cézanne's paintings.[9]

From this grouping of Merleau-Ponty's sources for constructing the essay, it becomes plain that "Cézanne's Doubt" should be classified together with the antiformalist Cézanne interpretations. The cubist and formalist geometrical interpretations of Cézanne's works had already emerged by the time Merleau-Ponty wrote his essay, particularly in Roger Fry's landmark formalist study published in 1927.[10] Formalist interpretations focused on Cézanne's design, pure form, and use of line

and planes on the two-dimensional surface. It took these to be of superior value to his evocation of three-dimensional space, his use of color,
and his representation of any particular subject matter. Merleau-Ponty
was also little concerned with chronological or art historical considerations regarding Cézanne's place in relation to his predecessors and
successors. Though Merleau-Ponty discusses the influence of the impressionists, particularly Pissarro, on Cézanne's turn to nature, he emphasizes that Cézanne broke with the impressionist aesthetic in his effort
to create a new expression of nature. To the extent that Merleau-ponty
was interested in Cézanne's life and his struggles to exist as an artist in
relation to the critics, the Ecole des Beaux-Arts, the salons and museums, his interpretation bears some affinity to the work of later social
historians on Cézanne such as that of Meyer Shapiro.[11] Nevertheless,
though Merleau-Ponty was keenly interested in political philosophy, especially Marxism, at this time, and in *Sense and Non-Sense* brought together his essay on Cézanne with essays on Marxism and politics, his
interpretation omits much that we might have expected him to say regarding Cézanne's poverty, class, and lack of social status. The essay
treats the case of Cézanne quite individualistically, at least three times
referring to Cézanne's "genius" (SNS, 9, 10, 14; *SNS*, 16, 17, 25; CD,
59, 60, 64).

Merleau-Ponty was clearly interested in Cézanne as a colorist and,
above all, for presenting us with a paradigm for prescientific perceptual
experience of the natural world in his landscapes and still lifes. "The
world is a mass without gaps, a system of colors," Merleau-Ponty wrote.
"If the painter is to express the world, the arrangement of his colors
must carry with it this indivisible whole" (SNS, 15; *SNS*, 26; CD, 65).
When the color is at its richest, the form will have reached its fullness.
Merleau-Ponty found in Cézanne a supreme example of phenomenological work with paint. We should now turn our attention more explicitly to
the philosophical themes expressed in "Cézanne's Doubt," and outline
the main features of the topography of Merleau-Ponty's 1945 phenomenological theory of painting.

Philosophical Themes:
Phenomenology and Painting

Merleau-Ponty developed the idea of phenomenology in *Phenomenology
of Perception* based on the philosophy of Edmund Husserl (1859–1938).

He took Husserl to have articulated not a doctrine or a system of thought, but a new way of describing the meaning of human experience in the world that would not fall prey to the impasses of either rationalism or empiricism—the problems of mind and body, solipsism, and skepticism. Husserl had introduced the phenomenological *epoché* (bracketing, reduction) as a means for consciousness to free itself from the presuppositions of the modern Galilean scientific and Cartesian philosophical tradition, particularly that of the subject-object, self-world split. Phenomenology sought to gain access to the phenomena and their essential forms in the way they actually appear, not as they are "supposed" to appear according to the scientific concepts of our "natural attitude." In *Ideas I*, Husserl had articulated the phenomenological "principle of principles": human experience (*Erfahrung*) is authoritative for knowledge, and what is given in human experience is to be accepted as it is given and within the limits of its givenness.[12]

Merleau-Ponty expressed Husserl's "principle of principles" as the thesis of the "primacy of perception." However, he did not only appropriate Husserl's phenomenology, he also deformed it by pushing Husserl's remnant intellectualism based on the primacy of *consciousness* downward toward a new philosophy of the human body. By "perception" Merleau-Ponty referred to our kinaesthetic, prescientific lived-bodily presence to the world. We are a living bodily system (*le corps propre*) prior to the body-object that is constructed by science or medicine. This lived body includes our customary spatial level for operating on the world, our grasp, our style of bodily movement, our protentional and retentional sense of time, and our sense of the constancy of colors and things. Both Husserl and Merleau-Ponty were phenomenologists, but what they meant by "experience" separated them. Husserl understood "phenomena" from within the immanent history of consciousness, Merleau-Ponty from the worldly standpoint of bodily incarnation and intersubjective, historical situation. Here is how Merleau-Ponty compactly elaborated the thesis of the "primacy of perception" shortly after publication of the *Phenomenology*:

> By these words, "the primacy of perception," we mean that the experience of perception is our presence at the moment when things, truths, values are constituted for us, that perception is a nascent *logos*; that it teaches us, outside all dogmatism, the true conditions of objectivity itself; that it summons us to the tasks of knowledge and action. It is not a question of reducing human knowledge to sensation, but of assisting at the birth of this

knowledge, to make it as sensible as the sensible, to recover the consciousness of rationality. (PrP, 25)[13]

Husserl's phenomenology had focused its descriptive attention on single, rather isolated, individual perceptions of a tone or a scene, that is, on *thetic* or judgmental intentionalities. When Husserl had turned his attention to questions of situation and tradition in his last writings, he was interested above all in the history of mathematics and science, such as in his essay entitled "The Origin of Geometry."[14] In *Phenomenology of Perception*, we find Merleau-Ponty's phenomenological attention shifted toward latent or operative intentionalities in an effort to comprehend body, desire, gesture, speech, and the arts as fields of meaning (*sens*). This reflects Merleau-Ponty's philosophical movement "downward" exchanging Husserl's idealist phenomenology centered on single perceptions, logic, geometry, and science for one centered on the traditions of painting, gesture, and speech, in short, on operative bodily existence and the entire range of human symbolic activities.

This brief background should enable us to imagine Merleau-Ponty's *philosophical* excitement in encountering the work of Cézanne and Cézanne's own words about what he was attempting. The problematic of Cézanne's art duplicated the problematic of Merleau-Ponty in *Phenomenology of Perception*, to articulate a philosophical way between naturalism (empiricism) and intellectualism (rationalism). The philosopher and the painter share the same problem, Merleau-Ponty wrote, namely "expressing what *exists*" (SNS, 15; *SNS*, 26; CD, 66). Cézanne "remain[ed] faithful to the phenomena" and painted "the lived perspective, that which we actually perceive" (SNS, 14; *SNS*, 23; CD, 64), rather than a geometric or photographic univocal perspective on the way the world is "supposed" to look. Merleau-Ponty, like Cézanne, did not take the linear, planimetric perspective established in the Italian Renaissance as natural, but as "one of the symbolic forms by which men have tried to conquer worlds."[15] In the preface to *Phenomenology of Perception*, Merleau-Ponty had written that "the most important lesson which the reduction teaches us is the impossibility of a complete reduction" (PhP, xiv; *PP*, viii), yet Merleau-Ponty found in Cézanne a paradigm of the phenomenological *epoché* and achievement of a prescientific perception of the visible. Merleau-Ponty, in the *Phenomenology*, quoted Novotny's analysis of Cézanne's art as the attempt to paint the "pre-world" (PhP, 322; *PP*, 372), the physiognomy of things in their sensible configuration as they effortlessly arise in nature.

Another singularity of Merleau-Ponty's phenomenology of paint-

ing is the philosopher's insistence on returning the meaning of Cézanne's work to "the speaking subject." This refers to Merleau-Ponty's
care in studying Cézanne's conversations and correspondence with
Emile Bernard and Joachim Gasquet. In the chapter of *Phenomenology of
Perception* entitled "The Body as Expression, and Speech," Merleau-
Ponty defended a gestural theory of language and traced out a genealogy
of linguistic meaning beginning from the facial and bodily gestures of
infants and their early sung tonalities, then to speech and written word
as abstractions from these. This is another deviation from Husserl, who
had ruled out bodily gestures as instances of linguistic meaning and
shifted the paradigm for "genuine" speech from the realm of communication to inner, silent, phantasized speaking to oneself.[16] Merleau-Ponty
argued that, to the contrary, there is no essential difference between
gesturing with face or hand and spoken gesturing with teeth and tongue
that takes up the tradition of tonality common to English, French, or
other human languages (PhP, 194; *PP*, 226). In his later 1951 essay on
Saussure entitled "Phenomenology of Language," Merleau-Ponty originated his reflections from the definition of phenomenology of language
as "a return to the speaking subject, to my contact with the language I
am speaking," and concluded with the assertion that "the phenomenology of speech is among all others best suited" to reveal this order of
linguistic meaning to us (S, 85, 97; *S*, 106, 121). This is why Merleau-
Ponty was more interested, in "Cézanne's Doubt," in Cézanne's gestural
brush strokes using the carefully chosen colors on his palette, in his long
and repeated meditations germinating with a scene, and in his own insistent words regarding his work, than he was interested in the schooled
and theoretical analyses of art historians and critics.

This "return to the speaking subject" needs to be qualified in important ways, for there is probably no area of Merleau-Ponty's philosophy that has opened it to more criticism than this one. The more
"objective" recent approaches to language and the artwork, including
structuralism, hermeneutics, and deconstruction, arose in France after
Merleau-Ponty's death in 1961. These make primary the text or artwork
itself for interpretation detached from author or artist, and authors of
these approaches have criticized Merleau-Ponty's emphasis on speech.[17]
The qualifications regarding Merleau-Ponty's first philosophy of language are these. The return to the speaking subject is not a version of the
intentional fallacy, for Merleau-Ponty does not *reduce* the meaning of
Cézanne's work to the artist's own interpretation of it. In fact, Merleau-
Ponty's approach is quite hermeneutical even at this early stage, for he
stresses what he calls the "ambiguity" or "overdetermination" (SNS, 24;

SNS, 41; CD, 74, 75) of the meaning of Cézanne's work. In "Cézanne's Doubt," Merleau-Ponty already took under serious consideration the psychoanalytic reading of Leonardo's work, saying that those who dismiss psychoanalysis by the rules of inductive logic "only triumph on paper" (SNS, 24; *SNS*, 42; CD, 74) and miss the richness of "the psychoanalyst's *hermeneutic* musing" (SNS, 25; *SNS*, 43; CD, 75; my emphasis). Finally, as we will see, Merleau-Ponty's reflections on literary and artistic meaning did not end with "Cézanne's Doubt," but moved through the 1952 and 1960 essays on painting in directions that laid down many of the themes of postmodernism, including trace, signature, erasure, and hyperdialectic (deconstruction).[18]

What Merleau-Ponty found in Cézanne's own interpretations of his painting was a nearly classical theory of painting containing strong elements of realism and naturalism. Cézanne said that what he was doing was to paint from nature; he did not want to make a picture, but to "attempt a piece of nature" (SNS, 12; *SNS*, 21; CD, 62). Yet, at the same time, Cézanne rejected the classical techniques of painting such as linear perspective and outline, resulting in canvases with distortions of objects and nature. Emile Bernard called this "Cézanne's suicide: aiming for reality while denying himself the means to attain it" (SNS, 12; *SNS*, 21; CD, 63), and demanded of Cézanne a more "intellectual" approach to painting in terms of linear perspective, composition, and distribution of light and shadows. This discordance between Cézanne's own interpretation of his efforts and the questions of Bernard and attacks by the critics provoked Merleau-Ponty to invoke his own phenomenological theory of "lived-perspective" and the primacy of perception as a philosophy of painting that could give philosophic credence both to the works of Cézanne and Cézanne's own words. "Cézanne's Doubt" stresses that the artist does not "imitate" nature, as a realist philosophy of art often says, nor is artistic creation an act of intellectual "imagination" projecting an inner world outward, like we do find in Cézanne's earliest work, for example his reinterpretation of Manet's *Olympia* entitled *A Modern Olympia* (1873). Rather, what we discover in Cézanne's new approach to painting is a faithful, observant, minutely ordered construction, a fusion of self and nature in which the visible world is re-constructed in its process of appearing to visual sensation as colored, solid, weighty, and monumental. One of the most forward-looking sentences in "Cézanne's Doubt" pertains to this self-world fusion in artistic creation. "The landscape thinks itself in me," Merleau-Ponty quoted Cézanne, "and I am its consciousness" (SNS, 17; *SNS*, 30; CD, 67). Later, in "Eye and Mind," Merleau-Ponty would speak of the reversibility of roles between the artist and the visible world, citing the words of André Marchand, after Paul Klee: "In a forest, I have felt many times over that it was not I who looked at the forest. Some days I felt that the trees were looking at me, were speaking to me" (PrP, 167; *OE*, 31; EM, 129).

Merleau-Ponty's stress upon Cézanne as a colorist reveals another feature in the topography of a phenomenology of painting. Color became the unique feature of Cézanne's fusion of self and world, for pigment is both a bit of nature and a visual sensation, therefore the element of construction that could bind object and sensation. Point, line, plane, and ratio are mathematical properties and they have been given the place of first importance in modern Western philosophy, science, and art, based on their epistemic repeatability and reliability. This prestige was revived from Plato by Leonardo, Galileo, and Descartes, and the mathematical properties were named "primary qualities" by John Locke. The sensible properties of the world, namely color, taste, sound, odor, and touch, were called "secondary qualities" and regarded with diminished status in knowing the world in light of their alleged subjectivity and privacy. Since these secondary qualities are the ones more closely connected with the emotional and valuing tone of our experience, emotions and values were also relegated to secondary and subjective status, resulting in an arid and sterile rationalism that Husserl called the "crisis of European sciences." Throughout *Phenomenology of Perception*, Merleau-Ponty sought to restore the solidity of the lived-qualities of the world, especially color and the tangible thickness of things, depth understood not as a linear third dimension constructed as an illusion but primordial depth as the "most existential dimension" (PhP, 256; *PP*, 296). This was part of Merleau-Ponty's phenomenology of our lived being-in-the-world, just as it was part of Cézanne's visual attention to the solid, dense local colors of things, rather than the atmospheric colors in impressionist construction. In light of this phenomenological stress on secondary qualities, especially color, we should look forward with anticipation to what Merleau-Ponty will have to say about "line" when he does turn his attention to that theme in "Eye and Mind."

Cézanne's alleged trouble with his eyes provides the link in "Cézanne's Doubt" between Merleau-Ponty's discussion of Cézanne in the balance of the essay and his appraisal of Valéry's and Freud's reading of Leonardo in the last pages. What is the role of "hereditary traits," "influences," and "accidents" such as Cézanne's eye troubles or Leonardo's troubled early childhood in determining the meaning of a work of art? Disputing determinism and any physiological reduction of the meaning of Cézanne's or Leonardo's painting, Merleau-Ponty defends a dialectical view of the relation between determinants that call for a work to be done and the freely created meaning of an artistic project once undertaken. This problematic and the position Merleau-Ponty takes make this portion of his essay sound somewhat existentialist. Nevertheless, it would be a mistake to construe it too strongly in that direction, for Jean-Paul Sartre had rejected Freud's notion of the unconscious. The *Phenomenology of Perception* had disputed and qualified Sartre's philosophy of radical freedom quite directly in the last chapter entitled "Freedom," and Merleau-Ponty had offered a phenomenological appreciation of the meaning of Freud's theory of sexuality in a lengthy footnote to the chapter entitled "The Body in Its Sexual Being." The dialectical view Merleau-Ponty develops in "Cézanne's Doubt" permits neither the Sartrean reduction of artistic meaning to the subject's *for-itself* project nor the mechanistic interpretation of psychoanalysis that would reduce artistic meaning to *the* unconscious of the body-object. In Merleau-Ponty's next essay on painting, "Indirect Language and the Voices of Silence," the philosopher will engage Sartre's existentialism much more directly, and in his last essay, "Eye and Mind," we will find a more explicit and deepened appreciation of the insights of psychoanalysis.

We can now draw together the main contours in the topography of Merleau-Ponty's phenomenology of painting as they apprear in "Cézanne's Doubt." They include: (1) the bracketing of the scientific assumptions of the natural attitude regarding what the world *should* look like; (2) emphasis on the lived perspective as the visible world arises in relation to our living body, not a univocal, planimetric perspective; (3) the return of the meaning of painterly work to the gesturing and speaking subject; (4) the primacy of the solidity and constancy of the secondary, lived qualities of the visible world, especially color and tangibility; (5) a theory of artistic creation as the fusion of self and world, not imitation of the world as object by painter as subject, nor a subjective projection of the world by the artist's imagination; and (6) defense of a nonreductionist view of the overdetermined richness of meaning in an artwork.

"Cézanne's Doubt" draws our attention to the standing of the artist and artwork in relation to the visible world. We find only passing reference regarding the artwork as a cultural object in relation to the viewer, institutions, or history, developing anything like a phenomenology of aesthetic appreciation and criticism. Merleau-Ponty's response to the museums is a dominant theme in the next essay, "Indirect Language and the Voices of Silence." Nevertheless, there is already ample richness in "Cézanne's Doubt," and such an abstract, topographical outline should not be taken as a total account of Merleau-Ponty's phenomenology of painting in this essay. The attentive reader will find much of his or her own to add or subtract based on the lucidity and elegance of Merleau-Ponty's own prose.

2

Structures and Painting: "Indirect Language and the Voices of Silence"

Galen A. Johnson

Merleau-Ponty's middle essay on painting is quite unlike "Cézanne's Doubt" or "Eye and Mind." "Indirect Language and the Voices of Silence" is not a direct philosophical interpretation of painting, but Merleau-Ponty's critical response to the aesthetic theories of André Malraux in *The Voices of Silence* and Jean-Paul Sartre in "What is Literature?" These provide him with the occasion for counterthinking, further developing indirectly his philosophy of painting regarding institutions, style, imagination, and signs. Though the influence of phenomenology remains quite visible, the essay is part of Merleau-Ponty's philosophical experiment in relation to structuralism during the middle of his career to form a new philosophy of expression, language, history, and truth.

Text and Context

"Indirect Language and the Voices of Silence" was first published in a two-part installment in successive numbers of *Les Temps Modernes* (June, July 1952). Both parts were subsequently published together without changes in the collection of Merleau-Ponty's essays entitled *Signs* in 1960. Prior to the publication of "Indirect Language and the Voices of Silence" in *Les Temps Modernes*, Merleau-Ponty had originally written the essay in 1951 as the third chapter of his never completed book entitled *The Prose of the World*, edited and published posthumously by Claude Lefort.[1] Merleau-Ponty subsequently extracted the third chapter, "The Indirect Language," from the book manuscript and edited it for publication in *Les Temps Modernes*. Merleau-Ponty did not publish the other chapters of *The Prose of the World*.[2]

There are differences between the two versions of the essay that are not without significance. The major textual difference is that for the later version published in *Les Temps Modernes*, Merleau-Ponty prefaced the third chapter from *The Prose of the World* with a ten-page reflection on philosophy of language that takes its departure from the work of Ferdinand Saussure. In addition, the text excerpted from *The Prose of the World* is quite heavily edited for *Les Temps Modernes*.[3] Two general shifts may be noted in the year between 1951 and 1952. The earlier version of the essay tends to be more appreciative of Malraux's "subjective" history and psychology of art. For example, the following sentence is omitted from the later published version: Malraux "goes further than anyone else since Husserl introduced the notion of *style* to translate our original relation to the world" (PW, 56; *PM*, 79). The earlier version of the essay also defends a stronger parallel between language and painting, more insistently returning the formalisms of written expression, including mathematical algorithms, to our bodily field of presence in the visible world for their meaning and truth. For example, the following sentence from *The Prose of the World* is omitted from the published version of the essay: "However far one proceeds with formalization, its signification remains in suspension, actually means nothing, and has no truth at all unless we refer its superstructures back to a visible object" (PW, 106; *PM*, 150–51). These shifts suggest that under the influence of structuralist philosophies of language and the human sciences, especially Saussure and Lévi-Strauss, Merleau-Ponty had, in the intervening year, moved further away from the gestural theory of expression and major theses of *Phenomenology of Perception* toward recognizing differences among gesture, painting, speech, and written and formal expression. He had begun to catch a glimpse of the new lines of thought that would carry him forward to the ontology of visibility and *invisiblity* that we will find in "Eye and Mind." Thus, in reading the "Indirect Language" essay, we should note the lines that come into the essay from the expressive theory of painting in "Cézanne's Doubt," and the lines leading beyond the essay toward "Eye and Mind."

A great deal transpired in Merleau-Ponty's career between "Cézanne's Doubt" (1945) and "Indirect Language and the Voices of Silence." Seven years had passed, and Merleau-Ponty had been pursuing a meteoric academic career. He had defended *The Structure of Behavior* and *Phenomenology of Perception* at the University of Paris, Sorbonne, and was awarded the highest degree in French letters, the Doctor ès Lettres, in July 1945. Subsequently, he moved from teaching at the University of Lyon (1945–48) into an appointment to the Chair of Child Psychology and Pedagogy at the Sorbonne (1948–51), the position vacated by the genetic psychologist and epistemologist Jean Piaget. Here his courses included "Consciousness and the Acquisition of Language," "The Child's Relations with Others," and "Phenomenology and the Human Sciences."[4] In 1952, Merleau-Ponty successfully competed for the Chair of Philosophy at Collège de France vacated by Louis Lavelle, and earlier held by Henri Bergson. His appointment to the Chair of Philosophy at the Collège de France was decreed 21 March 1952, effective 1 April 1952. At age forty-four, he was the youngest person ever appointed to this most prestigious chair in French philosophy. His chief rival had been the University of Paris aesthetician Etienne Souriau.[5]

Since "Indirect Language and the Voices of Silence" appeared in *Les Temps Modernes*, we should say a few words about the career of this journal and Merleau-Ponty's role in it. The review had been founded in 1945, with an original editorial committee of Sartre, Merleau-Ponty, Simone de Beauvoir, Raymond Aron, and three lesser-known French intellectuals.[6] These four principals had all been friends since their university days studying philosophy at the Ecole Normale Superieur. They founded the journal immediately following the Liberation in order to continue their activities during the Resistance, giving leftist French intellectuals a public voice in politics, the arts, and philosophy, playing the role of a critical conscience of engaged commitment in the major political and cultural events of modern times. Sartre was clearly the dominant personality within the group, and saw in the journal an opportunity to popularize and extend the tenets of existentialism as expressed in *Being and Nothingness* (1943). For example, he published "What is Literature?" in *Les Temps Modernes* in 1947. Merleau-Ponty was the political editor for the review, and given his academic prestige, functioned as the editorial liaison with the academic community. During the years from 1945 until 1950, Merleau-Ponty's major publication in *Les Temps Modernes* was his three part article entitled "The Yogi and the Proletarian" that became the basis for his controversial book entitled *Humanism and Terror* (1947), a detailed study of the transcripts of the Moscow Trials and defense of Marxism in reply to Arthur Koestler's novel, *Darkness at Noon*.[7] Merleau-Ponty also wrote briefer articles on Indochina, the Liberation, existentialism, Christianity, Hegel, Montaigne, Machiavelli, and the new cinema. These were later collected in *Sense and Non-Sense* and *Signs*. With the invasion of Korea in 1950, Merleau-Ponty imposed a political silence on the review, which largely held until his departure in 1952.

It is singularly important, in reading "Indirect Language and the Voices of Silence," to realize that it was Merleau-Ponty's last essay for *Les Temps Modernes*, and its publication preceded his resignation from the journal and public break with Sartre by a scant five months.[8] In the same July 1952 number of *Les Temps Modernes* in which the second installment of "Indirect Language and the Voices of Silence" appeared, Sartre published the first installment of his book, *The Communists and Peace*. This work by Sartre reflects the influence of Merleau-Ponty's *Humanism and Terror* from five years earlier, a favorable evaluation of the Marxist philosophy of history that Merleau-Ponty had long since abandoned in light of the Soviet labor camps and the Korean invasion. Yet, as a member of the editorial committee of *Les Temps Modernes*, Merleau-Ponty was directly implicated in Sartre's position, though he was unable to make a critical response to it in his own voice.[9] As Merleau-Ponty had been moving away from Marxism, Sartre had been moving closer to it. Merleau-Ponty had never been an existentialist nor a Marxist, and certainly never a disciple of Sartre. Philosophically, they had been moving steadily away from one another since their editorial collaboration in 1945, until the rupture in their editorial collaboration and friendship in 1952, culminating in Merleau-Ponty's attack on *The Communists and Peace* entitled "Sartre and Ultrabolshevism" published in *Adventures of the Dialectic* (1955). In that work, Merleau-Ponty wrote that what separated him from Sartre was both "as personal and as general as possible: it is philosophical" (AD, 188; *AD*, 275). "Indirect Language and the Voices of Silence" already contains the major contours of Merleau-Ponty's critique of Sartre's existentialism and Marxism. We will indicate the major themes of that critique below. Curiously, "Indirect Language and the Voices of Silence" is dedicated "To Jean-Paul Sartre."

Just as Merleau-Ponty had made "Cézanne's Doubt" the lead essay in *Sense and Non-Sense*, so "Indirect Language and the Voices of Silence" is the lead essay of *Signs*. Yet, by the time Merleau-Ponty wrote the preface to *Signs* in February and September of 1960, he had already completed his last essay on painting, "Eye and Mind," in July and August of 1960, and the preface to *Signs* has more to do with the ontological themes of "Eye and Mind" than the critical themes of "Indirect Language and the Voices of Silence." Nevertheless, we do find in the last part of the preface a moving commentary on his friendship with Sartre that goes in the direction of a reconciliation. The occasion was publication of a preface Sartre had written to a work entitled *Aden Arabie* by Paul Nizan, Sartre and Merleau-Ponty's mutual friend from university days. It was difficult to be a friend of Sartre, Merleau-Ponty said, yet Sartre reproached himself too greatly and judged his youth too harshly. We find the testimony of reconciliation between Sartre and Merleau-Ponty in Sartre's homage to Merleau-Ponty written a few months following his death and published in a special number of *Les Temps Modernes* dedicated to Merleau-Ponty:

> I have lost so many friends who are still alive. No one was to blame. It was they. It was myself. Events made us, brought us together, separated us. And I know that Merleau-Ponty said the same thing when he thought of the people who haunted, and then left his life. But he never lost me, and he had to die for me to lose him.[10]

Painters and Sources

Additional painters appear in "Indirect Language and the Voices of Silence." Cézanne and Leonardo are here again. Now there are also Matisse, Renoir, Van Gogh, Klee, Tintoretto, Delacroix, Ingres, and Vermeer. Among these, Van Gogh, Renoir, and Matisse receive special attention in the essay.

The story Merleau-Ponty recounts of Renoir working by the sea at Cassis, then making a change in a little corner of the brook in *The Bathers*, is repeated from Malraux's *The Voices of Silence*,[11] as is Merleau-Ponty's discussion of Van Gogh's painting entitled *The Crows*. The importance of Van Gogh for Malraux can scarcely be underestimated; it is second only to the importance of Picasso, whom Merleau-Ponty chooses never to discuss in any of his texts on painting.[12] Malraux wrote that "the modern artist's supreme aim is to subdue all things to his style, beginning with the simplest, least promising objects. And his emblem is Van Gogh's famous *Chair*."[13] Merleau-Ponty's objections to Malraux's subjective notion of "style" and his own reformulation of the concept will become one of the most important disputes in "Indirect Language and the Voices of Silence." We will return to it below.

Since Merleau-Ponty's interpretation of painting in "Indirect Language and the Voices of Silence" relies so heavily upon *The Voices of Silence*, we should say a few direct words about this work by André Malraux. Beginning in 1947 and continuing through 1950, André Malraux published his three-volume history of art titled *Psychologie de l'art*, subsequently collected in a one-volume Pléiade edition under the title *The Voices of Silence* (*Les voix du silence*), which found its way into Merleau-Ponty's title.[14] As has no doubt become clear, Malraux's fundamental thesis throughout this work was that modern painting is a "subjectivism" that breaks with the attempts at "objectivism" among the Renaissance classical artists. Merleau-Ponty could not have asked for an account of the meaning of modern painting more directly opposed to his own thought.

"Le musée imaginaire" is translated variously. The literal meaning, "the imaginary museum," alerts us to one of the central philosophical disputes between Merleau-Ponty on one side and Malraux and Sartre on the other: the nature of imagination and its relation to perception. The sense of "le musée imaginaire" has also been translated by the phrases "museum of the mind" and "museum without walls," and Malraux's work is one of the first and most important efforts to create an anthology of the metamorphosis of art across the centuries and across cultures. Malraux collected photographic reproductions of artistic "masterpieces," no lesser paintings from the picture-dealers' shops, and no profusion of works within an already existing aesthetic. By a masterpiece, Malraux meant "the most significant work by the inventor of a style," an artist's "most personal work, the one from which he has stripped all that is not his very own, and in which his style reaches its climax."[15] Malraux's imaginative bounds and the breadth of his gallery of reproductions is sweeping. He writes about the masks of New Guinea, the Ivory Coast, and Hopi Indians, the pottery of ancient China and Greece, the mummies and Sphinx of Egypt, Celtic and Germanic coins, the mosaics, frescoes, and stained glass of the cathedrals of Europe, Leonardo's *Mona Lisa*, Rembrandt's *Prodigal Son*, and Cézanne's many versions of Mont Sainte-Victoire. On the same page, one can move through the art of four cultures and three epochs, sometimes even in a subordinate clause. Though the three volumes of *Psychologie de l'art* were published in the space of four years, Malraux had worked on the project at least over the sixteen-year period from 1935 to 1951.

The sweep of Malraux's achievement in *The Voices of Silence* also leads to many of the work's defects. Malraux's photographic reproductions falsify important aspects of the works of art they are meant to represent. The photographs are black and white, making color disappear in favor of an emphasis on line and form. The photographs of coins are larger than the photograph of the towering *Winged Victory of Samothrace* in the Louvre. The detail studies of a small section of the Port Royal at Chartres or the Cathedral's stained glass are the same size as the photographs of the entire originals. Malraux's photographic museum also isolates the official masterpieces of world art from their social and personal background. Even bare chronological dates of the works are omitted. In contrast with Merleau-Ponty's careful attention to Cézanne's conversations and letters articulating his artistic problems and efforts, Malraux wrote that painters "speak of their art as if they were housepainters."[16] For Malraux to have included biographical, cultural, and historical context would have opened up a chasm of detail that would have curtailed his panorama. Art historian E. H. Gombrich, for example, has written that his studies thoroughly weaned him of Malraux's panoramic approach, "which now appeared to me somewhat hysterical and sensationalist."[17]

Malraux's museum without walls was an intentional isolation (*arrachement*) in order to present a history of human artistic creativity. The panorama enabled Malraux to construct his central theses about modern painting that engage Merleau-Ponty's essay: a critique of the limitations of the modern day art museum, an individualism and subjectivism regarding modern painting as an expression of the painter's personal style or inner world, an objectivist, Hegelian notion of a Spirit of painting that controls the style of an historical epoch even across cultures, and a cult of genius regarding the heroes of modern art that approaches religious fervor. Influenced by Nietzsche and Gide, Malraux finds in modern painting a return to the worship of the sublime and exotic that characterized primitive religion. Consequent upon the death of God, Malraux was determined to ward off the death of culture and to establish the artist as replacement for the divine: "What genius is not fascinated by that extremity of painting, by that appeal before which time itself vacillates? It is the moment of the possession of the world. Let painting go no further, and Hans the Elder becomes God."[18]

In his essay, Merleau-Ponty also writes of a film that recorded the work of Henri Matisse as the artist was drawing. The film is entitled *Matisse* or *A Visit with Matisse*, and was a 1946 documentary study of the artist made in Paris and Vence, near Nice. The most striking sequences, partly in slow motion, show Matisse drawing a flower he has just picked in his garden, then the head of his grandson. Here is what Matisse himself told Rosamond Bernier in February of 1949:

There was a passage showing me drawing in slow motion.
Before my pencil ever touched the paper, my hand made a
strange journey of its own. I never realized before that I did
this. I suddenly felt as if I were shown naked—that everyone
could see this—it made me deeply ashamed. You must understand this was not hesitation. I was unconsciously establishing
the relationship between the subject I was about to draw and
the size of my paper. *Je n'avais pas encore commence a chanter.*[19]

Merleau-Ponty agrees with Matisse, that the slow-motion camera's "eye"
should not be taken as revealing the truth about Matisse's gesture as a
painter, for Matisse acted in the world of human perception, gesture,
and time, and the film attempts to make us believe that the painter's
hand operated in the physical world of abstract scientific possibilities.

Not only does this interpretation reinforce Merleau-Ponty's attention to the primacy of perception and the lived world in contrast with
abstracted, scientific perspective, it also forces us to notice the privilege
he has steadily accorded painting over other arts, in this instance, photography and film. More recent philosophers, such as Jean-François
Lyotard, have criticized Merleau-Ponty for privileging painting over
photography within modern art.[20] There is a curious convergence between the views of Malraux and Merleau-Ponty in this regard, for *The
Voices of Silence*, with its photgraphic "museum without walls," depends
upon photography, yet Malraux does not include photography as part of
the essence of modern art. We will find the same in Merleau-Ponty's
"Eye and Mind," when he includes photographs of representative
artworks within the essay, yet privileges painting. Earlier, Merleau-Ponty
had written a more appreciative essay on film entitled "The Film and the
New Psychology," but he limited himself to narrative film in "lived time"
and his interpretation emphasizes filmic time as a "temporal gestalt."[21]
In "Indirect Language and the Voices of Silence," Merleau-Ponty does
not seek to incorporate film or photography within his aesthetic theory,
but emphasizes the ways in which photographs of artworks or films of
artists at work can abstract and intellectualize, thus falsifying, the work
of art. Malraux himself gives us the list of falsifications. Photographs
present artworks from one perspective only, in a chosen light, using in-
exact color reproduction, with little idea of original size.[22]

We find two additional literary sources at play in Merleau-Ponty's
essay. The first is an influential essay on Malraux by Maurice Blanchot
entitled "Le musée, l'art, et le temps," published in *Critique* in 1950.[23]
The second is the work by Jean-Paul Sartre that, in the literary world,

had commanded the attention of a wide readership, including Merleau-Ponty. Jean-Paul Sartre published his "What is Literature?" ("Qu'est-ce que la littérature?") in 1947. The work is an existentialist literary manifesto in three parts: I. What is Writing? II. Why Write? III. For Whom Does One Write? Sartre defended the privilege of literary prose over painting and poetry for responsibly engaging the political life of one's times. "The writer can guide you," Sartre wrote, "and, if he describes a hovel, make it seem the symbol of social injustice and provoke your indignation. The painter is mute. He presents you with a hovel, that's all."[24] Here is the second textual source for Merleau-Ponty's discussion of the silence of painting. We can best study Merleau-Ponty's response to Sartre's provocation in the context of a discussion of Sartre's aesthetic theory and theory of the imagination, and the philosophic themes of "Indirect Language and the Voices of Silence." Sartre, together with Malraux, are the implicit, sometimes explicit, provocateurs addressed by Merleau-Ponty in the second essay on painting. We should now turn to the philosophic themes of the published essay as we find it in *Signs*. It is in three parts. The philosophy of painting is sandwiched between opening and concluding sections on philosophy of language. That is as it should be, for the philosopher's goal was to "try out the parallel" between language and painting (S, 46-47; S, 58-59; ILVS, 84).

Philosophical Themes

"Indirect Language and the Voices of Silence" is a rich and turbulent text, filled with Merleau-Ponty's counterthinking in relation to Sartre and Malraux, and even in relation to his own earlier phenomenology of painting. We will draw attention to four major dialectical themes that inform the essay's philosophy of painting: the critique of the institutions of the museum and official art, style and the history of painting, imagination and perception, and language and truth in painting. This is an ambitious list, and indicative that during the middle period of his career, Merleau-Ponty was working on a general theory of expression that would elaborate a philosophy of art and language and extend it into a general philosophy of culture and history.[25] Merleau-Ponty's title theme is found in this sentence: "We shall see that the idea of *complete* expression is nonsensical, and that all language is indirect or allusive—that it is, if you wish, silence" (S, 43; S, 54; ILVS, 80).

I hope that the textual context and grouping of sources we have now indicated is sufficient explanation for saying that Jean-Paul Sartre is the principal philosopher addressed by Merleau-Ponty's essay, with Malraux in the shadows, even though the essay's explicit references are most often to Malraux. Merleau-Ponty found in Malraux's philosophy of art a nearly perfect analogue for the views of Jean-Paul Sartre, the same swing from subjectivism to objectivism founded on dualistic splits between mind and body, subject and world, individual and collective history, freedom and fate, real and unreal, imagination and perception, prose and painting. Merleau-Ponty's entire philosophical effort from *Phenomenology of Perception* forward had been to overcome dichotomies such as these and the philosophical impasses they had created in modern thought. He continues this effort in "Indirect Language and the Voices of Silence."

Institutions

We begin from a point of agreement among the three philosophers. Merleau-Ponty's essay contains a ringing critique of the museum, as does Malraux's *The Voices of Silence*. We also recall the sarcastic contempt of Sartre's description, in his novel *Nausea*, of the portrait gallery in Bouville that enshrined the worthy elders of the town, a satire that escalates into Roquentin's departing rage at the official portraits ("Salauds!"). Later in volume three of *Les chemins de la liberté* (*Roads to Freedom*) entitled *La mort dans l'âme* (*Sick at Heart* or *Troubled Sleep*), Sartre also gave a satirical fictional account of the New York Museum of Modern Art, characterizing it as organized, approved, enclosed, sanitary, and sterile.

Museums have existed for barely two hundred years and only in cultures influenced by modern Europe, yet for most of us, our awareness of what painting is depends nearly exclusively upon this institution. To the Asiatic, as Malraux puts it, especially one from the Far East, "artistic contemplation and the picture gallery are incompatible."[26] A painting was not to be exhibited pitted against others, but contemplated singly and in a spiritual mood of relaxation. The museum was born in the era of easel-pictures and is uniquely adapted to painting and small sculpture. Only what is portable and can be owned finds its way into museum rooms, legitimating the alliance among painting, money, and political power. Artworks are isolated from their historical setting, from their social function, and from the personal context of living problems an artist was attempting to solve at a particular moment in his or her work. Deprived of any context other than official museum approval, presented not in progress but in retrospective, they vie with one another as hostile, rival abstractions in an unjustified, aggressive modernity. These are some of the reasons that underlie Merleau-Ponty's remarks that the museum's function is not entirely beneficent. It gives us a thieves' conscience, and turns the living vehemence of painting into a morose, cruel "historicity of death" (S, 62–63; *S*, 78–79; ILVS, 99–100).

Almost all the painters Merleau-Ponty loved were outsiders, rejected by the official art world for most of their lives. Merleau-Ponty urges us to return painting to the painter's living work (*peindre*, to paint), rather than enshrine the completed or abandoned artwork (*la peinture*, the painting) as a fetish of capital exchange. Of course, when Merleau-Ponty attacks the museum in this way, one cannot help but notice that Malraux's "museum without walls" comes under many of these same criticisms. It would not be difficult to imagine that Malraux's imaginary museum and an actual museum might converge. In fact it happened when, in 1973, Malraux opened an exhibition at Saint-Paul-de-Vence sponsored by the Foundation Maeght named "André Malraux et le musée imaginaire."[27] Still minus the Sistine Chapel and other notable untransportables, the museum of the mind had become a museum of fact.

Merleau-Ponty's essay suggests a radical reinterpretation of the meaning of "institution" in stark contrast to the notion of an entrenched, rule-structured and often bureaucratic establishment of buildings, officers, money, and power. Once again relying upon Husserl, Merleau-Ponty introduces the term *Stiftung* to speak of a creative formation or establishment of a cultural meaning that continues, after its appearance, to have the value of opening up a field for further investigations. An original meaning formation (*Urstiftung*) is sedimented and reactivated in a tradition of retrieval (*Nachstiftung*), in the way, for example, that Matisse was nourished by thirty-seven years of living with Cézanne's oil study entitled *Three Bathers*, which he reports "sustained him spiritually in the critical moments of his career as an artist."[28] Merleau-Ponty refers in the essay to the paintings on the walls of caves at Lascaux as an original institution of the task of painting, sedimented in the work of Cézanne, Klee, and Matisse. He calls such institutions, in the terminology of the Christian calendar and adapted from Paul Ricoeur, an *advent* rather than mere historical event; they are a promise of events, the breaking forth of a new word that is carried forward in human interchanges in time. This is Husserl's philosophy of history developed in "The Origin of Geometry," but once again deintellectualized and pushed downward away from the written, textual histories of geometry, science, and mathematics toward the living work of modern artists. If we comprehend the meaning of institution in this living way, then we are able to speak of a fecundity and unity in the tradition of painting, the power to forget origins in order to give them a new life, "which is the noble form of memory" (S, 59; S, 74; ILVS, 96). This is not the forgetfulness of ignorance or partiality, but the power of work to be done drawing upon the generosity of what we have been given. Then as well, we will recognize that the empirical and external "cruel historicity" of works enshrined in museums as rivals should give way to a true, cumulative living historicity in which each new attempt to paint revives, recaptures, and renews the undertaking of painting as an expression of the visible world.

Style

Where is the bearer of this tradition from the caves at Lascaux to Leonardo and beyond to the paintings of Cézanne, Matisse, and Klee, if not the museums, if not the collected "masterpieces" of art? If we have followed Merleau-Ponty's thought, we know that the answer will be found closer to the living perception and work of painters, and "Indirect Language and the Voices of Silence" refers this problem to the notion of "style." Here Merleau-Ponty enters into his most severe dispute with Malraux.

Merleau-Ponty cites three formulations of the meaning of style from *The Voices of Silence* which he disapproves. Malraux wrote that style is the "means of re-creating the world according to the values of the man who discovers it"; it is "the expression of a meaning lent to the world, a call for and not a consequence of a way of seeing"; or, finally, it is "the reduction to a fragile human perspective of the eternal world which draws us along according to a mysterious rhythm into a drift of stars" (S, 53; S, 67; ILVS, 90).[29] One notices that the first two of these formulations refer the meaning of style to the individual, personal values or meanings of the painter. The third, on the other hand, swings to the opposite extreme away from the individual to the mystical powers of the eternal world, implying the work of a "super-artist" or "Spirit of painting" who draws the artist along, working out the style of an era across cultures by using individual artists. It should be clear that if "style" is defined at the beginning so individually and subjectivistically, Malraux has no alternative for understanding the apparent unity of style during an historical period but to appeal to some objectivistic notion of Spirit or fate. It is worth pointing out here that Malraux's incoherent swing between these subjective and objective notions of style is an analogue of Sartre's existentialist philosophy of the free for-itself subject over against the inert, determined in-itself object, as well as of the tension in Marx's thought between the humanism of proletarian action in conflict with the objective market forces of capital production and exchange.

Before we briefly give voice to Merleau-Ponty's alternative account of artistic style, we should point out his agreement with Malraux's critique of the type of approach to the meaning of style that searches for a catalog of unique traits in a painter's work; for example, Van Gogh's large, heavy brush strokes full of paint like the skeletons of trees after a forest fire; or his use of deep rich primary and secondary colors, especially yellows, greens, blues, and reds; or even Van Gogh's signature. If we made a catalog of all the objective qualities observable in Van Gogh's canvases, they would not "add up" to a Van Gogh painting, like a mathematical sum, like bytes of information we could program. This is to think from the point of view of copying or counterfeiting Van Gogh, that is, from the point of view of a student rather than Van Gogh himself. The style of a painter escapes the catalog of objects he or she painted, it escapes the catalog of techniques. Even if a painting would not be a Van Gogh without the everyday subject matter such as a chair or a pair of shoes, without the special techniques of brush, color, and composition, the only way to recognize the style of the painter is to bring ourselves into the presence of Van Gogh's painting.

An artist's style is as inaccessible to himself or herself as our own face and everyday gestures. Merleau-Ponty says that it "is just as recognizable for others and just as little visible to him as his silhouette" (S, 53; S, 67; ILVS, 90). Even the mirror freezes our own glance or smile into a surface without reference. Expression is reduced to configuration. The self-portraits by artists like Cézanne and Van Gogh, painted from their image in a mirror, stare out at us with a frozen ferocity.[30] Our face is available only to the look of others, and even for them is encountered, appreciated, and understood rather than inventoried like the electricity and gas in a neon smile. In pointing to this intersubjective quality of style, nevertheless, we should not now reduce style to the influences of a master or the brotherhood of a school. Matisse painted and drew the way he did because his teacher was Gustave Moreau, because he lived with Cézanne's *Three Bathers* which he studied minutely and cherished fervently, and because he was a friend of Picasso, Gauguin, and Renoir, but in the final analysis, because he was Matisse. In a discussion of style from the *Phenomenology*, Merleau-Ponty had written that through the experience we share with others in relation to the world, a certain open and indefinite consistency of style is born: "One day, once and for all, something was set in motion which, even during sleep, can no longer cease to see or not to see, to feel or not to feel, to suffer or be happy, to think or rest from thinking, in a word to 'have it out with the world.' My first perception . . . is an ever-present event, an unforgettable tradition" (PhP, 406–7; *PP*, 465–66).

Style is, therefore, an intersubjective and historical phenomenon. It is recognized by others, and recognizable for ourselves in retrospect. Artistic style is nothing else than the artist's vision of the world, it is what goes on *between* the subject in relation to others and the world, what Merleau-Ponty calls "the allusive logic of the perceived world" (S, 57; *S*, 71; ILVS, 94). This literally refers to Matisse, after years of education and experiment, looking at an interior against the background of a window, then putting down a dot of red against the blue background of *La Fenetre Bleue*. When an artist paints, sculpts, or draws, she lends her body to color, composition, and line. If this is so, what a painter does with eye and hand is not unlike what an athlete does when running, throwing, or swimming, or what all do when walking, smiling, gesturing, or speaking. Style begins as soon as any person perceives the world, and all perception stylizes because embodiment is a style of the world. Our own living body is a special way of accenting the variants the world offers. The artist is the one who is capable of condensing and expressing his or her bodily encounter with the world onto paper, canvas, stone, or clay. Merleau-Ponty summarizes his point of view by describing style as the system of equivalences an artist creates to make manifest the visible world, "the 'coherent deformation' by which he concentrates the still scattered meaning of his perception and makes it exist expressly" (S, 54–55; *S*, 68; ILVS, 91–92). The labor of the painter is the birth of expression and the world is a *call* or *demand* for this birth. These are maternal metaphors of labor and birth, but this is the travail of expression, and we should not underestimate or trivialize this work with notions of subjective projection or self-abandonment to the control of a Spirit-agent.

Imagination

Merleau-Ponty's work on institutions, history, and style in "Indirect Language and the Voices of Silence" continues the lines of thought coming into the essay from Husserl and the phenomenology of painting in "Cézanne's Doubt" based on the primacy of perception and the living body. When we now turn to the further issues of imagination and the status of the artwork as a sign in relation to language and truth, we embark upon issues of *invisibility* and lines of thought that will carry Merleau-Ponty forward to the new ontology at work in "Eye and Mind." This two-track movement explains the turbulence that readers will find at work in this essay.

For a philosophy of painting based on perception and body, imagination presents a unique problem. On the one hand, imagination seems impossible to ignore in developing an aesthetic theory, as exemplified by the modern tradition beginning from Kant to the romantics such as Schelling, Schopenhauer, and Hegel, and culminating in Sartre. On the other hand, imagination seems inevitably to refer us to a faculty or acts of consciousness that are different from perception: imagination is characterized as spontaneous and free, less bound, if at all bound, to the imposed givens of sensation. Though Malraux entitled his anthology of art *Le musée imaginaire*, it is difficult to know all that he meant by imagination. He uses the term to refer principally to the creative acts of consciousness artists perform in arriving at a work, what he calls the "mind's eye." Nevertheless, the problem of imagination is more complex than this, for in addition to referring to a creative mental act, imagination may also refer to an image, either a mental image "seen" by the mind or the actual images, that is, the photographs, collected in Malraux's book.

Thus, the complex of problems for philosophy of painting raised by the question of imagination includes description of what we mean by an imaginative mental act and the mental image, and clarification of the relation of actual images such as photographs or paintings to what they signify. For Merleau-Ponty's phenomenology of painting, only the latter would seem somewhat a matter of perception. In so emphasizing perception in his response to Malraux, the entire process before a painter first sets brush or pen to paper seems omitted from Merleau-Ponty's purview. I will try to show briefly how this is not so, but what we will find in both Merleau-Ponty's reflections on imagination as well as those on the nature of painting as sign is his first struggles to break free of the "perceptual monism"[31] that informed his phenomenology of painting. Eventually this would lead him to an entire reformulation of his philosophical outlook and philosophy of art, one less committed to privileging the works of "worldly" painters such as Cézanne, Renoir, Matisse, and Van Gogh.

Let us first indicate Merleau-Ponty's position on imagination as a unique kind of mental act and the question of the mental image. Whereas Malraux had left these matters where he received them from the aesthetic tradition, Jean-Paul Sartre had made imagination a central topic of his philosophical work. He had written two complete works on imagination, *Imagination* (1936) and *L'imaginaire* (1940), translated as *The Psychology of Imagination*. Sartre's thought, especially in these early works, was also deeply influenced by Husserl, and Sartre's theory of imagination was at pains to defeat the notion of imagination as the intuition of an immanent mental content, like a "mini-thing" trapped in the mind separate from the world. Imagination is an intentional act that therefore refers to an object as transcendent, beyond the subject and in the world. In this respect, imagination is like perception, yet it was a characteristic of Sartre's psychology to separate acts of consciousness into different modes or intentional attitudes such as perception, thinking, imagining, and emotionality, and his theory of imagination proceeded to differentiate sharply imaginative from perceptual intentionality. Imagination is not like perception, which is the consciousness of an external thing, object, or event, rather it is the awareness of something as *not being*. Images are distinguished from perceptions or sensations by a distinctive nothingness or nihilation. An image is the awareness of an object as nonexistent, or as absent, or as elsewhere, or as pure possibility. Whereas Merleau-Ponty argued that the task of painting is "expressing what exists," Sartre believed it to be the expression of what does *not* exist. This returns to imagination its characteristic freedom and spontaneity, which Sartre describes as the "magical" quality of imagination, which "magic" he also accorded to the emotions. Imagination is the only type of conscious act that is wholly spontaneous and unmotivated, for whereas both thought and emotion can also be consciousness of an object as not-being, both are somewhat imposed by objects or events external to consciousness, emotions precipitated by bodily behaviors and thoughts by words and the ideas they signify. In imagination, on Sartre's account, we find the exemplary case of a free, spontaneous act *ex nihilo* that is not bound to body, place, time, circumstance, or situation.[32]

In this psychology of imagination we find the characteristic Sartrean philosophy of nothingness, together with several of the dualistic bifurcations this philosophy generated in his thought, between for-itself subject and in-itself object, freedom and unfreedom, real and unreal, and imagination and perception. Yet Merleau-Ponty's *Phenomenology of Perception*, as well as a 1936 review he had written of Sartre's *Imagination*,[33] are surprisingly receptive to Sartre's theses on imagination. In fact, Merleau-Ponty takes Sartre's account as definitive, and given his own interests in the modalities of perception, employs Sartre's account as evidence for assigning an impoverished and reduced importance to imagination in comparison with perception. He wrote, for example, citing Sartre's *L'imaginaire*, that in contrast with perception, "the imaginary has no depth, and does not respond to our efforts to vary our points of view; it does not lend itself to observation. We never have a hold upon it" (PhP, 323–24; *PP*, 374). In the *Phenomenology*, Merleau-Ponty's references to imagination occur mostly in discussions of the brain-damaged patient Schneider's abnormalities and illusions.[34] This is surprising not only for the dualism of real and unreal it implicitly accepts, but also because Merleau-Ponty needed the notion of imagination in his account of the body to distinguish the physical body-object from our living body comprended in terms of "body-schema" and "body-image." Merleau-Ponty's phenomenology had knit the fabric of perception too tightly, and in spite of his own better intentions, he had given in to a dualism of perception and imagination, real and unreal, under Sartre's influence.

Nevertheless, in "Indirect Language and the Voices of Silence" we find the beginnings of a less monistic philosophy of perception that gives a new account of imagination and its place in the artistic endeavor. On the one hand, Merleau-Ponty does not object to Malraux's description of the Spirit of painting as an "imaginary spirit of art," in which the term "imaginary" for Merleau-Ponty would mean unreal. On the other hand, he says that our vision of the world is capable of leaping over distances, piercing the perceptual future, outlining hollows and reliefs, distances and deviations (*écarts*) in being (S, 67; *S*, 83; ILVS, 103–4). An image is not nothingness or a hole intuited in being, it is rather a hollow or deviation in the visible surface, the imminent, the latent or hidden meaning interwoven with the real. This conception comprehends imagination as an intentional act, therefore an act in relation to some feature of the world and not trapped in our minds, but a feature previously unnoticed or forgotten or repressed and unexpressed. Imagination remains a variant of perception, but the fabric of perception is more loosely knit, allowing interruptions and discontinuities, mixings, foldings and intertwinings between visible and invisible, real and imaginary. Referring to Stendhal's *Red and Black*, Merleau-Ponty says that Stendhal found for Julien Sorel "an imaginary body more agile than his own body" that operated according to a cadence of "what was visible and what was invisible." Julien's desire to kill Madame de Renal is found, not in Stendhal's explicit lines, but between the words and lines "in the hollows of space, time and signification they mark out, as movement at the cinema is between the immobile images which follow one another" (S, 76; *S*, 95; ILVS, 113). This is the language and philosophy we will find more fully enunciated in "Eye and Mind." There Merleau-Ponty would write that imagination "offers to vision its inward tapestries, the imaginary texture of the real" (PrP, 165; *OE*, 24; EM, 126). We find in "Eye and Mind" and *The Visible and the Invisible* explicit rejections of the Sartrean psychology of imagination (PrP, 164; *OE*, 23–24; EM, 126; and VI, 266; *VI*, 320).

Signs

Though much of Merleau-Ponty's essay disputes the importance of the completed work of art for comprehending the meaning of institutions, style, and art history, the essay does take up the question of the status of the artwork as a sign. We find these texts principally in the opening and closing pages on language, as well as near the middle of the essay in a discussion of art and truth in relation to Sartre's "What is Literature?" Here Merleau-Ponty enters into his sharpest and most explicit dispute with Sartre. Together with his separation of perception from imagination, Sartre also drew a sharp line between prose on one side, and poetry and painting on the other. Since he understood the latter as arts of the image, of the picture or word-picture, he portrayed them as the least worldly and most subjective. Though they best exemplified magical spontaneity and freedom, they were least capable of engaging the life of one's times and least capable of expressing knowledge or truth about the world. " 'As always in art, one must lie to tell the truth,' Sartre rightly says" (S, 57; *S*, 71; ILVS, 94). To the extent that this was Sartre's denial of a copying or representational theory of painting, Merleau-Ponty agreed. However, it was much more than that. It was an expression of Sartre's view that a work of art does not refer or signify anything at all. It is a spontaneous, imaginative projection of the subject, incapable of true signification. Sartre thus joins the long line of rationalist philosophies since Descartes that devalue the image as impoverished or barren in comparison with reflective thought and knowledge. If a viewer comes into the presence of an artwork such as Tintoretto's, Sartre contended, the yellow of the sky over Golgotha may evoke in us a feeling of anguish, but this is an affective reaction between the viewer and the painting. The work of art itself is opaque, a thing like all in-itself objects, without translucency or transparency of reference. "Does anyone think," Sartre wrote, that Picasso's *Guernica* "won over a single heart to the Spanish cause?"[35] Only the words of prose convey a transparency of reference to a world and meanings beyond the ink marks of a page. "The painter is mute."

These Sartrean formulas published in *Les Temps Modernes* are much harsher and hastier than the account of the reference of an artwork that Sartre had earlier given in *The Psychology of Imagination*. There he had not departed from the view of the painting as a physical thing, but he had accorded to the artwork the status of a "material analogue" that we surpass toward an imagined aesthetic object, either real or unreal. Paintings are thus like photographs, caricatures, or faces in the flame.[36] The painting is what he calls a "picture-sign," or what we may call an "iconic sign," and this category of signs includes not only paintings and photographs, but also fiction, poetry, and drama, in contrast with the "word-signs" of nonfictional prose writing, which we may call "indexical signs." Given Sartre's own literary achievements as a novelist and author of short stories and plays, it is surprising to find fiction included in the list of iconic signs. An iconic sign is one in which there is a relationship of resemblance between the sign and its referent, between, for example, a photograph and a person or between an actor and the character he or she portrays, whereas for an indexical sign no resemblance binds sign and signified. Again, like the case of an emotion evoked by an artwork, the imagined aesthetic object is generated in the relation between the viewer and the work or the viewer and the performance, rather than between the work and the world.

Merleau-Ponty seeks, in his essay, to defeat two central aspects of the Sartrean view: on the one side, Sartre's notion of the transparency and univocity of nonfictional linguistic reference, and on the other, Sartre's treatment of the work of art as a thing with no reference to the world. To complicate this mix, Merleau-Ponty also entertains and rejects the possibility that the meaning of an artwork rests in its internal references, its diacritical differentiations between colors, lines, or planes. This possibility was implied by Saussure's linguistics, which maintained that taken singly, signs do not signify anything, but gain their sense and reference by their divergence from other signs.[37] To this possibility Merleau-Ponty replies definitively and unequivocally near the end of the essay: "Signs do not simply evoke other signs for us and so on without end, and language is not like a prison we are locked into or a guide we must blindly follow" (S, 81; S, 101; ILVS, 118).

To summarize briefly, Merleau-Ponty's conclusion seems to be that no sharp difference can be made between the physical work of art and the aesthetic object, even though works of art can exist in multiple copies or performances and can be lost or destroyed. This bestows a fragility on the aesthetic object that is objectionable to more idealist philosophies of art such as that of Roman Ingarden.[38] To come before the material work is essential to the aesthetic experience. Nevertheless, the aesthetic object is not the work of art *simpliciter*, rather the aesthetic object just is the world itself, but the world as revealed by the work, that is, the world-cum-work. The aesthetic object signified by a work of art is not a feeling or imagined object found in the truncated relation between viewer and work, as Sartre had maintained. The work reveals the world in a new way. The work is not an opaque thing, but if not transparent, at least a translucent window through which the world appears. The distinction between indexical and iconic signs is therefore too sharply drawn by Sartre. Though Merleau-Ponty denies that the relation of the painting to the world is a resemblance, he views the relation as one of revealing or disclosing (*dévoiler*). This begins to move Merleau-Ponty's aesthetic theory away from Sartre and in the direction of Heidegger's *The Origin of the Work of Art*. The aesthetic experience that intends the aesthetic object, world-cum-work, requires the viewer's imagination, but since imagination is characterized by Merleau-Ponty as attention to the imminent, latent, hidden, or repressed hollows of the world, not nihilation of the world in favor of not-being, it is just as well to say that the aesthetic experience requires vision of all that is *in* the *visible*.

Near the end of "Indirect Language and the Voices of Silence," Merleau-Ponty directly takes up the question of the privilege of linguistic expression over the expression of painting. It is surely Sartre's position on the supposed cognitive supremacy of nonfictional writing over the alleged cognitive impoverishment of painting, poetry, drama, and fiction that is being addressed. Professional writers like Sartre, Merleau-Ponty says, underestimate the "language of painting," like what happens to us when we hear a foreign language that we speak poorly. In contrast, Merleau-Ponty had often referred to the fact that "painting speaks," that Cézanne "writes in paint" and "thinks in paint." Therefore, it is with some surprise, perhaps consternation, that we find Merleau-Ponty's conclusion to be that "in short, language speaks, and the voices of painting are the voices of silence" (S, 81; S, 101; ILVS, 117).

On its surface, this may seem a concession to the cognitive privilege Sartre assigned to nonfictional writing, but it surely is not. Silence is not a negative phenomenon for Merleau-Ponty, the sheer absence of thought or meaning. Within speaking and writing, silence is "the voice of the spirit" that dwells in the pauses and spaces between signs and in what is omitted, in what is not said rather than said. In painting, silence is the style of an artist's work that resists formalism and complete analysis, and no language, including nonfictional prose, ever frees itself from "the precariousness of mute forms of expression." In other places, Merleau-

Ponty often quoted the words of Paul Claudel found at the end of *Art poétique*: "Time is the way offered to all that will be to be no longer. It is the *invitation to die*, for every phrase to decompose in the explicative and total concordance, to consummate the speech of adoration addressed to *Sigé* the Abyss"[39] (*sigé* = silence).

Having established the resonances of silence, now finding a new philosophical voice, Merleau-Ponty enunciates important differences between the ways in which painting, speech, and writing signify. These differences had been glossed over earlier by the philosopher, but he now articulates three differences clearly and unequivocally. Painting absorbs its history more discontinuously and aggressively than does language, language has a greater reflexive power than painting in its ability to speak about speaking or write about writing, and ancient works of painting are more accessible but also less informative than ancient works of prose, which are less accessible but more informative. In interpreting Merleau-Ponty's account of these differences, the reader is urged to discover whether Merleau-Ponty is referring to the painter's living work (*peindre*, to paint) or the artwork (*la peinture*, the painting) on the one side of the comparison and whether he is referring to speech, writing, or the sedimented language system on the other. If these references are sometimes unclear, Merleau-Ponty's conclusion about the alleged cognitive privilege of language is quite clear. The various forms of expression of meaning are not reducible one to the other. A painting is not substitutable for a thousand words, nor may a thousand words replace a painting. In the end what we must say is that language is neither primary nor secondary to painting, both are different modes of signification for the expression of meaning. This conclusion foreshadows *The Visible and the Invisible*, where language will be described as "another less heavy, more transparent body" (VI, 153; *VI*, 200), and this casts our attention forward to "Eye and Mind."

3

Ontology and Painting: "Eye and Mind"

Galen A. Johnson

E ye and Mind" is Merleau-Ponty's climactic philosophical study of modern painting. It is a rich and deep text that marks Merleau-Ponty's return to the study of painting itself as a renewed inspiration for philosophical work, in this case for developing a new metaphysics. "[A]ny theory of painting is a metaphysics" (PrP, 171; OE, 41–42; EM, 132), Merleau-Ponty wrote, and his essay undertakes a study of modern painting in order to develop his philosophy beyond phenomenology and beyond structuralism toward a new post-Cartesian ontology of visibility and invisibility. The new philosophical terms of that ontology are introduced throughout the text: element, Flesh, chiasm, reversibility, depth, transcendence, and vertical time. It is this experiment with a new ontology amidst an essay on painting that led the artist Rene Magritte to his ironic appraisal of "Eye and Mind": "Merleau-Ponty's very brilliant thesis is very pleasant to read, but it hardly makes one think of painting—which he nevertheless appears to be dealing with."[1]

Nevertheless, the philosophy of painting that emerges in "Eye and Mind" is less narrowly focused on Cézanne, Matisse, and other "worldly" or representational painters, and one more capable of encompassing the work of recent abstract artists such as Paul Klee, Nicholas de Staël, and even Magritte himself. Before we turn to the philosophical themes of the essay directly, we should once again briefly situate the text of "Eye and Mind" in its context and say a few words regarding the painters and sources that are involved.

Text and Context

"Eye and Mind" was first published in January 1961 as an essay in the first volume of *Art de France*, and was subsequently published as a separate short monograph by Gallimard in 1964. It was the last work Merleau-Ponty published prior to his sudden, premature death on 3 May 1961, at the age of fifty-three. The essay is signed and dated July and August 1960 and was written at Le Tholonet, a small village in the south of France near Aix-en-Provence where Cézanne had a studio during the last years of his career. Nine years had passed between the appearance of "Indirect Language and the Voices of Silence" (June and July 1952) and the publication of "Eye and Mind." Merleau-Ponty had given his inaugural lecture at Collège de France entitled *Eloge de la philosophie* (*In Praise of Philosophy*) on 15 January 1953, and offered two courses each year at the Collège between 1952 and 1961.[2] His critique of Marxism and strident critique of Sartre had appeared in 1955 in his book entitled *Adventures of the Dialectic*. From 1953 to 1956, Merleau-Ponty had edited a history of philosophy for the series published by Lucien Mazenod called "Galerie des hommes célèbres," and entitled *Les philosophes célèbres*.[3] Merleau-Ponty wrote the introductions to each of the major periods in the history of philosophy, most of which were later published in *Signs*, and recruited some of the leading philosophers of Europe to write the introductions to the thought of each of the world's major philosophers. For example, Jean Beaufret wrote the essays on Parmenides and Zeno, Gilbert Ryle wrote on Hume, Gilles Deleuze on Bergson, Alfred Schutz on Scheler, and Alphonse de Waehlens on Heidegger and Sartre.

In addition to being an anthology of the history of philosophy, *Les philosophes célèbres* is an art edition with 115 plates of portraits, drawings, paintings, and sculptures of the world's celebrated philosophers collected from the museums of western Europe. These include full-page color portraits of Pascal and Malebranche, a drawing of Max Stirner in profile by Friedrich Engels, and a full-page photograph of the young Sartre by a Paris photographer. The book opens with a drawing Albert Giacometti made especially for the volume as frontispiece (and included here). *Les philosophes célèbres* is a testimony to Merleau-Ponty's ongoing interest in painting and the plastic arts during the years that separate the

"Indirect Language" essay and "Eye and Mind," as well as to the common task of philosophy and painting in which Merleau-Ponty believed. The writing of "Eye and Mind" in July and August of 1960 is chronologically interlaced with two other texts on which Merleau-Ponty was at work. The first is the preface to *Signs*, which Merleau-Ponty had completed in February 1960, but to which he returned in September 1960 following completion of "Eye and Mind," to add the last section on his broken friendship with Sartre. The earlier portion of this preface gives us the intellectual itinerary of Merleau-Ponty's development from the philosophy of expression and language that occupied him in "Indirect Language and the Voices of Silence" toward ontology. "The whole description of our landscape and the lines of our universe," Merleau-Ponty wrote, "needs to be redone. Colors, sounds, and things—like Van Gogh's stars—are the focal points and radiance of being" (S, 15; *S*, 22). As the "Indirect Language" essay had argued, if every statement is incomplete and every expression is situated upon a silent tacit comprehension, then it must be that "things are said and are thought by a Speech and by a Thought which we do not have but which has us" (S, 19; *S*, 27). It must be that the visible world appears in union with an invisibility that is the outline and depth of the visible. This mystery, this intertwining, this chiasm between visible and in-the-visible, has been poorly handled by the modern philosophical tradition from Descartes to Sartre that opposes being to nothingness. Merleau-Ponty believed that the invisible depth and richness of the visible had been better approached through the colors of painters than through philosophy, "which paints without colors in black and white, like copperplate engravings" (S, 22; *S*, 31). We need a new philosophical language that would not ignore the strangeness of the world, even if it would of necessity speak indirectly and in half-silence.

The second text with which "Eye and Mind" is chronologically and intellectually interlaced is *The Visible and the Invisible*. In the same way that "Eye and Mind" was written between the first and second parts of the preface to *Signs*, so did "Eye and Mind" fall in between the early and later chapters of *The Visible and the Invisible*. Merleau-Ponty began his work on this text in January of 1959, and from March through June of 1959 he wrote the first three chapters. He then interrupted his work for a period of sixteen months before renewing it in November 1960 to work on a fourth and most original chapter entitled "The Intertwining—The Chiasm."[4] The work on "Eye and Mind" in July and August of 1960 is positioned just prior to Merleau-Ponty's resumption of *The Visible and the Invisible* when he wrote chapter 4 with his most arresting ontological ideas. At the time of his death, Merleau-Ponty left us a 200-page manuscript in progress together with 110 pages of titled and dated working notes that were edited and published posthumously as *The Visible and the Invisible* by Claude Lefort in 1964. This double textual nesting of "Eye and Mind" within *Signs* and *The Visible and the Invisible* shows us how crucial renewed reflections on modern painting were to the inspiration of Merleau-Ponty's late ontology.

"Eye and Mind" condenses what it seems would have been the continuation of *The Visible and the Invisible* according to Merleau-Ponty's last outline for the three major sections of his new book on ontology: (1) Visible and Invisible, (2) Nature, and (3) Logos. If we assume that the fourth and last completed chapter of *The Visible and the Invisible* on "The Intertwining—The Chiasm" would have marked the approximate conclusion of part 1, then "Eye and Mind" may best be taken as the nearest chronological experiment that Merleau-Ponty wrote toward the development of part 2 (Nature) and Part 3 (Logos). This is not to say that the essays immediately preceding "Eye and Mind" during the sixteen month interruption of work on *The Visible and the Invisible* should be disregarded either, especially Merleau-Ponty's provocative essay on Husserl's *Ideas II* from October 1959, entitled "The Philosopher and His Shadow," nor should the courses be disregarded from Collège de France beginning from 1956 to 1957 on "The Concept of Nature."

An example of the power of Merleau-Ponty's reflections on painting for the development of his new ontology is found at the very opening of the decisive fourth chapter of *The Visible and the Invisible*. There Merleau-Ponty begins his reflections on the mysterious union of visible with invisible by speaking of the hidden depths that are indexed within a color like red. A certain precise color red is bound up with a woolly, metallic, or porous texture and is already a variant or difference in its relations with the other reds and the other colors in its surroundings. As a concretion of visibility, it is also an opening to a fabric of invisibility. It is a "punctuation in the field of red things, which includes the tiles of roof tops, the flags of gatekeepers and of the Revolution, certain terrains near Aix or in Madagascar, it is also a punctuation in the field of red garments, which includes, along with the dresses of women, robes of professors, bishops, and advocate generals, and also in the field of adornments and that of uniforms" (VI, 132; *VI*, 174). In short, a visible thing is not a chunk of absolutely hard being that stops our vision, but "a fossil drawn up from the depths of imaginary worlds," a crystallization of visibility that our vision goes through toward invisible possibilities and latencies.

Merleau-Ponty's reference to the "depths of imaginary worlds" in *The Visible and the Invisible* reminds us of the alternative account of imagination he had developed over against Sartre, but also signals that Merleau-Ponty's essay on "Eye and Mind" is formulated in implicit dialogue and dispute with Heidegger's "The Origin of the Work of Art." In a play on a famous Heideggerian text on language, Merleau-Ponty condensed in "Eye and Mind" both his agreement and his deformation of Heidegger's philosophy by writing: "The eye lives in this texture [of visible and invisible] as a man lives in his house" (PrP, 166; *OE*, 27; EM, 127).[5] Heidegger's thesis was that an artwork is the unique blend of thing and sign that gathers a historical world, in the way that Van Gogh's painting of peasant shoes gathers the entire world of the peasant or a Greek temple gathers the world of ancient Greek culture and religion. In a similar way, Italian Renaissance perspective painting and drawing is the visible sign of a world of scientific and technological domination. In Merleau-Ponty's language, these are visibles through which appear invisibles. Yet Merleau-Ponty already knew that painting was a way of entering into visibility and invisibility that remained closer to the palpating life of things and that it was therefore a mistake to collapse the expressions of painting, speech, dialogue, and writing. Painting was a disclosure of the world in the form of a heavier, less transparent, less ductile body than language, with the attendant unique advantages and disadvantages that Merleau-Ponty had studied in "Indirect Language and the Voices of Silence." Nevertheless, Merleau-Ponty's work on "Eye and Mind" awakened his desire for a more concentrated study of Heidegger, which he undertook during the ensuing year in his course at Collège de France entitled "Philosophy and Non-Philosophy Since Hegel."[6]

Painters and Sources

When Merleau-Ponty published "Eye and Mind," he selected several photographic reproductions of artworks for inclusion with the written text. These include oil paintings by Paul Klee and Nicholas de Staël, a watercolor by Cézanne, drawings by Giacometti and Matisse, and sculptures by Rodin and Germaine Richier. In addition to these seven works, the photograph of an eighth work of art was included in the first *Art de France* publication of Merleau-Ponty's essay that did not make its way into the Gallimard edition of the book, a painting by Alain de la Bourdonnaye entitled *Composition* (1960). There are a number of features of interest regarding these selections.

Of the three paintings that were chosen, the Klee work from 1938 entitled *Park near Lucerne* and the Bourdonnaye *Composition*, consisting of the juxtaposition of several angular planes, are nonrepresentational works. The painting by de Staël entitled *Corner of a Studio* or *Green Studio* from 1954, though somewhat representational, is quite abstract. De Staël (1914–55) was a Russian-born painter who was a friend of Georges Braque in Paris and whose life and painting had evident affinities with Van Gogh.[7] De Staël's abstract compositions were built up from large planes and free architecture, which toward the last three years of his career edged back toward representation such as we find in the 1954 composition selected by Merleau-Ponty. Merleau-Ponty's painting selections indicate the progress of his interest in painting toward more abstract forms of expression in which the integrity of the canvas as a two-dimensional surface is more prominent. This is a quite different selection of illustrations than the list of paintings to which Merleau-Ponty referred in "Cézanne's Doubt," for example. The difference between figurative and nonfigurative art, Merleau-Ponty says in "Eye and Mind," "is badly posed; . . . no grape was ever what it is in the most figurative painting and no painting, no matter how abstract, can get away from Being" (PrP, 188; *OE*, 87; EM, 147).

The direction of Merleau-Ponty's philosophy of painting is also indicated in the choice of a late watercolor to represent the presence of Cézanne, a watercolor of Mont Sainte-Victoire from 1900. In Cézanne's watercolors the many shifting planes superimposed on top of each other or blended into one another together with their different levels of depth are more prominently visible than in Cézanne's oils. The orchestration of color harmonies from the transparencies of each color modulates toward more delicate and less resounding chords, such as we find in the modulation of blue, green, and pink in the painting of Mont Sainte-Victoire selected by Merleau-Ponty. Moreover, the blank spaces of white paper are not filled in, but are surrounded by colors and thus incorporated into the scene as more and less brilliant highlights, unifying visible with invisible. In the watercolors of Cézanne's last years, Merleau-Ponty comments, space "radiates around planes that cannot be assigned any place at all" (PrP, 181; *OE*, 68; EM, 141). Without losing the objectivity of his oil paintings, both these features of Cézanne's watercolors draw our attention to the surface composition of the painter's late work and its sublimity and spirituality rather than the features of mass, monumentality, and solidity Merleau-Ponty had stressed in "Cézanne's Doubt."[8]

The painting by Paul Klee, in addition to its nonrepresentational character, also highlights the use of line as a distinct element of composition in creating a hieroglyphic or sign system against a subdued background of color. Merleau-Ponty's interest in secondary qualities, especially color, as bearing special ontological force remains steadfast in "Eye and Mind" (PrP, 172; *OE*, 43; EM, 133). Merleau-Ponty quoted Paul Klee's words that color gets us nearer to "the heart of things" (PrP, 181; *OE*, 67; EM, 141). Yet Merleau-Ponty was now also interested in what he called the "logos of lines," and he included a drawing by Matisse entitled *Bather with Long Hair* that eloquently displays the facility of Matisse's line independent of color. Matisse's linear arabesques move toward simplification, in which the power of a single organic line discloses the essence of a scene. We also find a drawing by Giacometti entitled *Portrait of Aimé Maeght* that moves toward complexity: a face emerges from a tangle of relatively straight lines drawn from a multitude of different positions and planes. The Giacometti drawing done as original frontispiece for *Les philosophes célèbres* employs a cluster of more curved lines to bring forth an image of a face. Though "Eye and Mind" does not retract Merleau-Ponty's criticism of the mechanical, prosaic line of Renaissance perspective painting and drawing as a form of domination that imposes a fixed, univocal perspective of godlike survey, he expresses a new appreciation for the "flexuous line" as a constituting power. A line is a generating axis for perception and creation that balances and unbalances; a line, Merleau-Ponty says, sets in motion a certain disequilibrium within the space of a surface. Therefore, lines, like color, also trace a metaphysics of space, and painters like Klee and Matisse, who more than anyone believed in color, had found a way to "let a line muse," to "go line"—*d'aller ligne* (PrP, 183; *OE*, 74; EM, 143). In *The Visible and the Invisible*, Merleau-Ponty wrote that a line is a certain value. It is a "ray of the world" that impacts on vision and gives vision "the value of a curvature of space" (VI, 247; *VI*, 301). Surprisingly, given the association between Italian Renaissance art and the mechanical line, Merleau-Ponty invokes Leonardo da Vinci's *Treatise on Painting* on behalf of the sinuous, flexuous, bending and swaying lines of bodies, of melodies, of lineage, of chiasm between visible and invisible: "The secret of the art of drawing is to discover in each object the particular way in which a certain flexuous line, which is, so to speak, its generating axis, is directed through its whole extent" (PrP, 183; *OE*, 72; EM, 142).[9]

"Eye and Mind" also includes photographs of two works of sculpture and Merleau-Ponty's first comments on this plastic art. The works are August Rodin's *Femme Accroupie* (*Crouching Woman*) from 1882 and Germaine Richier's *La Sauterelle* (*The Leaper*) from 1945. Germaine Richier (1904–59), from a small town near Arles, France, is known for her eccentric animal sculptures of insects like bats, toads, and grasshoppers, such as her *Spider* (1946), as well as her dark, brutal and almost monstrous allegorical personifications of the forces of nature in works like *Storm* (1947–48) and *Hurricane* (1949). One of her works entitled *Christ* (1950) raised violent controversies at the church at Assy for its fantastic, flayed representation of the Christ figure.[10]

Merleau-Ponty comments on the facility painters often show as sculptors, and the remarkable "transubstantiations" eye and hand are able to undertake from one medium to another, all the while retaining their essential unity and style (PrP, 182; *OE*, 71; EM, 142). He introduces Rodin's reflections on the possibility for sculpture in stone or bronze or wood to present motion by portraying arms, legs, trunk, and head at different instants. By presenting the body in an attitude that it never actually holds at any one particular instant, the artist sculptures the invisible from the visible, and this mingling of real with fictive permits transition and duration to arise from bronze or stone before our eyes. Perhaps now, Merleau-Ponty says, we will have a better sense of that little verb "to see." "Vision is not a certain mode of thought or presence to self; it is the means given me for being absent from myself" (PrP, 186; *OE*, 81; EM, 146).

As there is this mingling between presence and absence, actual and imaginary, in our vision of short-term motion, a longer-term intertwining of presence with absence is found in the history of art. Merleau-Ponty comments that fragments of Rodin's sculptures are almost already statues by Richier, though the works are separated by more than sixty years.[11] In spite of Richier's departure from the smooth, full shapes of Rodin in favor of hollows, perforations, and defacements, a work such as her *Storm* (1947–48) is animated by the same posture and plastic energy as the torso of Rodin's *Walking Man* (1977–78).[12] This is also evident in the postural analogies between *Femme Accroupie* and *La Sauterelle* selected by Merleau-Ponty. The rather remarkable continuity between two sculptors who seem so different leads Merleau-Ponty to his reflections near the end of the essay on the question of progress in art history. He proposes a notion of vertical time with layers and depths that remain latently present, as opposed to linear time with its vanishing present and specious notion of progress.

In addition to these artists whose works illustrate "Eye and Mind," there are also passing references in the essay to Robert Delaunay, Marey, Jean Dubuffet, and Marcel Duchamp. Obviously a new and extensive range of sources was at work in the background of Merleau-Ponty's renewed philosophy of painting. The footnotes to the essay cite twenty-one different works. Noteworthy among these are Paul Claudel's *Introduction a la peinture hollandaise*, two works on abstract painting by C. P. Bru and Robert Delaunay, a work by Schmidt on Cézanne's watercolors, and Rainer Maria Rilke's book on Rodin. Merleau-Ponty also continued his practice of studying interviews and conversations with the artists about whom he wrote, adding to Bernard and Gasquet's accounts of their conversations with Cézanne, Paul Gsell's conversations with Rodin published in Rodin's *Art*, and the interviews by Georges Charbonnier with Max Ernst, Albert Giacometti, and Henri Matisse published in Charbonnier's two volume *Le monologue du peintre*.

It is vital to call attention to the number of works Merleau-Ponty cites in relation to Paul Klee. He refers to Klee's 1924 Jena Lecture published in Grohmann's *Paul Klee* as well as Klee's four-volume pedagogical *Journals* which were edited and published in German in 1956 and had just appeared in French translation in 1959[13] prior to the summer of 1960 when Merleau-Ponty wrote "Eye and Mind." Volume 1 of Klee's *Journals* is entitled *The Thinking Eye*, ever so close to Merleau-Ponty's own title, "Eye and Mind." Paul Klee is the strongest new voice in "Eye and Mind," approaching the authority of Cézanne for Merleau-Ponty's philosophy of painting, who was the other likely source for the title. Emile Bernard had recorded this opinion from Cézanne: "There are two things in the painter, the eye and the mind; each of them should aid the other. It is necessary to work at their mutual development, in the eye by looking at nature, in the mind by the logic of organized sensations which provides the means of expression."[14] The strength of Klee's voice in "Eye and Mind" is heightened with the discovery that the work by Henri Michaux entitled "Aventures de lignes" that is the source for many of Merleau-Ponty's insights regarding line was written as the preface to the French edition of Will Grohmann's *Paul Klee*.[15]

In one respect at least Merleau-Ponty is not well served by the choice of Klee as painterly spokesperson for his new ontology. Klee had a formalist interest in color relationships, and formalized color relationships arithmetically in his Bauhaus course notes, using circles, triangles, and proportions to create what he named "The Canon of Color Totality."[16] It was probably against this totalizing tendency in Klee, the theoretician and teacher, that Merleau-Ponty wrote "there is no one master key to the visible" (PrP, 181; *OE*, 67; EM, 141). Nevertheless, it was in the reflections of Paul Klee on the art of painting that Merleau-Ponty found some of the most germinating insights for "Eye and Mind." It was in the words of André Marchand, expressing the sentiment of Paul Klee in Marchand's interview with Charbonnier, that we find the purest expression of reversibility: "In a forest, I have felt many times over that it was not I who looked at the forest. Some days I felt that the trees were looking at me, were speaking to me" (PrP, 167; *OE*, 31; EM, 129). This was a sentiment that had haunted Merleau-Ponty's thoughts on painting since he had first encountered it in Cézanne's expression: "The landscape thinks itself in me and I am its consciousness" (SNS, 17; *SNS*, 30; CD, 67). It was also Paul Klee who gave Merleau-Ponty the text: "I cannot be caught in immanence" (PrP, 188; *OE*, 87; EM, 148). These words were chosen by Klee for his tombstone during his long struggle with a terminal illness to express the emblem of his life and work, and Merleau-Ponty also chose Klee's words in "Eye and Mind" as expressing to us "the ontological formula of painting" (PrP, 188; *OE*, 87; EM, 147–48). It is now time to turn directly to the themes of transcendence and immanence, visibility and invisibility, as found in Merleau-Ponty's ontology of painting.

Philosophical Themes

"Eye and Mind" sets out into new waters. Its task is to "interrogate painting itself" regarding the nature of what exists, in order to return "to the 'there is,' to the site, the soil of the sensible and opened world such as it is in our life and for our body" (PrP, 160; *OE*, 12; EM, 122). Merleau-Ponty is explicit about granting painting and the plastic arts such as sculpture an ontological privilege over other arts such as music, as well as over science and philosophy. Music, Merleau-Ponty says without further explanation, is "too far on the hither side of the world" to depict anything other than "certain outlines of Being" (PrP, 161; *OE*, 14; EM, 123). Claude Lévi-Strauss has noted the paradox in Merleau-Ponty's dismissal in "Eye and Mind" of the significance of music for ontology, for in other of Merleau-Ponty's works we find a different appraisal of music.[17] *The Visible and the Invisible* gives us a rich text on invisibility and depth in musical performance: the musician "feels himself, and others feel him to be at the service of the sonata; the sonata sings through him or cries out so suddenly that he must 'dash on his bow' to follow it" (VI, 151; *VI*, 199).[18] *The Visible and the Invisible* also speaks of the reversibility between sonority and listening as a more "agile" reversibility than touch-touching for it is the crossing-over between flesh and expression, between visible and the invisibilities of speech and thought: "If I am close enough to the other who speaks to hear his breath and feel his effervescence and his fatigue, I almost witness, in him as in myself, the awesome birth of vociferation" (VI, 144; *VI*, 190).[19] *Phenomenology of Perception* had spoken of the way an infant learns to speak a language by first "singing the world" and mastering the tonalities of a tongue (PhP, 187; *PP*, 218).

Painting is also closer to the palpable life of things than science or philosophy, Merleau-Ponty says, for modern science, unlike classical science, "has given up living in things" (PrP, 159; *OE*, 9; EM, 121) in favor of manipulation, operations, and theoretical models, and philosophy is too tied to language, advice, and opinions in comparison with the "innocence" of painting (PrP, 161; *OE*, 13; EM, 123). Merleau-Ponty's term "innocence" reinvokes the painterly *epoché* of "Cézanne's Doubt," the suspension or bracketing of the presuppositions of the modern scientific and philosophical traditions in order to gain access to the essential forms of phenomena as they appear in pretheoretical experience. The painter lends his or her body to the world to bring forth a metamorphosis of the visible, an imaginative expression of the mute meanings and richness of the prereflective world. Merleau-Ponty joins a line of philosophers originating in Schelling and coming forward through Nietzsche to Heidegger who accord special prominence to artistic work in tracing the ribs and joints of Being. The painter "lives in fascination" with the "there is" (*il y a*)—that there is something, and this is the miracle or "delirium" of vision (PrP, 166; *OE*, 26; EM, 127). The quotation from Cézanne's conversations with Gasquet that prefaces "Eye and Mind" expresses equally the goal of the painter and the philosopher: "What I am trying to translate to you is more mysterious; it is entwined in the very roots of being, in the impalpable source of sensations" (PrP, 159; *OE*, ix; EM, 121).

Herein lies the stylistic and methodological dilemma of the essay. If Emile Bernard referred to "Cézanne's suicide" as the painter's attempt to express nature on canvas while denying himself the means for doing so, "Eye and Mind" might be referred to as "Merleau-Ponty's suicide," in which the philosopher seeks to bring to written expression the silent and mute meanings of prereflective brute Being. This accounts for the allusive, poetic, Proust-like style of the essay which at once makes it such a pleasure to read but so difficult to think. Merleau-Ponty praised Proust's prose, saying that "no one had gone further in fixing the relations between the visible and the invisible" (VI, 149; *VI*, 195). "Eye and Mind" is an indirect ontology, filled with allusions, themes that appear and disappear winding in and out, and startling new philosophical vocabulary. In the opening chapter of *The Visible and the Invisible*, Merleau-Ponty introduced the method of "hyperreflection" (*surréflex-*

ion) that would characterize his indirect ontology. To reflect in thought cannot mean to coincide with the object precisely because thought is *re*flection, re-turn, re-conquest, or re-covery (VI, 45; *VI*, 69). Reflection is retrospective, therefore a temporal beat behind the genesis of its object; reflection is the activity of a self-in-genesis in relation to an object, therefore a temporal beat behind the genesis of itself. The source of the world and the source of the self slip away from reflective view. Hyperreflection is the effort to take seriously these spaces of genesis, meaning that ontology is possible only indirectly, in an interrogative mood that remains sensitive to the silence of what cannot be said.

In hyperreflection there is a decentering of Merleau-Ponty's philosophy away from the authority of the subject and the philosopher-author that has evident affinities with postmodernism,[20] and that alters Merleau-Ponty's voice significantly in the essay. He is now a philosopher close to the poet seeking to listen to the painter's evocation of "the silent logos of the world," indicating indirectly a "conceptless presentation of universal Being" (PrP, 182; *OE*, 71; EM, 142). The reader who enters into this paradoxical enterprise with patience and energy will be fascinated by a deepened comprehension of what exists. Judgments vary. Michel de Certeau wrote that in Merleau-Ponty's lyricism he "got lost at sea."[21] Sartre commented that "Eye and Mind" "says it all providing one can decipher it."[22] We will make an approach to the essay, with no confidence that we will decipher everything in it, but with the intent of a reading that makes an address to postmodernism and the praise and criticisms the essay has absorbed in the decades since it appeared.

By the time of "Eye and Mind," Merleau-Ponty recognized that his earlier phenomenology and thesis of the primacy of perception and the lived-body had remained too closely tied to the unity of the subject as transcendental ground of the unity of the world.[23] "Eye and Mind" sought to explore and articulate a depth or laterality of the self that is at a distance from itself, from things and the world, and from the significances given things in language. Merleau-Ponty conveyed these distances, gaps, or spreads in the word *écart*. Themes from his earlier essays on painting appear in "Eye and Mind," but they are now redone. It is as if Merleau-Ponty had decided his earlier work had enunciated themes on the surface of painting and expression, and now he wanted to get to the heart of the matter. The earlier themes are now set in motion around the central question of *depth*, depth in painting, depth in space, depth in self and in Being. The problem of depth collects together the work of Merleau-Ponty's later ontology and the work of modern painting.

Merleau-Ponty takes his departure from the painter's body and "thinking eye." Why is it that painters have so often said, in the manner of Klee, that the forest was speaking in them, or the trees were looking at them, or why did Cézanne say that "nature is on the inside"? It must be that there is a system of exchanges between body and world such that eye and hand become the obverse side of things, the inside of an outside in which are both enveloped. This extraordinary overlapping or envelopment is one in which seer and seen are capable of reversing their roles as subject and object, and the maturation of vision in the life of a painter is this opening up of self to the world as "the other side" of its power of looking. The body seeing becomes the body looked at; the body touching becomes the body touched. Things, for the painter, become an annex or prolongation of self, Merleau-Ponty says, incrusted in its flesh, necessarily "made of the same stuff as the body" (PrP, 163; OE, 19; EM, 125). Merleau-Ponty refers to this as a good or profound "narcissism" in which the seer is caught up in the seen, not to see in the outside the contour of one's own body, but to emigrate into the world, to be seduced and captivated by it, "so that the seer and the visible reciprocate one another and we no longer know which sees and which is seen" (VI, 139; VI, 183). It is this generality, this anonymity that is called Flesh. "There is a human body when, between the seeing and the seen, between touching and the touched, between one eye and the other, between hand and hand, a blending of some sort takes place—when the spark is lit between sensing and sensible, lighting the fire that will not stop burning" (PrP, 163; OE, 21; EM, 125). Painting expresses nothing other than these "inversions" (ces renversements) between vision and the visible. It is "the genesis, the metamorphosis of Being in vision" (PrP, 166; OE, 28; EM, 128).

These opening reflections on vision and visibility introduce us to two of the most important technical terms of Merleau-Ponty's ontology—namely, reversibility and Flesh. With these terms, Merleau-Ponty seems well on his way toward some form of ontological monism of underlying substance that envelops painter and world. The perceptual monism of the thesis of the primacy of perception from Phenomenology of Perception, which we found in "Cézanne's Doubt" but which began to be relaxed and more loosely knit in "Indirect Language and the Voices of Silence," seems in danger of sedimenting and rigidifying into a more basic frozen monistic metaphysic. This is precisely what Merleau-Ponty avoids in the notion of Flesh. Such a monism would collapse the depth of the world, the distance between painter and thing and the movement of things that is sought through the color and line of Klee or Matisse and through the bronze or stone of Rodin or Richier. Flesh and reversibility are notions meant to express both envelopment and distance, the paradox of unity at a distance or sameness with difference, finding a new ontological way between monism and dualism. Let us take a brief but more detailed look at these terms to see how this might be so.

The term "Flesh" occurs in both sections 2 and 4 of "Eye and Mind," and Merleau-Ponty introduces it with an account of what he means by reversibility. The reversibility of subject and object that the painter experiences is exemplified in our own bodies as a fundamental manifestation of Being. When my right hand touches my left, the right hand is touched in reply, and in the next instant the relation may be reversed. This reversibility is called "chiasm" from the Greek rhetorical form of reversing the order of an expression from first to last into last to first. Chiasm expresses the overlapping, criss-crossing, inclining and reclining found in the Greek letter *chi* (X). What does Merleau-Ponty mean in saying that vision is similarly reversible between self and world? It does not mean the absurdity that the trees and things we see also see us in return, thus imputing consciousness and vision to inanimate things as a heightened and exaggerated Leibnizian panpsychism. Rather it means that the seer is caught up in the midst of the visible, that in order to see, the seer must in turn be capable of being seen. Merleau-Ponty's thought is here driving toward the fact that our body announces a kind of "natural reflection."[24] *The Visible and the Invisible* says that "the flesh is a mirror phenomenon and the mirror is an extension of my relation with my body" (VI, 255; *VI*, 309), for in the mirror I both see and see myself seeing. In "Eye and Mind," Merleau-Ponty discusses the painterly fascination with mirrors as an outline of the metaphysical structure of Flesh. In the mirror, the entire room is digested in reverse, what is on my left becomes what is on my right. Artists have often painted themselves in the act of painting, adding to what they saw of things what things saw of them. This is the metamorphosis of seeing into seen that defines both the Flesh and the painter's vocation (PrP, 169; *OE*, 34; EM, 130). In his essay included in this volume, "Cezanne's Mirror Stage," Hugh Silverman has given us a detailed study of the painter's use of mirrors in self-portraiture and the left-right reversibility that inevitably occurs.

Thus, reversibility is an aesthetic rather than a logical phenomenon and does not imply the symmetry of subject and object, their substitutability in meaning, as would be implied by the logical biconditional. In the mirror, the reflection of the right hand is transposed as the left hand. There is asymmetrical reversibility, reflexivity with difference. Touching is changed in being touched, "transubstantiated," Merleau-Ponty says, "through the offices of an agile hand" (PrP, 165; *OE*, 26; EM, 127). This priestly metaphor captures the metamorphosis of subject into object and back that refers to a strife between things and between self and things that nevertheless does not destroy their bonding synergy, that therefore does not announce a divorce into separate substances or categories of Being. This doubling with difference (*écart*) between self and world is the meaning of Flesh. The strife and rivalry among colors, shadings, and lines is both their bond and their separation.[25] The artist bears bodily witness to this genesis in the metamorphosis of world into artwork, thus conferring memory and duration upon genesis.[26] Véronique Fóti, in her essay included here, "The Dimension of Color," extends the suggestions of Merleau-Ponty in *Eye and Mind* regarding the "logos of color" in order to vindicate his view that the secondary qualities give us a more profound opening onto the world. Her discussion leads us back to theories of color proposed prior to Cartesian optics among the Pre-Socratics and by Plato and Aristotle.

We can now see that the ontology Merleau-Ponty finds implicit in the work of painting is very far removed from a metaphysics of substance and sameness, a monism of the One. In *The Visible and the Invisible*, Merleau-Ponty wrote that Flesh "is not matter, is not mind, is not substance. To designate it, we should need the old term 'element,' in the sense it was used to speak of water, air, earth, and fire . . . a sort of incarnate principle that brings a style of being wherever there is a fragment of being" (VI, 139; *VI*, 184). Merleau-Ponty's account of Flesh in terms of strife as a unity of opposites should have already signaled the influence, not only of Heidegger's essay on "The Origin of the Work of Art," but of Heraclitus. This important direct reference to the Greek Presocratic philosophers alerts us to figures like water, air, and fire that occur throughout "Eye and Mind," and point us on from depth to desire as an *ontological*, not merely psychological, feature of the world. Being itself, for Merleau-Ponty, as the incarnate principle of Flesh, is imbued with a kind of energy, longing, desire or *conatus*. What is this synergy that binds the folds of my ragged, "vagabond" body—left and right, front and back, and binds it equally to its world?

Merleau-Ponty invokes the element of air in "Eye and Mind." "We speak of . . . inspiration and expiration of Being, . . . action and passion so slightly discernible that it becomes impossible to distinguish between what sees and what is seen, what paints and what is painted" (PrP, 167; *OE*, 31–32; EM, 129). Merleau-Ponty also conveys the binding synergy in the heart of Being with images of water. He speaks of the froth and crest of waves, the water's thickness as it bends the tiling at the bottom of a pool, and the nostalgic longing for "that place where there persists, like the mother water in crystal, the undividedness of the sensing and the sensed" (PrP, 179, 182, 163; *OE*, 62, 70, 20; EM, 139, 142, 125). Nevertheless, through repetition of terms like spark, fission, explosion, and dehiscence, it is the figure of fire that dominates the account of the element called *Flesh* in "Eye and Mind," and fire speaks to us of desire.[27]

Before we enter further into this discussion of fire and desire, we should again remind ourselves that when Merleau-Ponty speaks this way, he means that things are fleshly and fiery, not that Flesh or fire are some all-pervasive cosmic substance.[28] The world is made of the things we see around us, with their surfaces, textures, colors, and lines. Flesh is an "incarnate principle" of doubling, difference, and desire crocheted into all that is *there*. Jean-François Lyotard, whose *Discours, figure* is helpful about so much in "Eye and Mind," completely missed both the difference and the desire in Merleau-Ponty's treatment of depth in "Eye and Mind." Two works by Lyotard highly critical of Merleau-Ponty are included in this volume, one of them consisting of excerpts from this major early work (1971). Lyotard claims to find in Merleau-Ponty's ontology of painting a lingering phenomenological demand for unity and continuity of experience and ontological knowledge that is figured in his text as a nostalgic longing for the mother. Nethertheless, Merleau-Ponty's account does not overlook the gaps, splits, and disunities within world and self, eliminating what is strange, foreign and Other in favor of conceptual sameness, and Merleau-Ponty's account has much to do with desire, dreams, and Eros. It was Merleau-Ponty who said that painting mixes up the imaginary and the real "in laying out its oneiric universe of carnal essences" (PrP, 1.69; *OE*, 35; EM, 130).

Merleau-Ponty rejects the thesis that desire is a positivity, a thing or force in our bodies like an instinct or mechanical unconscious that overtakes the painter, such as we find expressed in mechanical, physiological renderings of Freud's theory of libido or Nietzsche's Dionysian. Likewise, Merleau-Ponty also rejects Sartre's thesis on the emotions which, like his account of imagination, renders desire a lack or sheer nothingness, the negative intuition of absence. Rather, what Merleau-Ponty meant by the desire that is figured within the genesis of Being is best approached through the Greek term "element." The Milesian sense of element meant that which is always presupposed but always forgotten, that from which everything comes and to which everything returns. The Greek elements were, therefore, eternal. Merleau-Ponty's term *Flesh* was meant to convey a genesis and growth in contrast to this eternality. In the "Working Notes" to *The Visible and the Invisible*, Merleau-Ponty was quite direct on this point: "I call the world flesh," he wrote, "in order to say that it is a *pregnancy* of possibles" (VI, 250; *VI*, 304). Paired with this term "pregnancy" we also find the birthing term "labor": "in the patient and silent labor of desire, begins the paradox of expression" (VI, 144; *VI*, 189). The painter's vision, "Eye and Mind" says, "is a continued birth" (PrP, 168; *OE*, 32; EM, 129).

The figure of fire and the notion of desire it indexes refers us to genesis and growth, the possibility for new and renewed expression of the visible *simpliciter*. The longing within the Flesh is the longing for vision, new and renewed comprehension and self-comprehension. This is not some new "end" or "teleology of history," nor is it a nostalgic quest to return us to a lost origin, as Merleau-Ponty makes clear in the last section of "Eye and Mind." The idea of a universal painting and history of painting, of "a totalization of painting," and the idea of a perfect painting found either at a "beginning" of history in a pagan or primitive origin like the caves at Lascaux or at an "end" of history in some misty future, are ideas that make no sense. In terms of the ontology of painting and the expression of what exists, the very first painting "went to the farthest reach of the future" (PrP, 190; *OE*, 92; EM, 149) and every painting stands on its own as an experience, exaltation, and re-creation of the visible world. The desire or *conatus* of the Flesh is the demand for expression, the demand that the world be brought forth over and over again into visibility. In *The Visible and the Invisible*, Merleau-Ponty spoke of the "promiscuity" (VI, 239; *VI*, 292) of Reason with Being and the world in this ongoing movement of genesis, self-genesis, and expression for its own sake, and introduced the notions of "vertical time" and "vertical history." Against linear seriality, vertical time refers us to a variety of experiences that have as their inner structure losing oneself to the world: joy, euphoria, fascination, infatuation, and artistic creation. The flow of time is stopped up. The vertical moment is *simply being there* in the world in what Merleau-Ponty calls a "transversal ecstasis" (VI, 271; *VI*, 325).[29] The meanings and depths of such experiences are not plumbed by referring to backward and forward temporal references, they are understood by referring to the magnetism of the world. The history of Being is the generous explosion of the world into ever new and renewed forms. The history of cultural expression is intensifying, deepening astonishment (wonder) in the face of this "there is." This is the desire within the difference which is Flesh.

These ideas on depth and desire in "Eye and Mind" might be taken as indications of what would have become the philosophy of space and time in the new philosophy of nature Merleau-Ponty projected as part 2 of *The Visible and the Invisible*. They were developed from a departure in the painter's body on the "eye" side of the conjunction "eye and mind." There are also important but less well-formed indications in "Eye and Mind" of some of Merleau-Ponty's ideas with respect to "mind" and invisibility which would have found their way into part 3 of *The Visible and the Invisible* to have been entitled "Logos." "The proper essence of the visible," "Eye and Mind" says, "is to have a layer of invisibility in the strict sense, which makes it present as a certain absence" (PrP, 187; *OE*, 85; EM, 147). In his essay in this volume entitled "Eye and Mind," Mikel Dufrenne takes up the question of the positive content of the term "mind" (*esprit*) in Merleau-Ponty's title, given Merleau-Ponty's stress upon the "eye." Dufrenne pursues the remainder of that term after Merleau-Ponty's critique of "Cartesian mind" and scientific operationalism. Robert Burch's essay analyses the relation of art to ontological truth in the thought of Merleau-Ponty in comparison with Heidegger, and argues that there are *aporias* in both philosophers' attempts to privilege art as a region of transcendence in the comprehension of ontological truth.

The painter's line expresses the nature of the visible world and in so doing also conveys to us the visible world's lining of invisibility. What is this invisible Logos correlative with Flesh? We do find references in the text of "Eye and Mind" to "the unfathomable God" and "abyssal Being" (PrP, 177; *OE*, 58; EM, 138): "God's being for us is an abyss" (PrP, 177; *OE*, 56; EM, 137). The Notes to *The Visible and the Invisible* cite Heidegger: the abyss is upsurge of a *Hoheit* which supports from above, "we fall into the high" (VI, 250; *VI*, 303–4). The attentive reader must wonder regarding the meaning of such references and the spiritual tone that is sometimes found in the adoration of painting and Being in the essay. Nevertheless, it should be remembered that Merleau-Ponty broke with Catholicism early in his adult life and withdrew his participation from Emmanuel Mounier and the journal *Esprit*.[30] The reader of "Eye and Mind" should not confuse Merleau-Ponty's references to invisibility and spirit with the distortion of God into the omniscient and absolute Other, nor the distortion into a rationalistic principle of sufficient reason. This sort of false piety or philosophical absolutism are the exact opposite of the philosopher's basic sensitivities centering on contingency, porosity, openness, and genesis. Paradoxical as it may sound, Merleau-Ponty's position on "spirit" (*esprit*) in "Eye and Mind" is quite consistent with a certain qualified atheism.

In "Eye and Mind," the invisible is not the nonvisible. The word "invisible" is perfectly chosen. The lines of visible things are doubled by a lining of invisibility that is *in* the visible. Merleau-Ponty stresses this, and by doing so decenters the aesthetic task and desire away from the pursuit of an invisibility that would be a separate reality, a heavenly world apart from this world. In May 1960, just prior to the writing of "Eye and Mind," Merleau-Ponty wrote a four-part outline of invisibility in the Notes for *The Visible and the Invisible*:

> The invisible is
> 1) what is not actually visible, but could be (hidden or inactual aspects of the thing—hidden things, situated "elsewhere"— "Here" and "elsewhere")
> 2) what, relative to the visible, could nevertheless not be seen as a thing (the existentials of the visible, its dimensions, its non-figurative inner framework)
> 3) what exists only as tactile or kinesthetically, etc.
> 4) the *lekta*, the Cogito. (VI, 257; *VI*, 310–11)

The meaning of invisibility and the aesthetic insight Merleau-Ponty found in painting pertains to noticing the hidden things, having eyes that genuinely see and minds that genuinely think. It also pertains to the *lekta* and the cogito. *Lekta* is not the same as the cogito, as their grouping above might lead one to think. *Lekta* is from the Greek noun *lektos*, and means both (1) that which is gathered, chosen and picked out; and (2) that which is capable of being spoken. The painter's vision is a gathering that makes possible a speaking. The painter's line is an expression of a particular color or thing but also is a transcendent line tracing the *Wesen* (essence) of things. This is what we *see* in the lines of Matisse and Klee, the presentation of a universal in a particular. Merleau-Ponty explicitly denies that this is a *hylomorphism* (VI, 250; *VI*, 304), yet undoubtedly Aristotle's account of form and matter is the one Merleau-Ponty had in mind as an approximation for the intertwining of world and word. There is an essence of red, which is not the essence of green. This essence, though, like a painting, is accessible only through the seeing and not through a thinking separate from the seeing. The essence exists (*este*) in the red, Merleau-Ponty says, and for the painter whose canvas is given a title, there are two possibilities. Either one may decide, with Paul Klee, to hold to the genesis of the visible on a surface and the principle of absolute painting, and then give the work no title or bestow a title post facto as Klee used to do in his christening ceremonies. Or one may decide, with Matisse, to put into a single line of a drawing the *visible essence* of a thing as nude, as face, or flower (PrP, 184; *OE*, 75-76; EM, 143–44). In either case, the title is within the frame of the work, and word and world are interlaced. This relation between thing and essence is one that we could well have wished from Merleau-Ponty further detail and elaboration.

Invisibility is also the cogito, an invisibility to myself. The eye does not see itself for reasons of principle, *The Visible and the Invisible* says, for the eye contains a blind spot. What the eye does not see is what in it prepares and makes possible the vision of everything else, as the retina is blind at the point where the fibers that permit vision spread out into it (VI, 248; *VI*, 301). Merleau-Ponty made note of the blind spot in self-consciousness in May of 1960, again just prior to "Eye and Mind." Self-portraiture and the fascination with mirrors are the artist's attempt to coincide with himself or herself, to be present at the heart of one's own being and make oneself visible. Even if this attempt at coincidence is ever frustrated, and the invisibility of the cogito is an invisibility in principle, the *question* of self-comprehension persists in the ragged and tattered folds of our bodies, lives, and histories, and in the manifold expressions of art. In interrogating the depths of the world, the seer and painter interrogate the depths of the self. "Light must have its *imaginaire*. . . . The question is to make space and light, which are *there*, speak to us. There is no end to this question, since the vision to which it addresses itself is itself a question" (PrP, 178; *OE*, 59–60; EM, 138).

In the end, Merleau-Ponty's interrogation of painting in order to return us to the site and soil of the sensible world has led us to an ontology of Flesh, desire, and invisibility. Flesh is the pregnancy of the world, a genesis of doubling with difference and without fusion in the desire for new and renewed expressions of visibility. As the visual is a metamorphosis of desire, so this desire is transubstantiated into the mystery of invisibility, of the word and self-comprehension. The lyricism, depths, and heights of this new metaphysics of painting may seem to overburden the humble artisan of the studio and to display a haste in its movement toward Being out of keeping with our times. "Eye and Mind" was published in the very same year that Emmanuel Levinas published his devastating critique of metaphysics entitled *Totality and Infinity* (1961). *The Visible and the Invisible* appeared in the very same year as Jacques Derrida's essay entitled "Violence and Metaphysics" (1964). Nevertheless, perhaps the reader will find in this account of the work of the painter and of "polymorphous Being" some of the germs of a "postmodern metaphysic" that does not succumb to either the excesses of philosophical totalization or skeptical negation. "Everything happens," Merleau-Ponty once wrote, "as if man encountered at the roots of his constituted being a generosity which is not a compromise with the adversity of the world and which is on his side against it" (IPP, 26–27; *EP*, 33). Upon his return to Paris after completing "Eye and Mind," Merleau-Ponty wrote in the preface to *Signs*: "Underneath the clamor a silence is growing, an expectation. Why could it not be a hope?" (S, 23; *S*, 32).

PART   2

MERLEAU-PONTY'S ESSAYS ON PAINTING

4

Cézanne's Doubt

Maurice Merleau-Ponty

I t took him one hundred working sessions for a still life, one hundred fifty sittings for a portrait. What we call his work was, for him, only an attempt, an approach to painting. In September of 1906, at the age of sixty-seven—one month before his death—he wrote: "I was in such a state of mental agitation, in such great confusion that for a time I feared my weak reason would not survive. . . . Now it seems I am better and that I see more clearly the direction my studies are taking. Will I ever arrive at the goal, so intensely sought and so long pursued? I am still working from nature, and it seems to me I am making slow progress." Painting was his world and his mode of existence. He worked alone, without students, without admiration from his family, without encouragement from the critics. He painted on the afternoon of the day his mother died. In 1870 he was painting at l'Estaque while the police were after him for dodging the draft. And still he had moments of doubt about this vocation. As he grew old, he wondered whether the novelty of his painting might not come from trouble with his eyes, whether his whole life had not been based upon an accident of his body. The hesitation or muddle-headedness of his contemporaries equaled this strain and self-doubt. "The painting of a drunken privy cleaner," said a critic in 1905. Even today, C. Mauclair finds Cézanne's admissions of powerlessness an argument against him. Meanwhile, Cézanne's paintings have spread throughout the world. Why so much uncertainty, so much labor, so many failures, and, suddenly, the greatest success?

Zola, Cézanne's friend from childhood, was the first to find genius in him and the first to speak of him as a "genius gone wrong." An observer of Cézanne's life such as Zola, more concerned with his character than with the meaning of his painting, might well consider it a manifestation of ill-health.

For as far back as 1852, upon entering the Collège Bourbon at Aix, Cézanne worried his friends with his fits of temper and depression. Seven years later, having decided to become an artist, he doubted his talent and did not dare to ask his father—a hatter and later a banker—to send him to Paris. Zola's letters reproach him for his instability, his weakness, and his indecision. When finally he came to Paris, he wrote: "The only thing I have changed is my location: my ennui has followed me." He could not tolerate discussions, because they wore him out and he could never give his reasoning. His nature was basically anxious. Thinking that he would die young, he made his will at the age of forty-two; at forty-six he was for six months the victim of a violent, tormented, overwhelming passion of which no one knows the outcome and to which he would never refer. At fifty-one he withdrew to Aix, where he found landscape best suited to his genius but where also he returned to the world of his childhood, his mother and his sister. After the death of his mother, Cézanne turned to his son for support. "Life is terrifying," he would often say. Religion, which he then set about practicing for the first time, began for him in the fear of life and the fear of death. "It is fear," he explained to a friend; "I feel I will be on earth for another four days—what then? I believe in life after death, and I don't want to risk roasting *in aeternum*." Although his religion later deepened, its original motivation was the need to put his life in order and be relieved of it. He became more and more timid, mistrustful, and sensitive. Occasionally he would visit Paris, but when he ran into friends he would motion to them from a distance not to approach him. In 1903, after his pictures had begun to sell in Paris at twice the price of Monet's and when young men like Joachim Gasquet and Emile Bernard came to see him and ask him questions, he unbent a little. But his fits of anger continued. (In Aix a child once hit him as he passed by; after that he could not bear any contact.) One day when Cézanne was quite old, Emile Bernard steadied him as he stumbled. Cézanne flew into a rage. He could be heard striding around his studio and shouting that he wouldn't let anybody "get his hooks into me." Because of these "hooks" he pushed women who could have modeled for him out of his studio, priests, whom he called "pests," out of his life, and Emile Bernard's theories out of his mind, when they became too insistent.

This loss of flexible human contact; this inability to master new situations; this flight into established habits, in an atmosphere which presented no problems; this rigid opposition between theory and practice, between the "hook" and the freedom of a recluse—all these symptoms permit one to speak of a morbid constitution and more precisely, as, for example, in the case of El Greco, of schizothymia. The notion of painting "from nature" could be said to arise from the same weakness. His extremely close attention to nature and to color, the inhuman character of his paintings (he said that a face should be painted as an object), his devotion to the visible world: all of these would then only represent a flight from the human world, the alienation of his humanity.

These conjectures nevertheless do not give any idea of the positive side of his work; one cannot thereby conclude that his painting is a phenomenon of decadence and what Nietzsche called "impoverished" life or that it has nothing to say to the educated person. Zola's and Emile Bernard's belief in Cézanne's failure probably arises from their having put too much emphasis on psychology and their personal knowledge of Cézanne. It is nonetheless possible that Cézanne conceived a form of art which, while occasioned by his nervous condition, is valid for everyone. Left to himself, he was able to look at nature as only a human being can. The meaning of his work cannot be determined from his life.

This meaning will not become any clearer in the light of art history—that is, by considering influences (the Italian school and Tintoretto, Delacroix, Courbet, and the impressionists), Cézanne's technique, or even his own pronouncements on his work.

His first pictures—up to about 1870—are painted fantasies: a rape, a murder. They are therefore almost always executed in broad strokes and present the moral physiognomy of the actions rather than their visible aspect. It is thanks to the impressionists, and particularly to Pissarro, that Cézanne later conceived painting not as the incarnation of imagined scenes, the projection of dreams outward, but as the exact study of appearances: less a work of the studio than a working from nature. Thanks to the impressionists, he abandoned the baroque technique, whose primary aim is to capture movement, for small dabs placed close together and for patient hatchings.

He quickly parted ways with the impressionists, however. Impressionism was trying to capture, in the painting, the very way in which objects strike our eyes and attack our senses. Objects were depicted as they appear to instantaneous perception, without fixed contours, bound together by light and air. To capture this envelope of light, one had to exclude siennas, ochres, and black and use only the seven colors of the spectrum. The color of objects could not be represented simply by putting on the canvas their local tone, that is, the color they take on isolated from their surroundings; one also had to pay attention to the phenomena of contrast which modify local colors in nature. Furthermore, by a sort of reversal, every color we perceive in nature elicits the appearance of its complement; and these complementaries heighten one another. To achieve sunlit colors in a picture which will be seen in the dim light of apartments, not only must there be a green—if you are painting grass— but also the complementary red which will make it vibrate. Finally, the impressionists break down the local tone itself. One can generally obtain any color by juxtaposing rather than mixing the colors which make it up, thereby achieving a more vibrant hue. The result of these procedures was that the canvas—which no longer corresponded point by point to nature—afforded a generally true impression through the action of the separate parts upon one another. But at the same time, depicting the atmosphere and breaking up the tones submerged the object and caused it to lose its proper weight. The composition of Cézanne's palette leads one to suppose that he had another aim. Instead of the seven colors of the spectrum, one finds eighteen colors—six reds, five yellows, three blues, three greens, and black. The use of warm colors and black shows that Cézanne wants to represent the object, to find it again behind the atmosphere. Likewise, he does not break up the tone; rather, he replaces this technique with graduated colors, a progression of chromatic nuances across the object, a modulation of colors which stays close to the object's form and to the light it receives. Doing away with exact contours in certain cases, giving color priority over the outline—these obviously mean different things for Cézanne and for the impressionists. The object is no longer covered by reflections and lost in its relationships to the atmosphere and other objects: it seems subtly illuminated from within, light emanates from it, and the result is an impression of solidity and material substance. Moreover, Cézanne does not give up making the warm colors vibrate but achieves this chromatic sensation through the use of blue.

One must therefore say that Cézanne wished to return to the object without abandoning the impressionist aesthetics which takes nature as its model. Emile Bernard reminded him that, for the classical artists, painting demanded outline, composition, and distribution of light. Cézanne replied: "They created pictures; we are attempting a piece of nature." He said of the old masters that they "replaced reality with imagination and by the abstraction which accompanies it." Of nature, he said, "the artist must conform to this perfect work of art. Everything comes to us from nature; we exist through it; nothing else is worth remembering."

He stated that he wanted to make of impressionism "something solid, like the art in the museums." His painting was paradoxical: he was pursuing reality without giving up the sensuous surface, with no other guide than the immediate impression of nature, without following the contours, with no outline to enclose the color, with no perspectival or pictorial arrangement. This is what Bernard called Cézanne's suicide: aiming for reality while denying himself the means to attain it. This is the reason for his difficulties and for the distortions one finds in his pictures between 1870 and 1890. Cups and saucers on a table seen from the side should be elliptical, but Cézanne paints the two ends of the ellipse swollen and expanded. The work table in his portrait of Gustave Geffroy stretches, contrary to the laws of perspective, into the lower part of the picture. In giving up the outline Cézanne was abandoning himself to the chaos of sensation, which would upset the objects and constantly suggest illusions, as, for example, the illusion we have when we move our heads that objects themselves are moving—if our judgment did not constantly set these appearances straight. According to Bernard, Cézanne "submerged his painting in ignorance and his mind in shadows." But one cannot really judge his painting in this way except by closing one's mind to half of what he said and one's eyes to what he painted.

It is clear from his conversations with Emile Bernard that Cézanne was always seeking to avoid the ready-made alternatives suggested to him: sensation versus judgment; the painter who sees against the painter who thinks; nature versus composition; primitivism as opposed to tradition. "We have to develop an optics," Cézanne said, "by which I mean a logical vision—that is, one with no element of the absurd." "Are you speaking of our nature?" asked Bernard. Cézanne: "It has to do with both." "But aren't nature and art different?" "I want to make them the same. Art is a personal apperception, which I embody in sensations and which I ask the understanding to organize into a painting."[1] But even these formulas put too much emphasis on the ordinary notions of "sensitivity" or "sensations" and "understanding"—which is why Cézanne could not convince by his arguments and preferred to paint instead. Rather than apply to his work dichotomies more appropriate to those who sustain traditions than to those—philosophers or painters—who found them, we would do better to sensitize ourselves to his painting's own, specific meaning, which is to challenge those dichotomies. Cézanne did not think he had to choose between feeling and thought, as if he were deciding between chaos and order. He did not want to separate the stable things which we see and the shifting way in which they appear; he wanted to depict matter as it takes on form, the birth of order through spontaneous organization. He makes a basic distinction not between "the senses" and "the understanding" but rather between the spontaneous organization of the things we perceive and the human organization of ideas and sciences. We see things; we agree about them; we are anchored in them; and it is with "nature" as our base that we construct our sciences. Cézanne wanted to paint this primordial world, and his pictures therefore seem to show nature pure, while photographs of the same landscapes suggest man's works, conveniences, and imminent presence. Cézanne never wished to "paint like a savage." He wanted to put intelligence, ideas, sciences, perspective, and tradition back in touch with the world of nature which they were intended to comprehend. He wished, as he said, to confront the sciences with the nature "from which they came."

By remaining faithful to the phenomena in his investigations of perspective, Cézanne discovered what recent psychologists have come to formulate: the lived perspective, that which we actually perceive, is not a geometric or photographic one. The objects we see close at hand appear smaller, those far away seem larger than they do in a photograph. (This is evident in films: an approaching train gets bigger much faster than a real train would under the same circumstances.) To say that a circle seen obliquely is seen as an ellipse is to substitute for our actual perception what we would see if we were cameras: in reality we see a form which oscillates around the ellipse without being an ellipse. In a portrait of Mme Cézanne, the border of the wallpaper on one side of her body does not form a straight line with that on the other: and indeed it is known that if a line passes beneath a wide strip of paper, the two visible segments appear dislocated. Gustave Geffroy's table stretches into the bottom of the picture, and indeed, when our eye runs over a large surface, the images it successively receives are taken from different points of view, and the whole surface is warped. It is true that I freeze these distortions in repainting them on the canvas; I stop the spontaneous movement in which they pile up in perception and tend toward the geometric perspective. This is also what happens with colors. Pink upon gray paper colors the background green. Academic painting shows the background as gray, assuming that the picture will produce the same effect of contrast as the real object. Impressionist painting uses green in the background in order to achieve a contrast as brilliant as that of objects in nature. Doesn't this falsify the color relationship? It would if it stopped there, but the painter's task is to modify all the other colors in the picture so that they take away from the green background its characteristics of a real color. Similarly, it is Cézanne's genius that when the overall composition of the picture is seen globally, perspectival distortions are no longer visible in their own right but rather contribute, as they do in natural vision, to the impression of an emerging order, an object in the act of appearing, organizing itself before our eyes. In the same way, the contour of an object conceived as a line encircling the object belongs not to the visible world but to geometry. If one outlines the shape of an apple with a continuous line, one makes an object of the shape, whereas the contour is rather the ideal limit toward which the sides of the apple recede in depth. Not to indicate any shape would be to deprive the objects of their identity. To trace just a single outline sacrifices depth—that is, the dimension in which the thing is presented not as spread out before us but as an inexhaustible reality full of reserves. That is why Cézanne follows the swelling of the object in modulated colors and indicates *several* outlines in blue. Rebounding among these, one's glance captures a shape that emerges from among them all, just as it does in perception. Nothing could be less arbitrary than these famous distortions which, moreover, Cézanne abandoned in his last period, after 1890, when he no longer filled his canvases with colors and when he gave up the closely-woven texture of his still lifes.

The outline should therefore be a result of the colors if the world is to be given in its true density. For the world is a mass without gaps, a system of colors across which the receding perspective, the outlines, angles, and curves are inscribed like lines of force; the spatial structure vibrates as it is formed. "The outline and the colors are no longer distinct from each other. As you paint, you outline; the more the colors harmonize, the more the outline becomes precise. . . . When the color is at its richest, the form has reached plenitude." Cézanne does not try to use color to *suggest* the tactile sensations which would give shape and depth. These distinctions between touch and sight are unknown in primordial perception. It is only as a result of a science of the human body that we finally learn to distinguish between our senses. The lived object is not rediscovered or constructed on the basis of the contributions of the senses; rather, it presents itself to us from the start as the center from which these contributions radiate. We *see* the depth, the smoothness, the softness, the hardness of objects; Cézanne even claimed that we see their odor. If the painter is to express the world, the arrangement of his colors must bear within this indivisible whole, or else his painting will only hint at things and will not give them in the imperious unity, the presence, the insurpassable plenitude which is for us the definition of the real. That is why each brushstroke must satisfy an infinite number of conditions. Cézanne sometimes pondered hours at a time before putting down a certain stroke, for, as Bernard said, each stroke must "contain the air, the light, the object, the composition, the character, the outline, and the style." Expressing what *exists* is an endless task.

Nor did Cézanne neglect the physiognomy of objects and faces: he simply wanted to capture it emerging from the color. Painting a face "as an object" is not to strip it of its "thought." "I agree that the painter must interpret it," said Cézanne. "The painter is not an imbecile." But this interpretation should not be a reflection distinct from the act of seeing. "If I paint all the little blues and all the little browns, I capture and convey his glance. Who gives a damn if they have any idea how one can sadden a mouth or make a cheek smile by wedding a shaded green to a red." One's personality is seen and grasped in one's glance, which is, however, no more than a combination of colors. Other minds are given to us only as incarnate, as belonging to faces and gestures. Countering with the distinctions of soul and body, thought and vision is of no use here, for Cézanne returns to just that primordial experience from which these notions are derived and in which they are inseparable. The painter who conceptualizes and seeks the expression first misses the mystery— renewed every time we look at someone—of a person's appearing in nature. In *La peau de chagrin* Balzac describes a "tablecloth white as a layer of fresh-fallen snow, upon which the place settings rose symmetrically, crowned with blond rolls." "All through my youth," said Cézanne, "I wanted to paint that, that tablecloth of fresh-fallen snow. . . . Now I know that one must only *want* to paint 'rose, symmetrically, the place settings' and 'blond rolls.' If I paint 'crowned' I'm done for, you understand? But if I really balance and shade my place settings and rolls as they are in nature, you can be sure the crowns, the snow and the whole shebang will be there."

We live in the midst of man-made objects, among tools, in houses, streets, cities, and most of the time we see them only through the human actions which put them to use. We become used to thinking that all of this exists necessarily and unshakably. Cézanne's painting suspends these habits of thought and reveals the base of inhuman nature upon which man has installed himself. This is why Cézanne's people are strange, as if viewed by a creature of another species. Nature itself is stripped of the attributes which make it ready for animistic communions: there is no wind in the landscape, no movement on the Lac d'Annecy; the frozen objects hesitate as at the beginning of the world. It is an unfamiliar world in which one is uncomfortable and which forbids all human effusiveness. If one looks at the work of other painters after seeing Cézanne's paintings, one feels somehow relaxed, just as conversations resumed after a period of mourning mask the absolute change and restore to the survivors their solidity. But indeed only a human being is capable of such a vision, which penetrates right to the root of things beneath the imposed order of humanity. All indications are that animals cannot *look at* things, cannot penetrate them in expectation of nothing but the truth. Emile Bernard's statement that a realistic painter is only an ape is therefore precisely the opposite of the truth, and one sees how Cézanne was able to revive the classical definition of art: man added to nature.

Cézanne's painting denies neither science nor tradition. He went to the Louvre every day when he was in Paris. He believed that one must learn how to paint and that the geometric study of planes and forms is a necessary part of this learning process. He inquired about the geological structure of his landscapes, convinced that these abstract relationships, expressed, however, in terms of the visible world, should affect the act of painting. The rules of anatomy and design are present in each stroke of his brush just as the rules of the game underlie each stroke of a tennis match. But what motivates the painter's movement can never be simply perspective or geometry or the laws governing the breakdown of color, or, for that matter, any particular knowledge. Motivating all the movements from which a picture gradually emerges there can be only one thing: the landscape in its totality and in its absolute fullness, precisely what Cézanne called a "motif." He would start by discovering the geological foundations of the landscape; then, according to Mme Cézanne, he would halt and look at everything with widened eyes, "germinating" with the countryside. The task before him was, first, to forget all he had ever learned from science and, second, *through* these sciences to recapture the structure of the landscape as an emerging organism. To do this, all the partial views one catches sight of must be welded together; all that the eye's versatility disperses must be reunited; one must, as Gasquet put it, "join the wandering hands of nature." "A minute of the world is going by which must be painted in its full reality." His meditation would suddenly be consummated: "I have a hold on my *motif*," Cézanne would say, and he would explain that the landscape had to be tackled neither too high nor too low, caught alive in a net which would let nothing escape. Then he began to paint all parts of the painting at the same time, using patches of color to surround his original charcoal sketch of the geological skeleton. The picture took on fullness and density; it grew in structure and balance; it came to maturity all at once. "The landscape thinks itself in me," he would say, "and I am its consciousness." Nothing could be farther from naturalism than this intuitive science. Art is not imitation, nor is it something manufactured according to the wishes of instinct or good taste. It is a process of expression. Just as the function of words is to name—that is, to grasp the nature of what appears to us in a confused way and to place it before us as a recognizable object—so it is up to the painter, said Gasquet, to "objectify," "project," and "arrest." Words do not *look like* the things they designate; and a picture is not a *trompe-l'oeil*. Cézanne, in his own words, "writes in painting what had never yet been painted, and turns it into painting once and for all." We, forgetting the viscous, equivocal appearances, go through them straight to the things they present. The painter recaptures and converts into visible objects what would, without him, remain walled up in the separate life of each consciousness: the vibration of appearances which is the cradle of things. Only one emotion is possible for this painter—the feeling of strangeness—and only one lyricism—that of the continual rebirth of existence.

Leonardo da Vinci's motto was persistent rigor, and all the classical works on the art of poetry tell us that the creation of art is no easy matter. Cézanne's difficulties—like those of Balzac or Mallarmé—are of a different nature. Balzac (probably based on Delacroix's comments) imagined a painter who wants to express life through the use of color alone and who keeps his masterpiece hidden. When Frenhofer dies, his friends find nothing but a chaos of colors and elusive lines, a wall of painting. Cézanne was moved to tears when he read *Le chef-d'oeuvre inconnu* and declared that he himself was Frenhofer. The quest of Balzac, himself obsessed with "realization," sheds light on Cézanne's. In *La peau de chagrin* Balzac speaks of "a thought to be expressed," "a system to be built," "a science to be explained." He makes Louis Lambert, one of the abortive geniuses of the Comédie Humaine, say: "I am heading toward certain discoveries . . . , but how shall I describe the power which binds my hands, stops my mouth, and drags me in the opposite direction from my vocation?" To say that Balzac set himself to understand the society of his time is not sufficient. It is no superhuman task to describe the typical traveling salesman, to "dissect the teaching profession," or even to lay the foundations of a sociology. Once he had named the visible forces such as money and passion, once he had described the manifest workings of things, Balzac wondered where it all led, what the impetus behind it was, what the *meaning* was of, for example, a Europe "whose efforts tend toward some unknown mystery of civilization." In short, he wanted to understand what inner force holds the world together and causes the proliferation of visible forms. Frenhofer had the same idea about the meaning of painting: "A hand is not simply part of the body, but the expression and continuation of a thought which must be captured and conveyed. . . . That is the real struggle! Many painters triumph instinctively, unaware of this theme of art. You draw a woman, but you do not see her." The artist is the one who arrests the spectacle in which most men take part without really seeing it and who makes it visible to the most "human" among them.

There is thus no art for pleasure's sake alone. One can invent pleasurable objects by linking old ideas in a new way and by presenting forms that have been seen before. This way of painting or speaking "second hand" is what is generally meant by culture. Cézanne's or Balzac's artist is not satisfied to be a cultured animal but takes up culture from its inception and founds it anew: he speaks as the first man spoke and paints as if no one had ever painted before. What he expresses cannot, therefore, be the translation of a clearly defined thought, since such clear thoughts are those that have already been said within ourselves or by others. "Conception" cannot precede "execution." Before expression, there is nothing but a vague fever, and only the work itself, completed and understood, will prove that there was *something* rather than *nothing* to be found there. Because he has returned to the source of silent and solitary experience on which culture and the exchange of ideas have been built in order to take cognizance of it, the artist launches his work just as a man once launched the first word, not knowing whether it will be anything more than a shout, whether it can detach itself from the flow of individual life in which it was born and give the independent existence of an identifiable *meaning* to the future of that same individual life, or to the monads coexisting with it, or the open community of future monads. The meaning of what the artist is going to say *does not exist* anywhere— not in things, which as yet have no meaning, nor in the artist himself, in his unformulated life. It summons one away from the already constituted reason in which "cultured men" are content to shut themselves, toward a reason which would embrace its own origins.

To Bernard's attempt to bring him back to human intelligence, Cézanne replied: "I am oriented toward the intelligence of the *Pater Omnipotens*." He was, in any case, oriented toward the idea or project of an infinite Logos. Cézanne's uncertainty and solitude are not essentially explained by his nervous temperament but by the purpose of his work. Heredity may well have given him rich sensations, strong emotions, and a vague feeling of anguish or mystery which upset the life he might have wished for himself and which cut him off from humanity; but these qualities cannot create a work of art without the expressive act, and they have no bearing on the difficulties or the virtues of that act. Cézanne's difficulties are those of the first word. He thought himself powerless because he was not omnipotent, because he was not God and wanted nevertheless to portray the world, to change it completely into a spectacle, to make *visible* how the world *touches* us. A new theory of physics can be proven because calculations connect the idea or meaning of it with standards of measurement already common to all human beings. It is not enough for a painter like Cézanne, an artist, or a philosopher, to create and express an idea; they must also awaken the experiences which will make their idea take root in the consciousness of others. If a work is successful, it has the strange power of being self-teaching. The reader or spectator, by following the clues of the book or painting, by establishing the concurring points of internal evidence and being brought up short when straying too far to the left or right, guided by the con-fused clarity of style, will in the end find what was intended to be communicated. The painter can do no more than construct an image; he must wait for this image to come to life for other people. When it does, the work of art will have united these separate lives; it will no longer exist in only one of them like a stubborn dream or a persistent delirium, nor will it exist only in space as a colored piece of canvas. It will dwell undivided in several minds, with a claim on every possible mind like a perennial acquisition.

Thus, the "hereditary traits," the "influences"—the accidents in Cézanne's life—are the text which nature and history gave him to decipher. They give only the literal meaning of his work. But an artist's creations, like a person's free decisions, impose on this given a figurative sense which did not exist before them. If Cézanne's life seems to us to carry the seeds of his work within it, it is because we get to know his work first and see the circumstances of his life through it, charging them with a meaning borrowed from that work. If the givens for Cézanne which we have been enumerating, and which we spoke of as pressing conditions, were to figure in the web of projects which he was, they could have done so only by presenting themselves to him as *what* he had to live, leaving *how* to live it undetermined. An imposed theme at the start, they become, when replaced in the existence of which they are part, the monogram and the symbol of a life which freely interpreted itself.

But let us make no mistake about this freedom. Let us not imagine an abstract force which could superimpose its effects on life's "givens" or cause breaches in life's development. Although it is certain that a person's life does not *explain* his work, it is equally certain that the two are connected. The truth is that *that work to be done called for that life.* From the very start, Cézanne's life found its only equilibrium by leaning on the work that was still in the future. His life was the preliminary project of his future work. The work to come is hinted at, but it would be wrong to take these hints for causes, although they do make a single adventure of his life and work. Here we are beyond causes and effects; both come together in the simultaneity of an eternal Cézanne who is at the same time the formula of what he wanted to be and what he wanted to do. There is a relationship between Cézanne's schizoid temperament and his work because the work reveals a metaphysical meaning of his illness (schizothymia as the reduction of the world to the totality of frozen appearances and the suspension of expressive values); because the illness thus ceases being an absurd fact and destiny to become a general possibility of human existence confronting, in a consistent, principled way, one of its paradoxes—the phenomenon of expression— and because in this to be schizoid and to be Cézanne are one and the same thing. It is therefore impossible to separate creative freedom from that behavior, as far as possible from deliberate, already evident in Cézanne's first gestures as a child and in the way he reacted to things. The meaning Cézanne gave to objects and faces in his paintings presented itself to him in the world as it appeared to him. Cézanne simply released that meaning: it was the objects and the faces themselves as he saw them that demanded to be painted, and Cézanne simply expressed what they *wanted* to say. How, then, can any freedom be involved? True, the conditions of existence can only affect consciousness indirectly, through raisons d'être and the justifications consciousness offers to itself. We can only see before us, and in the form of goals, what it is that we are—so that our life always has the form of a project or choice, and thus seems to us self-caused. But to say that we are from the start our way of aiming at a particular future would be to say that our project has already been determined with our first ways of being, that the choice has already been made for us with our first breath. If we experience no external constraints, it is because we are our whole exterior. That eternal Cézanne whom we see springing forth from the start and who then brought upon the human Cézanne the events and influences deemed *exterior*, and who planned all that happened to the latter—that attitude toward humanity and toward the world which was not chosen through deliberation—may be free from external causes, but is it free in respect to itself? Is the choice not pushed back beyond life, and can a choice exist where there is as yet no clearly articulated field of possibilities, only one probability and, as it were, only one temptation? If I am a certain project from birth, the given and the created are indistinguishable in me, and it is therefore impossible to name a single gesture which is merely hereditary or innate, a single gesture which is not spontaneous—but also impossible to name a single gesture which is absolutely new in regard to that way of being in the world which, from the very beginning, is myself. There is no difference between saying that our life is completely constructed and that it is completely given. If there is true freedom, it can only come about in the course of our life by our going beyond our original situation and yet not ceasing to be the same. Such is the problem. Two things are certain about freedom: that we are never determined and yet that we never change, since, looking back on what we were, we can always find hints of what we have become. It is up to us to understand both these things simultaneously, as well as the way freedom dawns in us without breaking our bonds with the world.

Such bonds are always there, even and above all when we refuse to admit they exist. Inspired by the paintings of da Vinci, Valéry described a monster of pure freedom, without mistresses, creditors, anecdotes, or adventures. No dream intervenes between himself and the things themselves; nothing taken for granted supports his certainties; and he does not read his fate in any favorite image, such as Pascal's abyss. Instead of struggling against the monsters he has understood what makes them tick, has disarmed them by his attention, and has reduced them to the state of known things. "Nothing could be more free, that is, less human, than his judgments on love and death. He hints at them in a few fragments from his notebooks: 'In the full force of its passion,' he says more or less explicitly, 'love is something so ugly that the human race would die out (la natura si perderebbe) if lovers could see what they were doing.' This contempt is brought out in various sketches, since the leisurely examination of certain things is, after all, the height of scorn. Thus, he now and again draws anatomical unions, frightful cross-sections of love's very act."[2] He has complete mastery of his means, he does what he wants, going at will from knowledge to life with a superior elegance. Everything he did was done knowingly, and the artistic process, like the act of breathing or living, is not beyond his ken. He has discovered the "central attitude," on the basis of which it is equally possible to know, to act, and to create because action and life, when turned into exercises, are not contrary to detached knowledge. He is an "intellectual power"; he is a "man of the mind."

Let us look more closely. For Leonardo there was no revelation; as Valéry said, no abyss yawned at his right hand. Undoubtedly true. But in Saint Anne, the Virgin, and Child, the Virgin's cloak suggests a vulture where it touches the face of the Child. There is that fragment on the flight of birds where da Vinci suddenly interrupts himself to pursue a childhood memory: "I seem to have been destined to be especially concerned with the vulture, for one of the first things I remember about my childhood is how a vulture came to me when I was still in the cradle, forced open my mouth with its tail, and struck me several times between the lips with it."[3] So even this transparent consciousness has its enigma, whether truly a child's memory or a fantasy of the grown man. It did not come out of nowhere, nor did it sustain itself alone. We are caught in a secret history, in a forest of symbols. One would surely protest if Freud were to decipher the riddle from what we know about the meaning of the flight of birds and about fellatio fantasies and their relation to the period of nursing. But it is still a fact that to the ancient Egyptians the vulture was a symbol of maternity because they believed all vultures were female and that they were impregnated by the wind. It is also a fact that the Church Fathers used this legend to refute, on the grounds of natural history, those who were unwilling to believe in a virgin birth, and it is probable that Leonardo came across the legend in the course of his endless reading. He found in it the symbol of his own fate: he was the illegitimate son of a rich notary who married the noble Donna Albiera the very year Leonardo was born. Having no children by her, he took Leonardo into his home when the boy was five. Thus Leonardo spent the first four years of his life with his mother, the deserted peasant girl; he was a child without a father, and he got to know the world in the sole company of that unhappy mother who seemed to have miraculously created him. If we now recall that he was never known to have a mistress or even to have felt anything like passion; that he was accused—but acquitted—of sodomy; that his diary, which tells us nothing about many other, larger expenses, notes with meticulous detail the costs of his mother's burial, as well as the cost of linen and clothing for two of his students—it is no great leap to conclude that Leonardo loved only one woman, his mother, and that this love left no room for anything but platonic tenderness he felt for the young boys surrounding him. In the four decisive years of his childhood he had formed a fundamental attachment, which he had to give up when he was recalled to his father's home, and into which he had poured all his resources of love and all his power of abandon. As for his thirst for life, he had no other choice but to use it in the investigation and knowledge of the world, and, since he himself had been *"detached,"* he had to become that intellectual power, that man who was all mind, that stranger among men. Indifferent, incapable of any strong indignation, love or hate, he left his paintings unfinished to devote his time to bizarre experiments; he became a person in whom his contemporaries sensed a mystery. It was as if Leonardo had never quite grown up, as if all the places in his heart had already been spoken for, as if the spirit of investigation was a way for him to escape from life, as if he had invested all his power of assent in the first years of his life and had remained true to his childhood right to the end. His games were those of a child. Vasari tells how "he made up a wax paste and, during his walks, he would model from it very delicate animals, hollow and filled with air; when he breathed into them, they would fly; when the air had escaped, they would fall to the ground. When the wine-grower from Belvedere found a very unusual lizard, Leonardo made wings for it out of skin of other lizards and filled these wings with mercury so that they waved and quivered whenever the lizard moved; he likewise made eyes, a beard, and horns for it in the same way, tamed it, put it in a box, and used the lizard to terrify his friends."[4] He left his work unfinished, just as his father had abandoned him. He paid no heed to authority and trusted only nature and his own judgment in matters of knowledge, as is often the case with people who have not been raised in the shadow of a father's intimidating and protective power. Thus even that pure power of examination, that solitude, that curiosity—which are the essence of mind—only developed in da Vinci in relation to his personal history. At the height of his freedom he was, *in that very freedom*, the child he had been; he was free on one side only because bound on the other. Becoming a pure consciousness is just another way of taking a stand in relation to the world and other people. Leonardo had learned this attitude in assuming the situation into which his birth and childhood had put him. There can be no consciousness that is not sustained by its primordial involvement in life and by the manner of this involvement.

Whatever is arbitrary in Freud's *explanations* cannot in this context discredit *psychoanalytic intuition*. True, the reader is stopped more than once by the lack of evidence. Why this and not something else? The question seems all the more pressing since Freud often offers several interpretations, each symptom being "over-determined" according to him. Finally, it is obvious that a doctrine which brings in sexuality everywhere cannot, by the rules of inductive logic, establish its effectiveness anywhere, since, excluding all differential cases beforehand, it deprives itself of any counterevidence. This is how one triumphs over psychoanalysis, but only on paper. For if the suggestions of the analyst can never be proven, neither can they be eliminated: how would it be possible to credit chance with the complex correspondences which the psychoanalyst discovers between the child and the adult? How can we deny that psychoanalysis has taught us to notice echoes, allusions, repetitions from one moment of life to another—a concatenation we would not dream of doubting if Freud had stated the theory correctly? Unlike the natural sciences, psychoanalysis was not meant to give us necessary relations of cause and effect but to point to motivational relationships which are in principle simply possible. We should not take Leonardo's fantasy of the vulture, or the infantile past which it masks, for a force which determined his future. Rather, it is like the words of the oracle, an ambiguous symbol which applies in advance to several possible chains of events. To be more precise: in every life, one's birth and one's past define categories or basic dimensions which do not impose any particular act but which can be found in all. Whether Leonardo yielded to his childhood or whether he wished to flee from it, he could never have been other than he was. The very decisions which transform us are always made in reference to a factual situation; such a situation can of course be accepted or refused, but it cannot fail to give us our impetus nor to be for us, as a situation "to be accepted" or "to be refused," the incarnation of the value we give to it. If it is the aim of psychoanalysis to describe this exchange between future and past and to show how each life muses over riddles whose final meaning is nowhere written down, then we have no right to demand inductive rigor from it. The psychoanalyst's hermeneutic musing, which multiplies the communications between us and ourselves, which takes sexuality as the symbol of existence and existence as symbol of sexuality, and which looks in the past for the meaning of the future and in the future for the meaning of the past, is better suited than rigorous induction to the circular movement of our lives, where the future rests on the past, the past on the future, and where everything symbolizes everything else. Psychoanalysis does not make freedom impossible; it teaches us to think of this freedom concretely, as a creative revival of ourselves, always, in retrospect, faithful to ourselves.

Thus it is true both that the life of an author can teach us nothing and that—if we know how to interpret it—we can find everything in it, since it opens onto his work. Just as we may observe the movements of an unknown animal without understanding the law that inhabits and controls them, so Cézanne's observers did not divine the transmutations he imposed on events and experiences; they were blind to *his* significance, to that glow from out of nowhere which surrounded him from time to time. But he himself was never at the center of himself: nine days out of ten all he saw around him was the wretchedness of his empirical life and of his unsuccessful attempts, the debris of an unknown celebration.[5] Yet it was in the world that he had to realize his freedom, with colors upon a canvas. It was from the approval of others that he had to await the proof of his worth. That is why he questioned the picture emerging beneath his hand, why he hung on the glances other people directed toward his canvas. That is why he never finished working. We never get away from our life. We never see ideas or freedom face to face.

5

Indirect Language and the Voices of Silence

Maurice Merleau-Ponty

to Jean-Paul Sartre

What we have learned from Saussure is that, taken singly, signs do not signify anything, and that each one of them does not so much express a meaning as mark a divergence of meaning between itself and other signs. Since the same can be said for all other signs, we may conclude that language is made of differences without terms; or more exactly, that the terms of language are engendered only by the differences which appear among them. This is a difficult idea, because common sense tells us that if term *A* and term *B* do not have any meaning at all, it is hard to see how there could be a difference of meaning between them; and that if communication really did go from the whole of the speaker's language to the whole of the hearer's language, one would have to know the language in order to learn it. But the objection is of the same kind as Zeno's paradoxes; and as they are overcome by the act of movement, it is overcome by the use of speech. And this sort of circle, according to which language, in the presence of those who are learning it, precedes itself, teaches itself, and suggests its own deciphering, is perhaps the marvel which defines language.

Language is learned, and in this sense one is certainly obliged to go from the parts to the whole. The prior whole which Saussure is talking about cannot be the explicit and articulated whole of complete language as it is recorded in grammars and dictionaries. Nor does he have in mind a logical totality like that of a philosophical system, all of whose elements can (in principle) be deduced from a single idea. Since what he is doing is rejecting any other than a "diacritical" meaning of signs, he cannot base language upon a system of positive ideas. The unity he is talking about is a unity of coexistence, like that of the sections of an arch which shoulder one another.

In a unified whole of this kind, the learned parts of a language have an immediate value as a whole, and progress is made less by addition and juxtaposition than by the internal articulation of a function which is in its own way already complete. It has long been known that for a child the word first functions as a sentence, and perhaps even certain phonemes as words. But contemporary linguistics conceives of the unity of language in an even more precise way by isolating, at the origin of words—perhaps even at the origin of form and style—"oppositive" and "relative" principles to which the Saussurian definition of sign applies even more rigorously than to words, since it is a question here of components of language which do not for their part have any assignable meaning and whose sole function is to make possible the discrimination of signs in the strict sense. Now these first phonemic oppositions may well have gaps and be enriched subsequently by new dimensions, and the verbal chain may well find other means of self-differentiation. The important point is that the phonemes are from the beginning variations of a unique speech apparatus, and that with them the child seems to have "caught" the principle of a mutual differentiation of signs and at the same time to have acquired *the meaning of the sign.* For the phonemic oppositions—contemporaneous with the first attempts at communication—appear and are developed without any relation to the child's babbling. His babbling is often repressed by the oppositions, and in any case retains only a marginal existence without its materials being integrated to the new system of true speech. This lack of relation between babbling and phonemic oppositions seems to indicate that possessing a sound as an element of babbling which is addressed only to itself is not the same as possessing a sound as a stage in the effort to communicate. It can be said that beginning with the first phonemic oppositions the child *speaks,* and that thereafter he will only learn to apply the principle of speech in diverse ways.

Saussure's insight becomes more precise: with the first phonemic oppositions the child is initiated to the lateral liaison of sign to sign as the foundation of an ultimate relation of sign to meaning—in the special form it has received in the language in question. Phonologists have succeeded in extending their analysis beyond words to forms, to syntax, and even to stylistic differences because the language in its entirety as a style of expression and a unique manner of handling words is anticipated by the child in the first phonemic oppositions. The whole of the spoken language surrounding the child snaps him up like a whirlwind, tempts him by its internal articulations, and brings him *almost* up to the moment when all this noise begins to mean something. The untiring way in which the train of words crosses and recrosses itself, and the emergence one unimpeachable day of a certain phonemic scale according to which discourse is visibly composed, finally sways the child over to the side of those who speak. Only a language taken as an integral whole enables one to understand how language draws the child to itself and how he comes to enter that domain whose doors, one might think, open only from within. It is because the sign is diacritical from the outset, because it is composed and organized in terms of itself, that it has an interior and ends up laying claim to a meaning.

This meaning arising at the edge of signs, this immanence of the whole in the parts, is found throughout the history of culture. There is that moment at which Brunelleschi built the cupola of the cathedral in Florence in a definite relation to the configuration of the site. Should we say that he broke with the closed space of the Middle Ages and discovered the universal space of the Renaissance?[1] But *one* operation of art is still a long way from being a deliberate use of space as the medium of a universe. Should we say then that this space is not yet there? But Brunelleschi did make for himself a strange device in which two views of the Battistero and the Palazzo della Signoria, with the streets and the squares which frame them, were reflected in a mirror, while a disc of polished metal projected the light of the sky upon the scene.[2] Thus he had done research and had raised a question of space. It is just as difficult to say when the generalized number begins in the history of mathematics. "In itself" (that is, as Hegel would say, for us who project it into history), it is already present in the fractional number which, before the algebraic number, inserts the whole number in a continuous series. But it is there as if it were unaware of its existence; it is not there "for itself." In the same way one must give up trying to establish the moment at which Latin becomes French. Grammatical forms begin to be efficacious and outlined in a language before being systematically employed. A language sometimes remains a long time pregnant with transformations which are to come; and the enumeration of the means of expression in a language does not have any meaning, since those which fall into disuse continue to lead a diminished life in the language and since the place of those which are to replace them is sometimes already marked out—even if only in the form of a gap, a need, or a tendency.

Even when it is possible to date the emergence of a principle which exists "for itself," it is clear that the principle has been previously present in the culture as an obsession or anticipation, and that the realization that lays it down as an explicit signification merely completes its long incubation in the form of operative meaning. Now, realization is never complete. The space of the Renaissance will in turn be thought of later as a very particular case of possible pictorial space. Culture thus never gives us absolutely transparent significations; the genesis of meaning is never completed. What we rightly call our truth we never contemplate except in a symbolic context which dates our knowledge. We always have to do only with sign structures whose meaning, being nothing other than the way in which the signs behave toward one another and are distinguished from one another, cannot be set forth independently of them. We do not even have the morose consolation of a vague relativism, since each stage of our knowledge is indeed a truth and will be preserved in the more comprehensive truth of the future.

As far as language is concerned, it is the lateral relation of one sign to another which makes each of them significant, so that meaning appears only at the intersection of and as it were in the interval between words. This characteristic prevents us from forming the usual conception of the distinction and the union between language and its meaning. Meaning is usually thought to transcend signs in principle (just as thought is supposed to transcend the sounds or sights which indicate it), and to be immanent in signs in the sense that each one of them, having *its* meaning once and for all, could not conceivably slip any opacity between itself and us, or even give us food for thought. Signs are supposed to be no more than monitors which notify the hearer that he must consider such and such of *his* thoughts. But meaning does not actually dwell in the verbal chain or distinguish itself from the chain in this way. Since the sign has meaning only in so far as it is profiled against other signs, its meaning is entirely involved in language. Speech always comes into play against a background of speech; it is always only a fold in the immense fabric of language. To understand it, we do not have to consult some inner lexicon which gives us the pure thoughts covered up by the words or forms we are perceiving; we have only to lend ourselves to its life, to its movement of differentiation and articulation, and to its eloquent gestures. There is thus an opaqueness of language. Nowhere does it stop and leave a place for pure meaning; it is always limited only by more language, and meaning appears within it only set in a context of words. Like a charade, language is understood only through the interaction of signs, each of which, taken separately, is equivocal or banal, and makes sense only by being combined with others.

For the speaker no less than for the listener, language is definitely something other than a technique for ciphering or deciphering ready-made significations. Before there can be such ready-made significations, language must first make significations exist as available entities by establishing them at the intersection of linguistic gestures as that which, by common consent, the gestures reveal. Our analyses of thought give us the impression that before it finds the words which express it, it is already a sort of ideal text that our sentences attempt to *translate*. But the author himself has no text to which he can compare his writing, and no language prior to language. His speech satisfies him only because it reaches an equilibrium whose conditions his speech itself defines, and attains a state of perfection which has no model.

Language is much more like a sort of being than a means, and that is why it can present something to us so well. A friend's speech over the telephone brings us the friend himself, as if he were wholly present in that manner of calling and saying goodbye to us, of beginning and ending his sentences, and of carrying on the conversation through things left unsaid. Because meaning is the total movement of speech, our thought crawls along in language. Yet for the same reason, our thought moves through language as a gesture goes beyond the individual points of its passage. At the very moment language fills our minds up to the top without leaving the smallest place for thought not taken into its vibration, and exactly to the extent that we abandon ourselves to it, it passes beyond the "signs" toward their meaning. And nothing separates us from that meaning any more. Language does not *presuppose* its table of correspondence; it unveils its secrets itself. It teaches them to every child who comes into the world. It is entirely a showing. Its opaqueness, its obstinate reference to itself and its turning and folding back upon itself are precisely what make it a spiritual power; for it in turn becomes something like a universe, in which it is capable of lodging things themselves—after it has transformed them into their meaning.

Now if we rid our minds of the idea that our language is the translation or cipher of an original text, we shall see that the idea of *complete* expression is nonsensical, and that all language is indirect or allusive—that it is, if you wish, silence. The relation of meaning to the spoken word can no longer be a point for point correspondence that we always envisage. Saussure notes that the English "the man I love" expresses just as completely as the French "l'homme *que* j'aime." We say that the English does not express the relative pronoun. The truth is that instead of being expressed by a word, the relative pronoun passes into the language by means of a blank between the words. But we should not even say that it is implied. This notion of implication naively expresses our conviction that a language (generally our native tongue) has succeeded in capturing things themselves in its forms; and that any other language, if it wants to reach things themselves too, must at least tacitly use the same kind of instruments. Now the reason French seems to us to go to things themselves is certainly not that it has actually copied the articulations of being. French has a distinct word to express relation, but it does not distinguish the function of being the object of a verb by means of a special flexional ending. It could be said that French implies the declension that German expresses (and the aspect that Russian expresses, and the optative that Greek expresses). The reason French seems to us to be traced upon things is not that it is, but that it gives us the illusion of being so by the internal relation of one sign to another. But "the man I love" does so just as well. The absence of a sign can be a sign, and expression is not the adjustment of an element of discourse to each element of meaning, but an operation of language upon language which suddenly is thrown out of focus toward its meaning.

To speak is not to put a word under each thought; if it were, nothing would ever be said. We would not have the feeling of living in the language and we would remain silent, because the sign would be immediately obliterated by its own meaning and because thought would never encounter anything but thought—the thought it wanted to express and the thought which it would form from a wholly explicit language. We sometimes have, on the contrary, the feeling that a thought has been *said*—not replaced by verbal counters but incorporated in words and made available in them. And finally, there is a power of words because, working against one another, they are attracted at a distance by thought like tides by the moon, and because they evoke their meaning in this tumult much more imperiously than if each one of them brought back only a listless signification of which it was the indifferent and predestined sign.

Language speaks peremptorily when it gives up trying to express the thing itself. As algebra brings unknown magnitudes under consideration, speech differentiates significations no one of which is known separately; and it is by treating them as known (and giving us an abstract picture of them and their interrelations) that language ends up imposing the most precise identification upon us in a flash. Language signifies when instead of copying thought it lets itself be taken apart and put together again by thought. Language bears the meaning of thought as a footprint signifies the movement and effort of a body. The empirical use of already established language should be distinguished from its creative use. Empirical language can only be the result of creative language. Speech in the sense of empirical language—that is, the opportune recollection of a preestablished sign—is not speech in respect to an authentic language. It is, as Mallarmé said, the worn coin placed silently in my hand. True speech, on the contrary—speech which signifies, which finally renders "l'absente de tous bouquets" present and frees the meaning captive in the thing—is only silence in respect to empirical usage, for it does not go so far as to become a common noun. Language is oblique and autonomous, and if it sometimes signifies a thought or a thing directly, that is only a secondary power derived from its inner life. Like the weaver, the writer works on the wrong side of his material. He has to do only with language, and it is thus that he suddenly finds himself surrounded by meaning.

If this account is true, the writer's act of expression is not very different from the painter's. We usually say that the painter reaches us across the silent world of lines and colors, and that he addresses himself to an unformulated power of deciphering within us that we control only after we have blindly used it—only after we have enjoyed the work. The writer is said, on the contrary, to dwell in already elaborated signs and in an already speaking world, and to require nothing more of us than the power to reorganize our significations according to the indications of the signs which he proposes to us. But what if language expresses as much by what is between words as by the words themselves? By that which it does not "say" as by what it "says"? And what if, hidden in empirical language, there is a language raised to the second power in which signs once again lead the vague life of colors, and in which significations never free themselves completely from the intercourse of signs?

There are two sides to the act of painting: the spot or line of color put on a point of the canvas, and its effect in the whole. The two are incommensurable, since the former is almost nothing yet suffices to change a portrait or a landscape. One who, with his nose against the painter's brush, observed the painter from too close would see only the wrong side of his work. The wrong side is a slight movement of the brush or pen of Poussin; the right side is the sunshine's breaking through, which that movement releases. A camera once recorded the work of Matisse in slow motion. The impression was prodigious, so much so that Matisse himself was moved, they say. That same brush that, seen with the naked eye, leaped from one act to another, was seen to meditate in a solemn, expanded time—in the imminence of a world's creation—to try ten possible movements, dance in front of the canvas, brush it lightly several times, and crash down finally like a lightning stroke upon the one line necessary. Of course, there is something artificial in this analysis. And Matisse would be wrong if, putting his faith in the film, he believed that he really chose between all possible lines that day and, like the God of Leibniz, solved an immense problem of maximum and minimum. He was not a demiurge; he was a human being. He did not have in his mind's eye all the gestures possible, and in making his choice he did not have to eliminate all but one. It is slow motion which enumerates the possibilities. Matisse, set within a human's time and vision, looked at the still open whole of his work in progress and brought his brush toward the line which called for it in order that the painting might finally be that which it was in the process of becoming. By a simple gesture he resolved the problem which in retrospect seemed to imply an infinite number of data (as the hand in the iron filings, according to Bergson, achieves in a single stroke the arrangement which will make a place for it). Everything happened in the human world of perception and gesture; and the camera gives us a fascinating version of the event only by making us believe that the painter's hand operated in the physical world where an infinity of options is possible. And yet, Matisse's hand did hesitate. Consequently, there was a choice, and the chosen line was chosen in such a way as to observe, scattered out over the painting, a score of conditions which were unformulated and even informulable for anyone but Matisse, since they were only defined and imposed by the intention of executing *that particular painting which did not yet exist.*

The case is no different for the truly expressive word and thus for all language in the phase in which it is being established. The expressive word does not simply choose a sign for an already defined signification, as one goes to look for a hammer in order to drive a nail or for a claw to pull it out. It gropes around a significative intention which is not guided by any text, and which is precisely in the process of writing the text. If we want to do justice to it, we must evoke some of the other words that might have taken its place and were rejected, and we must feel the way in which they might have touched and shaken the chain of language in another manner and the extent to which this particular word was really the only possible one if that signification was to come into the world. In short, we must consider the word before it is spoken, the background of silence which does not cease to surround it and without which it would say nothing.

Or to put the matter another way, we must uncover the threads of silence with which speech is intertwined. In already acquired expressions there is a direct meaning which corresponds point for point to figures, forms, and established words. There are no apparent gaps or expressive silences there. But the meaning of expressions which are in the process of being accomplished cannot be of that sort; it is a lateral or oblique meaning which runs between words. It is another way of shaking the linguistic or narrative apparatus in order to tear a new sound from it. If we want to understand language as an originating operation, we must pretend never to have spoken, submit language to a reduction without which it would once more escape us by referring us to what it signifies for us, *look* at it as deaf people look at those who are speaking, compare the art of language to other arts of expression, and try to see it as one of these mute arts. It is possible that the meaning of language has a decisive privilege, but it is in trying out the parallel that we will perceive what may in the end make that parallel impossible. Let us begin by understanding that there is a tacit language, and that painting speaks in its own way.

Malraux says that painting and language are comparable only when they are detached from what they "represent" and are brought together under the category of creative expression. It is then that they are both recognized as two forms of the same endeavor. Painters and writers have worked for centuries without a suspicion of their relationship. But it is a fact that they have experienced the same adventure. At first, art and poetry are consecrated to the city, the gods, and the sacred, and it is only in the mirror of an external power that they can see the birth of their own miracle. Later, both know a classic age which is the secularization of the sacred age; art is then the representation of a Nature that it can at best embellish—but according to formulas taught to it by Nature herself. As La Bruyère would have it, speech has no other role than finding the exact expression assigned in advance to each thought by a language of things themselves; and this double recourse to an art before art, to a speech before speech, prescribes to the work a certain point of perfection, completeness, or fullness which makes all human beings assent to it as they assent to the things which fall under their senses. Malraux has made a good analysis of this "objectivist" prejudice, which is challenged by modern art and literature. But perhaps he has not measured the depth at which the prejudice is rooted; perhaps he was too quick to concede that the domain of the visible world is "objective"; and perhaps it is this concession which led him, by contrast, to define modern painting as a return to subjectivity—to the "incomparable monster"—and to bury it in a secret life outside the world. His analysis needs to be reexamined.

To begin with, oil painting seems to enjoy a special privilege. For more than any other kind of painting it permits us to attribute a distinct pictorial representative to each element of the object or of the human face and to look for signs which can give the illusion of depth or volume, of movement, of forms, of tactile qualities or of different kinds of material. (Think of the patient studies which brought the representation of velvet to perfection.) These processes, these secrets augmented by each generation, seem to be elements of a general technique of *representation* which ultimately should reach the thing itself (or the person himself), which cannot be imagined capable of containing any element of chance or vagueness, and whose sovereign function painting should try to equal. Along this road one takes steps that need not be retraced. The career of a painter, the productions of a school, and even the development of painting all go toward *masterpieces* in which what was sought after up until then is finally obtained; masterpieces which, at least provisorily, make the earlier attempts useless and stand out as landmarks in the progress of painting. Classical painting wants to be as convincing as things and does not think that it can reach us except as things do—by imposing an unimpeachable spectacle upon *our senses*. It relies in principle upon the perceptual apparatus, considered as a natural, given means of communication between human beings. Don't we all have eyes which function more or less in the same way? And if the painter has succeeded in discovering the sufficient signs of depth or velvet, won't we all, in looking at the painting, see the same spectacle, which will rival that of Nature?

The fact remains that the classical painters were painters and that no valuable painting has ever consisted in simply representing. Malraux points out that the modern conception of painting as creative expression has been a novelty for the public much more than for the painters themselves, who have always practiced it, even if they did not construct the theory of it. That is why the works of the classical painters have a different meaning and perhaps more meaning than the painters themselves thought, why these painters frequently anticipate a kind of painting that is free from their canons, and why they are still necessary mediators in any initiation to painting. At the very moment when, their eyes fixed upon the world, they thought they were asking it for the secret of a sufficient representation, they were unknowingly bringing about that *metamorphosis* of which painting later became aware. Consequently, classical painting cannot be defined by its representation of nature or by its reference to "our senses," nor modern painting by its reference to the subjective. The perception of classical painters already depended upon their culture, and our culture can still give form to our perception of the visible. It is not necessary to abandon the visible world to classical formulas or shut modern painting up in a recess of the individual. There is no choice to be made between the world and art, or between "our senses" and absolute painting, for they blend into one another.

Sometimes Malraux speaks as if "sense data" had never varied throughout the centuries, and as if the classical perspective had been imperative as long as painting referred to sense data. Yet it is clear that the classical perspective is only one of the ways humanity has invented for projecting the perceived world before itself, and not the copy of that world. The classical perspective is an optional interpretation of spontaneous vision, not because the perceived world contradicts the laws of classical perspective and imposes others, but rather because it does not require any particular one, and is not of the order of laws. In free perception, objects spread out in depth do not have any definite "apparent size." We must not even say that the perspective "deceives us" and that the faraway objects are "bigger" for the naked eye than their projection in a drawing or a photograph would lead us to believe—at least not according to that size which is supposed to be a common measure of backgrounds and foregrounds. The size of the moon on the horizon cannot be measured by a certain number of aliquot parts of the coin that I hold in my hand; it is a question of a "size-at-a-distance," and of a kind of quality which adheres to the moon as heat and cold adhere to other objects. Here we are in the order of the "ultra-things" which H. Wallon[3] speaks about and which do not arrange themselves according to a single graduated perspective in relation to nearby objects. Beyond a certain size and distance, we encounter the absolute of size in which all the "ultra-things" meet; and that is why children say that the sun is as "big as a house."

If I want to come back from that way of seeing to perspective, I must stop perceiving the whole freely. I must circumscribe my vision, mark (on a standard of measurement I hold) what I call the "apparent size" of the moon and of the coin, and, finally, transfer these measurements onto paper. But during this time the perceived world has disappeared along with the true simultaneity of objects, which is not their peaceful coexistence in a single scale of sizes. When I was seeing the coin and the moon together, my glance had to be fixed on one of them. Then the other one appeared to me in marginal vision—"little-object-seen-up-close" or "big-object-seen-far-away"—incommensurable with the first. What I transfer to paper is not this coexistence of perceived things as rivals in my field of vision. I find the means of arbitrating their conflict, which makes depth. I decide to make them co-possible on the same plane, and I succeed by coagulating a series of local and monocular views, no one of which may be superimposed upon the elements of the living perceptual field. Once things competed for my glance; and, anchored in one of them, I felt in it the solicitation of the others which made them coexist with the first—the demands of a horizon and its claim to exist. Now I construct a representation in which each thing ceases to call the whole of vision to itself, makes concessions to the other things, and no longer occupies on the paper any more than the space which they leave to it. Before, my glance, running freely over depth, height, and width, was not subjected to any point of view, because it adopted them and rejected them in turn. Now I renounce that ubiquity and agree to let only that which could be seen from a certain reference point by an immobile eye fixed on a certain "vanishing point" of a certain "vanishing line" figure in my drawing. (A deceptive modesty, for if I renounce the world itself by precipitating the narrow perspective upon the paper, I also cease to see like a human being, who is open to the world because he is situated in it. I think of and dominate my vision as God can when he considers his *idea* of me.) Before, I had the experience of a world of teeming, exclusive things which could be taken in only by means of a temporal cycle in which each gain was at the same time a loss. Now the inexhaustible being crystallizes into an ordered perspective within which backgrounds resign themselves to being only backgrounds (inaccessible and vague as is proper), and objects in the foreground abandon something of their aggressiveness, order their inner lines according to the common law of the spectacle, and already prepare themselves to become backgrounds as soon as it is necessary. A perspective, in short, within which nothing holds my glance and takes the shape of a present.

The whole scene is in the mode of the completed or of eternity. Everything takes on an air of propriety and discretion. Things no longer call upon me to answer, and I am no longer compromised by them. And if I add the artifice of aerial perspective to this one, the extent to which I who paint and they who look at my landscape dominate the situation is readily felt. Perspective is much more than a secret technique for imitating a reality given as such to all humanity. It is the invention of a world dominated and possessed through and through by an instantaneous synthesis, which is at best roughed out by our glance when it vainly tries to hold together all these things seeking individually to monopolize it. The faces of the classical portrait, always in the service of the subject's character, passion, or love—always signifying—or the babies and animals of the classical painting, so desirous to enter the human world, so unconcerned with rejecting it, manifest the same "adult" relation of human to the world, except when, giving in to his favorable daemon, the great painter adds a new dimension to this world too sure of itself by making contingency vibrate within it.

Now if "objective" painting is itself a creation, the fact that modern painting seeks to be a creation no longer provides any reasons for interpreting it as a movement toward the subjective and a ceremony glorifying the individual. And here Malraux's analysis seems to me to be on tenuous ground. There is only one subject in today's painting, he says— the painter himself.[4] Painters no longer look for the velvet of peaches, as Chardin did, but, like Braque, for the velvet of the painting. The classical painters were unconsciously themselves; the modern painter wants first of all to be original and for him his power of expression is identical to his individual difference.[5] *Because* painting is no longer for faith or beauty, it is for the individual;[6] it is "the annexation of the world by the individual."[7] The artist is thus supposed to be "of the tribe of the ambitious and the drugged,"[8] and like them devoted to stubborn self-pleasure, to daemonic pleasure—that is, to the pleasure of all in humanity which destroys humanity.

It is clear, however, that it would be hard to apply these definitions to Cézanne or Klee, for example. There are two possible interpretations of that tolerance for the incomplete shown by those moderns who present sketches as paintings, and whose every canvas, as the signature of a moment of life, demands to be seen on "show" in a series of successive canvases. It may be that they have given up the *work*, and no longer look for anything but the immediate, perceived and individual— the "brute expression" as Malraux says. Or else, completion in the sense of a presentation that is objective and convincing for the *senses* may no longer be the means to or the sign of a work that is really *complete*, because henceforth expression must go from person to person across the common world they *live*, without passing through the anonymous realm of the *senses* or of Nature. Baudelaire wrote—in an expression very opportunely recalled by Malraux—"that a complete work was not necessarily finished, and a finished work not necessarily complete."[9] The accomplished work is thus not the work which exists in itself like a thing, but the work which reaches its viewer and invites him to take up the gesture which created it and, skipping the intermediaries, to rejoin, without any guide other than a movement of the invented line (an almost incorporeal trace), the silent world of the painter, henceforth uttered and accessible.

There is the improvisation of childlike painters who have not learned their own gesture and who believe, under the pretext that a painter is no more than a hand, that it suffices to have a hand in order to paint. They extract petty wonders from their body as a morose young man who observes his body with sufficient complacency can always find some little peculiarity in it to nourish his private religion. But there is also the improvisation of the artist who has turned toward the world that he wants to express and (each word calling for another) has finally composed for himself an acquired voice which is more his than his original cry. There is the improvisation of automatic writing and there is that of the *Charterhouse of Parma*. Since perception itself is never complete, since our perspectives give us a world to express and think about that envelops and exceeds those perspectives, a world that announces itself in lightning signs as a spoken word or an arabesque, why should the expression of the world be subjected to the prose of the *senses* or of the concept? It must be poetry; that is, it must completely awaken and recall our sheer power of expressing beyond things already said or seen. Modern painting presents a problem completely different from that of the return to the individual: the problem of knowing how one can communicate without the help of a preestablished Nature which all men's senses open upon, the problem of knowing how we are grafted to the universal by that which is most our own.

This is one of the philosophies toward which Malraux's analysis may be extended. It just has to be detached from the philosophy of the individual or of death which, with its nostalgic inclination toward civilizations based upon the sacred, is at the forefront of his thought. The painter does not put his immediate self—the very nuance of feeling—into his painting. He puts his *style* there, and he has to win it as much from his own attempts as from the painting of others or from the world. How long it takes, Malraux says, before a writer learns to speak with his own voice. Similarly, how long it takes the painter—who does not, as we do, have his work spread out before him, but who creates it—to recognize in his first paintings the features of what will be his completed work, provided that he is not mistaken about himself.

Even more: he is no more capable of *seeing* his paintings than the writer is capable of reading his work. It is in others that expression takes on its relief and really becomes signification. For the writer or painter, there is only the allusion of self to self, in the familiarity of one's personal hum, which is also called inner monologue. The painter works and leaves his wake; and except when he or she indulges in examining his earlier works to try to recognize what he has become, he does not like very much to look at his work. He has something better in his own possession; the language of his maturity eminently contains the feeble accent of his first works. Without going back to them, and by the sole fact that they have fulfilled certain expressive operations, he finds himself endowed with new organs; and experiencing the excess of what is to be said over and beyond their already verified power, he is capable (unless, as it has more than once occurred, a mysterious fatigue intervenes) of going "further" in the same direction. It is as if each step taken called for and made possible another step, or as if each successful expression prescribed another task to the spiritual automaton or founded an institution whose efficacy it will never stop testing anew.

This "inner schema" which is more and more imperious with each new painting—to the point that the famous chair becomes, Malraux says, "a brutal ideogram of the very name of Van Gogh"—is legible *for Van Gogh* neither in his first works, nor even in his "inner life" (for in this case Van Gogh would not need painting in order to be reconciled with himself; he would stop painting). It *is* that very life, to the extent that it emerges from its inherence, ceases to be in possession of itself and becomes a universal means of understanding and of making something understood, of seeing and of presenting something to see— and is thus not shut up in the depths of the mute individual but diffused throughout all he sees. Before the style became an object of predilection for others and an object of delectation for the artist himself (to the great detriment of his work), there must have been that fecund moment when the style germinated at the surface of the artist's experience, and when an operant and latent meaning found the emblems which were going to disengage it and make it manageable for the artist and at the same time accessible to others. Even when the painter has already painted, and even if he has become in some respects master of himself, what is given to him with his style is not a manner, a certain number of procedures or tics that he can inventory, but a mode of formulation that is just as recognizable for others and just as little visible to him as his silhouette or his everyday gestures.

Thus when Malraux writes that style is the "means of re-creating the world according to the values of the one who discovers it";[10] or that it is "the expression of a meaning lent to the world, a call for and not a consequence of a way of seeing";[11] or finally, that it is "the reduction to a fragile human perspective of the eternal world which draws us along according to a mysterious rhythm into a drift of stars";[12] he does not get inside the functioning of style itself. Like the public, he looks at it from the outside. He indicates some of its consequences, which are truly sensational ones—the victory of humanity over the world—but ones the painter does not intend. The painter at work knows nothing of the antithesis of humanity and world, of meaning and the absurd, of style and "representation." He is far too busy expressing his communication with the world to become proud of a style which is born almost as if he were unaware of it. It is quite true that style for the moderns is much more than a means of representing. It does not have any external model; painting does not exist before painting. But we must not conclude from this, as Malraux does, that the representation of the world is only a *stylistic means*[13] for the painter, as if the style could be known and sought after outside all contact with the world, as if it were an *end*. We must see it developing in the hollows of the painter's perception as a painter; style is an exigency that has issued from that perception.

Malraux says as much in his best passages: perception already stylizes. A woman passing by is not first and foremost a corporeal contour for me, a colored mannequin, or a spectacle; she is "an individual, sentimental, sexual expression." She is a certain manner of being flesh which is given entirely in her walk or even in the simple click of her heel on the ground, just as the tension of the bow is present in each fiber of wood— a most remarkable variant of the norm of walking, looking, touching, and speaking that I possess in my self-awareness because I am body. If I am also a painter, what will be transmitted to the canvas will no longer be only a vital or sensual value. There will be in the painting not just "a woman" or "an unhappy woman" or "a hatmaker." There will also be the emblem of a way of inhabiting the world, of treating it, and of interpreting it by her face, by clothing, the agility of the gesture and the inertia of the body—in short, the emblems of a certain relationship with being.

But even though this truly pictorial style and meaning are not in the woman seen—for in that case the painting would be already completed—they are at least called for by her. "All style is a shaping of the elements of the world, allowing it to be oriented toward one of its essential parts." There is meaning when we submit the data of the world to a "coherent deformation."[14] That convergence of all the visible and intellectual vectors of the painting toward the same meaning, x, is already sketched out in the painter's perception. It begins as soon as he perceives—that is, as soon as he arranges certain gaps or fissures, figures and grounds, a top and a bottom, a norm and a deviation, in the inaccessible fullness of things. In other words, as soon as certain elements of the world take on the value of dimensions to which from then on we relate all the rest, and in whose *language* we express them. For each painter, style is the system of equivalences that he sets up for himself for that labor of manifestation. It is the universal index of the "coherent deformation" by which he concentrates the still scattered meaning of his perception and makes it exist expressly. The work is not brought to fulfillment far from things and in some intimate laboratory to which the painter and the painter alone has the key. Whether he is looking at real flowers or paper flowers, he always goes back to *his* world, as if the principle of the equivalences by means of which he is going to manifest it had been buried there since the beginning of time.

Writers must not underestimate the painter's labor and study, that effort which is so like an effort of thought and which allows us to speak of a language of painting. It is true that, scarcely having drawn his system of equivalences from the world, the painter invests it again in colors and a quasi space on a canvas. The painting does not so much *express* the meaning as the meaning impregnates the painting. "That yellow rent in the sky over Golgotha . . . is an anguish made thing, an anguish which has turned into a yellow rent in the sky, and which is immediately submerged and thickened by thing-like qualities."[15] More than being manifested by the painting, the meaning sinks into it and trembles around it "like a wave of heat."[16] It is "like an immense and futile effort, always arrested halfway between heaven and earth," to express what the nature of painting prevents it from expressing. For professional users of language, the preceding impression is perhaps inevitable. The same thing happens to them that happens to us when we hear a foreign language which we speak poorly; we find it monotonous and marked with an excessively heavy accent and flavor, precisely because it is not our own, and we have not made it the principal instrument of our relations with the world. The meaning of the painting remains *captive* for those of us who do not communicate with the world through painting. But for the painter, and even for us if we set ourselves to living in painting, the meaning is much more than a "wave of heat" at the surface of the canvas, since it is capable of demanding *that* color and *that* object in preference to all others, and since it commands the arrangement of a painting just as imperiously as a syntax or a logic. For not all the painting is in those little anguishes or local joys with which it is sown: they are only the components of a total meaning which is less moving, more *legible*, and more enduring.

Malraux is quite right to relate the anecdote of the innkeeper at Cassis who, seeing Renoir at work by the sea, comes up to him: "There were some naked women bathing in some other place. Goodness knows what he was looking at, and he changed only a little corner." Malraux comments, "The blue of the sea had become that of the brook in *The Bathers*. His vision was less a way of looking at the sea than the secret elaboration of a world to which that depth of blue whose immensity he was recapturing pertained."[17] Nevertheless, Renoir was looking at the sea. And why did the blue of the sea pertain to the world of his painting? How was it able to teach him something about the brook in *The Bathers*? Because each fragment of the world—and in particular the sea, sometimes riddled with eddies and ripples and plumed with spray, sometimes massive and immobile in itself—contains all sorts of shapes of being and, by the way it has of joining the encounter with one's glance, evokes a series of possible variants and teaches, over and beyond itself, a general way of expressing being. Renoir can paint women bathing and a freshwater brook while he is by the sea at Cassis because he only asks the sea— which alone can teach what he asks—for its way of interpreting the liquid element, of exhibiting it, and of making it interact with itself. In short, because he only asks for the prototypical manifestations of water.

The painter can paint while he is looking at the world because it seems to him that he finds in appearances themselves the style which will define him in the eyes of others, and because he thinks he is spelling out nature at the moment he is recreating it. "A certain peremptory equilibrium or disequilibrium of colors and lines overwhelms the person who discovers that the half-opened door over there is that of another world."[18] *Another world*—by this we mean the same world that the painter sees and that speaks his own language, only freed from the nameless weight which held it back and kept it equivocal. How would the painter or poet express anything other than his encounter with the world? What does abstract art itself speak of, if not of a negation or refusal of the world? Now austerity and the obsession with geometrical surfaces and forms (or the obsession with infusorians and microbes; for the interdict put upon life, curiously enough, begins only with the Metazoon) still have an odor of life, even if it is a shameful or despairing life. Thus the painting always says something. It is a new system of equivalences which demands precisely this particular upheaval, and it is in the name of a *truer* relation between things that their ordinary ties are broken.

A vision or an action that is finally free throws out of focus and regroups objects of the world for the painter and words for the poet. But breaking or burning up language does not suffice to write the *Illuminations*, and Malraux profoundly remarks of modern painters that "although no one of them spoke of truth, all, faced with the works of their adversaries, spoke of imposture."[19] They want nothing to do with a truth defined as the resemblance of painting and the world. They would accept the idea of a truth defined as a painting's cohesion with itself, the presence of a unique principle in it which affects each means of expression with a certain contextual value. Now when one stroke of the brush replaces the (in principle) complete reconstruction of appearances in order to give us a sense of wool or flesh, what replaces the object is not the subject—it is the allusive logic of the perceived world.

The painter always intends to signify something; there is always something he or she has to say and progressively approaches. It is just that Van Gogh's "going farther" at the moment he paints *The Crows* no longer indicates some reality to be approached, but rather what still must be done in order to restore the encounter between his glance and the things which solicit it, the encounter between the one who has yet to be and what exists. And that relation is certainly not one of copying. "As always in art, one must lie to tell the truth," Sartre rightly says. It is said that the exact recording of a conversation which had seemed brilliant later gives the impression of poverty. The presence of those who were speaking, the gestures, the physiognomies, and the feeling of an event which is taking place and of a continuous improvisation, all are lacking in the recording. Henceforth the conversation no longer exists; it *is*, flattened out in the unique dimension of sound and all the more disappointing because this wholly auditory medium is that of a text read. In order to fill our mind as it does, the work of art—which often addresses itself to only one of our senses and never assails us from all sides as our lived experience does—must thus be something other than frozen existence. It must be, as Gaston Bachelard[20] says, "superexistence." But it is not arbitrary or, as we say, fictional. Modern painting, like modern thought generally, obliges us to admit a truth which does not resemble things, which is without any external model and without any predestined instruments of expression, and which is nevertheless truth.

If we put the painter back in contact with his world, as we are trying to, perhaps we will be better able to understand the metamorphosis which, through him, transforms the world into painting, changes him into himself from his beginnings to his maturity, and, finally, gives certain works of the past a meaning in each generation that had not been perceived before. When a writer considers painting and painters, he is a little in the position of readers in relation to the writer, or the man in love who thinks of the absent woman. Our conception of the writer begins with his work; the man in love captures the essence of the absent woman in a few words and attitudes by which she expressed herself most purely. When he meets her again, he is tempted to repeat Stendhal's famous "What? Is this all?" When we make the writer's acquaintance, we feel foolishly disappointed at not finding, in each moment of his presence, that essence and impeccable speech that we have become accustomed to designating by his name. So that's what he does with his time? So that's the ugly house he lives in? And these are his friends, the woman with whom he shares his life? These, his mediocre concerns? But all this is only reverie—or even envy and secret hate. One admires as one should only after having understood that there are not any supermen, that there is no one who does not have a human's life to live, and that the secret of the woman loved, of the writer, or of the painter, does not lie in some realm beyond his empirical life, but is so mixed in with his mediocre experiences, so modestly confused with his perception of the world, that there can be no question of meeting it separately, face to face.

In reading the *Psychologie de l'art*, we sometimes get the impression that Malraux, who certainly knows all this as a writer, forgets it where painters are concerned and dedicates the same kind of cult to them which we believe he would not accept from his readers. In short, he makes painters divine. "What genius is not fascinated by that extremity of painting, by that appeal before which time itself vacillates? It is the moment of possession of the world. Let painting go no further, and Hals the Elder becomes God."[21] This is perhaps the painter seen by others. The painter himself is a person at work who each morning finds in the shape of things the same questioning and the same call he never stops responding to. In his eyes, his work is never completed; it is always in progress, so that no one can exalt it above the world. One day, life slips away; the body falls, cut off. In other cases, and more sadly, it is the question spread out through the world's spectacle which is no longer heard. Then the painter is no more, or he has become an honorary painter. But as long as he paints, his painting concerns visible things; or if he is or becomes blind, it concerns that unimpeachable world which he has access to through his other senses and which he speaks of in terms of one who sees. And that is why his labor, which is obscure for him, is nevertheless guided and oriented. It is always only a question of advancing the line of the already opened furrow and of recapturing and generalizing an accent which has already appeared in the corner of a previous painting or in some instant of his experience, without the painter himself ever being able to say (since the distinction has no meaning) what comes from him and what comes from things, what his new work adds to the previous ones, or what he has taken from others as opposed to what is his own.

This triple reworking, which makes a sort of provisional eternity of the operation of expression, is not simply a metamorphosis in the fairytale sense of miracle, magic, and absolute creation in an aggressive solitude. It is also a response to what the world, the past, and the painter's own completed works demanded. It is accomplishment and brotherhood. Husserl has used the fine word *Stiftung*—foundation or establishment—to designate first of all the unlimited fecundity of each present which, precisely because it is singular and passes, can never stop having been and thus being universally; but above all to designate that fecundity of the products of a culture which continue to have value after their appearance and which open a field of investigations in which they perpetually come to life again. It is thus that the world as soon as he has seen it, his first attempts at painting, and the whole past of painting all deliver up a *tradition* to the painter—*that is*, Husserl remarks, *the power to forget origins* and to give to the past not a survival, which is the hypocritical form of forgetfulness, but a new life, which is the noble form of memory.

Malraux emphasizes what is misleading and pathetic in the comedy of the mind: those rival contemporaries, Delacroix and Ingres, whom posterity recognizes as twins, those painters who wanted to be classic and are only neoclassical, that is, the contrary, and those styles which escaped the view of their creators and become visible only when the museum gathered together works scattered about the earth, and photography enlarged miniatures, transformed a section of a painting by its way of framing it, changed rugs, coins, and stained glass windows into paintings, and brought to painting a consciousness of itself which is always retrospective. But if expression recreates and transforms, the same was already true of times preceding ours and even of our perception of the world before painting, since that perception already marked things with the trace of human elaboration. The productions of the past, which are the data of our time, themselves once went beyond yet earlier productions toward a future which we are, and in this sense called for (among others) the metamorphosis which we impose upon them. One can no more inventory a painting (say what is there and what is not) than, according to the linguists, one can inventory a vocabulary—and for the same reason. In both cases it is not a question of a finite sum of signs, but of an open field or of a new organ of human culture.

We cannot deny that in painting such and such a fragment of a painting, that classical painter had already invented the very gesture of this modern one. But we must not forget that he did not make it the principle of his painting and that in this sense he did not invent it, as St. Augustine did not invent the cogito as a central thought but merely encountered it. And yet what Aron[22] called each age's dreamlike quest for ancestors is possible only because all ages pertain to the same universe. The classical and the modern pertain to the universe of painting conceived of as a single task, from the first sketches on the walls of caves to our "conscious" painting. No doubt one reason why our painting finds something to recapture in types of art which are linked to an experience very different from our own is that it transfigures them. But it also does so because they prefigure it, because they at least have something to say to it, and because their artists, believing that they were continuing primitive terrors, or those of Asia and Egypt, secretly inaugurated another history which is still ours and which makes them present to us, while the empires and beliefs to which they thought they *belonged* have disappeared long ago.

The unity of painting does not exist in the museum alone; it exists in that single task which all painters are confronted with and which makes the situation such that one day they *will be* comparable in the museum, and such that these fires answer one another in the night. The first sketches on the walls of caves set forth the world as "to be painted" or "to be sketched" and called for an indefinite future of painting, so that they speak to us and we answer them by metamorphoses in which they collaborate with us. There are thus two historicities. One is ironic or even derisory, and made of misinterpretations, for each age struggles against the others as against aliens by imposing its concerns and perspectives upon them. This history is forgetfulness rather than memory; it is dismemberment, ignorance, externality. But the other history, without which the first would be impossible, is constituted and reconstituted step by step by the *interest* which bears us toward that which is not us and by that life which the past, in a continuous exchange, brings to us and finds in us, and which it continues to lead in each painter who revives, recaptures, and renews the entire undertaking of painting in each new work.

Malraux often subordinates this cumulative history, in which paintings join each other by what they affirm, to the cruel history in which paintings oppose each other because they deny. For him, reconciliation takes place only in death, and it is always in retrospect that one perceives the single problem to which rival paintings are responding and which makes them contemporaneous. But if the problem were really not already present and operative in the painters—if not at the center of their consciousness, at least at the horizon of their labors—what could the museum of the future derive it from? What Valéry said of the priest applies pretty well to the painter: he leads a double life, and half of his bread is consecrated. He is indeed that irascible and suffering person for whom all other painting is a rival. But his angers and hatreds are the waste-product of a work. Wherever he goes, this poor wretch enslaved by his jealousy brings along an invisible double who is free from his obsessions—his self as he is defined by his painting—and he can easily recognize the filiations or kinships manifested by what Péguy called his "historical inscription" if only he consents not to take himself for God and not to venerate each gesture of his brush as unique.

Malraux shows perfectly that what makes "a Vermeer" for us is not the fact that this canvas was one day painted by Vermeer the human being. It is the fact that the painting observes the system of equivalences according to which each of its elements, like a hundred pointers on a hundred dials, marks the same deviation—the fact that it speaks the language of Vermeer. And if the counterfeiter succeeded in recapturing not only the processes but the very style of the great Vermeers, he would no longer be a counterfeiter; he would be one of those painters who painted for the old masters in their studios. It is true that such counterfeiting is impossible: one cannot spontaneously paint like Vermeer after centuries of other painting have gone by and the meaning of the problem of painting itself has changed. But the fact that a painting has been copied in secret by one of our contemporaries qualifies him as a counterfeiter only to the extent that it prevents him from truly reproducing the style of Vermeer.

The fact is that the name of Vermeer and of each great painter comes to stand for something like an institution. And just as the business of history is to discover, behind "Parliament under the *ancien régime*" or "the French Revolution," what they really signify in the dynamics of human relations and what modulation of these relations they represent, and just as it must designate this as accessory and that as essential in order to accomplish its task—so a true history of painting must seek, beyond the immediate aspect of the canvases attributed to Vermeer, a structure, a style, and a meaning against which the discordant details (if there are any) torn from his brush by fatigue, circumstance, or self-imitation cannot prevail. The history of painting can judge the authenticity of a canvas only by examining the painting, not simply because we lack information concerning origins, but also because the complete catalog of the work of a master does not suffice to tell us what is really *his*, because he himself is a certain word in the discourse of painting which awakens echoes from the past and future to the exact degree that it does not look for them, and because he is linked to all other attempts to the exact degree that he busies himself resolutely with his world. Retrospection may well be indispensable for this true history to emerge from empirical history, which is attentive only to events and remains blind to advents, but it is traced out to begin with in the total will of the painter. History looks toward the past only because the painter first looked toward the work to come; there is a fraternity of painters in death only because they live the same problem.

In this respect the museum's function, like the library's, is not entirely beneficent. It certainly enables us to see works of art scattered about the world and engulfed in cults or civilizations they sought to ornament as unified aspects of a single effort. In this sense our consciousness of painting as painting is based upon the museum. But painting exists first of all in each painter who works, and it is there in a pure state, whereas the museum compromises it with the somber pleasures of retrospection. One should go to the museum as the painters go there, in the sober joy of work; and not as we go there, with a somewhat spurious reverence. The museum gives us a thieves' conscience. We occasionally sense that these works were not after all intended to *end up* between these morose walls, for the pleasure of Sunday strollers or Monday "intellectuals." We are well aware that something has been lost and that this meditative necropolis is not the true milieu of art—that so many joys and sorrows, so much anger, and so many labors were not *destined* one day to reflect the museum's mournful light.

By transforming attempts into "works," the museum makes a history of painting possible. But perhaps it is essential to men to attain greatness in their works only when they do not look for it too hard. Perhaps it is not bad that the painter and the writer do not clearly realize that they are establishing a human community. Perhaps, finally, they have a truer and more vital feeling for the history of art when they carry it on in their work than when they make "art lovers" of themselves in order to contemplate it in the museum. The museum adds a false prestige to the true value of the works by detaching them from the chance circumstances they arose from and making us believe that the artist's hand was guided from the start by fate. Whereas style lived within each painter like his heartbeat, and was precisely what enabled him to recognize every effort which differed from his own, the museum converts this secret, modest, nondeliberated, involuntary, and, in short, living historicity into official and pompous history.

The imminence of a regression gives our liking for such and such a painter a nuance of pathos which was quite foreign to him. He *labored* the whole lifetime of a human being; we see his work like flowers on the brink of a precipice. The museum makes the painters as mysterious for us as octopuses or lobsters. It transforms these works created in the fever of a life into marvels from another world, and in its pensive atmosphere and under its protective glass, the breath which sustained them is no more than a feeble flutter on their surface. The museum kills the vehemence of painting as the library, Sartre said, changes writings which were originally a man's gestures into "messages." It is the historicity of death. And there is a historicity of life of which the museum provides no more than a fallen image. This is the historicity which lives in the painter at work when with a single gesture he links the tradition that he carries on and the tradition that he founds. It is the historicity which in one stroke welds him to all which has ever been painted in the world, without his having to leave his place, his time, or his blessed or accursed labor. The historicity of life reconciles paintings by virtue of the fact that each one expresses the whole of existence—that they are all successful—instead of reconciling them in the sense that they are all finite and like so many futile gestures.

If we put painting back into the present, we shall see that it does not admit of the barriers between the painter and others, and between the painter and his own life, that our purism would like to impose. Even if the innkeeper at Cassis does not understand Renoir's transmutation of the blue of the Mediterranean into the water of *The Bathers*, it is still true that he wanted to see Renoir work. That *interests* him too—and after all, nothing stops him from discovering the path that the cave dwellers one day opened without tradition. Renoir would have been quite wrong to ask his advice and try to please him. In this sense, he was not painting for the innkeeper. By his painting, he himself defined the conditions under which he intended to be approved. But he did paint; he questioned the visible and made something visible. It was the world, the water of the sea, that he asked to reveal the secret of the water of *The Bathers*; and he opened the passage from one to the other for those who were caught up in the world with him. As Vuillemin[23] says, there was no question of speaking their language, but of expressing them in expressing himself.

And the painter's relation to his own life is of the same order: his style is not the style of his life, but he draws his life also toward expression. It is understandable that Malraux does not like psychoanalytic *explanations* in painting. Even if St. Anne's cloak is a vulture, even if one admitted that while da Vinci painted it as a cloak, a second da Vinci in da Vinci, head tilted to one side, deciphered it as a vulture like a reader of riddles (after all, it is not impossible: in the life of da Vinci there is a frightening taste for mystification which could very well have inspired him to enshrine his monsters in a work of art), no one would be discussing this vulture any more if the painting did not have another meaning. The explanation only accounts for the details—at most for the materials. Admitting that the painter likes to handle colors (the sculptor, clay) because he is an "anal erotic," this still does not tell us what it is to paint or sculpt.[24] But the contrary attitude, the cult of the artist which forbids us to know anything about their lives and places their work beyond private or public history and outside the world like a miracle, hides their true greatness from us. The reason why Leonardo is something other than one of the innumerable victims of an unhappy childhood is not that he has one foot in the great beyond, but that he succeeded in making a means of interpreting the world out of everything he lived—it is not that he did not have a body or sight, but that he constituted his corporeal or vital situation in language.

When one goes from the order of events to that of expression one does not change worlds; the same circumstances which were previously submitted to now become a signifying system. Hollowed out, worked from within, and finally freed from that weight upon us which made them painful or wounding, they become transparent or even luminous, and capable of clarifying not only the aspects of the world which resemble them but the others too; yet transformed as they may be, they still do not cease to exist. The knowledge of them we may gain will never replace our experience of the work itself. But it helps measure the creation and it teaches us about that immanent transcending of one's situation which is the only irrevocable transcendence. If we take the painter's point of view in order to be present at that decisive moment when what has been given to him to live by way of physical destiny, personal odyssey, or historical circumstances crystallizes into "the motif," we will recognize that his work, never a result, is always a response to these givens, and that the body, life, landscapes, schools, mistresses, creditors, the police, and revolutions which might suffocate painting, are also the bread his painting consecrates. To live in painting is still to breathe the air of this world— above all for the man who sees in the world something to paint. And there is a little of him in every human being.

To get to the heart of the problem. Malraux meditates upon miniatures and coins in which photographic enlargement miraculously reveals the very same style that is found in full-sized works; or upon works uncovered beyond the limits of Europe, far from all "influences"—works in which moderns are astonished to find the same style which a conscious painter has reinvented somewhere else. If one shuts art up in the most secret recess of the individual, he can explain the convergence of separate works only by invoking some destiny which rules over them.

As if an imaginary spirit of art pushed forward from miniature to painting and from fresco to stained-glass window in a single

conquest which it suddenly abandoned for another, parallel or
suddenly opposed, as if a subterranean torrent of history unified all these scattered works by dragging them along with it,
. . . a style known in its evolution and metamorphoses becomes
less an idea than the illusion of a living fatality. Reproduction,
and reproduction alone, has brought into art these imaginary
super-artists of indistinct birth, possessed of a life, of conquests
and concessions to the taste for wealth or seduction, of death
and resurrection—known as styles.[25]

Thus Malraux encounters, at least as a metaphor, the idea of a history
which unites the most disparate attempts, a painting that works behind
the painter's back, and a Reason in history of which he is the instrument.
These Hegelian monstrosities are the antithesis and complement of
Malraux's individualism. What do they become when the theory of perception puts the painter back into the visible world and retrieves the
body as spontaneous expression?

Let us begin with the simplest fact (which we have already clarified in part). The magnifying glass reveals the very same style in a medal-
lion or miniature as the one found in full-sized works because one's hand
has its own ubiquitous style, which is undivided in one's gesture and does
not need to lean heavily upon each point of the tracing in order to mark
the material with its stripe. Our handwriting is recognized whether we
trace letters on paper with three fingers of our hand or in chalk on the
blackboard at arm's length; for it is not a purely mechanical movement
of our body which is tied to certain muscles and destined to accomplish
certain materially defined movements, but a general motor power of formulation capable of the transpositions which constitute the constancy of
style.

Or rather, there is not even any transposition; we simply do not
write in space "in itself" with a thing-hand and a thing-body for which
each new situation presents new problems. We write in perceived space,
where results with the same form are immediately analogous—if we ignore differences of scale—just as the same melody played at different
pitches is immediately identified. And the hand with which we write is a
phenomenon-hand which possesses, in the formula of a movement,
something like the effectual law of the particular cases in which the
movement may have to be executed. The whole marvel of a style already
present in the invisible elements of a work thus comes down to the fact
that, working in the human world of perceived things, the artist comes to
put his stamp upon even the inhuman world revealed by optical instru-

ments—just as the swimmer unknowingly skims over a whole buried universe which would frighten him if he looked at it with undersea goggles; or as Achilles, in the simplicity of one step, effects an infinite summation of spaces and instants.

There is no doubt that this marvel, whose strangeness the word *human* should not hide from us, is a very great one. But we can at least recognize that this miracle is natural to us, that it begins with our incarnate life, and that there is no reason to look for its explanation in some World Spirit which allegedly operates within us without our knowledge and perceives in our place, beyond the perceived world, on a microscopic scale. Here, the spirit of the world is ourselves, as soon as we know how to *move* and *look*. These simple acts already enclose the secret of expressive action. As the artist makes his style radiate into the very fibers of the material he is working on, I move my body without even knowing which muscles and nerve paths should intervene, nor where I must look for the instruments of that action. I want to go over there, and here I am, without having entered into the inhuman secret of the bodily mechanism or having adjusted that mechanism to the givens of the problem. For example: without having adjusted the bodily mechanism to the position of a goal defined by its relation to some system of coordinates, I look at the goal, I am drawn by it, and the bodily apparatus does what must be done in order for me to be there. For me, everything happens in the human world of perception and gesture, but my "geographical" or "physical" body submits to the demands of this little drama which does not cease to bring about a thousand natural marvels in it.

Just my glance toward the goal already has its own miracles. It too takes up its dwelling in being with authority and conducts itself there as in a conquered country. It is not the object which obtains movements of accommodation and convergence from my eyes. It has been shown that on the contrary I would never see anything clearly, and there would be no object for me, if I did not use my eyes in such a way as to make a view of a single object possible. And it is not the mind which takes the place of the body and anticipates what we are going to see. No; it is my glances themselves—synergy, their exploration, and their prospecting—which bring the imminent object into focus; and our corrections would never be rapid and precise enough if they had to be based upon an actual calculation of effects.

We must therefore recognize that what is designated by the terms *glance*, *hand*, and in general *body* is a system of systems destined for the inspection of a world and capable of leaping over distances, piercing the perceptual future, and outlining hollows and reliefs, distances and deviations—a meaning—in the inconceivable flatness of being. The movement of the artist tracing his arabesque in infinite matter amplifies, but also prolongs, the simple marvel of oriented locomotion or grasping movements. Already in its pointing gestures the body not only flows over into a world whose schema it bears in itself but possesses this world at a distance rather than being possessed by it. So much the more does the gesture of expression, which undertakes to delineate what it intends and make it appear "outside," retrieve the world. But already with our first oriented gesture, *the* infinite relationships of a *someone* to his situation had invaded our mediocre planet and opened an inexhaustible field to our behavior. All perception, all action which presupposes it, and in short every human use of the body is already *primordial expression*. Not that derivative labor which substitutes for what is expressed signs which are given elsewhere with their meaning and rule of usage, but the primary operation which first constitutes signs as signs, makes that which is expressed dwell in them through the eloquence of their arrangement and configuration alone, implants a meaning in that which did not have one, and thus—far from exhausting itself in the instant at which it occurs—inaugurates an order and founds an institution or tradition.

Now if the presence of style in miniatures which no one had ever seen (*and in a sense no one had ever made*) is one with the fact of our corporeality and does not call for any occult explanation, it seems to me that one can say as much of the singular convergences which, outside all influences, make works which *resemble one another* appear from one end of the world to another. We ask for a cause which explains these resemblances, and we speak of a Reason in history or of Superartists who guide artists. But to begin with, to speak of resemblances is to put the problem badly. Resemblances are, after all, of little importance in respect to the innumerable differences and varieties of cultures. The probability, no matter how slight, of a reinvention without guide or model suffices to account for these exceptional recurrences. The true problem is to understand why such different cultures become involved in the same search and have the same task in view (and when the opportunity arises, encounter the same modes of expression). We must understand why what one culture produces has meaning for another culture even if it is not its original meaning; why we take the trouble to transform fetishes into art. In short, the true problem is to understand why there is *one* history or one universe of painting.

But this is a problem only if we have begun by placing ourselves in the geographical or physical world, and by placing works of art there as so many separate events whose resemblance or mere connection then becomes improbable and calls for an explanatory principle. We propose on the contrary to consider the order of culture or meaning an original order of *advent*,[26] which should not be derived from that of mere events, if it exists, or treated as simply the effect of extraordinary conjunctions. If it is characteristic of the human gesture to signify beyond its simple existence in fact, to inaugurate a meaning, it follows that every gesture is *comparable* to every other. They all arise from a single syntax. Each is both a beginning and a continuation which, insofar as it is not walled up in its singularity and finished once and for all like an event, points to a continuation or recommencements. Its value exceeds its simple presence, and in this respect it is allied or implicated in advance with all other efforts of expression.

The difficult and essential point here is to understand that in positing a field distinct from the empirical order of events, we are not positing a Spirit of Painting which is already in possession of itself on the other side of the world that it is gradually manifested in. There is not, above and beyond the causality of events, a second causality which makes the world of painting a "suprasensible world" with its own laws. Cultural creation is ineffectual if it does not find a vehicle in external circumstances. But if circumstances lend themselves in the least to creation, a preserved and transmitted painting develops a creative power in its inheritors which is without proportion to what it is—not only as a bit of painted canvas, but even as a work endowed by its creator with a definite meaning. This significance which the work has in excess of the painter's intended meaning involves it in a multitude of relationships which are only faintly reflected in short histories of painting and even in psychological studies of the painter, just as the body's gesture toward the world introduces it into an order of relations of which pure physiology and biology do not have the least idea. Despite the diversity of its parts, which makes it fragile and vulnerable, the body is capable of gathering itself into a gesture which for a time dominates its dispersion and puts its stamp upon everything it does. In the same way, we may speak of a unity of human style which transcends spatial and temporal distances to bring the gestures of all painters together in one sole expressive effort, and their works in a single cumulative history—a single art. The enveloping movement which the unity of culture extends beyond the limits of the individual life is of the same type as that which unites all the moments of the individual life itself in advance at the moment of its institution or birth, when a consciousness (as they say) is sealed up in a body and a new being appears in the world. We know not what will happen in this new life, only that from now on something cannot fail to happen, be it but the end of what has just begun.

Analytic thought breaks up the perceptual transition from moment to moment, from place to place, from one perspective to the next, and then seeks in the mind to guarantee a unity which is already there when we perceive. It also breaks the unity of culture and then tries to reconstruct it from without. After all, it says, there are only the works themselves—which in themselves are a dead letter—and individuals who freely give them a meaning. How is it then that works resemble one another and that individuals understand one another? It is at this conjuncture that the Spirit of Painting is brought in. But just as we must recognize the existential spanning of diversity, and in particular the bodily possession of space, as a fundamental fact; and just as our body, insofar as it *lives* and makes itself gesture, sustains itself only through its effort to be in the world, holds itself upright because its inclination is toward the top and because its perceptual fields draw it toward that risky position, and could not possibly receive this power from a separate spirit; so the history of painting, which runs from one work to another, rests upon itself and is borne only by the caryatid of our efforts, which converge by the sole fact that they are efforts to express.

The intrinsic order of meaning is not eternal. Although it does not follow each zigzag of empirical history, it sketches out, it calls for, a series of successive steps. For it is not (as we stated provisionally) defined simply by the kinship all of its moments bear to one another within a single task. Precisely because these moments are all those of painting, each one of them (if preserved and transmitted) modifies the situation of that overarching enterprise and requires precisely that those moments which come after it be different. Two cultural gestures can be identical only if they are unaware of one another. It is thus essential to art to develop: that is, both to change and, in Hegel's words, to "return to itself," and thus to present itself in the form of history, and the meaning of the expressive gesture upon which we have based the unity of painting is on principle a meaning in genesis.

Advent is a promise of events. The domination of the many by the one in the history of painting, like that domination which we have encountered in the functioning of the perceiving body, does not swallow up succession into an eternity. On the contrary, it insists upon succession; it needs it at the same time that it establishes it in meaning. And there is more than just an analogy between the two problems: it is the expressive operation of the body, begun by the least perception, that develops into painting and art. The field of pictorial meaning has been open since people appeared in the world. The first cave drawing founded a tradition only because it had received one—that of perception. The quasi-eternity of art is of a piece with the quasi-eternity of incarnate existence; and in the use of our bodies and our senses, insofar as they involve us in the world, we have the means of understanding our cultural gesticulation insofar as it involves us in history. The linguists sometimes say that since there is strictly no means of marking the date in history when, for example, Latin ends and French begins, not only are specific tongues all forms of language in general, but there is almost only one specific tongue, constantly fermenting change within itself. Let us say more generally that the continued attempt at expression founds one single history, as the hold our body has upon every possible object founds one single space.

Thus understood, history would escape—here we cannot elaborate—the confused discussions it is the object of today and become once more what it should be for the philosopher: the center of his reflections. Not, certainly, as a *"nature simple,"* absolutely clear in itself, but on the contrary as the locus of all our questionings and wonderments. Whether it be to worship or to hate it, we conceive of history and the dialectic of history today as an external power. Consequently, we are forced to choose between this power and ourselves. To choose history means to devote ourselves body and soul to the advent of a future humanity not even outlined in our present life. For the sake of that future, we are asked to renounce all judgment upon the means of attaining it; and for the sake of efficaciousness, all judgment of value and all "self-consent to ourselves." This history idol secularizes a rudimentary conception of God, and it is not by accident that contemporary discussions return so willingly to a parallel between what is called the "horizontal transcendence" of history and the "vertical transcendence" of God.

The fact is that we doubly misstate the problem when we draw such a parallel. The finest encyclicals in the world are powerless against the fact that for at least twenty centuries Europe and a good part of the world have renounced so-called vertical transcendence. And it is a little too much to forget that Christianity is, among other things, the recognition of a mystery in the relations of man and God, which stems precisely from the fact that the Christian God wants nothing to do with a vertical relation of subordination. He is not simply a principle of which we are the consequence, a will whose instruments we are, or even a model of which human values are only the reflection. There is a sort of impotence of God without us, and Christ attests that God would not be fully God without becoming fully human. Claudel goes so far as to say that God is not above but beneath us—meaning that we do not find Him as a suprasensible idea, but as another ourself, who dwells in and authenticates our darkness. Transcendence no longer hangs over humanity: we become, strangely, its privileged bearer.

Furthermore, no philosophy of history has ever transferred all the substance of the present into the future or *destroyed* the self to make room for the other person. Such a neurotic attitude toward the future would be exactly nonphilosophy, the deliberate refusal to know what one believes in. No philosophy has ever consisted in choosing between transcendences—for example between that of God and that of a human future. They have all been concerned with mediating them (with understanding, for example, how God makes himself man or how man makes himself God) and with elucidating that strange enveloping movement which makes the choice of means already a choice of ends and the self become world, culture, history—but which makes the culture decline at the same time it does. According to Hegel, as is endlessly repeated, all that is real is rational, and thus justified—but justified sometimes as a true acquisition, sometimes as a pause, and sometimes as an ebbing withdrawal for a new surge. In short, all is justified relatively as a moment in total history on condition that this history be realized, and thus in the sense that our errors themselves are said to perform a positive task and that our progress is our mistakes understood—which does not erase the difference between growth and decline, birth and death, regression and progress.

It is true that in Hegel's works the theory of the state and the theory of war seem to reserve the judgment of historical works for the absolute knowledge of the philosopher, and take it away from all other persons. This is not a reason for forgetting that even in the *Philosophy of Right* Hegel rejects judging action by its results alone as well as by its intention alone. "The principle of not taking consequences into account in action, and that other of judging actions according to what follows from them and of taking these consequences as the measure of what is just and good, both pertain to abstract understanding."[27] The twin abstractions Hegel wishes to avoid are lives so separated that one can limit the responsibilities of each to the deliberate and necessary consequences of what it has desired or conceived of, and a history that is one of equally unmerited failures and successes, and which consequently labels human beings glorious or infamous according to the external accidents which have come to deface or embellish what they have done. What he has in mind is the moment when the internal becomes external, that turning or veering by which we merge with others and the world as the world and others merge with us. In other words, action.

By action, I make myself responsible for everything; I accept the aid of external accidents just as I accept their betrayals—"the transformation of necessity into contingence and vice versa."[28] I mean to be master not only of my intentions, but also of what events are going to make of them. I take the world and others as they are. I take myself as I am and I answer for all. *"To act is . . . to deliver oneself up to this law."*[29] Action makes the event its own to such an extent that the botched crime is punished more lightly than the successful one, and Oedipus thinks of himself as a parricide and an incestuous person, even though he is so in fact only.

Confronted with the folly of action, which assumes responsibility for the course of events, one may be tempted to conclude with equal justice that we are all guilty—since to act or even to live is already to accept the risk of infamy along with the chance for glory, and that we are all innocent—since nothing, not even crime, has been willed *ex nihilo*, no one having chosen to be born. But beyond these philosophies of the internal and the external before which all is equivalent, what Hegel suggests (since when all is said and done there is a difference between the valid and the invalid, and between what we accept and what we refuse) is a judgment of the attempt, of the undertaking, or of the *work*. Not a judgment of the intention or the consequences only, but of the use which we have made of our good will, and of the way in which we have evaluated the factual situation. A person is judged by neither intention nor fact but by his or her success in making values become facts.

When this happens, the meaning of the action does not exhaust itself in the situation which has occasioned it, or in some vague judgment of value; the action remains as an exemplary type and will survive in other situations in another form. It opens a field. Sometimes it even institutes a world. In any case it outlines a future. History according to Hegel is this maturation of a future in the present, not the sacrifice of the present to an unknown future; and the rule of action for him is not to be efficacious at any cost, but to be first of all fecund.

The polemics against "horizontal transcendence" in the name of "vertical transcendence" (admitted or simply regretted) are thus no less unjust toward Hegel than toward Christianity. And by throwing overboard along with history not only, as they think, a blood-smeared idol, but also the duty of carrying principles over into events, they have the drawback of reintroducing a false simplicity which is no remedy for the abuses of the dialectic. Both the pessimism of the neo-Marxists and the laziness of non-Marxist thought, today as always one another's accomplice, present the dialectic—within and without us—as a power of lying and failure, a transformation of good into evil, and an inevitable disappointment. According to Hegel, this is only one side of the dialectic. It is also something like a grace in events which draws us away from evil toward the good, and which, for example, throws us toward the universal when we think we are pursuing only our own interest. The dialectic is, Hegel said approximately, *a movement which itself creates its course and returns to itself,* and thus a movement which has no other guide but its own initiative and which nevertheless does not escape outside itself but doubles back to confirm itself from time to time. So the Hegelian dialectic is what we call by another name the phenomenon of expression, which gathers itself up and launches itself again through the mystery of rationality. And we would undoubtedly recover the concept of history in the true sense of the term if we were to get used to modeling it after the example of the arts and language. For the fact that each expression is closely connected within one single order to every other expression brings about the junction of the individual and the universal. The central fact to which the Hegelian dialectic returns in a hundred and one ways is that we do not have to choose between the *pour soi* and the *pour autrui,* between thought according to us and according to others, but that at the moment of expression the other to whom I address myself and I who express myself are linked together without concessions. The others such as they are (or will be) are not the sole judges of what I do. If I wanted to deny myself for their benefit, I would deny them too as "selves." They are worth exactly what I am worth, and all the powers I give them I give simultaneously to myself. I submit myself to the judgment of another *who is himself worthy of that which I have attempted,* that is to say, in the last analysis, to the judgment of a peer whom I myself have chosen.

History is the judge—not history as the power of a moment or of a century, but history as the inscription and accumulation, beyond the limits of countries and epochs, of what, given the situation, we have done and said that is most true and valuable. Others will judge what I have done, because I painted in the realm of the visible and spoke for those who have ears—but neither art nor politics consists in pleasing or flattering them. What they expect of the artist or of the politician is that he draw them toward values in which they will only later recognize their values. The painter or the politician moulds others much more often than he follows them. The public he aims at is not given; it is precisely the one which his oeuvre will elicit. The others he thinks of are not empirical "others," defined by what they expect of him at this moment. He thinks even less of *humanity* conceived of as a species which possesses "human dignity" or "the honor of being a human" as other species have a cara-pace or an air-bladder. No, his concern is with others who have become such that he is able to live with them. The history that the writer partici-pates in (and the less he thinks about "making history"—about making his mark in the history of letters—and honestly produces *his* work, the more he will participate) is not a power before which he must bend his knee. It is the perpetual conversation carried on between all spoken words and all valid actions, each in turn contesting and confirming the other, and each recreating all the others. The appeal to the judgment of history is not an appeal to the complacency of the public (and even less, it must be said, an appeal to the lay public). It is inseparable from the inner certainty of having said what waited to be said in the particular situation and what consequently could not fail to be understood by x. "I shall be read in one hundred years," Stendhal thinks. This means that he wants to be read, but also that he is willing to wait a century, and that his free-dom invites a world as yet in limbo to become as free as he is by recogniz-ing as acquired what he has had to invent.

This unvarnished appeal to history is an invocation of truth, which is never created by what is inscribed in history, but which, insofar as it is truth, requires that inscription. It dwells not only in literature or art but also in every undertaking of life. Except perhaps in the case of some wretched souls who think only of winning or of being right, all action and all love are haunted by the hope for an account which will transform them into their truth—the coming of the day it will finally be known just what the situation was. Was it one person's reserve hiding under an apparent respect for others which one day definitively put the other off, who reflected that reserve back, magnified one hundredfold, or was the die cast from that moment on, and that impossible love . . . ? Perhaps this hope for a final, clear accounting will forever be in some way disappointed. People borrow from one another so constantly that each movement of our will and thought receives its impetus from contact with others, so that in this sense it is impossible to have more than a rough idea of what is due to each individual. It is nevertheless true that this desire for a total manifestation animates life as it does literature, and that beyond the petty motives it is this desire which makes the writer want to be read, sometimes prompts people to become writers, and in any case makes them speak, makes everyone want to account for him or herself in the eyes of x—which means that everyone thinks of his life and all lives as something that can be told, as both a story and as history.

True history thus gets its life entirely from us. It is in our present that it gets the force to make everything else present. The other whom I respect gets his life from me as I get mine from him. A philosophy of history does not take away any of my rights or initiatives. It simply adds to my obligations as a solitary person the obligation to understand situations other than my own and to create a path between my life and that of others, that is, to express myself. Through the action of culture, I take up my dwelling in lives which are not mine. I confront them, I make one known to the other, I make them co-possible in an order of truth, I make myself responsible for all of them, and I create a universal life, just as by the thick and living presence of my body, in one fell swoop I take up my dwelling in space. And like the functioning of the body, that of words or paintings remains obscure to me. The words, lines, and colors which express me come out of me as gestures. They are torn from me by what I want to say as my gestures are by what I want to do. In this sense, there is in all expression a spontaneity which will not take orders, not even those which I would like to give to myself. Words, even in the art of prose, carry the speaker and the hearer into a common universe by drawing both toward a new meaning through their power to designate in excess of their accepted definition, through the muffled life they have led and continue to lead in us, and through what Ponge[30] appropriately called their "semantic thickness" and Sartre their "signifying soil." This spontaneity of language which unites us is not a command, and the history which it establishes is not an external idol: it is ourselves with our roots, our growth, and, as we say, the fruits of our toil.

Perception, history, expression—it is only by bringing together these three problems that we can rectify Malraux's analyses in keeping with their own direction. And, at the same time, we shall be able to see why it is legitimate to treat painting as a language. This way of dealing with the problem will emphasize a perceptual meaning which is captured in the visible configuration of the painting and yet capable of gathering up a series of antecedent expressions into an eternity ever to be recreated. The comparison benefits not only our analysis of painting but also that of language. For it will perhaps lead us to detect beneath spoken language an operant or speaking language whose words live a little-known life and unite with and separate from one another as their lateral or indirect meaning demands, even though these relations seem *evident* to us once the expression is accomplished. The transparency of spoken language, that brave clarity of the word that is all sound and the meaning that is all meaning, the property it apparently has of extracting the meaning from signs and isolating it in its pure state (which is perhaps simply the anticipation of several different formulations in which it would really remain *the same*), and its presumed power of recapitulating and enclosing a whole process of expression in a single act—are these not simply the highest point of a tacit and implicit accumulation of the same sort as that of painting?

Like a painting, a novel expresses tacitly. Its subject matter, like that of a painting, can be recounted. But Julien Sorel's trip to Verrières and his attempt to kill Mme de Rênal after he learns she has betrayed him are not as important as that silence, that dreamlike journey, that unthinking certitude, and that eternal resolution which follow the news. Now these things are nowhere *said*. There is no need of a "Julien thought" or a "Julien wished." In order to express them, Stendhal had only to insinuate himself into Julien and make objects, obstacles, means, and chance occurrences appear before our eyes with the swiftness of the journey. He had only to decide to narrate in one page instead of five. That brevity, that unusual proportion of things omitted to things said, is not even the result of a *choice*. Consulting his own sensitivity to others, Stendhal suddenly found an imaginary body for Julien which was more agile than his own body. As if in a second life, he made the trip to Verrières according to a cadence of cold passion which itself decided what was visible and what invisible, what was to be said and what to remain unspoken. The desire to kill is thus not in the words at all. It is between them, in the hollows of space, time, and meaning they mark out, as movement at the cinema is between the immobile images which follow one another.

The novelist speaks for his reader, and every person to every other, the language of the initiated—initiated into the world and into the universe of possibilities confined in a human body and a human life. What he has to say he presumes known. He takes up his dwelling in a character's behavior and gives the reader only a suggestion of it, its nervous and peremptory trace in the surroundings. If the author is a writer, that is, if he is capable of finding the elisions and caesuras which indicate the behavior, the reader responds to his appeal and joins him at the virtual center of the writing, *even if neither one of them is aware of it*. The novel as a report of events and a statement of ideas, theses, or conclusions (as manifest or prosaic meaning) and the novel as an expression of style (as oblique and latent meaning) are in a simple relationship of homonymy. Marx clearly understood this when he adopted Balzac. We can be sure that there was no question here of some return to liberalism. Marx meant that a certain way of *making visible* the world of money and the conflicts of modern society was worth more than Balzac's theses—even political—and that this vision, once acquired, would have its consequences, with or without Balzac's consent.

It is certainly right to condemn formalism, but it is ordinarily forgotten that its error is not that it esteems form too much, but that it esteems it so little that it detaches it from meaning. In this respect formalism is no different than a literature of "subject matter," which also separates the meaning of the work from its configuration. The true contrary of formalism is a good theory of style, or of speech, which puts both above "technique" or "device." Speech is not a means in the service of an external end. It contains its own rule of usage, ethics, and view of the world, as a gesture sometimes bears the whole truth about a person. This living use of language, ignored by both formalism and the literature of "subject matter" is literature itself as quest and acquisition. A language which only sought to reproduce reality itself would exhaust its instructive power in factual statements. On the contrary, a language which gives our perspectives on things and hollows out relief in them opens up a discussion that goes beyond the language and itself invites further investigation. What is irreplaceable in the work of art, what makes it, far more than a means of pleasure, a spiritual organ whose analogue is found in all productive philosophical or political thought, is the fact that it contains, better than ideas, *matrices of ideas*—providing us with emblems whose meaning we never stop developing. Precisely because it dwells and makes us dwell in a world we do not have the key to, the work of art teaches us to see and ultimately gives us something to think about as no analytical work can; for when we analyze an object, we find only what we have put into it.

What is hazardous in literary communication, and ambiguous and irreducible to the theme in all the great works of art, is not a provisional weakness which we might hope to overcome. It is the price we must pay to have a literature, that is, a conquering language which introduces us to unfamiliar perspectives instead of confirming us in our own. We would not see anything if our eyes did not give us the means of catching, questioning, and giving form to an indefinite number of configurations of space and color. We would not do anything if our body did not enable us to leap over all the neural and muscular means of locomotion in order to move to the goal. Literary language fills the same kind of office. In the same imperious and brief way the writer transports us without transitions or preparations from the world of established meanings to something else. And as our body guides us among things only on condition that we stop analyzing it and make use of it, language is literary, that is, productive, only on condition that we stop asking justifications of it at each instant and follow it where it goes, letting the words and all the means of expression of the book be enveloped by that halo of signification that they owe to their singular arrangement, and the whole writing veer toward a second-order value where it almost rejoins the mute radiance of painting.

The meaning of a novel too is perceptible at first only as a *coherent deformation* imposed upon the visible. Nor will it ever be so otherwise. Criticism may compare one novelist's mode of expression with another's and incorporate one type of narrative in a family of other possible ones. This work is legitimate only if it is preceded by a perception of the novel in which the particularities of "technique" merge with those of the overall project and meaning, and if it is only intended to explain to us what we ourselves have already perceived. As the description of a face does not allow us to imagine it, though it may specify certain of its characteristics, the language of the critic, who claims to possess the object of his criticism, does not replace that of the novelist, who shows us what is true or makes it show through without touching it. It is essential to what is true to be presented first and forever in a movement which throws our image of the world out of focus, distends it, and draws it toward fuller meaning. It is thus that the auxiliary line introduced into a geometrical figure opens the road to new relations. It is thus that the work of art works and will always work upon us—as long as there are works of art.

But these remarks are far from exhausting the question. There are still the exact forms of language—and philosophy—to be considered. We may wonder whether their ambition to recover the slippery hold on our experience that literature gives us and gain actual possession of what is said does not express the essence of language much better than literature does. This problem would involve logical analyses which cannot be considered here. Without dealing with it completely, we can at least situate it and show that in any case no language ever wholly frees itself from the precariousness of the silent forms of expression, reabsorbs its own contingency, and melts away to make the things themselves appear; that in this sense the privilege language enjoys over painting or the practices of life remains relative; and, finally, that expression is not one of the curiosities that the mind may propose to examine but is its existence in act.

Certainly one who decides to write takes an attitude in respect to the past which is his alone. All culture prolongs the past. Today's parents see their childhood in their own children's and adopt toward them the behavior of their own parents. Or, through ill-will, they go to the opposite extreme. If they have been subjected to an authoritarian upbringing, they practice a permissive one. And by this detour they often come back to the tradition, for in twenty-five years the vertiginous heights of freedom will bring the child back to a system of security and make him an authoritarian father. The novelty of the arts of expression is that they bring tacit culture out of its mortal circle. Even the artist is not content to continue the past by veneration or revolt: he resumes its venture on his own terms. One reason why the painter takes up his brush is that in a sense the art of painting still remains to be created.

But the arts of language go much farther toward true creation. Precisely because painting is always something to be created, the works which the new painter produces will be added to already created works. The new do not make the old useless, nor do they expressly contain them; they rival them. Today's painting denies the past too deliberately to be able truly to free itself from it. It can only forget it while exploiting it. The cost of its novelty is that in making what came before it seem an unsuccessful effort, it foreshadows a different painting tomorrow which will make it seem in turn another unsuccessful effort. Thus painting as a whole presents itself as an abortive effort to say something which still remains to be said. Although the writer is not content simply to extend existing language, he is no more anxious to replace it by an idiom which, like a painting, is sufficient unto itself and closed in upon its intimate signification. If you wish, he destroys ordinary language, but by realizing it. The given language, which penetrates him through and through and already offers a general representation of his most secret thoughts, does not stand before him as an enemy. It is entirely *ready to* convert everything new he stands for as a writer into an acquisition. It is as if it had been made for him, and he for it; as if the task of speaking to which he was destined in learning the language were more legitimately he than his heartbeat; and as if the established language called into existence, along with him, one of *his* possibilities.

Painting fulfills a vow of the past. It has the power to act in the name of the past, but it does not contain it in its manifest state. It is memory for us, if we happen to know the history of painting, but it is not memory "for itself"—it does not claim to sum up what has made it possible. Speech, not content to push beyond the past, claims to recapitulate, retrieve, and contain it in substance. And since without repeating it textually speech could not give us the past in its presence, it makes the past undergo a preparation which is the property of language—it offers us the *truth* of it. It is not content to push the past aside in making a place for itself in the world: it wants to preserve it in its spirit or its meaning. Thus speech twists back upon itself, takes itself up, and gets possession of itself once more.

There is a critical, philosophical, universal use of language which claims to retrieve things as they are—whereas painting transforms them into painting—to retrieve everything, both language itself and the use other doctrines have made of it. From the moment he seeks the truth, the philosopher does not think that it had to wait for him in order to be true; he seeks it as what has always been true for everyone. It is essential to truth to be integral, whereas no painting has ever pretended to be. The Spirit of Painting appears only in the museum, because it is a Spirit external to itself. Speech, on the contrary, tries to gain possession of itself and conquer the secret of its own inventions. Man does not paint painting, but he speaks about speech, and the spirit of language wants to depend upon nothing but itself.

A painting makes its charm dwell from the start in a dreaming eternity where we easily rejoin it many centuries later, even without knowing the history of the dress, furnishings, utensils, and civilization whose stamp it bears. Writing, on the contrary, relinquishes its most enduring meaning to us only through a precise history which we must have some knowledge of. The *Provincial Letters* put the theological discussions of the seventeenth century back in the present; *The Red and the Black*, the gloom of the Restoration. But painting pays curiously for this immediate access to the enduring that it grants itself, for it is subject much more than writing to the passage of time. The pleasure of an anachronism is mixed with our contemplation of paintings, whereas Stendhal and Pascal are entirely in the present. To the exact extent that it renounces the hypocrite eternity of art and, boldly confronting time, displays it instead of vaguely evoking it, literature surges forth victorious and founds time on meaning. Although the statues of Olympia play a great part in attaching us to Greece, they also foster (in the state in which they have come down to us—bleached, broken, detached from the work as a whole) a fraudulent myth about Greece. They cannot resist time as a manuscript, even incomplete, torn, and almost illegible, does. Heraclitus's writing casts light for us as no broken statues can, because its signification is deposited and concentrated in it in another way than theirs is in them, and because nothing equals the ductility of speech. In short, language speaks, and the voices of painting are the voices of silence.

This is because statements venture to unveil the thing itself; language goes beyond itself toward what it signifies. It is of no avail that (as Saussure explains) each word draws its meaning from all the others, the fact remains that at the moment it occurs the task of expressing is no longer deferred and referred to other words—it is accomplished, and we understand something. Saussure may show that each act of expression becomes significant only as a modulation of a general system of expression and only insofar as it is differentiated from other linguistic gestures. The marvel is that before Saussure we did not know anything about this, and that we forget it again each time we speak—as this very moment, as we speak of Saussure's ideas. This proves that each partial act of expression, as an act common to the whole of the given language, is not limited to expending an expressive power accumulated in the language, but recreates both the power and the language by making us verify in the obviousness of given and received meaning the power that speaking subjects have of going beyond signs toward their meaning. Signs do not simply evoke other signs for us and so on without end, and language is not like a prison we are locked into or a guide we must blindly follow; for at the crossroads of all these linguistic gestures, their meaning appears—to which we have been given such total access that it seems to us we no longer need the linguistic gestures to refer to it. Thus when we compare language to the silent forms of expression such as gestures or paintings, we must point out that unlike these forms language is not content to sketch out directions, vectors, a "coherent deformation," or a tacit meaning on the surface of the world, exhausting itself as animal "intelligence" does in kaleidoscopically producing a new landscape for action. Language is not just the replacement of one meaning by another, but the substitution of equivalent meanings. The new structure is given as already present in the old, the latter subsists in it, and the past is now understood.

There is no doubt that language is the presumption to a total accumulation; and present speech confronts the philosopher with the problem of this provisional self-possession, which is provisional yet no mean thing. The fact remains that language could deliver up the thing itself only if it ceased to be in time and in situation. Hegel is the only one who thinks that his system contains the truth of all the others, and one who knew the others only through Hegel's synthesis would not know them at all. Even if Hegel were true from one end to the other, we cannot dispense with reading the "pre-Hegelians," for he can contain them only "in what they affirm." By what they deny they offer the reader another situation of thought which is not eminently contained in Hegel—which is not there at all—and in which Hegel is visible in a light which he is himself unaware of. Hegel is the only one to think that he has no existence "for others," and that he is in the eyes of others exactly what he knows himself to be. Even if it is admitted that there has been progress from them to him, there may be a passage of Descartes's *Meditations* or Plato's dialogues—and precisely because of the "naivetés" that held them back from Hegel's "truth"—a contact with things, a spark of meaning that we cannot recognize in Hegel unless we have already found it in the originals, to which we must always return, if only to understand Hegel.

Hegel is the museum. He is if you wish all philosophies, but deprived of their finiteness and power of impact, embalmed, transformed, he believes, into themselves, but really transformed into Hegel. We only have to see how a truth wastes away when it is integrated into different ones (how the cogito, for example, in going from Descartes to the Cartesians, becomes almost a listlessly repeated ritual) to agree that the synthesis does not effectively contain all past systems of thought, that it is not all that they have been, that it is never a synthesis at once both "in and for itself"—that is, a synthesis which in the same movement is and knows, is what it knows, knows what it is, preserves and suppresses, realizes and destroys. If Hegel means that as the past becomes distant it changes into its meaning, and that we can, after the fact, trace an intelligible history of thought, he is right; but on condition that in this synthesis each term remains the whole of the world at the date considered, and that in linking philosophies together we keep them all in their place like so many open significations and let an exchange of anticipations and metamorphoses subsist between them. The meaning of philosophy is the meaning of a genesis. Consequently, it could not possibly be summed up outside of time, and it is still expression.

It is all the more true of nonphilosophical writing that the writer can have the feeling of attaining things themselves only by using language and not by going beyond language. Mallarmé himself was well aware that nothing would fall from his pen if he remained absolutely faithful to his vow to say everything without leaving anything unsaid, and that he was able to write minor books only by giving up the Book which would dispense with all the others. The signification without any sign, the thing itself—that height of clarity—would be the disappearance of all clarity. And whatever clarity we can have is not at the beginning of language, like a golden age, but at the end of its efforts. Language and the system of truth do displace our life's center of gravity by suggesting that we cross-check and resume our operations in terms of one another, in such a way that each one shifts into all of them and they seem independent of the step-by-step formulations which we first gave them. They do thereby reduce the other expressive operations to the rank of "mute" and subordinate ones. Yet language and the system of truth are not themselves lacking in reticence, and meaning is not so much designated by them as it is implied by their word structure.

We must therefore say the same thing about language in relation to meaning that Simone de Beauvoir says about the body in relation to mind: it is neither first nor second. No one has ever made the body simply a means or an instrument, or maintained for example that one can love by principles. And since it is no more true that the body loves all by itself, we may say that it does everything and nothing, that it is and is not ourselves. Neither end nor means, always involved in matters which go beyond it, always jealous nevertheless of its autonomy, it is powerful enough to oppose any end which is merely deliberate, but it has none to propose to us if we finally turn toward it and consult it. Sometimes—and then we have the feeling of being ourselves—it lets itself be animated and takes upon itself a life which is not simply its own. Then it is happy and spontaneous, and we with it. Similarly, language is not meaning's servant, and yet it does not govern meaning. There is no subordination between them. Here no one commands and no one obeys. What we *mean* is not before us, outside all speech, as sheer signification. It is only the excess of what we live over what has already been said. With our apparatus of expression we set ourselves up in a situation the apparatus is sensitive to, we confront it with the situation, and our statements are only the final balance of these exchanges. Political thought itself is of this order. It is always the elucidation of an historical perception in which all our understanding, all our experience, and all our values simultaneously come into play—and of which our theses are only the schematic formulation. All action and knowledge which do not go through this elaboration, and which seek to set up values which have not been embodied in our individual or collective ·history (*or*—what comes down to the same thing—which seek to choose means by a calculus and a wholly technical process), fall short of the problems they are trying to solve. Personal life, expression, understanding, and history advance obliquely and not straight toward ends or concepts. What we strive for too reflectively eludes us, while values and ideas come forth abundantly to him who, in his meditative life, has learned to free their spontaneity.

6

Eye and Mind

Maurice Merleau-Ponty

What I am trying to convey to you is more mysterious; it is entwined in the very roots of being, in the impalpable source of
sensations.

—J. Gasquet, *Cézanne*

I

Science manipulates things and gives up living in them.[1] Operating
within its own realm, it makes its constructs of things; operating upon
these indices or variables to effect whatever transformations are permit-
ted by their definition, it comes face to face with the real world only at
rare intervals. It is, and always has been, that admirably active, ingenious, and bold way of thinking whose fundamental bias is to treat everything as though it were an object-in-general—as though it meant
nothing to us and yet was predestined for our ingenious schemes.

But classical science clung to a feeling for the opaqueness of the
world, and it expected through its constructions to get back into the
world. For this reason it felt obliged to seek a transcendent or transcendental foundation for its operations. Today we find—not in science but
in a widely prevalent philosophy of the sciences—an entirely new approach. Constructive scientific activities see themselves and represent
themselves to be autonomous, and their thinking deliberately reduces
itself to a set of data-collecting techniques which it has invented. To think
is thus to test out, to operate, to transform—the only restriction being
that this activity is regulated by an experimental control that admits only

the most "worked-up" phenomena, more likely produced by the apparatus than recorded by it.

Whence all sorts of vagabond endeavors. Today more than ever, science is sensitive to intellectual fads and fashions. When a model has succeeded in one order of problems, it is tried out everywhere else. At the present time, for example, our embryology and biology are full of "gradients." Just how these differ from what classical tradition called "order" or "totality" is not at all clear. This question, however, is not raised; it is not even allowed. The gradient is a net we throw out to sea, without knowing what we will haul back in it. It is the slender twig upon which unforeseeable crystalizations will form. No doubt this freedom of operation will serve well to overcome many a pointless dilemma—provided only that from time to time we take stock, and ask ourselves why the apparatus works in one place and fails in others. For all its flexibility, science must understand itself; it must see itself as a construction based on a brute, existent world and not claim for its blind operations the constitutive value that "concepts of nature" were granted in a certain idealist philosophy. To say that the world is, by nominal definition, the object x of our operations is to treat the scientist's knowledge as if it were absolute, as if everything that is and has been was meant only to enter the laboratory. Thinking "operationally" has become a sort of absolute artificialism, such as we see in the ideology of cybernetics, where human creations are derived from a natural information process, itself conceived on the model of human machines. If this kind of thinking were to extend its dominion over humanity and history; and if, ignoring what we know of them through contact and our own situations, it were to set out to construct them on the basis of a few abstract indices (as a decadent psychoanalysis and culturalism have done in the United States)—then, since the human being truly becomes the *manipulandum* he thinks he is, we enter into a cultural regimen in which there is neither truth nor falsehood concerning humanity and history, into a sleep, or nightmare from which there is no awakening.

Scientific thinking, a thinking which looks on from above, and thinks of the object-in-general, must return to the "there is" which precedes it; to the site, the soil of the sensible and humanly modified world such as it is in our lives and for our bodies—not that possible body which we may legitimately think of as an information machine but this actual body I call mine, this sentinel standing quietly at the command of my words and my acts. Further, *associated bodies* must be revived along with my body—"others," not merely as my congeners, as the zoologist says, but others who haunt me and whom I haunt; "others" along with whom I haunt a single, present, and actual Being as no animal ever haunted those of his own species, territory, or habitat. In this primordial historicity, science's agile and improvisatory thought will learn to ground itself upon things themselves and upon itself, and will once more become philosophy. . . .

Now art, especially painting, draws upon this fabric of brute meaning which operationalism would prefer to ignore. Art and only art does so in full innocence. From the writer and the philosopher, in contrast, we want opinions and advice. We will not allow them to hold the world suspended. We want them to take a stand; they cannot waive the responsibilities of humans who speak. Music, at the other extreme, is too far on the hither side of the world and the designatable to depict anything but certain schemata of Being—its ebb and flow, its growth, its upheavals, its turbulence.

Only the painter is entitled to look at everything without being obliged to appraise what he sees. For the painter, we might say, the watchwords of knowledge and action lose their meaning and force. Political regimes which denounce "degenerate" painting rarely destroy paintings. They hide them, and one senses here an element of "one never knows" amounting almost to an acknowledgment. The reproach of escapism is seldom aimed at the painter; we do not hold it against Cézanne that he lived hidden away at L'Estaque during the Franco-Prussian War. And we recall with respect his "life is frightening," although the most insignificant student, after Nietzsche, would flatly reject philosophy if he or she were told that it did not teach us how to live life to the fullest. It is as if in the painter's calling there were some urgency above all other claims on him. Strong or frail in life, but incontestably sovereign in his rumination of the world, possessed of no other "technique" than the skill his eyes and hands discover in seeing and painting, he gives himself entirely to drawing from the world—with its din of history's glories and scandals—*canvases* which will hardly add to the angers or the hopes of humanity; and no one complains.[2] What, then, is the secret science which he has or which he seeks? That dimension which lets Van Gogh say he must go "still further"? What is this fundamental of painting, perhaps of all culture?

II

The painter "takes his body with him," says Valéry. Indeed we cannot imagine how a *mind* could paint. It is by lending his body to the world that the artist changes the world into paintings. To understand these transubstantiations we must go back to the working, actual body—not the body as a chunk of space or a bundle of functions but that body which is an intertwining of vision and movement.

I have only to see something to know how to reach it and deal with it, even if I do not know how this happens in the nervous system. My moving body makes a difference in the visible world, being a part of it; that is why I can steer it through the visible. Moreover, it is also true that vision is attached to movement. We see only what we look at. What would vision be without eye movement? And how could the movement of the eyes not blur things if movement were blind? If it were only a reflex? If it did not have its antennae, its clairvoyance? If vision were not prefigured in it?

All my changes of place figure on principle in a corner of my landscape; they are carried over onto the map of the visible. Everything I see is on principle within my reach, at least within reach of my sight, and is marked upon the map of the "I can." Each of the two maps is complete. The visible world and the world of my motor projects are both total parts of the same Being.

This extraordinary overlapping, which we never give enough thought to, forbids us to conceive of vision as an operation of thought that would set up before the mind a picture or a representation of the world, a world of immanence and of ideality. Immersed in the visible by his body, itself visible, the see-er does not appropriate what he sees; he merely approaches it by looking, he opens onto the world. And for its part, that world of which he is a part is not *in itself*, or matter. My movement is not a decision made by the mind, an absolute doing which would decree, from the depths of a subjective retreat, some change of place miraculously executed in extended space. It is the natural sequel to, and maturation of, vision. I say of a thing that it is moved; but my body moves itself; my movement is self-moved. It is not ignorance of self, blind to itself; it radiates from a self. . . .

The enigma derives from the fact that my body simultaneously sees and is seen. That which looks at all things can also look at itself and recognize, in what it sees, the "other side" of its power of looking. It sees itself seeing; it touches itself touching; it is visible and sensitive for itself. It is a self, not by transparency, like thought, which never thinks anything except by assimilating it, constituting it, transforming it into thought— but a self by confusion, narcissism, inherence of the see-er in the seen, the toucher in the touched, the feeler in the felt—a self, then, that is caught up in things, having a front and a back, a past and a future. . . .

This initial paradox cannot but produce others. Visible and mobile, my body is a thing among things; it is one of them. It is caught in the fabric of the world, and its cohesion is that of a thing. But because it moves itself and sees, it holds things in a circle around itself.[3] Things are an annex or prolongation of itself; they are incrusted in its flesh, they are part of its full definition; the world is made of the very stuff of the body. These reversals, these antinomies,[4] are different ways of saying that vision is caught or comes to be in things—in that place where something visible undertakes to see, becomes visible to itself and in the sight of all things, in that place where there persists, like the original solution still present within crystal, the undividedness of the sensing and the sensed.

This interiority no more precedes the material arrangement of the human body than it results from it. What if our eyes were made in such a way as to prevent our seeing any part of our body, or some diabolical contraption were to let us move our hands over things, while preventing us from touching our own body? Or what if, like certain animals, we had lateral eyes with no cross-blending of visual fields? Such a body would not reflect itself; it would be an almost adamantine body, not really flesh, not really the body of a human being. There would be no humanity.

But humanity is not produced as the effect of our articulations or by the way our eyes are implanted in us (still less by the existence of mirrors, though they alone can make our entire bodies visible to us). These contingencies and others like them, without which mankind would not exist, do not by simple summation bring it about that there *is* a single man. The body's animation is not the assemblage or juxtaposition of its parts. Nor is it a question of a mind or spirit coming down from somewhere else into an automation—which would still imply that the body itself is without an inside and without a "self." A human body is present when, between the see-er and the visible, between touching and touched, between one eye and the other, between hand and hand a kind of crossover occurs, when the spark of the sensing/sensible is lit, when the fire starts to burn that will not cease until some accident befalls the body, undoing what no accident would have sufficed to do. . . .

Once this strange system of exchanges is given, we find before us all the problems of painting. These problems illustrate the enigma of the body, which enigma in turn legitimates them. Since things and my body are made of the same stuff, vision must somehow come about in them; or yet again, their manifest visibility must be repeated in the body by a secret visibility. "Nature is on the inside," says Cézanne. Quality, light, color, depth, which are there before us, are there only because they awaken an echo in our bodies and because the body welcomes them.

Things have an internal equivalent in me; they arouse in me a carnal formula of their presence. Why shouldn't these correspondences in turn give rise to some tracing rendered visible again, in which the eyes of others could find an underlying motif to sustain their inspection of the world?[5] Thus there appears a "visible" to the second power, a carnal essence or icon of the first. It is not a faded copy, a *trompe l'oeil*, or another *thing*. The animals painted on the walls of Lascaux are not there in the same way as are the fissures and limestone formations. Nor are they *elsewhere*. Pushed forward here, held back there, supported by the wall's mass they use so adroitly, they radiate about the wall without ever breaking their elusive moorings. I would be hard pressed to say *where* the painting is I am looking at. For I do not look at it as one looks at a thing, fixing it in its place. My gaze wanders within it as in the halos of Being. Rather than seeing it, I see according to, or with it.

The word "image" is in bad repute because we have thoughtlessly believed that a drawing was a tracing, a copy, a second thing, and that the mental image was such a drawing, belonging among our private bric-a-brac. But if in fact it is nothing of the kind, then neither the drawing nor the painting belongs to the in-itself any more than the image does. They are the inside of the outside and the outside of the inside, which the duplicity of feeling [*le sentir*] makes possible and without which we would never understand the quasi presence and imminent visibility which make up the whole problem of the imaginary. The picture, the actor's mimicry—these are not devices borrowed from the real world in order to refer to prosaic things which are absent. For the imaginary is much nearer to, and much farther away from, the actual—nearer because it is in my body as a diagram of the life of the actual, with all its pulp and carnal obverse exposed to view for the first time. In this sense, Giacometti says energetically, "What interests me in all paintings is likeness—that is, what likeness is for me: something that makes me uncover the external world a little."[6] And the imaginary is much farther away from the actual because the painting is an analogue or likeness only according to the body; because it does not offer the mind an occasion to rethink the constitutive relations of things, but rather it offers the *gaze* traces of vision, from the inside, in order that it may espouse them; it gives vision that which clothes it within, the imaginary texture of the real.[7]

Shall we say, then, that there is an inner gaze, that there is a third eye which sees the paintings and even the mental images, as we used to speak of a third ear which grasps messages from the outside through the noises they caused inside us? But how would this help us when the whole point is to understand that our fleshly eyes are already much more than receptors for light rays, colors, and lines? They are computers of the world, which have the gift of the visible, as we say of the inspired man that he has the gift of tongues. Of course this gift is earned by exercise; it is not in a few months, or in solitude, that a painter comes into full possession of his vision. But that is not the question; precocious or belated, spontaneous or cultivated in museums, his vision in any event learns only by seeing and learns only from itself. The eye sees the world, and what it would need to be a painting, sees what keeps a painting from being itself, sees—on the palette—the colors awaited by the painting, and sees, once it is done, the painting that answers to all these inadequacies just as it sees the paintings of others as other answers to other inadequacies.

It is no more possible to make a restrictive inventory of the visible than it is to catalog the possible expressions of a language or even its vocabulary and turns of phrase. The eye is an instrument that moves itself, a means which invents its own ends; it is *that which* has been moved by some impact of the world, which it then restores to the visible through the traces of a hand.

In whatever civilization it is born, from whatever beliefs, motives, or thoughts, no matter what ceremonies surround it—and even when it appears devoted to something else—from Lascaux to our time, pure or impure, figurative or not, painting celebrates no other enigma but that of visibility.

What we have just said amounts to a truism. The painter's world is a visible world, nothing but visible: a world almost mad, because it is complete though only partial. Painting awakens and carries to its highest pitch a delirium which is vision itself, for to see is *to have at a distance*; painting extends this strange possession to all aspects of Being, which must somehow become visible in order to enter into the work of art. When, apropos of Italian painting, the young Berenson spoke of an evocation of tactile values, he could hardly have been more mistaken; painting evokes nothing, least of all the tactile. What it does is entirely different, almost the inverse. It gives visible existence to what profane vision believes to be invisible; thanks to it we do not need a "muscular sense" in order to possess the voluminosity of the world. This voracious vision, reaching beyond the "visual givens," opens upon a texture of Being of which the discrete sensorial messages are only the punctuations or the caesurae. The eye lives in this texture as a man in his house.

Let us remain within the visible in the narrow and prosaic sense. The painter, any painter, *while he is painting*, practices a magical theory of vision. He is obliged to admit that objects before him pass into him or else that, according to Malebranche's sarcastic dilemma, the mind goes out through the eyes to wander among objects; for he never ceases adjusting his clairvoyance to them. (It makes no difference if he does not paint from "nature"; he paints, in any case, because he has seen, because the world has at least once emblazoned in him the ciphers of the visible.) He must affirm, as one philosopher has said, that vision is a mirror or concentration of the universe or that, in another's words, the *idios kosmos* opens by virtue of vision upon a *koinos kosmos*; in short, that the same thing is both out there in the world and here at the heart of vision—the same or, if you will, a *similar* thing, but according to an efficient similarity which is the parent, the genesis, the metamorphosis of being into its vision. It is the mountain itself which from out there makes itself seen by the painter; it is the mountain that he interrogates with his gaze.

What exactly does he ask of it? To unveil the means, visible and not otherwise, by which it makes itself mountain before our eyes. Light, lighting, shadows, reflections, color, all these objects of his quest are not altogether real objects; like ghosts, they have only visual existence. In fact they exist only at the threshold of profane vision; they are not ordinarily seen. The painter's gaze asks them what they do to suddenly cause something to be and to be *this* thing, what they do to compose this talisman of a world, to make us see the visible. The hand pointing toward us in *The Nightwatch* is truly there only when we see that its shadow on the captain's body presents it simultaneously in profile. The spatiality of the captain lies at the intersection of the two perspectives which are incompossible and yet together. Everyone with eyes has at some time or other witnessed this play of shadows, or something like it, and has been made by it to see things and a space. But it worked in them without them; it hid to make the object visible. To see the object, it was necessary *not* to see the play of shadows and light around it. The visible in the profane sense forgets its premises; it rests upon a total visibility which is to be recreated and which liberates the phantoms captive in it. The moderns, as we know, have liberated many others; they have added many a muted tone to the official gamut of our means of seeing. But the interrogation of painting in any case looks toward this secret and feverish genesis of things in our body.

And so it is not a question asked of someone who doesn't know by someone who does—the schoolmaster's question. The question comes from one who does not know, and it is addressed to a vision, a seeing, which knows everything and which we do not make, for it makes itself in us. Max Ernst (with the surrealists) says rightly, "Just as the role of the poet since [Rimbaud's] famous *Lettre du voyant* consists in writing under the dictation of what is being thought, of what articulates itself in him, the painter's role is to circumscribe and project what is making itself seen within himself."[8] The painter lives in fascination. The actions most proper to him—those gestures, those tracings of which he alone is capable and which will be revelations to others because they do not lack what he lacks—to him they seem to emanate from the things themselves, like figures emanating from the constellations.

Inevitably the roles between the painter and the visible switch. That is why so many painters have said that things look at them. As André Marchand says, after Klee: "In a forest, I have felt many times over that it was not I who looked at the forest. Some days I felt that the trees were looking at me, were speaking to me. . . . I was there, listening. . . . I think that the painter must be penetrated by the universe and not want to penetrate it. . . . I expect to be inwardly submerged, buried. Perhaps I paint to break out."[9]

We speak of "inspiration," and the word should be taken literally. There really is inspiration and expiration of Being, respiration in Being, action and passion so slightly discernible that it becomes impossible to distinguish between who sees and who is seen, who paints and what is painted. We say that a human being is born the moment when something that was only virtually visible within the mother's body becomes at once visible for us and for itself. The painter's vision is an ongoing birth.

In paintings themselves we could seek a figured philosophy[10] of vision—its iconography, perhaps. It is no accident, for example, that frequently in Dutch paintings (as in many others) an interior in which no one is present is "digested" by the "round eye of the mirror."[11] This prehuman way of seeing things is emblematic of the painter's way. More completely than lights, shadows, and reflections, the mirror image anticipates, within things, the labor of vision. Like all other technical objects, such as tools and signs, the mirror has sprung up along the open circuit *between* the seeing and the visible body. Every technique is a "technique of the body," illustrating and amplifying the metaphysical structure of our flesh. The mirror emerges because I am a visible see-er, because there is a reflexivity of the sensible; the mirror translates and reproduces that reflexivity. In it, my externality becomes complete. Everything that is most secret about me passes into that face, that flat, closed being of which I was already dimly aware, from having seen my reflection mirrored in water. Schilder observes that, smoking a pipe before a mirror, I feel the sleek, burning surface of the wood not only where my fingers are but also in those otherworldly fingers, those merely visible ones inside the mirror.[12] The mirror's phantom draws my flesh into the outer world, and at the same time the invisible of my body can invest its psychic energy in the other bodies I see.[13] Hence my body can include elements drawn from the body of another, just as my substance passes into them; man is a mirror for man. Mirrors are instruments of a universal magic that converts things into spectacle, spectacle into things, myself into another, and another into myself. Artists have often mused upon mirrors because beneath this "mechanical trick," they recognized, as they did in the case of the "trick" of perspective,[14] the metamorphosis of seeing and seen that defines both our flesh and the painter's vocation. This explains why they have so often chosen to draw themselves in the act of painting (they still do—witness Matisse's drawings), adding to what *they* could see of things at that moment, what *things* could see of them—as if to attest to there being a total or absolute vision, leaving nothing outside, including themselves. Where in the realm of the understanding can we place these occult operations, together with the potions and idols they concoct? What can we call them? Consider, as Sartre did in *Nausea*, the smile of a long-dead monarch which keeps producing and reproducing itself on the surface of a canvas. It is too little to say that it is there as an image or essence; it is there as itself, as that which was always most alive about it, the moment I look at the painting. The "world's instant" that Cézanne wanted to paint, an instant long since passed away, is still hurled toward us by his paintings.[15] His *Mont. Sainte-Victoire* is made and remade from one end of the world to the other in a way different from but no less energetic than in the hard rock above Aix. Essence and existence, imaginary and real, visible and invisible—painting scrambles all our categories, spreading out before us its oneiric universe of carnal essences, actualized resemblances, mute meanings.

III

How crystal clear everything would be in our philosophy if only we would exorcise these specters, make illusions or objectless perceptions out of them, brush them to one side of an unequivocal world!

Descartes's *Dioptrics* is an attempt to do just that. It is the breviary of a thought that wants no longer to abide in the visible and so decides to reconstruct it according to a model-in-thought. It is worthwhile to remember this attempt and its failure.

Here there is no concern to cling to vision. The problem is to know "how it happens," but only enough to invent, whenever the need arises, certain "artificial organs" which correct it.[16] We are to reason not so much upon the light we see as upon the light which, from outside, enters our eyes and regulates our vision. And for that we are to rely upon "two or three comparisons which help us to conceive it [light]" in such a way as to explain its known properties and to deduce others.[17] The question being so formulated, it is best to think of light as an action by contact—not unlike the action of things upon the blind man's cane. The blind, says Descartes, "see with their hands."[18] The Cartesian model of vision is modeled after the sense of touch.

At one swoop, then, Descartes eliminates action at a distance and relieves us of that ubiquity which is the whole problem of vision (as well as its peculiar virtue). Why should we henceforth puzzle over reflections and mirrors? These unreal duplications are a class of things; they are real effects like a ball bouncing back. If the reflection resembles the thing itself, it is because this reflection acts upon the eyes more or less as a thing would. It deceives the eye by engendering a perception which has no object, yet this perception does not affect our conception of the world. In the world there is the thing itself, and outside this thing itself there is that other thing which is only reflected light rays and which happens to have an ordered correspondence with the real thing; there are two individuals, then, bound together externally by causality. As far as the thing and its mirror image are concerned, their resemblance is only an external denomination; the resemblance belongs to thought. The dubious relationship of likeness is—among things—an unequivocal relationship of projection.

The Cartesian does not see *himself* in the mirror; he sees a puppet, an "outside," which, he has every reason to believe, other people see in the very same way, but which is no more for himself than for others a body in the flesh. His "image" in the mirror is an effect of the mechanics of things. If he recognizes himself in it, if he thinks it "looks like him," it is his thought that weaves this connection. The mirror image is in no sense *a part of* him. For him, icons lose their powers.[19] However vividly an etching may "represent" forests, towns, men, battles, storms, it does not resemble them. It is only a bit of ink put down here and there on the paper. A figure flattened down onto a plane surface scarcely retains the forms of things; it is a deformed figure that *must* be deformed—the square becomes a lozenge, the circle an oval—*in order to* represent the object. It is an image only as long as it does not resemble its object. If not through resemblance, how, then, does it work? It "excites our thought" to "conceive," as do signs and words "which in no way resemble the things they signify."[20] The etching gives us sufficient indices, unequivocal "means" for forming an idea of the thing that does not come from the icon itself; rather, it arises in us, as "occasioned" by the icon. The magic of intentional species—the old idea of effective resemblance so strongly suggested to us by mirrors and paintings—loses its final argument if the entire potential of a painting is that of a text to be read, a text totally free of promiscuity between the seeing and the seen. We need no longer try to understand how a painting of things in the body could make them felt in the soul— an impossible task, since the very resemblance between this painting and those things would have to be seen in turn, since we would "have to have other eyes in our minds with which to apperceive it,"[21] and since the problem of vision remains intact even after we have introduced these simulacra, wandering between things and us. What the light casts upon our eyes, and thence upon our brain, does not resemble the visible world any more than etchings do. Nothing goes from things to the eyes, and from the eyes to vision, no more than from things to a blind man's hands, and from his hands to his thoughts.

Vision is not the metamorphosis of things themselves into the sight of them; it is not a matter of things' belonging simultaneously to the world at large and a little private world. It is a thinking that unequivocally decodes signs given within the body. Resemblance is the result of perception, not its basis. Thus, the mental image, the visualization which renders present to us what is absent, is a fortiori nothing like a breakthrough to the heart of Being. It too is a thought relying upon bodily indices—this time insufficient ones—which are made to say more than they mean. Nothing is left of the oneiric world of analogy. . . .

What interests us in these famous analyses is that they make us aware of the fact that every theory of painting is a metaphysics. Descartes does not say much about painting, and one might think it unfair on our part to make so much of a few pages on engravings. And yet the very fact that he speaks of painting only in passing is itself significant. Painting for him is not a central operation contributing to the definition of our access to Being; it is a mode or a variant of thinking, where thinking is canonically defined as intellectual possession and self-evidence. His very brevity is the indication of a choice; a closer study of painting would lead to a different philosophy. It is significant, too, that when he speaks of "pictures" [tableaux] he takes line drawings as typical. We shall see that the whole of painting is present in each of its modes of expression; there is a kind of drawing, even a single line, that can embrace all of painting's bold potential.

But what Descartes likes most about engravings is that they preserve the form of objects, or at least give us sufficient signs of their forms. They present the object by its outside, or its envelope. If he had examined that other, deeper opening upon things given us by the secondary qualities, especially color, then—since there is no rule-governed or projective relationship between them and the true properties of things, and we understand their message all the same—he would have found himself faced with the problem of a conceptless universality and opening upon things. He would have been obliged to find out how the uncertain murmur of colors can present us with things, forests, storms—in short the world. He would have been obliged, perhaps, to integrate perspective, as a particular case, into a broader ontological power. But for him it goes without saying that color is an ornament, mere coloring, and that the real power of painting lies in drawing, whose power in turn rests upon the ordered relationship between it and objective space established by perspectival projection. Pascal's famous saying that painting is frivolous because it attaches us to images whose originals would not move us is a Cartesian saying. For Descartes it is self-evident that one can paint only existing things, that their existence consists in being extended, and line drawing alone makes painting possible by making possible the representation of extension. Thus painting is only an artifice that puts before our eyes a projection similar to the one things themselves would (and do, according to the commonsense view) inscribe in them. Painting causes us to see, without real objects, just as we see things in everyday life; and in particular it makes us see empty space where there is none.[22]

The picture is a flat thing contriving to give us what we would see in the presence of "diversely positioned" things, by offering sufficient diacritical signs, through height and width, of the missing dimension.[23] Depth is a *third dimension* derived from the other two.

It will be worth our while to dwell for a moment upon this third dimension. There is, at first glance, something paradoxical about it. I see objects that hide each other and that consequently I do not see; each one stands behind the other. I see depth and yet it is not visible, since it is reckoned from our bodies to things, and we are [as Cartesians] confined to our bodies. There is no real mystery here. I do not really see depth or, if I do, it is only another *size*. On the line from my eyes to the horizon, the foreground forever hides all the other planes, and if on either side I think I see things staggered at intervals, it is because they do not completely hide each other. Thus I see each thing outside the others, according to a width measured differently.[24] We are [as Cartesians] always on the hither side of depth, or beyond it. It is never the case that things really *are* one behind the other. The encroachment and latency do not enter into their definition. They express only my incomprehensible solidarity with one of them—my body; and by their positivity they are thoughts of mine and not attributes of things. I know that at this very moment another person, situated elsewhere—or better, God, who is everywhere—could penetrate their hiding place and see them openly deployed. What I call depth is either nothing, or else it is my participation in a Being without restriction, first and foremost a participation in the being of space beyond every particular point of view. Things encroach upon one another *because they are outside one another*. The proof of this is that I can see depth in a painting which everyone agrees has none and which organizes for me an illusion of an illusion. . . . This two-dimensional being,[25] which makes me see a third, is a being that is pierced [*troué*]—as the men of the Renaissance said, a window. . . . But in the final analysis the window opens only upon *partes extra partes*, upon height and breadth merely seen from another angle—upon the absolute positivity of Being.

It is this space without hiding places which in each of its points is only what it is, neither more nor less, this identity of Being that underlies the analysis of engravings. Space is in itself; rather, it is the in-itself par excellence. Its definition is *to be* in itself. Every point of space is, and is thought as being, right where it is—one here, another there; space is the self-evidence of the "where." Orientation, polarity, envelopment are, in space, derived phenomena linked to my presence. *Space* remains absolutely in itself, everywhere equal to itself, homogeneous; its dimensions, for example, are by definition interchangeable.

Like all classical ontologies, this one elevates certain properties of beings into a structure of Being, and in so doing it is both true and false. Reversing Leibniz's remark, we might say that it is true in what it denies and false in what it affirms. Descartes's space is true, when contrasted with a thought too empirically dominated, which dares not construct. It was necessary first to idealize space, to conceive of that being—perfect of its kind, clear, manageable, and homogeneous—which an unsituated thinking glides over without a vantage point of its own: a being which thought transcribes in its entirety onto three right-angled axes—so that subsequent thinkers could one day experience the limitations of that construction and understand that space does not have precisely three dimensions, (as an animal has either four or two legs), and that dimensions are taken by different systems of measurement from a single dimensionality, a polymorphous Being, which justifies all of them without being fully expressed by any. Descartes was right in liberating space: his mistake was to erect it into a positive being, beyond all points of view, all latency and depth, devoid of any real thickness.

He was also right in taking his inspiration from the perspectival techniques of the Renaissance; they encouraged painting to experiment freely with depth and the presentation of Being in general. These techniques were false only in that they presumed to bring an end to painting's quest and history, to found once and for all an exact and infallible art of painting. As Panofsky has shown concerning the men of the Renaissance, this enthusiasm was not without bad faith.[26] The theoreticians tried to forget the spherical visual field of the ancients, their angular perspective which relates the apparent size not to distance but to the angle from which we see the object. They wanted to forget what they disdainfully called *perspectiva naturalis*, or *communis*, in favor of a *perspectiva artificialis* capable in principle of founding an exact construction. To accredit this myth, they went so far as to expurgate Euclid, omitting from their translations the eighth theorem, which was inconvenient. But the painters knew from experience that no technique of perspective is an exact solution and that there is no projection of the existing world which respects it in all aspects and deserves to become the fundamental law of painting. They knew that linear perspective was far from being an ultimate breakthrough; on the contrary, it opened several pathways for painting. For example, the Italians took the way of representing the object, but the Northern painters discovered and worked out the formal technique of *Hochraum*, *Nahraum*, and *Schrägraum*. Thus plane projection does not always stimulate our thought to rediscover the true form of things, as Descartes believed. Beyond a certain degree of deformation, it refers us back, on the contrary, to our own vantage point; as for the things, they flee into a remoteness out of reach of all thought. Something about space evades our attempts to survey it from above.

The truth is that no means of expression, once mastered, resolves the problems of painting or transforms it into a technique. For no symbolic form ever functions as a stimulus. Symbolic form works and acts only in conjunction with the entire context of the *work*, and not at all by means of a *trompe-l'oeil*. The *Stilmoment* never dispenses with the *Wermoment*.[27] The language of painting is never "instituted by nature"; it must be made and remade. The perspective of the Renaissance is no infallible "gimmick." It is only one particular case, a date, a moment in a poetic information of the world which continues after it.

Yet Descartes would not have been Descartes if he had thought to *eliminate* the enigma of vision. For him, there is no vision without thought: but *it is not enough* to think in order to see. Vision is a conditioned thought; it is born "as occasioned" by what happens in the body; it is "incited" to think by the body. It does not *choose* either to be or not to be or to think this thing or that. It must carry in its heart that heaviness, that dependence which cannot come to it by some intrusion from outside. Such bodily events are "instituted by nature" in order to bring us to see this thing or that. The thinking that belongs to vision functions according to a program and a law which it has not given itself. It does not possess its own premises; it is not a thought altogether present and actual; there is in its center a mystery of passivity.

Thus the Cartesian situation is as follows. Everything we say and think of vision has to make a *thought* of it. When, for example, we wish to understand how we see the location of objects, we have no other recourse than to suppose the soul to be capable, knowing where the parts of its body are, of "transferring its attention from there" to all the points of space that lie along the prolongation of its bodily members.[28] But so far this is only a "model" of the event. For how does the soul know that space of its body which it extends toward things, that primary *here* from which all the *theres* will come? This space is not, like them, just another mode or specimen of extension; it is the place of the body the soul calls "mine," a place the soul inhabits. The body it animates is not, for it, an object among objects, and it does not deduce from its body all the rest of space as an implied premise. The soul thinks according to the body, not according to itself, and space, or exterior distance, is also stipulated within the natural pact that unites them. If, at a certain degree of ocular accommodation and convergence the soul becomes aware of a certain distance, the thought which draws the second relationship from the first is as if immemorially encoded in our inner workings. "Usually this comes about without our reflecting upon it—just as, when we clasp a body with our hand, we conform the hand to the size and shape of the body and thereby sense the body, without having need to think of those movements of the hand."[29] The body is both the soul's native space, and the matrix of every other existing space. Thus vision doubles. There is the vision upon which I reflect; I cannot think it except *as* thought, the mind's inspection, judgment, a reading of signs. And then there is the vision that actually occurs, an honorary or established thought, collapsed into a body—its own body, of which we can have no idea except in the exercise of it, and which introduces, between space and thought, the autonomous order of the composite of soul and body. The enigma of vision is not done away with; it is shifted from the "thought of seeing" to vision in act.

Still, this de facto vision and the "there is" which it contains do not upset Descartes's philosophy. Since it is thought united with a body, it cannot, by definition, truly be conceived. One can practice it, exercise it, and, so to speak, exist it; yet one can draw nothing from it which deserves to be called true. If, like Queen Elizabeth,[30] we want at all costs to think *something* about it, all we can do is go back to Aristotle and scholasticism, to conceive thought as a corporeal something which cannot be conceived but which is the only way to formulate, for our understanding, the union of soul and body. The truth is that it is absurd to submit to pure understanding the mixture of understanding and body. These would-be thoughts are the emblems of "the practice of everyday life," the verbal blazons of union, permissible only if not taken to be thoughts. They are indices of an order of existence—of humanity and world as existing—of which we are not held to produce a concept. For this order there is no *terra incognita* on our map of Being. It does not confine the reach of our thoughts, because it, just as much as they, is sustained by a Truth which grounds its obscurity as well as our own lights.[31]

We have to go to these lengths to find in Descartes something like a metaphysics of depth. For we are not present at the birth of this Truth; God's being is for us an abyss. An anxious trembling quickly mastered; for Descartes it is just as futile to plumb that abyss as it is to think the space of the soul and the depth of the visible. Our very position, he would say, disqualifies us from looking into such things. That is the secret of Cartesian equilibrium: a metaphysics which gives us definitive reasons to leave off doing metaphysics, which validates our self-evidence while limiting it, which opens up our thinking without rending it.

The secret has been lost, and lost for good, it seems. If we are ever again to find a balance between science and philosophy, between our models and the obscurity of the "there is," it must be of a new kind. Our science has rejected the justifications as well as the restrictions which Descartes assigned to its domain. It no longer pretends to deduce its invented models from the attributes of God. The depth of the existing world and an unfathomable God no longer stand over against the flatness of "technicized" thought. Science manages without the excursion into metaphysics that Descartes had to make at least once in his life; it begins from the point he ultimately reached. Operational thought claims for itself, in the name of psychology, that domain of contact with oneself and with the world which Descartes reserved for a blind but irreducible experience. Operational thought is fundamentally hostile to philosophy as thought-in-contact, and if it rediscovers a sense of such a philosophy, it will be through the very excess of its daring; when, having introduced all sorts of notions that Descartes would have held to arise from confused thought—quality, scalar structures, solidarity of observer and observed—it suddenly realizes that one cannot summarily speak of all these beings as *constructs*. Meanwhile, philosophy maintains itself against such operationalist thinking, plunging itself into that dimension of the composite of soul and body, of the existent world, of the abyssal Being that Descartes opened up and so quickly closed again. Our science and our philosophy are two faithful and unfaithful offshoots of Cartesianism, two monsters born of its dismemberment.

Nothing is left for our philosophy but to set out to prospect the actual world. We *are* the compound of soul and body, and so there must be a thought of it. It is to this knowledge by position or situation that Descartes owes what he himself says of it, or what he sometimes says of the presence of the body "against the soul," or of the exterior world "at the tip" of our hands. Here the body is no longer the means of vision and touch, but their depository.

Our organs are not instruments; on the contrary, our instruments are added-on organs. Space is not what it was in the *Dioptrics*, a network of relations between objects such as would be seen by a third party, witnessing my vision, or by a geometer looking over it and reconstructing it from outside. It is, rather, a space reckoned starting from me as the null point or degree zero of spatiality. I do not see it according to its exterior envelope; I live it from the inside; I am immersed in it. After all, the world is around me, not in front of me. Light is found once more to be action at a distance. It is no longer reduced to the action of contact or, in other words, conceived as it might be by those who cannot see.[32] Vision reassumes its fundamental power of manifestation, of showing more than itself. And since we are told that a bit of ink suffices to make us see forests and storms, light must have its own power to generate the imaginary. Its transcendence is not delegated to a reading mind which deciphers the impacts of the light qua thing upon the brain and which could do this quite as well if it had never inhabited a body. No longer is it a matter of speaking about space and light, but of making space and light, which are *there*, speak to us. There is no end to this questioning, since the vision to which it is addressed is itself a question. All the inquiries we believed closed have been reopened. What is depth, what is light, τί τо ὄν? What are they—not for the mind that cuts itself off from the body but for the mind Descartes says is suffused throughout the body? And what are they, finally, not only for the mind but for themselves, since they pass through us and surround us?

This philosophy, which is yet to be elaborated, is what animates the painter—not when he expresses opinions about the world but in that instant when his vision becomes gesture, when, in Cézanne's words, he "thinks in painting."[33]

IV

The entire history of painting in the modern period, with its efforts to detach itself from illusionism and acquire its own dimensions, has a metaphysical significance. There can be no question of demonstrating this here. Not because of the limits of objectivity in history and the inevitable plurality of interpretations, which would forbid linking a philosophy and an event, for the metaphysics we have in mind is not a separate body of ideas for which inductive justifications could then be sought in the experiential realm—and there are, in the flesh of contingency, a structure of the event and a virtue peculiar to the scenario that do not prevent the plurality of interpretations but in fact are the deepest reason for it. They make the event a durable theme of historical life, and have a right to philosophical status. In a sense everything that may have been said and will be said about the French Revolution has always been and will henceforth be within it, in that wave arising from a roil of discrete facts, with its froth of the past and its crest of the future. And it is always by looking more deeply into *how it came about* that we make and will go on making new representations of it. As for the history of works of art, in any case, if they are great, the sense we give to them later on has issued from them. It is the work itself that has opened the perspective from which it appears in another light. It transforms *itself* and *becomes* what follows; the interminable interpretations to which it is *legitimately* susceptible change it only into itself. And if the historian unearths beneath its manifest content a surplus and thickness of meaning, a texture which held the promise of a long history, then this active manner of being, this possibility he unveils in the work, this monogram he finds there—all are grounds for a philosophical meditation. But such a labor demands a long familiarity with history. I lack everything for its execution, both competence and space. But since the power or the fecundity of works of art exceeds every positive causal or linear relation, it is not illegitimate for a layman such as myself, speaking from his memory of a few paintings and books, to express how painting enters into his reflections, and to register his sense of a profound dissonance, a transformation in the relationship between humanity and Being, when he holds up a universe of classical thought, contrasting it en bloc with the explorations of modern painting. A sort of history by contact, that perhaps does not go beyond the limits of one person, though it owes everything to his frequentation of others. . . .

"I believe Cézanne was seeking depth all his life," says Giacometti.[34] Says Robert Delaunay, "Depth is the new inspiration."[35] Four centuries after the "solutions" of the Renaissance and three centuries after Descartes, depth is still new, and it insists on being sought, not "once in a lifetime" but all through life. It cannot be merely a question of an unmysterious interval, as seen from an airplane, between these trees nearby and those farther away. Nor is it a matter of the way things are conjured away, one by another, as we see so vividly portrayed in a perspective drawing. These two views are very explicit and raise no problems. The enigma, though, lies in their bond, in what is between them. The enigma consists in the fact that I see things, each one in its place, precisely because they eclipse one another, and that they are rivals before my sight precisely because each one is in its own place—in their exteriority, known through their envelopment, and their mutual dependence in their autonomy. Once depth is understood in this way, we can no longer call it a third dimension. In the first place, if it were a dimension, it would be the *first* one; there are forms and definite planes only if it is stipulated how far from me their different parts are. But a *first* dimension that contains all the others is no longer a dimension, at least in the ordinary sense of a *certain relationship* according to which we make measurements. Depth thus understood is, rather, the experience of the reversibility of dimensions, of a global "locality" in which everything is in the same place at the same time, a locality from which height, width, and depth are abstracted, a voluminosity we express in a word when we say that a thing is *there*. In pursuing depth, what Cézanne is seeking is this deflagration of Being, and it is all in the modes of space, and in form as well. Cézanne already knew what cubism would restate: that the external form, the envelope, is secondary and derived, that it is not what makes a thing to take form, that that shell of space must be shattered—the fruit bowl must be broken. But then what should be painted instead? Cubes, spheres, and cones—as he said once? Pure forms having the solidity of what could be defined by an internal law of construction, forms which taken together, as traces or cross-sections of the thing, let it appear between them like a face in the reeds? This would be to put Being's solidity on one side and its variety on the other. Cézanne had already made an experiment of this kind in his middle period. He went directly to the solid, to space—and came to find that inside this space—this box or container too large for them—the things began to move, color against color; they began to modulate in the instability.[36] Thus we must seek space and its content *together*. The problem becomes generalized; it is no longer solely that of distance, line, and form; it is also, and equally, the problem of color.

Color is the "place where our brain and the universe meet," he says in that admirable idiom of the artisan of Being which Klee liked to quote.[37] It is for the sake of color that we must break up the form *qua* spectacle. Thus the question is not of colors, "simulacra of the colors of nature."[38] The question, rather, concerns the dimension of color, that dimension which creates—from itself to itself—identities, differences, a texture, a materiality, a something. . . .

Yet there is clearly no one master key of the visible, and color alone is no closer to being such a key than space is. The return to color has the virtue of getting somewhat nearer to "the heart of things,"[39] but this heart is beyond the color envelope just as it is beyond the space envelope. The *Portrait of Vallier* sets white spaces between the colors which take on the function of giving shape to, and setting off, a being more general than yellow-being or green-being or blue-being. Similarly, in the water colors of Cézanne's last years, space (which had been taken to be self-evidence itself and of which it was believed that the question of *where* was not to be asked) radiates around planes that cannot be assigned to any place at all: "a superimposing of transparent surfaces," "a flowing movement of planes of color which overlap, advance and retreat."[40]

As we can see, it is not a matter of adding one more dimension to those of the flat canvas, of organizing an illusion or an objectless perception whose perfection consists in simulating an empirical vision to the maximum degree. Pictorial depth (as well as painted height and width) comes "I know not whence" to alight upon, and take root in, the sustaining support. The painter's vision is not a view upon the *outside*, a merely "physical-optical"[41] relation with the world. The world no longer stands before him through representation; rather, it is the painter to whom the things of the world give birth by a sort of concentration or coming-to-itself of the visible. Ultimately the painting relates to nothing at all among experienced things unless it is first of all "autofigurative."[42] It is a spectacle of something only by being a "spectacle of nothing,"[43] by breaking the "skin of things"[44] to show how the things become things, how the world becomes world. Apollinaire said that in a poem there are phrases which do not appear to have been *created*, which seem to have *shaped themselves*. And Henri Michaux said that sometimes Klee's colors seem to have been born slowly upon the canvas, to have emanated from some primordial ground, "exhaled at the right spot"[45] like a patina or a mold. Art is not construction, artifice, the meticulous relationship to a space and a world existing outside. It is truly the "inarticulate cry," as Hermes Trismegistus said, "which seemed to be the voice of the light." And once it is present it awakens powers dormant in ordinary vision, a secret of preexistence. When through the water's thickness I see the tiled bottom of the pool, I do not see it *despite* the water and the reflections; I see it through them and because of them. If there were no distortions, no ripples of sunlight, if it were without that flesh that I saw the geometry of the tiles, then I would cease to see it *as* it is and where it is—which is to say, beyond any identical, specific place. I cannot say that the water itself—the aqueous power, the syrupy and shimmering element—is *in* space; all this is not somewhere else either, but it is not in the pool. It inhabits it, is materialized there, yet it is not contained there; and if I lift my eyes toward the screen of cypresses where the web of reflections plays, I must recognize that the water visits it as well, or at least sends out to it its active, living essence. This inner animation, this radiation of the visible, is what the painter seeks beneath, the words *depth*, *space*, and *color*.

Anyone who thinks about the matter finds it astonishing that very often a good painter can also produce good drawings or good sculpture. Since neither the means of expression nor the creative gestures are comparable, this is proof that there is a system of equivalences, a Logos of lines, of lighting, of colors, of reliefs, of masses—a nonconceptual presentation of universal Being. The effort of modern painting has been directed not so much toward choosing between line and color, or even between figurative depiction and the creation of signs, as it has been toward multiplying the systems of equivalences, toward severing their adherence to the envelope of things. This effort may require the creation of new materials or new means of expression, but it may well be realized at times by the reexamination and reuse of those already at hand.

There has been, for example, a prosaic conception of the line as a positive attribute and property of the object in itself. Thus, it is the outer contour of the apple or the border between the plowed field and the meadow, considered as present in the world, such that, guided by points taken from the real world, the pencil or brush would only have to pass over them. But this line has been contested by all modern painting, and probably by all painting, as we are led to think by da Vinci's comment in his *Treatise on Painting*: "The secret of the art of drawing is to discover in each object the particular way in which a certain flexuous line, which is, so to speak, its generating axis, is directed through its whole extent."[46] Both Ravaisson and Bergson sensed something important in this, without daring to decipher the oracle all the way. Bergson scarcely looked for the "sinuous outline [*serpentement*]" outside living beings, and he rather timidly advanced the idea that the undulating line "could be no one of the visible lines of the figure," that it is "no more here than there," and yet "gives the key to the whole."[47] He was on the threshold of that gripping discovery, already familiar to the painters, that there are no lines visible in themselves, that neither the contour of the apple nor the border between field and meadow is in *this* place or that, that they are always on the near or the far side of the point we look at. They are always between or behind whatever we fix our eyes upon; they are indicated, implicated, and even very imperiously demanded by the things, but they themselves are not things. They were thought to circumscribe the apple or the meadow, but the apple and the meadow "form themselves" from themselves, and come into the visible as if they had come from a prespatial world behind the scenes.

Yet this challenging of the prosaic line is far from ruling out all lines in painting, as the impressionists may have thought. It is simply a matter of freeing the line, of revivifying its constituting power; and we are not faced with a contradiction when we see it reappear and triumph in painters like Klee or Matisse, who more than anyone believed in color. For henceforth, as Klee said, the line no longer imitates the visible; it "renders visible"; it is the blueprint of a genesis of things. Perhaps no one before Klee had "let a line muse."[48] The beginning of the line's path establishes or installs a certain level or mode of the linear, a certain manner for the line to be and to make itself a line, "to go line."[49] Relative to it, every subsequent inflection will have a diacritical value, will be another aspect of the line's relationship to itself, will form an adventure, a history, a meaning of the line—all this according as it slants more or less, more or less rapidly, more or less subtly. Making its way in space, it nevertheless corrodes prosaic space and its *partes extra partes*; it develops a way of extending itself actively into that space which sub-tends the spatiality of a thing quite as much as that of a man or an apple tree. It is just that, as Klee said, to give the generating axis of a man the painter "would have to have a network of lines so entangled that it could no longer be a question of a truly elementary representation."[50]

In view of this situation two alternatives are open, and it makes little difference which one is chosen. First, the painter may, like Klee, decide to hold rigorously to the principle of the genesis of the visible, the principle of fundamental, indirect, or—as Klee used to say—absolute painting, and then leave it up to the *title* to designate by its prosaic name the entity thus constituted, in order to leave the painting free to function more purely as a painting. Or alternatively he may undertake, with

Matisse (in his drawings), to put into a single line both the prosaic, identifying characteristics of the entity and the hidden operation which combines such indolence or inertia and such force in it as are required to constitute it as *nude*, as *face*, as *flower*.

There is a painting by Klee of two holly leaves, done in the most representational manner. At first glance the leaves are thoroughly indecipherable, and they remain to the end monstrous, unbelievable, ghostly, *on account of their exactness*. And Matisse's women (let us keep in mind his contemporaries' sarcasm) were not immediately women; they became women. It is Matisse who taught us to see his shapes not in a "physical-optical" way but rather as structural filaments [*des nervures*], as the axes of a corporeal system of activity and passivity. Whether it be representational or nonrepresentational, the line is no longer a thing or an imitation of a thing. It is a certain disequilibrium contrived within the indifference of the white paper; it is a certain hollow opened up within the in-itself, a certain constitutive emptiness—an emptiness which, as Moore's statues show decisively, sustains the supposed positivity of things. The line is no longer the apparition of an entity upon a vacant background, as it was in classical geometry. It is, as in modern geometries, the restriction, segregation, or modulation of a pregiven spatiality.

Just as painting has created the latent line, it has made for itself a movement without displacement, a movement by vibration or radiation. And well it should, since, as they say, painting is an art of space, is carried out upon a canvas or sheet of paper and so lacks the wherewithal to devise things that actually move. But an immobile canvas could suggest a change of place, just as a shooting star's track on my retina suggests a transition, a motion not contained in it. The painting itself would then offer to my eyes almost the same thing offered them by real movements: a series of appropriately mixed, instantaneous glimpses along with, if a living thing is involved, attitudes unstably suspended between a before and an after—in short, the externals of a change of place which the spectator would read from the imprint it leaves. Here Rodin's well-known remark reveals its full weight: instantaneous glimpses, unstable attitudes petrify movement, as is shown by so many photographs in which an athlete-in-motion is forever frozen. We could not thaw him out by multiplying the glimpses. Marey's photographs, the cubists' analyses, Duchamp's *La Mariée* do not move; they give a Zenonian reverie on movement. We see a rigid body as if it were a piece of armor going through its motions; it is here and it is there, magically, but it does not *go* from here to there. Cinema portrays movement, but *how*? Is it, as we are inclined to believe, by copying more closely the changes of place? We may presume not, since slow motion shows a body being carried along, floating among objects like seaweed, but not *moving itself*.

Movement is given, says Rodin, by an image in which the arms, the legs, the trunk, and the head are each taken at a different instant, an image which therefore portrays the body in an attitude which it never at any instant really held and which imposes fictive linkages between the parts, as if this mutual confrontation of incompossibles could—and alone could—cause transition and duration to arise in bronze and on canvas.[51] The only successful instantaneous glimpses of movement are those which approach this paradoxical arrangement—when, for example, a walking man or woman is taken at the moment when both feet are touching the ground; for then we almost have the temporal ubiquity of the body which brings it about that the person *bestrides* space. The picture makes movement visible by its internal discordance. Each member's position, precisely by virtue of its incompatibility with that of the others (according to the body's logic), is dated differently or is not "in time" with the others; and since all of them remain visibly within the unity of one body, it is the body which comes to bestride duration. Its movement is something conspired between legs, trunk, arms, and head in some locus of virtuality, and it breaks forth only subsequently by actual change of place. When a horse is photographed at that instant when he is completely off the ground, with his legs almost folded under him—an instant, therefore, when he must be moving—why does he look as if he were leaping in place? And why, by contrast, do Géricault's horses really *run* on canvas, in a posture impossible for a real horse at a gallop? It is because the horses in *Epsom Derby* bring me to see the body's grip upon the ground and that, according to a logic of body and world I know well, these "grips" upon space are also ways of taking hold of duration. Rodin said profoundly, "It is the artist who is truthful, while the photograph lies; for, in reality, time never stops."[52] The photograph keeps open the instants which the onrush of time closes up forthwith; it destroys the overtaking, the overlapping, the "metamorphosis" [Rodin] of time. This is what painting, in contrast, makes visible, because the horses have in them that "leaving here, going there,"[53] because they have a foot in each instant. Painting searches not for the outside of movement but for its secret ciphers, of which there are some still more subtle than those of which Rodin spoke. All flesh, and even that of the world, radiates beyond itself. But whether or not one is, depending on the era and the "school," attached more to manifest movement or the monumental, the art of painting is never altogether outside time, because it is always within the carnal.

Now perhaps we have a better sense of how much is contained in that little word "see." Seeing is not a certain mode of thought or presence to self; it is the means given me for being absent from myself, for being present from within at the fission of Being only at the end of which do I close up into myself.

Painters have always known this. Da Vinci invoked a "pictorial science" which does not speak in words (and still less in numbers) but in works that exist in the visible just as natural things do—yet pass on that science "to all the generations of the universe."[54] A silent science, says Rilke (apropos of Rodin), that brings into the work the forms of things "whose seal has not been broken"; it comes from the eye and addresses itself to the eye.[55] We must understand the eye as the "window of the soul." "The eye . . . through which the beauty of the universe is revealed to our contemplation is of such excellence that whoever should resign himself to losing it would deprive himself of the knowledge of all the works of nature, the sight of which makes the soul live happily in its body's prison, thanks to the eyes which show him the infinite variety of creation: whoever loses them abandons his soul in a dark prison where all hope of once more seeing the sun, the light of the universe, must vanish." The eye accomplishes the prodigious work of opening the soul to what is not soul—the joyous realm of things and their god, the sun.

A Cartesian can believe that the existing world is not visible, that the only light is of the mind, and that all vision takes place in God. A painter cannot agree that our openness to the world is illusory or indirect, that what we see is not the world itself, or that the mind has to do only with its thoughts or another mind. He accepts, with all its difficulties, the myth of the windows of the soul; what is without place must be subjected to a body—or, what is even more: what is without place must be initiated *by* the body to all the others and to nature. We must take literally what vision teaches us: namely, that through it we touch the sun and the stars, that we are everywhere at once, and that even our power to imagine ourselves elsewhere—"I am in Petersburg in my bed, in Paris, my eyes see the sun"[56]—or freely to envision real beings, wherever they are, borrows from vision and employs means we owe to it. Vision alone teaches us that beings that are different, "exterior," foreign to one another, are yet absolutely *together*, are "simultaneity"; which is a mystery psychologists handle the way a child handles explosives. Robert Delaunay says succinctly, "The railroad track is the image of succession which comes closest to the parallel: the parity of the rails."[57] The rails converge and do not converge; they converge *in order to* remain equidistant farther away. The world is in accordance with my perspective *in or-*

der to be independent of me, is for me in *order to be* without me, to be a world. The "visual quale" gives me, and is alone in doing so, the presence of what is not me, of what *is* simply and fully.[58] It does so because, as a texture, it is the concretion of a universal visibility, of one sole Space that separates and reunites, that sustains every cohesion (and even that of past and future, since there would be no such cohesion if they were not essentially parts of the same space). Every visual something, as individual as it is, functions also as a dimension, because it is given as the result of a dehiscence of Being. What this ultimately means is that the hallmark of the visible is to have a lining of invisibility in the strict sense, which it makes present as a certain absence. "In their time, our erstwhile opposites, the Impressionists, were perfectly right in electing domicile among the scrub and stubble of the daily spectacle. As for us, our heart throbs to get closer to the depths. . . . These oddities will become . . . realities . . . because instead of being limited to the diversely intense restoration of the visible, they also annex the occultly perceived portion of the invisible."[59] There is that which reaches the eye head on, the frontal properties of the visible; but there is also that which reaches it from below—the profound postural latency whereby the body raises itself to see—and that which reaches vision from above like the phenomena of flight, of swimming, of movement, where it participates no longer in the heaviness of origins but in free accomplishments.[60] Through vision, then, the painter touches both extremities. In the immemorial depth of the visible, something has moved, caught fire, which engulfs his body; everything he paints is in answer to this incitement, and his hand is "nothing but the instrument of a distant will." Vision is the meeting, as at a crossroads, of all the aspects of Being. "A certain fire wills to live; it wakes. Working its way along the hand's conductor, it reaches the canvas and invades it; then, a leaping spark, it arcs the gap in the circle it was to trace: the return to the eye, and beyond."[61] There is no break at all in this circuit; it is impossible to say that here nature ends and the human being or expression begins. It is, then, silent Being that itself comes to show forth its own meaning. Herein lies the reason why the dilemma between figurative and nonfigurative art is wrongly posed; it is at once true and uncontradictory that no grape was ever what it is in the most figurative painting and that no painting, no matter how abstract, can get away from Being, that even Caravaggio's grape is the grape itself.[62] This precession of what is upon what one sees and makes seen, of what one sees and makes seen upon what is—this is vision itself. And to give the ontological formula of painting we hardly need to force the painter's own words,

Klee's words written at the age of thirty-seven and ultimately inscribed on his tomb: "I cannot be grasped in immanence."[63]

V

Because depth, color, form, line, movement, contour, physiognomy are all branches of Being and because each entwines the tufts of all the rest, there are no separated, distinct "problems" in painting, no really opposed paths, no partial "solutions," no cumulative progress, no irretrievable options. There is nothing to prevent the painter from going back to one of the emblems he has shied away from—making it, of course, speak differently. Rouault's contours are not those of Ingres. Light is the "old sultana," says Georges Limbour, "whose charms withered away at the beginning of this century."[64] Expelled at first by the painters of matter, it reappears finally in Dubuffet as a certain texture of matter. One is never immune to these avatars or to the least expected convergences; some of Rodin's fragments are statues by Germaine Richier *because they were sculptors*—that is to say, enmeshed in a single, identical network of Being.

For the same reason nothing is ever finally acquired and possessed for good. In "working over" a favorite problem, even if it is just the problem of velvet or wool, the true painter unknowingly upsets the givens of all the other problems. His quest is total even where it looks partial. Just when he has reached proficiency in some area, he finds that he has reopened another one where everything he said before must be said again in a different way. Thus what he has found he does not yet have. It remains to be sought out; the discovery itself calls forth still further quests. The idea of universal painting, of a totalization of painting, of painting's being fully and definitively accomplished is an idea bereft of sense. For painters, if any remain, the world will always be yet to be painted; even if it lasts millions of years . . . it will all end without having been completed.

Panofsky shows that the "problems" of painting that structure its history are often solved obliquely, not in the course of inquiries instigated to solve them but, on the contrary, at some point when painters, having reached an impasse, apparently forget those problems and allow themselves to be attracted by other things. Then suddenly, their attention elsewhere, they happen upon the old problems and surmount the obstacle. This hidden historicity, advancing through the labyrinth by detours, transgression, slow encroachments and sudden drives, does not imply that the painter does not know what he wants, but that what he wants is on the hither side of means and goals, commanding and overseeing all our *useful* activity.

We are so fascinated by the classical idea of intellectual adequation that painting's mute "thought" sometimes leaves us with the impression of a vain swirl of significations, a paralyzed or miscarried utterance. And if one answers that no thought ever detaches itself completely from a sustaining support; that the sole privilege of speaking thought is to have rendered its own support manageable; that the figurations of literature and philosophy are no more settled than those of painting and are no more capable of being accumulated into a stable treasure; that even science learns to recognize a zone of the "fundamental," peopled with dense, open, rent beings of which an exhaustive treatment is out of the question—like the cyberneticians' "aesthetic information" or mathematico-physical "groups of operations"; that, in the end, we are never in a position to take stock of everything objectively or to think of progress in itself; and that the whole of human history is, in a certain sense, stationary: *What*, says the understanding, like [Stendhal's] Lamiel, *is that all there is to it?* Is this the highest point of reason, to realize that the soil beneath our feet is shifting, to pompously call "interrogation" what is only a persistent state of stupor, to call "research" or "quest" what is only trudging in a circle, to call "Being" that which never fully is?

But this disappointment issues from that spurious fantasy[65] which claims for itself a positivity capable of making up for its own emptiness. It is the regret of not being everything, and a rather groundless regret at that. For if we cannot establish a hierarchy of civilizations or speak of progress—neither in painting nor even elsewhere—it is not because some fate impedes us; it is, rather, because the very first painting in some sense went to the farthest reach of the future. If no painting completes painting, if no work is itself ever absolutely completed, still, each creation changes, alters, clarifies, deepens, confirms, exalts, re-creates, or creates by anticipation all the others. If creations are not permanent acquisitions, it is not just that, like all things, they pass away: it is also that they have almost their entire lives before them.

PLATES

Alberto Giacometti, *Portrait d'Aime Maeght,* 1960. © 1992 ARS, N.Y. / ADAGP, Paris.

Paul Cézanne, *Mont Sainte-Victoire* (watercolor, v. 1900). Paris: Musee d'Orsay. Photo:
Scala / Art Resource, N.Y.

Nicholas de Stael, *Atelier Vert,* 1954. © 1992 ARS, N.Y. / ADAGP, Paris.

Henri Matisse, *Baigneuse aux cheveux longs*, 1942. © 1992 Succession H. Matisse / ARS, N.Y.

Paul Klee, *Park bei Lu(zern)*, 1938. Photo: Paul Klee–Stiftung, Kunstmuseum Bern. © 1992 by VG Bild-Kunst, Bonn.

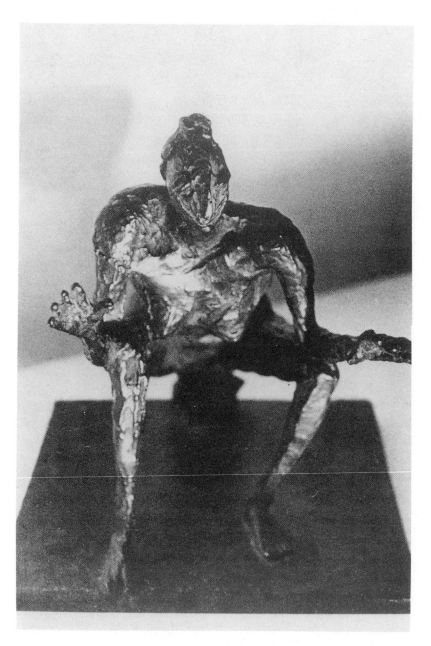

Germaine Richier, *La Sauterelle (Moyenne)*, 1945. © 1992 ARS, N.Y. / ADAGP, Paris.

Auguste Rodin, *Femme Accroupie,* 1882. Paris: Musee Rodin. Photo: Marburg / Art Resource, N.Y.

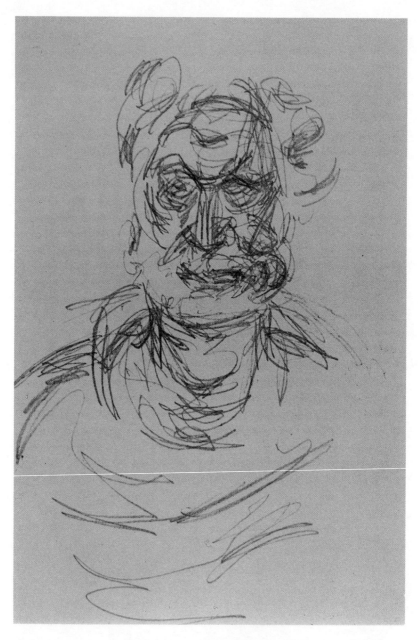

Alberto Giacometti, Frontispiece (untitled). In *Les philosophes célèbres,* Maurice Merleau-Ponty. Paris: Editions d'Art, Lucien Mazenod, 1956. © 1992 ARS, N.Y. / ADAGP, Paris.

PART 3

CRITICAL ESSAYS ON MERLEAU-PONTY'S PHILOSOPHY OF PAINTING

7

Cézanne, Phenomenology, and Merleau-Ponty

Forrest Williams

D ue to whatever common cultural formations that may serve to link
philosophical thought and artistic insight, the dominant philosophical system in France today known as "phenomenology," and
in particular, that of Maurice Merleau-Ponty, on the one hand,
and the art of Cézanne, on the other hand, appear to agree in origin,
method, and outcome.[1] Their common origin was a response to a certain
subjectivism of much of nineteenth-century art and philosophy; their
common method, to search by minute scrutiny of their own experience
for the outwardly given, objectively real; and their common achievement, to have avoided the opposite extreme to subjectivism, by discovering the real as the invariant structure of a given appearance. It is this
commonality that explains the repeated references by Merleau-Ponty to
the art of Cézanne, and the fact that he devoted an entire essay, "Le
doute de Cézanne," to the painter.[2]

Similarities between phenomenology in France and the art of
Cézanne have so far scarcely been noticed; on the part of philosophers and
art critics, there have been only a few indications. The aim of this paper is to
investigate the possibility of some common ground between a modern artistic genius and a current philosophical development. The possibility is worth
exploring that there may be a connection originating deep in the problems
of our times, especially in the reaction late in the nineteenth century to the
immoderacies of subjectivism in both philosophy and art.

The early work of Cézanne, e.g., *Le Meurtre* (1867–70) or *Le Christ aux Limbes* (1864–68),[3] reveals powerful subjective urges in the painter's preference for extravagantly "baroque" compositions that expressed intensely subjective states of mind for which the subject matter itself seemed to serve mainly as pretext. What nonetheless distinguished these early paintings of Cézanne from works by most painters similarly obsessed with inner states was, paradoxically, an objective concern with fidelity to feeling which was itself, almost dispassionate. Consequently, the later achievement of Cézanne, namely, *objectivity without the sacrifice of individual perception*, is especially noteworthy in view of the psychological strength of his subjective urges, thereby testifying to the magnitude of his eventual transcendence of them. The first point to be noticed in connection with the course of French phenomenology to be analyzed later is this necessity under which Cézanne found himself to *begin* with his own subjectivity, and yet the equal necessity to turn toward objective realities, toward mountains and houses and people. (For purposes of artistic contrast, one might of course consider the work of Van Gogh.)

Cézanne and other artists of the time had to confront an entrenched opinion which had been expressed a century earlier by Lessing, a view that not only stated a belief of Lessing's day but remained largely reflected in subsequent painting in Cézanne's time. Lessing had declared landscape painting to be the mere work of eye and hand, in which genius could have no share because the inorganic and vegetable worlds are incapable of an ideal.[4] By an "ideal" was meant a meaning or reality that is specifically human and entirely inward. "The highest bodily beauty exists only in man, and in him only because of the ideal. . . . There is no ideal of that in which Nature has proposed to herself nothing definite."[5] And who, echoed Cézanne's contemporary, Bernard Bosanquet, a century later, who indeed can say of two mountain shapes, which is the *right* one?[6] Yet this supposedly unanswerable question was precisely the sort of query to which Cézanne did try to give a correct "answer" within his paintings. Indeed, we witness in the course of Cézanne's development from, say, the landscape *La Neige Fondue a l'Estaque* (ca. 1870) to the landscape *La Montagne Sainte-Victoire* (1885–87, Barnes Foundation),[7] the emergence of an objectivity and realism within the very dynamic of Cézanne's subjectivity.

Although Cézanne underwent the powerful influence of French impressionism, his interest in objectivity was still not satisfied. To have stopped with impressionism would surely—we may say in the convenient wisdom of hindsight—have amounted to only a specious solution of the problem of objectivity with which Cézanne was concerned as an artist. As an impressionist, Cézanne could have gained only a *semblance* of the objectivity for which he was struggling in his vocation as a painter. Instead, Cézanne went on to "show" in his art that even if Monet was a superb eye,[8] he was nonetheless in principle as immersed in subjectivity as the most fantastic of painters. Philosophically viewed, one might say that sensory observation is by itself as subjective as any emotional urge, in the absence of a certain sort of reflective awareness which can apprehend and consciously identify structures. To be able to "see through" impressionism, in both senses of the phrase, was Cézanne's revolutionary achievement. This, too, had its parallel in phenomenology, in its concentration upon appearance that "saw through" phenomenalism (e.g., the epistemology of Hume).

Henceforth, painting for Cézanne was neither to distort the things of the world under the influence of the ardent emotions of his inner self, nor to represent on canvas his visual impressions, as the impressionists were doing. Thoughtful discernment, an assiduously reflective search for invariant structures, enabled him to approach that objective reality which he sought with increasing determination. His aim, as he was wont to put it, was to *"faire la chose,"* i.e., to paint *the visual thing*, not the mere impression. Thus, contrary to Bosanquet's idealist dictum, Cézanne was in effect declaring that there *is* a right shape to the mountain, the apple, the human body. The landscape, the still life, had its definite form—Nature *had* "proposed to herself" something *definite* after all, and Cézanne was determined to identify these objective forms through his painting. Probably in none of his works did he feel that he had succeeded completely in his goal. Yet the conviction that the human subject carries within its consciousness a capacity to apprehend objectively real structures was central to his conception of his work as an artist. The challenge was not for Cézanne, to be sure, a philosophical one in the technical sense that occupies philosophers. It was always for him a besetting artistic challenge, a problem of rendering "the right shape of the mountain." Yet his solutions, in their concrete and visual modalities, by way of paints, canvas, and brushstrokes, were as much an advance beyond the subjective tradition of modern thought as any mode of epistemological analysis can aspire to.

The exact nature of Cézanne's achievement is not easily described in words or in philosophical terms. To rehearse in any detail the artistic characteristics of his maturest works would certainly be an impractical undertaking. Speaking generally, however, critics are almost universally agreed upon the radically *objective* character of Cézanne's maturest works. Some have been particularly clear and succinct in their verbal characterizations of this central feature of Cézanne's later works. For example, such perceptive writers as Herbert Read, Roger Fry, and Rainer Maria Rilke struggled about as successfully as seems possible to communicate the specific significance of Cézanne's paintings for the larger context of contemporary thought, and to describe the unique figure which Cézanne cuts to this day against the background of certain long-standing theoretical challenges. Let us look at each of these commentators in turn.

"To renew one's sensibility toward one's environment," wrote Read, "is the method of both the traditionalist and the revolutionary."[9] It was in this context of renewed sensibility to nature that Read first associated Cézanne with what we shall see to be a phenomenological orientation (even while erroneously using the term "phenomenalism," which is entirely inconsistent with the intent of his analysis):

> [Modern painting from 1840 to 1910] is all a persistent attempt to correlate art and reality. It is the research not of the absolute, but of the concrete, of the *image*, and behind it all is not only the divorce of the artist from the processes of production, but also the concurrent attempt to establish a philosophy of reality, a [sic] phenomenalism that owes nothing to divine relevation or universal truths, but brings to the analysis of human existence the same faculties that the artist brings to the analysis of nature. Constable, Cézanne, Picasso—Hegel, Husserl, Heidegger: these names represent parallel movements in the evolution of human experience.[10]

Like Constable, Read held, Cézanne was an artist who regarded landscape painting as "a branch of natural philosophy."[11] For our purposes, the importance of Read's analysis lies in his clear expression of the realistic bent and philosophical character of Cézanne's art, and the implied parallel to phenomenology (miscalled "phenomenalism").

The artistic objectivity and realism of Cézanne was not, as we have seen, the sembling or impressionist realism of the seemingly more disinterested temperament of Monet. Ironically enough, the passionately reflective mind of Cézanne, not the superbly sensitive eye of Monet, actually proved to be the better observer. This is not to say that Cézanne himself ever formulated conceptually any philosophically profound doctrine of appearance and objectivity. It is quite enough that he was a profound *painter* of appearing objects of perception.[12] In his analysis, Read went on to say that Cézanne "felt a certain opposition between the *surface sensuousness* of objects and their *real nature*—his eyes were, as it were, dazzled by the brilliance of light and colour. Light and colour were not the same thing as *lucidity*."[13] This distinction between surface sensuousness and real nature was precisely what moved Cézanne beyond the semblances of impressionism to a far more significant objectivity and realism. Thus, contrasting him to both Gauguin and Van Gogh, Read calls our attention to Cézanne's conviction that "*the laws of beauty reside in the verities of nature*."[14] In this connection, Read introduces the concept of "eidetic purity."[15] Cézanne, in sum, sought to present on canvas what in phenomenological parlance has been termed the constitutive eidos of the given.

The critic Roger Fry described Cézanne's greatest achievement somewhat similarly, as "the acceptance and final assimilation of appearances" over against "willed and a priori inventions of the ego."[16] This characterization correctly emphasizes the descriptive, discovering nature of Cézanne's approach to the given which links his art to phenomenological reflection. Although Fry did not distinguish here phenomenalistic impressionism from this more realistic regard for the given, his meaning was clearly no more phenomenalistic than was Read's. Thus, Fry pointed out that the principal "question" put to nature by the painter concerned the relation between impressions and objective structure.[17] And he noted that Cézanne's method of resolving this problem was prolonged,[18] humble[19] contemplation of appearances (generically, the problem and method fundamental to Husserl's phenomenology).

Not surprisingly, it was the poet Rilke who expressed most vividly what he called "Cézanne's immense forward stride":[20]

> [Cézanne] considered the most indispensable thing [to be]: *La réalisation*. . . . The convincing quality, the becoming a thing, the reality heightened into the indestructible through his own experience of the object, it was that which seemed to him the aim of his innermost work.[21]

> It is this unlimited objectivity . . . that makes Cézanne's portraits so outrageous and absurd to people.[22]

> With Cézanne, [fruits] cease to be entirely edible, they become such very real things, so simply indestructible in their obstinate existing.[23]

> But I really wanted to say further about Cézanne, that it has never before been so demonstrated to what extent painting takes place among the colors themselves, how one must leave

them completely alone so that they may come to terms with
each other.[24]

This dedication of Cézanne to the objective structure of the subjectively given was precisely, it might fairly be said, the driving principle
of Husserl's phenomenology. It is clear that what Cézanne accepted was
not "mere" appearances, in any subjective sense of the term, but the
appearing-*of-something-as-given*: the appearing of the *thing*. By contrast,
the impressionists simply accepted what was arbitrarily impressed, so to
say, on the retina at a certain place and at a certain time of day, in a
certain light. Their well-known concern with returning to the same conditions of place, light, time, and atmosphere at each session is consequently understandable, since for all artistic purposes there are no
things. This punctiliousness, moreover, probably did help to draw Cézanne out of his early subjective manner of painting, compelling him to
look outward, and to look closely. But Cézanne began to look more reflectively than his mentors (than Pissarro, for example). What he found
was not impressions—not, in philosophical terms, the data of phenomenalism—but appearing things. As he came to "see through" impressionism, Cézanne was able to dispense with its scrupulousness about
reproducing the sheer surface sensuousness of the given, and was free to
introduce consciously into his paintings, where necessary, perfectly contradictory data, e.g., shadows that could not possibly be seen in reality as
they were placed on the canvas.[25] Far from betraying a willful subjectivity
or arbitrariness regarding things, his violations of the impressionist conception of fidelity to appearance was now reflectively controlled by a
fidelity to something more important than the surface sensuousness of
visual phenomena: the real, appearing thing.

Two conclusions emerge so far: First, by its rediscovery of the real
in the apparent the later work of Cézanne was his answer in artistic terms
to what he came to regard as the overweening subjectivity of his early
paintings. Second, this artistic advance anticipated in its own way the
phenomenological corrective to the subjectivism of a preceding epistemological tradition. In both cases, one begins with subjective appearances and finds one's way beyond them. This second conclusion has been
explored so far chiefly from the vantage point of Cézanne's art. Further
grounds for it may be adduced, however, by some consideration of phenomenology itself, first in Husserl, and then in Merleau-Ponty.

Husserl's phenomenology originated, as is well known, in a philosophical atmosphere of idealism, voluntarism, and subjectivism. His original

impetus was outgoing—*Zu den Sachen selbst!* ("Back to the things themselves!"), away from a priori constructions and toward objects that are
given *to*, not found *in*, consciousness. This outward or "intentional" orientation of phenomenological philosophy is what is meant by its realism,
in contrast with the idealism of either Kantian or the "sense-data" varieties. At first, this philosopher of mathematics and logic was thinking primarily of the objective transcendence of mathematical and logical
objects, e.g., numbers, propositions. In thus opposing both the idealism
of Kant and the psychologism of Mill on behalf of the objectivity of
mathematics and logic, Husserl found himself on the verge of a near-
Platonic logicism that threatened to ignore perceptual experience. He
came to realize, however, that the act of mathematical and logical intuition, in which indeed something was given that must not be confused
with the subjective act of consciousness, was yet a mode of *seeing*. Even
logical or mathematical intuition, in other words, is a mode of evidential
vision in which the evidence is direct and (what amounts to the same) the
objectivity is "natively" given—given "in flesh and blood." Husserl was
thus led to recognize an analogous state of affairs with respect to sense
experience. There, too, something objective is given *to*, not *in*, consciousness. A variety of modes of intuition, from the abstractly logical to
the most richly imaginative, came to radiate in his philosophy around the
founding "protovision" of sense perception. This acknowledgment of
the primacy of the perceptual mode of intuition might of course have led
Husserl back into the psychologism of Hume and Mill which his early
logical writings had opposed. The "thing itself" was preserved by the
principle of the intentionality of consciousness. As his former teacher
Franz Brentano had insisted, the self-immured mental states presupposed by various kinds of idealism are an invention never actually found
in any sort of experience, logical, perceptual, or otherwise. Consequently, the primacy of perceptual evidence, in which alone is found the
full meaning of real evidence, was entirely compatible for Husserl with a
philosophy in which real objects may be given to intentional consciousness as quite distinct from psychic acts. The famous method of "reduction," which opens up the field of the given and its invariant or "eidetic"
structures, is a *philosophical* implementation of the powers of intentional
consciousness. The hypothesis of this paper is that Cézanne's art involved an analogous *artistic* implementation of the same capacities, and
had an analogous aim.

    Merleau-Ponty's phenomenology is an original synthesis of Hus-
serl's phenomenological realism and the processual, antidualistic approaches of both Martin Heidegger's *Daseinsanalytik* and Husserl's later

writings. In addition, Merleau-Ponty's early work in psychology led him to give an important place in his phenomenology of perception to the Gestalt Principle. (This principle was in fact already implicit, and sometimes explicit, in the work of Husserl and Heidegger, though without the centrality that it acquired in Merleau-Ponty's thought.) Now a phenomenology of perception is, first and foremost, a phenomenology of visual perception, since that is the most cognitively interesting of our senses. Cézanne's paintings, in addition to their extraordinary artistic merit, offered to the thought of Merleau-Ponty the exceptional philosophical merit of Cézanne's particular approach or "method." Cézanne was, in effect, seeking the invariant structure of the thing he was paining. Thus, Merleau-Ponty's fascination with the painting of Cézanne may be interpreted as revealing far more than an understandable interest in perhaps the greatest of modern painters.

Moreover, without of course holding any philosophical or psychological theory on the subject, Cézanne painted as if perception were geared to Gestalts. Indeed, what Merleau-Ponty wrote in *Phénoménologie de la perception* could apply word for word to what appears to have been the governing principle of Cézanne's painting: "The Gestalt [is] no psychological event *of the order of an impression* but *an ensemble which develops an inner law of its own constitution.*"[26] In "Le doute de Cézanne," Merleau-Ponty proceeded to trace carefully Cézanne's transitions from a subjective style of painting to an increasing concern with appearance in an impressionist sense, and finally to a concern with the objective structure of reality, with "the right shape of the mountain," as it were.[27] Cézanne's artistic project thus became a seeming paradox to many minds: a search for reality without abandoning sense experience, which his admirer Emile Bernard once termed a "suicidal" attempt to reach reality while excluding the means of getting there.[28] Yet this "suicidal" approach, this paradoxical conception, was precisely Husserl's phenomenological approach as well: the determination to discover in reflection intentionally given objective structures without abandoning perceptual experience. In this connection, Merleau-Ponty underscores again and again the parallel effort of Cézanne to escape the ready-made alternatives of the painter who sees and the painter who thinks, the alternatives in philosophy of mere sensations, on the one hand, and mere intellectual construction on the other.[29] Indeed, these alternatives constitute the Scylla and Charybdis through which Merleau-Ponty attempts to steer his phenomenological philosophy.[30] Thus, he could well have said word for word of his phenomenology what he said of Cézanne's painting: "[He] does not want to separate the fixed things which appear to our gaze and their fleeting manner of appearing, he wants to paint matter as it gives itself form."[31] Cézanne's concern was thus, according to Merleau-Ponty, identical with that of his own phenomenology: "the object in the course of appearing."[32] "The experienced thing is not uncovered or constructed from the data of sense, but offers itself from the start as the center from which they radiate."[33] Phenomenology is thus defined as "the study of the apparition of being to consciousness."[34] The identity of its philosophical project with Cézanne's artistic project becomes obvious in Merleau-Ponty's sensitive description of Cézanne's painting that, mutatis mutandis, could stand equally as a perceptive gloss on his own phenomenology:

> If the painter wishes to express the world, the arrangement of colors must carry in it this individual Whole [of the subject]; otherwise, his painting will be an allusion to things and will not give them in that imperious unity, that presence, that unsurpassable plenitude which is for all of us the definition of the real.[35]

It is not surprising, therefore, that Merleau-Ponty invoked one of his key phenomenological terms, *la suspension*, as the procedure by which Cézanne was able to reveal through his works "the foundation of non-human nature on which man stands."[36]

> Nothing but a man is capable of this [Cézannean] vision which goes to the roots, on the hither side of [*en deçà de*] any already constituted humanity. Everything goes to show that animals cannot *look* [*ne savent pas* regarder], cannot immerse themselves in things for nothing but the truth.[37]

Consequently, Merleau-Ponty's particular interest, as France's leading phenomenological philosopher, in the development of Cézanne's art— from its early subjective distortions, through its absorption of the lessons of the new impressionism, to its mature and most genial works—as well as his repeated consideration of Cézanne in his phenomenological writings, seems best explained by considering the deep theoretical affinity that links their respective phenomenological and artistic projects.

8

Merleau-Ponty: Philosopher of Painting

Alphonse de Waelhens

Translated by Michael B. Smith

How can there be any doubt that there is a philosophy of painting in Merleau-Ponty, since he writes that "the entire history of painting in the modern period, with its efforts to detach itself from illusionism and acquire its own dimensions, has a metaphysical significance" (EM, 139, 132)? Which is at the same time to say that this "metaphysics" of painting cannot be rendered explicit otherwise than through the fundamental elements of all philosophy, namely perception, the body, language, the world, and meaning. But it also means that our experience of painting will in turn enrich the philosopher's articulation of those fundamental notions with a new perspective.[1]

And it is self-evident that this ontological interpretation of painting will find but little assistance (and more frequently an obstacle) in the opinions that painters express about what they do, and the world they see. Just as physics is not in itself a *theory* of science, just as the physicist is not in a position to generate such a theory independently, so painting is not a *view* of the act of painting, nor is the painter the philosopher of the thinking that he causes to exist through painting. Therefore the philosopher who takes on the impossible task of bringing to itself (or rendering "for itself") the intelligibility which every human work, including that of perception, establishes spontaneously and without "knowing" it, must (if he has chosen to focus on painting) try to surprise the painter "in that instant when his vision becomes gesture, when, in Cézanne's words, he 'thinks in painting' " (EM, 138–39).

Why do people paint? *Wozu Dichter?* Normally people frequent the visible world in which everything, or almost everything, goes without saying; thus the world offers little or nothing to see. Utensils, things, and people no longer indicate anything but general actions, as invariable as possible, for which these "objects" are destined to serve as props. We no longer look at them; we rest upon them as upon the unshakable ground of our installment in the world, without a care for that "real nature"[2] they cover up and colonize, but in which, from their perspective, they are totally rooted. Now, first of all, painting is a way of returning to that "real nature."[3] That is what warrants Merleau-Ponty's saying truly of one of the greatest among those who dedicated their lives to painting, Cézanne: "Painting was his world and his mode of existence" (CD, 59).

But let us beware. The meaning of that "conversion" is not to restore an in-itself of reality, the only truly real, that it would be the painter's task to present to us by reproducing it. The equivocation of naturalism and of "likeness"[4] resides precisely in their (vain) attempt to bolster their dubious ontology with this imperative mission of return— whereas painting, being language, must also be expression, and therefore a creative process. "Words do not *look like* the things they designate; and a picture is not a *trompe-l'oeil*" (CD, 68). But again like the word, though otherwise, painting *presents and unfolds in universality* that which prior to and without it lay unformed, unknown, within the private experience of the lone and largely inattentive consciousness. It transposes "the vibration of appearances which is the cradle of things" into a visible object open to all (ibid.), similarly to the way in which language embodies within the concrete universality of words and spoken melodies a mode of thought that first was only mine and therefore not fully itself—merely nascent thought. This thesis finds in the works of impressionism overwhelming confirmation, but should hold true for all painting.

Let us return, then, to our exegesis. There is a well-known anecdote about Renoir at Cassis. His hotelkeeper was aghast to find him one day before a deserted seashore, painting bathers frolicking in a brook. Why these transformations of places, objects, or "subjects"?

> Because each fragment of the world—and in particular the sea, sometimes riddled with eddies and ripples and plumed with spray, sometimes massive and immobile in itself—contains all sorts of shapes of being and, by the way it has of joining the

encounter with one's glance, evokes a series of possible variants and teaches, over and beyond itself, a general way of
expressing being. Renoir can paint women bathing and a freshwater brook while he is by the sea at Cassis because he only
asks the sea—which alone can teach what he asks—for its way
of interpreting the liquid element, of exhibiting it, and of making it interact with itself. In short, because he only asks for the
prototypical manifestations of water. (ILVS, 93)[5]

The thing is therefore less important than *the qualities of things*, in that
they are at the origin of all appearances, composing them. But what is to
be learned from that example goes well beyond the specific case. First,
the term "real" to which the painter thinks he is giving himself over is, in
fact, a creation that "invents" (and here I intend invention in the double
meaning of discovery and of promotion to self)[6] "nature." Secondly, it is
the structural obligation and necessity—the need to construct (in order
to reach nature) emblematic systems of expression (such as words are in
language), all of which see themselves as "realist," since they all aspire to
present being in the modality of visibility, and none of which *is* realist,
since they never tend to "duplicate" a scene already complete in itself—
no more than do sentences simply duplicate that of which they speak.
But we must take care to note that the relation between the signifier and
the signified, which is essential to all language, is not, as we shall see, the
same in painting and in words.[7]

From this perspective the controversy over abstract art becomes,
let us note in passing, devoid of any real significance.

How would the painter or the poet express anything other
than his encounter with the world? What does abstract art itself speak of, if not of a negation or refusal of the world? Now
austerity and the obsession with geometrical surfaces and forms
(or the obsession with infusorians and microbes; for the interdict put upon life, curiously enough, begins only with the Metazoon) still have an odor of life, even if it is a shameful or
despairing life. (Ibid.)

It is impossible for a painting to free itself from all reference to the real,
since that reference is constitutive of humanity's being, and the goal of
art is to constitute it at a certain level. Conversely, even painting's so-
called figurative modes of expression are also emblematic. If they appear
to be *simulacra* of things, it is because the system of equivalents upon

which they are based—through length of time and generality of use—
has become *selbstverständlich*, "obvious," "natural," deleting its value as
expression in the disastrous favor of a nonexistent value of *reproduction*
that it never was—neither in its function nor its means of exalting. The
changing of this system of equivalents implies no distancing in the relation to the real—a relation the painter cannot not establish—but only
that that system has lost, for the painter, rightly or wrongly, its power as a
language, and that it must be replaced by another one that will better
articulate that relation. "But it does not suffice to shatter or burn language to be able to write *Illuminations*" (ibid.). "There is always something to be said" (ibid., 94) and to say better what is to be said is the sole
principle of these changes.

But if this argument for or against abstract art lacks substance,
one can only, for the same reasons, declare Malraux in error in attempting to base the distinction between so-called modern and classical art on
the movement from objectivity to subjectivity. Picasso is no more at the
service of himself than was Giotto at the service of faith or Botticelli at
the service of beauty. They are at the service of a world, which is our
world, but insofar as the world gives itself to what is properly painting.

"The painter at work knows nothing of the antithesis of humanity
and world, of meaning and the absurd, of style and 'representation.' He
is far too busy expressing his communication with the world to become
proud of a style which is born almost as if he were unaware of it" (ibid.,
90–91). And the problem we must pose is always the same, whatever
period of painting it may be we refer to. Style is not an end, and even less
a means of representation: it is a mode of approach. It has no existence
outside this commerce with the world seen by the painter, and its mission
is to present it by expressing it. Here again the difficulty is not without an
analogy: perception can instruct us. It, too, stylizes. A woman seen from
my window is not *immediately* a human form, "a colored mannequin, or a
spectacle," but "a certain manner of being flesh which is given entirely in
her walk or even in the simple click of her heel on the ground, just as the
tension of a bow is present in every fiber of the wood—a most remarkable variant of the norm of walking, looking, touching and speaking that
I possess in my self-awareness because I am body" (ibid., 91). But if I am
a painter, besides these revelations of life, sense experience and humanity taken together in the unity of a lone, fleeting individual being, it will
be my task to bring into existence visual emblems "of a way of inhabiting
the world, of treating it, and of interpreting it by her face, her clothing,
the agility of the gesture and the inertia of the body—in short, the emblems of a certain relationship with being" (ibid.). As for the style that

makes this possible, and in which these equivalents are organized into the unity of a vision at once real and emblematic (as is the case with every language), I shall have to invent it. It is never given; otherwise paintings would be found in the real world just as trees are. But it is also required by reality, as its truest meaning, which reality relinquishes exclusively to the artist's creative expression. Style is what orients and shapes in view of a revelation—in the painter's case, proper to vision—denied to the pragmatic handling of objects, to their enjoyment in the world of every-day life, and to the contemplation of their reasons for being as they are, or for existing. This implies, it is true, "deformations" with respect to the various modalities of vision just enumerated, since the presentation of the thing by the painter must be *signifying* of what is inaccessible to those visions. But these deformations will also be *coherent*, since they all refer, in signifying, to one sole, visible meaning they organize.[8]

It remains true that—thinking back to what Merleau-Ponty has written on perception—the painter forms the first rough draft of his work in his own perception. But it is a painter's perception. It is the deployment of a language, as is the case with all perception, but in this case of a painterly language. The painter's perception "arranges certain gaps and fissures, figures and grounds, a top and a bottom, a norm and a deviation, in the inaccessible fullness of things . . . as soon as certain ele-ments of the world take on the value of dimensions to which from then on we relate all the rest, and in whose *language* we express them" (ibid.). It is this perception and the language included within it that the painter attempts to make manifest—it is out of this still "diffuse" meaning which the painter suggests to himself that he will produce an established mean-ing offered to all. To paint is not to take leave of things in order to give oneself over to an ultimately inviolable inner life of which the work of art would translate a few more or less felicitous fragments.[9]

And that is why Merleau-Ponty criticizes Sartre for having said in his study on Tintoretto that the language of the painter remains a *captive* one. It is not captive in any sense: quite to the contrary. But it can be so *to us*, if we do not undertake the "passage" into the world of painting, if that language is for us but the copy of another, the only one in which we have confidence. In itself, for itself, it is as imperiously exacting "as a syntax or a logic" (ibid., 92).[10]

But the language we are considering here can only be constituted and communicated by the use of line, form, and color. It is that original-ity that we must now attempt to circumscribe more precisely.

First, let us take care not to confuse vision with a "mode of thought" or "presence to oneself." Descartes, who attempted to do so, is instructive by the consequences he arrived at, to which we shall return. On the contrary, vision "is the means given me for being absent from myself" (EM, 146), that is, the means by which we can, by leaving ourselves, bring things to ourselves. I see, if I am not myself what I see, if I pass over into what is to be seen, installing myself in it to become myself visible, but in such a way that this seeing seenness is also that which organizes into a spectacle and world everything that is to be seen. To be a visible see-er is a way of "being present from within at the fissure of Being" (ibid.) that, failing this magic, would be but a compact mass, full, sense-less, the being of which—in the absence of any eye to make the distinction—would be indistinguishable from nonbeing. And it is only at the end point (doubtless never reached) of the constitution of the differentiated totality of the world into a single, unified visibility, that I could turn away toward myself, "close" myself in upon myself, and complete myself by the completion of my task. Here again is something painters have "always known." Cézanne "wanted to depict matter as it takes on form, the birth of order through spontaneous organization. . . . Cézanne wanted to paint this primordial world, and his pictures therefore seem to show nature pure, while photographs of the same landscapes suggest man's works, conveniences, and imminent presence" (CD, 63–64).[11]

Thus painting, and painting alone, makes it manifest to us that "different beings, 'external,' foreign to one another, are nevertheless absolutely *together*, 'simultaneity' " (EM, 146). Such is the dimension of experience, the meaning, and the revelation of ourselves that painting introduces into and imposes upon our minds. Painting expresses the meaning of vision and is thus more than vision.

But that originality of vision, and a fortiori of painting which is its expression, has not always been recognized. Descartes in particular went to some length to instruct us on what might be the basis of the credibility of the "line engraving" without accepting anything of what is precisely the specificity of an art of vision. He challenges the view that its authority is derived from resemblance, since "forests, towns, men, battles, storms," are nothing but "a bit of ink put down here and there on the paper" (ibid., 131). True, there is shape—but it is flat and deformed. It is a likeness only on the condition of being dissimilar. But then, whence its prestige? It comes from the fact that it leads us, prompts us to *conceptualize*, after the manner of signs and words "which in no way resemble the words they signify."[12] This clearly proves that although Descartes discerned in painting (or rather in drawing) a manner of language, the properly pictorial originality of this language escaped him. It also shows that Descartes remained the prisoner of a general conception of words that reduces them to the role of *translating* thought. Be that as it may, our quotation shows that for Descartes the graphic work is assimilated to the interpretation of a text, and that he conceived of no internal complicity between the thing painted and the real thing. Yet that is precisely what must be done. The "resemblance" between the painted and the real thing, even if it existed, would not solve anything, since that resemblance would in turn have to be "seen." The putative existence of "simulacra, wandering between things and us" (ibid., 132) merely postpones the problem. It is a problem the crucial nature of which Descartes did not understand. A victim of his own dualism, he missed the essential. "Painting for him is not a central operation contributing to the definition of our access to Being; it is a mode or a variant" (and, I would add, a *subordinate* one) "of thinking, where thinking is canonically defined as intellectual possession and self-evidence" (ibid.). This is also evident from the fact that Descartes, proposing to speak of pictures, deals directly and exclusively with drawing. That is because outlines, though they do not, as we have seen, reproduce the exact shapes of objects, remain closer to them than do painted colors to the real ones. Thus drawing is better suited to providing a sign based on a real analogy. This serves the ends of Cartesian intellectualism, but also contributes to setting the ontology of painting off on the wrong track. If Descartes had consented to consider that deeper and (in a non-Cartesian perspective) more essential "opening onto the world of things" we get from the secondary qualities, and, more specifically in the case of painting, from color, the impasse would have been avoided. Thus he could or should have seen that, in a picture, we perceive the "message" without any "rule-governed or projective relationship between them [the secondary qualities] and the true properties of things" (ibid., 133). This raises the question of access to reality—*universal* access—*without concepts*, freeing color from serving a merely decorative function, a notion radically challenged by the entire history of painting. For if the problem of painting and drawing comes down to that of an exact sign qua substitute, we could make those arts into a science, even a strict science, capable of producing a simulacrum of the world. Such a science would be as totally indisputable and free from the personal style of painters as the much-vaunted universal language would have been devoid of the variety of approaches to reality peculiar to every linguistic group. Descartes, while continuing to share the second illusion, which is apparently ineradicable, does not even dare to formulate the first, so clearly refuted by the absurdity of its goal.

This, as I have already intimated, is enough to transform the conception of *images*. If drawings are "tracings" (which they are not), images would be tracings of those tracings, but located *in mente*, within "our private bric-a-brac" (ibid., 126). Thus both fall away. Neither of these two images is based on an in-itself. They are both—and this includes the paintings and drawings considered as real images—"the inside of the outside and the outside of the inside, which the duplicity of feeling [*le sentir*] makes possible and without which we would never understand the quasi presence and imminent visibility which make up the whole problem of the imaginary" (ibid.).

The relationship between the imaginary and the real is therefore quite unrelated to that of an alleged tracing of the real. In a sense, the imaginary is even closer to the real than a duplicate, since it is the "carnal obverse" of the life led by the real in my own body, "exposed to view for the first time" (ibid.).[13] In another sense, the pictorial image is more distant from the real than an exact copy would be, since it is only an expression of it and an analogue "according to the body," and is not intended to set us back before pragmatic reality so that we may reconsider it more easily—as is the case with the figures in a geometry book—but rather offers "the *gaze* traces of vision, from the inside, in order that it may espouse them," and "gives vision that which clothes it within, the imaginary texture of the real" (ibid.).

Let us seek further confirmation of this view by examining the well-known case of perspective. Whatever perspectival system we may adopt, none offers a universally precise projection worthy of being raised to the rank of a universal language or a "fundamental law of painting." "Four centuries after the 'solutions' of the Renaissance and three centuries after Descartes, depth is still new, and insists on being sought, not 'once in a lifetime,' but all through life" (ibid., 135, 140). It seems quite clear, then, that the real question is not that of obtaining an exact projection. Contrary to the Cartesian thesis, it even seems that certain deformations, far from seeking to make us conceive of or find the depth of things per se, seek rather—and deliberately so—to return us to "our point of view." If the ideal of exact transposition is illusory—and explicitly rejected by many—must we not draw the following two conclusions? First, "no symbolic form ever functions as a stimulus" (ibid., 135), mechanically; its *virtue* being that of language, namely such that wherever it has been put to work and has acted, has *gone* to work, and has done so "only in conjunction with the entire context of the work, and not at all by means of *trompe-l'oeil*" (ibid.). Second, it is the nature of spatiality that we can never dominate it, master it, that "something in

space escapes our attempts to look at it from 'above' " (ibid.), and therefore nature cannot dictate, cannot institute a language. Nor can any language ever exhaust nature. A language must always "be made and
remade. The perspective of the Renaissance is no infallible 'gimmick.' It
is only one particular case, a date, a moment in a poetic information of
the world that continues after it" (ibid.).

This much having been established, the properly pictorial meaning of perspective remains to be understood. It may be that here, too,
the thesis of the copy, executed for the purpose of thought, will be found
wanting. Let us say at the outset that there are two extreme (to the point
of being opposite) modes of "presentation," both envisaged in any research on perspective; but this dichotomy will not be an obstacle, since
their intent is obvious. But the problem is precisely what meaning attaches to their combination, and, so to speak, to their mixture. There can
be no question but that perspective intends to show me, on one hand,
the "unmysterious interval" between things close and far, like people
seen from a plane or the forty-ninth floor of a skyscraper and, on the
other hand, "the way things are conjured away, one by another" (ibid.,
140), as we are taught by the experience (which is fundamental to the
structure of reality) of opacity. This one cannot fail to recognize.

But what needs to be understood, and what is behind the whole of
pictorial perspective, is the link, the meaning of the link that is insinu-
ated or declared by that dual presence, such that each presence is what it
is only through the other. What is the meaning of the statement "that I
see things, each one in its place precisely because they eclipse one another, and that they are rivals before my sight precisely because each one
is in its own place" (ibid.)? Here the issue is of a meaning not picked out
of things like stones picked out of a stream bed, but that must be *said* to
be present in them. Here it is a question of "picking out" according to
that very different acceptation that Heidegger attributes to λέγειν and
λόγος.[14] What does pictorial perspective, in its revisions and its permanence, say in this way? It says the meaning of *exteriority* and spatiality.
The exteriority of our surroundings is not the *partes extra partes* of the
geometrician or the Cartesian: it is "envelopment" *and* "mutual dependence" in "autonomy." Such is the reality of our surroundings when
they are truly seen in their actual exteriority through the painter's
creation.

In this respect, depth is not simply the third dimension. And, as
Merleau-Ponty maintains, if depth were to be considered as a dimension,
it would be the first. "There are forms and definite planes only if it is
stipulated how far from me their different parts are" (ibid.). But it isn't

that: a dimension that contains all the others is neither the first nor the third. In a sense it is no longer a dimension at all, that is, a simple relation of measurement. It is, rather, the expression of a "reversibility" of all the dimensions, the expression "of a global 'locality' in which everything is in the same place at the same time, a locality from which height, width, and distance are abstracted, of a voluminosity we express in a word when we say that a thing is *there*" (ibid.). The painter's quest for depth is an effort—that never reaches its goal—to say the "deflagration of Being" that is everywhere that anything is, in the dimensions, the form, the distance and the proximity. This is manifest in Cézanne, for example, and even more so, if possible, in cubism. The "pragmatic," apparent shapes are insufficient to form: they do not make a thing "take form" originarily. They are but a result, an end point, that must be broken open in order to find and express the origin of what is seen. There are no tried and true techniques for achieving this. The risk is always, even for the cubists, that "the solidity of Being" be put on one side and its "variety" on the other, and that its genesis be thus missed. At a certain time in his life, Cézanne became acutely aware of this danger. From it he derived the certainty, which is so characteristic of his work, that space cannot be described *alone*, as a pure container. "Thus we must seek space and its content together. The problem becomes generalized; it is no longer solely that of distance, line and form; it is also, and equally, the problem of color" (ibid., 140, 141).[15] It is therefore untrue that one system of perspective can assert its predominance because it is "natural"; particularly since the perceived world that it allegedly copies is itself not constant through the ages. Perception is itself already a language and an interpretation, and consequently more a fact of history than of laws. Objects have no "natural" apparent size, which is clear from the example of the moon, which observers cannot range within the scale of objects within one reach. Is it the size of a bagel, a circular billboard for "Martini," or the big clock outside the Gare de Lyon? "Perspective is much more than a secret technique for imitating a reality given as such to all humanity. It is the invention" (and, as I would put it, the myth) "of a world dominated and possessed through and through by an instantaneous synthesis, which is at best roughed out by our glance when it vainly tries to hold together all these things seeking individually to monopolize it" (ILVS, 87). The great painter, by his expressive reworking of perspective attempts to "make contingency vibrate" (ibid., 88).

For the same reasons, "there are no lines visible in themselves" (EM, 143). The shapes and outlines of things are not simply *here* or *there*. They cannot be *fixed* as in geometrical drawings, which are only *thought* drawings, not the expression of what we see. That does not mean that things have no shape or that they do not require them (even "very imperiously"), but that shape is not something outlining a thing. The impressionists, who were aware of this, tried to solve the problem by excluding line from their work. Now what needs to be done is not to omit lines, but to free their genetic power, their "constituting power," and show how, through them, things, "the apple and the meadow 'form themselves' of themselves and come into the visible as if they had come from a prespatial world behind the scenes" (ibid.). As Klee said, the line no longer imitates the visible: "it renders visible; it is the blueprint of a genesis of things" (ibid.).[16]

This allows us to understand that there is also, in a similar or proximate sense, for the painting, a "logic of lighting." Light, like line, plane, form, and color, joins in and contributes to the meaning expressed by the painting. And this is true not only for the lighting within the canvas, but also for that of the gallery in which it is shown, for the distance at which the spectator stands, which can betray the painter's work (PhP, 312–13), just as one can betray a conversation by the tone in which it is repeated, or a piece of music by the rhythm of its performance, or by its performance in general.

There is, finally, as has already been said (but we must now return to the theme), color. "It is for the sake of color that we must break up the form qua spectacle" (ibid., 141), just as, conversely, the deformations of contour rescue us from the illusions of so-called natural color. The color that painting speaks of is a color/dimension, "which creates—from itself to itself—identities, differences, a texture, a materiality, a something" (ibid.). The problem here is not (no more than it was in the case of depth) to create an "illusion" in order to return to an empirical view and to recopy "a view upon the *outside*" (ibid.). Painters do not try to *redo* the world that is really there before our eyes in the perception that is correlative to our natural attitude to this world. What they want to do is to constitute for all, by saying it (but in their own way and first of all for themselves), the "coming-to-itself of the visible" (ibid.). It is therefore not a question of wondering *where* the painting is in the empirical world, nor yet whether or not it is *figurative*. It is, as Merleau-Ponty explains, quoting an expression of Michaux's, who abruptly closes this irritatingly futile debate, "auto-figurative." Painting, says Merleau-Ponty, again with reference to Michaux, "is a spectacle of something only by being a 'spectacle of nothing,' by breaking the 'skin of things' to show how things become things and the world, world" (ibid.). The point is not to construct anything, nor even less to find an escape. Nor is it a matter, I would add, of the surreal. The origin is not more real than what it founds, but its presentation leads the real to its truth.

> When through the water's thickness I see the tiled bottom of the pool, I do not see it *despite* the water and the reflections; I see it through them and because of them. If there were no distortions, no ripples of sunlight, if it were without that flesh that I saw the geometry of the tiles, then I would cease to see it *as* it is and where it is—which is to say, beyond any identical, specific place. I cannot say that the water itself—the aqueous power, the syrupy and shimmering element—is *in* space; all this is not somewhere else either, but it is not in the pool. It inhabits it, is materialized there, yet it is not contained there; and if I lift my eyes toward the screen of cypresses where the web of reflections plays, I must recognize that the water visits it as well, or at least sends out to it its active, living essence. This inner animation, this radiation of the visible is what the painter seeks beneath, the words *depth*, *space*, and *color*. (Ibid., 142)[17]

These analyses have prepared us to pose or take up otherwise the decisive problem of the ontology of painting—Heidegger's question—stated at the beginning of these pages: *Wozu Maler?*[18]

There is in art, as in every language, an element of restitution, since vision is not simply a creative sense. But that restitution is not directed upon what we normally see, but precisely on what we do not see, but would be worthy of being seen. However, and indistinguishably, painting's "making seen" is expressive of what it presents. And this circumstance (of painting's being neither a beautification of what is nor spurious invention) precludes the possibility that that form of expression is "the translation of a clearly defined thought, since such clear thoughts are those that have already been said within ourselves or by others" (CD, 69); and also since, as we know, Merleau-Ponty does not believe, nor has he ever believed, in a "conception" that, at whatever level, could be brought to perfection in itself or fully accomplished before being realized in a work. If a painting copies nothing preexistent in nature, neither does it copy a private, preexistent view of the painter, which the latter would draw forth from himself or herself fully armed. "Before expression, there is nothing but a vague fever, and only the work itself, completed and understood, will prove that there was *something* rather than *nothing* to be found there" (ibid.). There is, indeed, in the painter, a prepictorial (in the sense in which philosophers speak of a pre-ontological understanding) and private orientation of his experience, committing him to the pictorial, to which he refers back in painting. But that is only a *beckoning toward* the work. No one knows, the painter least of all, if it will give birth to the work—the only locus in which painting exists. No one knows whether what the painter wants to do "will be able to work its way free from the flow of individual life in which it [the work] was born and give the independent existence of an identifiable *meaning* to the future of that same individual life, or to the monads coexisting with it, or the open community of future monads" (ibid.). This meaning, prior to the work, has no existence. It is not in things, which are unrelated to meaning before the encounter that illuminates them. Nor is it contained in the "private bric-a-brac." It is made, established, constituted in the "doing" of a presentation that, ultimately, would like to include everything—but never succeeds, and thus is also, in advance, its own failure. This is what Cézanne called turning "to the *Pater omnipotens.*" Merleau-Ponty comments upon this by appealing to (and this is a bit surprising in his expression) "the idea or project of an infinite Logos" (ibid.). But let us not be misled. There is no question here of the Logos of a transcendental thought, in which Merleau-Ponty never believed, but of the Logos as universal organizer, constituting the totality of Being (to use the capitalization Merleau-Ponty would later adopt). The expression must therefore be understood as if painters—because the meaning of their language is to present the birth of the visible (and not just of "this" that I see)—had the task, in each one of their works, of addressing themselves to the genesis of the All qua visible.[19] Now such an intent, if it is necessary in order for the work to be what it wants to be, is also necessarily impossible. The resolution is the infinity of discourse, the perennial nature of the vocation of painting, present from Lascaux to Picasso. The completion of the work is the call to another work, which takes up the challenge anew.[20] This, too, explains why Cézanne "thought himself powerless because he was not omnipotent" (ibid.).

It also explains how, in the long run at least, a successful work "has the strange power of being self-teaching" (ibid., 70; cf. also PhP, 179). Its truth, which has nothing to do with that of natural realism, awakens in each one of us fleeting experiences, fragmentary revelations that, had we followed up on them and had we been otherwise than we are, could have made of us a writer, painter, or philosopher. "The reader or spectator, by following the clues of the book or painting, by establishing the concurring points of internal evidence and being brought up short when straying too far to the left or right, guided by the con-fused clarity of style, will in the end find what was intended to be communicated" (ibid.). Also at this moment, and only then, the work will have completed its own birth—but certainly not its life. . . . It will have definitively won its wager of not being a "persistent delirium."

It is true that, in a sense, vision is itself delirium. This is true of the painter's vision more than of any other, since, besides its claim of making the whole reside within what cannot but be partial, it "raises to the last power" the paradox essential to seeing, which is "*to have at a distance*"; painting extends this strange possession to all aspects of Being, which must somehow become visible in order to enter into the work of art" (EM, 127). The painting gives visible presentation to what is not visible for the pragmatic eye, and is normally "possessed" by the senses of contact: movement, volume, lightness, or mass, as they obviously are presented in the work of Degas, for example.

The importance of this pictorial "imperialism" can be seen in the strange favor enjoyed, in the history of painting, by mirrors, or yet again by paintings of paintings, upon which a work as essential as *L'Enseigne de Gersaint* is constructed. This apparent "gimmick" declares and exemplifies that "metamorphosis of seeing and seen that defines both our flesh and the painter's vocation" (ibid., 130). This so-called technique presents the essence of the visible, and manifests its origin in its "intention" of equating being-in-the-world with vision—as poetry does for the verbal world—by adding to what painters see "what *things* saw of them—as if to attest to their being a total or absolute vision, leaving nothing outside, including themselves" (ibid.).[21] A vision that closes up? Not totally, however, since after all that entire power of the eye is restored, presented, by the hand's gesture. But that difficulty shows that the issues of painting are also those of the body and its enigmas. "It is by lending his body to the world that the painter transforms the world into paintings" (ibid., 123). Now, if the body is a thing by one of its dimensions, that means that vision is also somehow created within a thing, or, as we said earlier, that the see-er and the visible are convertible into one another. Just as in originary perception the distinctions between the senses are unknown and the qualities of objects imply one another (we can see the flexibility of a type of wood, the fragility of a glass, the viscous thickness of a bowl of soup), similarly painting seeks, by the disposition of its materials, not to suggest but to present the primordial world. "If the painter is to express the world, the arrangement of his colors must bear within itself this indivisible whole; or else his painting will only hint at things and will not give them the imperious unity, the presence, the unsurpassable plenitude which is for all of us the definition of reality. That is why each brushstroke must satisfy an infinite number of conditions" (CD, 65–66). The young Cézanne believed he could set to work directly from the start on the expression of a look or a face. The exercise of his art taught him that "expression is the language of the thing itself and springs from its configuration" (*PhP*, 322).

But then again, if the perception of what is never comes to completion, if the perspectives it takes up and organizes are linked to a reality "that envelops and exceeds those perspectives, a world that announces itself in lightning signs as a spoken word or an arabesque" (ILVS, 89), then the *presentation* of that reality must surely break free from "the prose of the *senses* or of the concept" (ibid.). Let us understand this to mean that painting is essentially poetic, since it "awakens," "recalls" and takes up our *pure power* of expression, beyond an exercise the world has given us and the pragmatic sights of daily life. It is, therefore, I repeat, a falsification of the problem to see, in painting, a return to subjectivity or a refusal of obvious forms. The real question is how to understand the incomprehensible: how to express, by the use of signs (new ones, to be sure, but old ones as well),[22] that which heretofore, while included in the world, has never intentionally appeared—and how to express it in such a way that everyone will henceforth be able to see it. Everyone? Those at least who have eyes to see.

That is what the painter will succeed in doing if he or she puts into the work, not the "I" that is hateful and loved, the refinements of the keenest sensitivity, but a "style." This style must be wrested from the world, the work of others, and "his own attempts" (ibid.). And he cannot *know* his style for himself. Others will make it become fully significant. For himself or herself, style is the very modality of access to reality—as is our body for each one of us. He cannot possess it "reflectively," and can but perceive in its texture a vague allusion to himself or herself. To himself or herself, style is the way what is to be painted must be painted.[23] The painter's style is his painterly body. He brings it to perfection in using it. He is interested in it only for the possibilities of expressive development and power that it once more contains for the future, "as if each step taken called for and made possible another step, or as if each successful expression prescribed another task to the spiritual automaton or founded an institution, the efficacy of which he would never stop testing anew" (ibid., 90). But the painter is lost if he "sees" this style for itself and makes an "object of delectation" of it. At that moment he begins copying himself and exhibiting himself. Style then has ceased being what it is: the means of finding emblems capable of bringing forth a latent meaning that was germinating within his entire experience as a human being and a painter (ibid.). That "bringing forth of meaning" (Heidegger) is at once an operational mode and a mode of communication. Style is neither a nervous tic nor a technique, but a manner "of formulation that is just as recognizable for others, and as little visible to him as his silhouette or his everyday gestures" (ibid.). It is thus the same thing with the painting and the spoken word; the painting *says* more than the literalness of sensible givens it offers, just as discourse says more than the literalness of the sentences in which it is couched. "The picture over and above the sense data, speech over and above linguistic data must, therefore, in themselves possess a signifying virtue, independently of any meaning that exists for itself, in the mind of the spectator or listener" (*PhP*, 389). The essential becomes presentation *as expression of itself*, which not only informs the observer or listener, but especially makes them participate in and contribute to the constitution of a novel, original truth of things.[24] For painting, that new truth is a "visible to the second power" (EM, 126), as convincing and indisputable as the other, though I cannot locate it in my pragmatic space (*where* is the painting's spectacle?), though I see "according to it and with it rather than seeing it" (ibid.); that is, if we take seeing to mean primarily to focus upon an object offered to my grasp.

Let us conclude.

Only the visual *puts me in the presence of* what is not myself, as the unity of the world. The other senses either retain a dimension of radical immanence, or, like hearing, only bring us the other as a piecemeal or evanescent presence. This privilege of sight, which is that of universal visibility, is derived from the fact that sight is the concretion "of one sole Space that separates and reunites, that sustains every cohesion (even that of the past and the future, since there would be no such cohesion if they were not parts of the same space)" (ibid., 147). Everything that is available to sight, although it is the exhibiting of an individual thing, manifests itself also as an express and adroit reference to other than itself and "functions also as a dimension, because it gives itself as the result of a dehiscence of Being" (ibid.). But that thesis also means (and here we find again on this occasion a classic affirmation of phenomenology, often taken up by Merleau-Ponty) "that the essence of the visible is to have a lining that, invisible in the strict sense, it makes present as a certain absence" (ibid.). It is again what we were saying, though differently, in discussing the exchange between the see-er and the visible in painting. The see-er is not visible as such; he is therefore the absence of the visible. But in making everything visible he must also include himself in the visible, to the extent that he is a visible *thing*. This movement of exchange, however, is only possible if there is in the visible itself that reference to the invisible that I am trying to explicate. Every view of what is seen from the front is also the view of a hidden other side—since it is an object we are looking at; it is also the view of an above that opens out and escapes "the weight of origins." "Vision is the meeting, as at a cross-roads, of all the aspects of Being" (ibid.). How can we think that this circuit is merely that of nature? No break in it gives us any indication of where that nature leaves off, and where the expressive power of humanity begins. Similarly, one cannot say of the painter's hand whether it is body or mind, whether the visible of the invisible or the invisible of the visible, whether it does or does not see. The truth is that this circuit is an episode of Being in which nature, humanity, and expression are "caught up" together. An episode that is silent, however, in itself, and that "comes to show forth its own meaning" in painting (ibid.).[25]

Yet the fact remains that painters come and go and sometimes do battle with one another. What we have said seems to exclude both any progress in painting (since the effort of expression to which we have referred by this term was already fully present from the start, since Lascaux) and any definitive perfecting of that same painting—since the expressive power of humanity, co-constitutive of Being, is inexhaustible, and renews itself as it continues to be carried out.

This situation is not peculiar to painting, and the difficulty has no other source than a surreptitious and stubborn tendency to return to the notion of a real, in-itself nature, that it would supposedly be our task to equal: the truth would be attained when things, such as they are in themselves, would in their entirety have passed through a mental translation that would deliver them up to us as if we were them.

From the point of view of this "prejudice," whose popularity this is not the time to explore, no form of art, thought or perhaps even science can succeed in justifying itself as it is, nor can it overcome the alternative we have outlined. It should be noted simply that an "objective assessment" is impossible, while being at the same time, strictly speaking, due upon request.[26]

But this disappointment issues from that spurious fantasy which claims for itself a positivity capable of making up for its own emptiness. It is the regret of not being everything, and a rather groundless regret at that. For if we cannot establish a hierarchy of civilizations or speak of progress—neither in painting nor even elsewhere—it is not because some fate impedes us; it is, rather, because the very first painting in some sense

went to the farthest reach of the future. If no painting completes painting, if no work is itself ever absolutely completed,
still, each creation changes, alters, clarifies, deepens, confirms,
exalts, re-creates, or creates by anticipation all the others. If
creations are not permanent acquisitions, it is not just that, like
all things, they pass away; it is also that they have almost their
entire lives still before them. (Ibid., 149)

9

Merleau-Ponty's Aesthetics

Michael B. Smith

T he purpose of these pages is to show that there is, in Merleau-Ponty's philosophy, a coherent theory of aesthetics, and that it appears, fully and less ambiguously than has at times been supposed, in his writings on painting. It is consistent with his thesis of the primacy of perception, of which it is, on the cultural plane, a necessary development. By a well-known reversal of the order of logic and discovery, the philosopher's reflection on aesthetics renewed and modified his original premises. Having meditated at length on the enigmas of artistic and verbal creation, he was led, in *The Visible and the Invisible*, a work interrupted by his death, to develop an indirect ontology. Drawing the necessary philosophical conclusions from an essential obliqueness he had discovered in all creation, he proposed a reformed idea of truth itself. In place of the false ideal of an identical truth (i.e., $A=A$) that would reduce the epistemological model to a coinciding in silence, mind pressed against thing, Merleau-Ponty has proposed a truth modeled upon vision. This model involves an inherent gap (*"écart"*) that does not separate us from things, at least not in any privative sense. On the contrary, it gives us our only possible access to them. In this view, "proximity through distance" (VI, 128) becomes the principle of perception and expression.

Alphonse de Waelhens, in a critical study on Merleau-Ponty's philosophy, affirms that "the doctrine we are studying truly contains the seeds of a coherent, complete aesthetics."[1] That opinion, from 1951, was based on only two texts involving aesthetics: "Cézanne's Doubt" and

"The Novel and Metaphysics" (appearing in *Cahiers du Sud* and *Fontaine*, respectively, in 1945, and collected in *Sense and Non-Sense* in 1948). I shall have occasion to confirm the later flowering of that germinating aesthetics in following the analyses of "Indirect Language and the Voices of Silence" (*Les Temps Modernes*, 1952, collected in *Signes*, 1960), until its culmination in "Eye and Mind" (1961). Some of the pages of these two last-mentioned works may be taken—crowded with imagery and a style that suggests a manner of harmonics between the physical and the metaphysical—as an instance as well as an exposition of his doctrine of expression.

But before approaching these texts systematically, it may be well to consider the main features of Merleau-Ponty's aesthetics in his work as a whole.

The Role of Aesthetics in Merleau-Ponty's Philosophy

Rémy Kwant distinguishes three phases in Merleau-Ponty's career.[2] The first, that of *The Structure of Behavior* (1942) and *Phenomenology of Perception* (1945), is devoted to establishing the foundation of his philosophy. The second, in broadening movement, is marked by the translation of that philosophy into the taking up of positions on issues of religion, art, and politics. Kwant sees the last phase as initiating a new turn, barely sketched out in the unfinished manuscript of *The Visible and the Invisible* and a certain number of essays of the same period. What was new was the revision of the role of contingency in favor of a teleology transcending the human. Kwant meticulously traces this revision to four autocritical notes found among the author's unfinished manuscripts.

This division, didactically clear-cut, obscures one point that is essential to the understanding of this existentialist thinker. Merleau-Ponty, ever opposed to "high-altitude thinking," never believed it possible that a philosopher could detach himself from his time in order to be purely contemplative, and then return to his contemporaries like Zarathustra descending from his mountain. It is not among his autocritical notes that we must seek the underlying reasons for the new direction in his philosophy, but in his energetic dialogue with all the intellectual currents of the day. This is not the place to retrace the history of that postwar era, the dialectic exchanges with a Marxism torn between Stalinism and Western humanism, a psychology in which Freudian, Gestalt, and existentialist elements were intermingled, and a young structuralist sociology, in search of both its methods and its objectives. Let us note, however, that it was the convergence of these forces with the internal logic of phenomenology that produced the complex movement of Merleau-Ponty's thought, and that it is impossible to follow that movement if we are overly fastidious about mixing levels of discourse.

But there is another objection to Kwant's schematization, which concerns us more closely. It is misleading insofar as it suggests that Merleau-Ponty's interest in art and expression in general was restricted to the middle and as it were worldly period of his career. In point of fact we shall see that it was not just in a few works written in response to circumstances but in an evenly diffused and increasingly insistent manner that he pursued his inquiry into the problems of painting and writing.

If, as I believe, Merleau-Ponty's entire philosophy must be understood as a radical empiricism (in the Husserlian sense) that, beginning with a critique of perception, extends to the field of expression and finally develops into an ontology founded on active/passive sentience (*le sentant sensible*), can we not recognize in that manifold a general theory of aesthetics? It is important to emphasize, in so doing, the philosophical and etymological sense of *aesthetics*, related to the Greek *aisthēsis*, that is, sensation. It is precisely with a critique of the classical theory of the sensation that Merleau-Ponty's magnum opus, *Phenomenology of Perception*, begins. Let us return briefly to the essential moments of these analyses of perception, then of expression; analyses that gradually revealed to their author the full significance of the hypotheses implicit in his research.

The Structure of Behavior demonstrates the shortcomings of contemporary[3] physiology and psychology in their effort to explain their own findings. Gestalt theory, more promising than behaviorism, seemed to shy away from the philosophical consequences of its methods. The relationship of the organism to its surroundings could not be explained by the causal action of an external stimulus, because the organism reacts globally to the lived context of the stimuli in a "milieu" that has no purely objective existence.[4] There is thus an a priori of the organism that contributes actively to the formation of the stimulus to which it reacts. This circular causality, the mutual interference of subject and object, mind and matter, is not an exceptional case but the norm, and the necessary condition of lived experience. It becomes a problem only upon reflection: it is therefore up to the latter to make accommodations. Only dialectic thinking remains faithful to this phenomenon of reciprocal solicitation and response between the interiority of the organism and the exteriority of the world—between consciousness and nature. With *Phenomenology of Perception* we move from the level of critique of the experimental sciences to the fuller exploration of the *Lebenswelt* adumbrated in Husserl's posthumous works; but with the difference that Merleau-Ponty continues to adduce supporting evidence for his speculations from the observations of the German Gestalt psychologists Gelb, Goldstein, and Köhler. The notion of the lived body ("*corps propre*," more specifically "one's own body"), introduced into French existentialism by Gabriel Marcel, becomes the "natural subject" of perception.[5] Space, time, and the objects of the surrounding world are less undergone than constituted by this lived body, of which science's physiological body is but a weakened derivative—a copy.

The body, seat of perception, is also the locus of expression. The gesture accomplishes a transcendence in inherence, for the virtual line extending from the tip of my finger to the object designated gives meaning and direction ("*sens*") to space and expresses at the same time *my* meaning (the extension of my intention) to other subjectivities. The spoken word, also, has a gestural meaning. Language, before being a code or a depository of established meanings, is but a generalized style, a way of "singing the world" (PhP, 187). But how does one move from a gestural or emotive use of words to their conceptual use? The process is described as being analogous, in its beginnings at least, to the body's transcendent acts.

> The meaning of a word is not contained in the word taken as a sound. But it is the definition of the human body to appropriate, in an indefinite series of discontinuous acts, signifying centers that transcend and transform its natural powers. That act of transcendence is first encountered in the acquisition of a behavior pattern, then in the gesture's silent communication. It is through the same power that the body opens itself to a new form of conduct, and renders it understandable to external witnesses. (PhP, 193)

In order for there to be communication, there must be a generalization of the signifier and the fund of common experience to make up a signified. In the case of corporeal gesture, it is the human body that provides the generality of signifier; the common perceived world furnishes a background of signified referents. This common perceived world already constitutes one of the necessary conditions for a spoken language to emerge. "The word is a gesture, and its meaning a world" (PhP, 184). But in place of the generality of the human body, that of a linguistic morphology is substituted. That institution, rigorously homologous with the lived body, is far more than a metaphor in Merleau-Ponty. The word is not the representative of a thought (and even less of a thing), nor its "clothing," but precisely "its emblem or body" and expression "makes meaning exist like a thing at the very heart of the text" (PhP, 182). Fifteen years later, in *The Visible and the Invisible*, the role of language as the body of all ideality is further affirmed and confirmed.

> Let us say only that pure ideality is itself not without flesh nor freed from horizon structures: it lives of them, though they be another flesh and other horizons. It is as though the visibility animating the sensible world were to emigrate, not outside of every body, but into a different, lighter, more transparent one, as though it were to change flesh, abandoning that of the body for that of language, and were thereby emancipated, but not freed from all conditionality. (VI, 153)

The problem preoccupying Merleau-Ponty here is the same one that had been raised during the oral defense of his thesis of the primacy of perception· in 1946 (see PrP, 12–42), namely: How can the passage from the originary lived world to the cultural one be explained? It is a constant problem for any philosophy that takes the genesis of its own reflection seriously. Merleau-Ponty's approach, as the preceding quotation shows, is to begin by qualifying the overly antithetical terms of the dilemma. On one hand, ideality is not "without conditions": it exists only in language. Inherence in a form is obvious in the case of musical and literary "ideas," as well as for the sort of ideality of coherence or style revealed in painting; these are the "ideas without equivalent" of which Marcel Proust speaks. But what should we say about his "ideas of the intelligence," those that are amenable to being transposed into algorithmic form? Merleau-Ponty approaches this problem by appealing to the principle Bergson called "the retrograde movement of the true,"[6] and Husserl *Rückgestaltung* (back-formation). What we call a "sign" does not take on the value of a sign until after its meaning has been given. This phenomenon makes it impossible for us to rid ourselves entirely of what we have ever thought, and causes us to find it in the perceived world. On the other hand, the raw, spiritual sensation on which the older empiricism of Hume was based does not exist as such. Perception is "inspired exegesis"; sight and touch interrogate things "according to their own wishes." The lived is already "spoken lived," before the letter. (Merleau-Ponty, quoting Lacan, says: "Vision itself, thought itself, are, it has been said, 'structured as a language,' are *articulation*" [VI, 126]).

Up to this point it may have been possible to think that Merleau-Ponty would be content to move the terms of the materialism/idealism dilemma closer together.[7] In fact he is preparing to open up a new path, at an equal distance from either, in the penumbra of lived experience. There is, in his view, a tendency to "construct perception out of the perceived, to construct our contact with the world out of what it has taught us about the world" (VI, 156). It is precisely the retrospective application of perception's accomplishments to its own definition that Merleau-Ponty criticizes on the part of physicalists as well as Husserl and Sartre. He terms that error "the prejudice of the world."

How can we rid ourselves of an error apparently so much a part of our experience of the world? That is the task that Merleau-Ponty undertakes in *The Visible and the Invisible*. We must first rid ourselves of the positivistic bric-a-brac, those correlations of the objective world called "state of consciousness," "matter," "form," "image," and even "perception" (to the extent that it implies the breakdown of lived experience into discontinuous acts and refers to "things," the status of which is not yet determined).

> The destruction of beliefs, the symbolic murder of the others and the world, the separation of seeing from the visible and of thought from being do not establish us, as they claim to do, in the negative. When all that has been removed, we take up residence in what is left—sensations, opinions. And what remains is not nothing, nor is it of a different nature than what was removed. What remains are mutilated fragments of the vague *omnitudo realitatis* about which our doubts were raised, and they resuscitate it under different names—appearance, dream, psyche, representation. It is in the name and for the profit of these floating realities that solid reality is placed in doubt. One never leaves the "something," and doubt as the destruction of certainty is not doubt. (VI, 105–6)

Perceptive faith remains intact and doubt, methodical or otherwise, can but displace its object. In order to avoid returning to the impasses it is our purpose to avoid, we must return to experiences that have not yet been worked over—before the separation into "object" or "subject," "essence" or "existence." These experiences are *seeing* and *speak-*

ing. (*Thinking* can only be included with certain reservations, because the absolute distinction between "speaking" and "thinking" would already place us on the reflective level.)

The intent here is not to renounce all reflection, but to make it sufficiently aware of its own operations to put it in touch with its origins; nor to abjure reason, but to bring it down to earth.

There can be no "model" or "schema" that remains faithful to perception, which is prior to all abstraction. And what would be the purpose of a philosophy's making it its goal to explain the possibility of the real world, once that philosophy has learned that "possibilities" are themselves but "mutilated fragments" of the real and derived from it? If the possible is founded on the real, it is the being of that reality, upon which our perception opens directly, that must be interrogated.

An ontology of the lived world cannot be established in the language of the positivists—a language whose clarity is the effect of lexical sparseness and a jejeune style. The visible, the invisible, voice and silence, flesh, the inside and the outside are elements of Merleau-Ponty's lived-world ontology. As for *flesh*, it is an "element" in the sense in which Greek and medieval philosophers used the term—for *fire*, *water*, *air*, and *earth*: "simple" notions, thinkable in and for themselves. (Gaston Bachelard makes interesting use of them in his psychoanalysis of literature.) "What we are calling flesh . . . has no name in any philosophy" (VI, 147), Merleau-Ponty writes. Let us try here to give some idea of what this element, flesh, is, since the aesthetics we are examining is based, not on an esthesiology of the organs of perception as these are described by physiology, but on the ontological framework of the lived body. That body—but also the lived world that is a prolongation of it—is a chiasma, an intertwining of movement, sight and touch, a narcissism of seeing visibility, the reversibility of inside and outside, the formative milieu of subject and object; it is the "barbaric Principle," prior to all objectivity—termed "flesh."

In the following passage, a generalized erotics of the encounter with the other evokes what would be reduced in analytic philosophy to the "problem of the perception of other subjectivities."

> For the first time the body is no longer coupled with the world; it entwines another body, applying itself carefully with its entire length, its hands tirelessly tracing the contours of the strange statue that in turn renders all it receives, lost beyond the world and its purposes, fascinated by the sole occupation

of floating in Being with another life, making itself the outside
of its inside and the inside of its outside. Henceforth movement, touch and sight, applying themselves to the other and to
themselves, climb back toward their source, and, in the patient,
silent labor of desire, the paradox of expression begins.
(VI, 144)

This is not an example of "metaphysical" poetry à la John Donne,
nor the didactic lyricism of a Fontanelle, to adorn a celestial mechanics.
And Sartre's descriptions of the Other, though closer in time, are very
distant from this one both in style and content. In Sartre, the Other's
body is usually reduced to the facticity of a thing for my gaze. We shall
have occasion to return to the very precise meaning Merleau-Ponty gives
to the expression "the inside of the outside" and vice versa, not in the
ontological drama of the encounter with the Other, but in connection
with the relation of image to reality in painting.

The "flesh" of the lived body and the world is not inert matter,
but "perpetual pregnancy, perpetual parturition, generativity and generality, brute essence and brute existence" (VI, 115). Matter is always
pregnant with its form, and the dimensions, "the pilings" of the lived
world occasionally show through, offering us a glimpse of a "wild
Logos." The first ideality is horizonal, unthematized, exposed at the articulations of my body and the world.

If I have understood the meaning of Merleau-Ponty's later philosophy, it concedes to anthropomorphism its share of truth, by virtue of the
fact that the ontological conditions of our being (as "being-in-the-world")
and the being of the world are the same. The thing is a variant of myself, the
latter being exemplary—and language, being the voice of no one, is, in a
sense, "the very voice of things, of the wave and the woods" (VI, 155).[8] To
say that things have a "presence" is to say that they "look at us," and that
one selfsame visibility, "sometimes wandering and sometimes reassembled"
(VI, 137–38) is responsible for the fact that we see the world and are ourselves visible. Ontogenesis is integrated into a general ontology. "We say
that a human being is born the moment when something that was only virtually visible within the mother's body becomes at once visible for us and for
itself. The painter's vision is an ongoing birth" (EM, 129). We must give an
account of this ontology of vision that surrounds Merleau-Ponty's aesthetics, running through it as well, pervading it, and shedding light particularly
on his texts on painting, which are constantly informed by a dialectic of the
visible and the invisible.

Painting

Merleau-Ponty's interest in painting dates from his 1945 thesis, developing out of his study of perception as its natural consequence. In a chapter of *Phenomenology of Perception* entitled "The Thing and the Natural World" he had already studied that quality of the real object that Husserl called its "transcendence": the source of increasingly deeper exploration, of an infinite series of *Abschattungen*, real things remain external to consciousness, absolutely "other." They come to us from that same antipredicative province from which hallucinations arise, and they are just as resistant as are the latter to the reductions of both idealism and realism. "Perceptive faith," which Husserl called *Urdoxa* or *Urglaube*, finds or constitutes, before it comes to the differentiated level of true and false or active and passive, that originating reality. The first moment of vision is "ecstasy," the losing of consciousness outside itself in the world of things, in objects. One of the consequences of this postulate, namely the unconscious elaboration of perception in the subject, will be examined only much later, in *The Visible and the Invisible*.[9]

The same year his *Phenomenology of Perception* was published, Merleau-Ponty wrote an essay on the painting of Paul Cézanne entitled "Cézanne's Doubt." The essay prolongs his reflections on Cézanne in *Phenomenology of Perception* (318–19, 323) and finds that the painter's practice resolves in a concrete, though always provisional manner, the philosophical dilemma of intellectualism versus empiricism. Cézanne's *painting*, in this view, constitutes an uneasy equilibrium between the logic of vision and nature in itself, or between brute sensation and thought.

"Cézanne's Doubt"

The essay sets out rather casually, stringing together a series of biographical notes, comments by the artist, and contemporary opinion. Through the fragmentary and anecdotal material of that life, a life nearly devoid of human relationships that seeks its justification and meaning in painting, the menacing figure of doubt appears. Cézanne takes refuge in his art, and is incapable, for the most part, of expressing the logic of that truth he practices, be it to his friends or to himself. "He himself is not at the center of himself; nine days out of ten he sees nothing around him but the wretchedness of his empirical life and his failed attempts, the debris of an unknown celebration" (CD, 75). He even came to the point of attributing the originality of his art to eye problems. But let us leave aside this existential aspect of the essay, which attempts to establish the subtle connections between the work and the life of this artist haunted by doubt.

Cézanne's art seems paradoxical in that it proposes to turn impressionism into "something solid like the art of the museums." Cézanne does in fact go through his impressionist period rather rapidly. In contrast with the volatile object of the impressionists, lost in the play of reflections, enveloped if not dissolved in giddy luminosity, Cézanne's object is "as if dully illuminated from within; light emanates from it, resulting in an effect of solidity and materiality." This is because Cézanne refuses to choose between thought and sensation. His gaze is present at the genesis of the object. The real object is perceived as the essential source, of which all impressions are an expression. There is a logic of vision that the eye understands without the intervention of reflection (which of course does not mean that reflection is absent from the technical stage of the painter's work of expression). Painting's fundamental bias is to express everything—tactile sensations, movement, even the way things smell, according to Cézanne—by vision alone. It is not a question of *suggesting* these sensations by means of an appropriate visual code: the painter *sees* the velvety or hard surface of the object itself. One should not desire, as Cézanne said, to paint expressions, physiognomies, or affective appearances *directly*. Painting is not a calligraphy.

> In *La peau de chagrin*, Balzac describes "a white tablecloth like a blanket of fresh-fallen snow upon which rose, symmetrically, the place settings crowned with blond rolls." "During my entire youth," Cézanne would say, "I wanted to paint that, the tablecloth of fresh-fallen snow. . . . Now I know that one must only *want* to paint 'rose, symmetrically, the place settings' and 'blond rolls.' If I paint 'crowned' I'm done for, you understand? But if I really balance and shade my place-settings and my rolls as they are in nature, you can be sure the crowns, the snow and the whole shebang will be there." (Ibid., 66)

Hence the effect of a "fund of inhuman nature" in his landscapes. The world is frozen, inanimate: there is not the least stirring on the surface of Lake Annecy. The movement, the meaning, is not thematized. All lies in waiting, as at the beginning of the earth. Nature is at the first day.

This essay leaves me with a sense of vague uneasiness. Is it perhaps because Merleau-Ponty, in implicitly associating the task of the painter par excellence, Cézanne in this case, with that of painting in general, offers us an aesthetics that is too narrowly defined? Did all the impressionists miss painting's authentic path? And what of abstract art? It is obvious that Cézanne's career and work are particularly apt to show certain elements of Merleau-Ponty's philosophy, and in a sense it is true that the best way to grasp the spirit of painting *in general* is by enthusiastically espousing the vision of one *particular* painter. Nevertheless, although the painter, whose form of expression is not discursive, is not required to formulate his artistic practice (not to mention that of others) adequately in words, the same does not hold for the philosopher. We shall see, in "Indirect Language and the Voices of Silence," which was published seven years after "Cézanne's Doubt," the appearance of a conception of the historicity of cultural works and painting as an institution that will broaden Merleau-Ponty's aesthetics markedly.

"Indirect Language and the Voices of Silence"

In 1952, Merleau-Ponty reworked a chapter of *The Prose of the World* (a book he eventually abandoned)[10] for publication in *Les Temps Modernes*. He titled it "Indirect Language and the Voices of Silence."

The author of the essay is in implicit dialogue with Saussure, Sartre (as the dedication shows) and especially Malraux. A substantial portion of the essay deals with verbal rather than visual expression, and therefore falls outside the purview of our present concern. But since the essay contrasts those two forms of expression in a very significant way, I must give an account of how painting and the word shed light upon one another.

Merleau-Ponty rejects the overly radical separation Sartre makes between painting and language in "What is Literature?" (S, 55). If meaning seems to be a "prisoner" in painting, if it appears to permeate the painting rather than be expressed by it, it is because we, as writers rather than painters, are too habituated to a more explicit expression of the word. Language gives the illusion of a world of autonomous meaning, and of a more direct, immediate access to the domain of the signified in all its purity. But painting speaks, in its own way: its voices are the voices of silence. Still, the autonomy of the signified of the words is not absolute, and in this sense the difference between the two modes of expression is relative. Language, too, has an essential relation to silence. Silence is not the opposite, but the *other side* of language: they grow at an equal rate.

As clearly as the essay on Cézanne was centered on the work of one sole painter, "Indirect Language and the Voices of Silence" just as clearly thematizes the general problems of expression and historicity. After a few introductory pages on Saussure's theory of the diacritical sign, the study of painting gets underway by critically examining Malraux's analyses (which were later anthologized under the title *The Voices of Silence*). Malraux points out that the theory (though not always the practice) of art of the classical masters considered the picture to be a somewhat embellished representation of objective nature. The moderns (in poetry as well as painting), according to Malraux, challenged this "objectivist" prejudice of art, replacing it with an individualistic and subjective aesthetics. Merleau-Ponty finds this analysis insufficient, because it mistakes the depth at which this objectivist prejudice is situated. Even if the modern conception of abstract art frees the artist from the imitation of nature, we continue to believe just as firmly as did the classical painters in a reality external to ourselves, perceptible through our senses, and capable of being visually represented by the application of certain procedures that would give us, as it were, a faithful illusion of it.

But does this not concede the entire domain of the visible world to the theory of the classical painters? Was not their perception an inseparable part of their culture, as ours is of ours? The "data" of the senses are not immutable facts located beyond cultural history. It is not just our relation to artistic creation that has changed: vision itself, that of the classics no less than our own, is a *metamorphosis*.[11]

Consider, for example, the classical conception of perspective. For the artists of the Renaissance it was an invention, a technique of representation, but it imposed itself progressively as an eternal truth about the world per se. Yet in spite of its persuasive power we must free ourselves from it and reawaken the polymorphous universe of which that perspective is but one possible expression: "The classical perspective is an optional interpretation of spontaneous vision, not because the perceived world contradicts the laws of classical perspective and imposes others, but rather because it does not require any particular one, and is not of the order of laws" (ILVS, 86).

The perspective in question reflects a fundamental bias: the transposition of incompatible possibilities on a plane surface, using a constant scale of magnitude. But size at a distance is not fully assimilable to the size of objects seen up close.[12] The simultaneous "incompossibility" of the baroque lived world leads to the wisdom of subordination, the "composition" of the sole, unifying point of view. Yet the apparent modesty that would characterize our seeing a landscape from one sole angle, on the basis of a geometrical projection ordered about a "vanishing point" is but false modesty. In fact, that landscape represents what we *can* see of a world that has become The Great Object. Hidden within the heart of this circumscribed ability to see is another perspective, that of God, that of the world seen from nowhere and from everywhere. The painter becomes this diminutive point of the retina that reflects an aspect of the Cartesian *omnitudo realitatis*. His modesty is the other side of this domination of the world, reducing the latter to the *uni-versum*.

What is uppermost for Merleau-Ponty is to reveal the polymorphous world that *gives rise to* all modalities of expression, though it *corresponds* to none. He evokes this "wild" world in an indirect style, with a jerky rhythm that piles up metaphors pêle-mêle. It is one of the modalities of the style of his last period.

> Things are no longer there simply according to their projective appearances and the requirements of the panorama, as in Renaissance perspective; but on the contrary upright, insistent, flaying our glance with their edges, each thing claiming an absolute presence which is not compossible with the absolute presence of the other things, and which they nevertheless have all together by virtue of a configurational meaning which is in no way indicated by its "theoretical meaning." (S, 181)

Despite the philosophical, psychological, and even political importance of the *Weltanschauung* related to Renaissance perspective, which tames the lived world's wild being, and despite the importance of that "step" in the empirical and, as it were, linear history of painting itself, there is another history of painting—a historicity without progress, without beginning or end. The "truth" of art, being neither correspondence with an external reality to which it would move ever closer, nor an arbitrary voluntarism, an absolute subjectivity having no relationship with an objective world (for what meaning could be assigned to a subjectivity in the absence of any external reality with which to contrast it?), can be nothing other than a perpetual return to that polymorphous being, a being no more objectively "perceived" than the painter is subjectively "expressed" in his work. In this view, all painting represents a unitary project, so to speak, and that is why rival schools and painters who hated each other appear to collaborate in the museum.

But that generality of painting, a common fund that gives meaning to a variety of techniques and aesthetics, is not to be understood with the help of idealist concepts, a Hegelian monster or "Spirit of Painting" realizing itself through history. It is rather below the official History of Painting, in the human body and its belonging to one sole world, not in *events* but in the *advent* of perception and the dimensionality it has opened up, that the generality of plastic expression is to be grasped. Being a generality of the body and not of the mind, a logic emerging at the cusps of the spatiality of the body and its world, the language of painting is not outside time and space, but omnitemporal and everywhere indigenous, universal to the extent that it is bound to the concrete individual: "The quasi-eternity of art is of a piece with the quasi-eternity of incarnate existence; and in the use of our bodies and our senses, insofar as they involve us in the world, we have the means of understanding our cultural gesticulation insofar as it involves us in history" (ILVS, 107).

Let us clarify the meaning of this historicity of expression, for that is what leads into Merleau-Ponty's ontology. Perception, history, and expression are problems that shed light upon one another in their relationship with Being. "Being is *that which requires creation of us* for us to experience it" (VI, 197). History is *Stiftung*, in Husserl's term, institution in the active sense of the word. It is thus tradition, but tradition defined as "*the power to forget origins* and to give to the past not a survival, which is the hypocritical form of forgetfulness, but a new life, which is the noble form of memory" (ibid., 96). As advent, institution, initiation, the opening up of a dimensionality that will never cease summoning a future, and the positing of a world "to be painted," the history of painting is diametrically opposed to the spirit of the museum, which makes painters as mysterious "as squid and lobsters." This parcelling out, this exteriority hides the "secret, modest, uncalculating, involuntary—in a word, free" history of painting.

It remains for us to examine precisely how perception, expression, and history, terms henceforth interconnected, will enter into the ontological configuration of "Eye and Mind." This task is made more difficult by the circumstance that the style of the essay is often allusive, oblique, an example of "indirect language" at work. There is another difficulty: underlying this text that "says it all" according to Sartre "provided you know how to decipher it,"[13] is the entire ontology of *The Visible and the Invisible*. It is an essay on painting, but, like Husserl's *The Origin of Geometry*, it is an exemplary essay, seeking the originary, the fundamental essence not only of painting, but of all culture.

"Eye and Mind"

All the themes of this essay, written in 1961, had already been introduced in earlier works. But a change in terminology reflects a radical change of perspective. Perception has become "vision," corporeity "flesh," and Being is now capitalized. Painting is no longer an anthropocentric function. The human being, through whom Being expresses itself, is the privileged locus in which the world turns back upon itself, becomes a "visible seer."

What is involved, then, is a metaphysics of painting. But the text itself tells us that it is not an attempt to give a philosophical interpretation to the history of modern painting: "The metaphysics we have in mind is not a separate body of ideas for which inductive justifications could be sought in the experiental realm" (EM, 139). Merleau-Ponty's intention (with respect to his views on modern art, at least) is worded far more modestly, in a way that brings to mind that other essayist he admired so much, Michel de Montaigne.

> It is not illegitimate for a layman such as myself, speaking from his memory of a few paintings and books, to express how painting enters into his reflections, and to register his sense of a profound dissonance, a transformation in the relationship between humanity and Being, when he holds up a universe of classical thought, contrasting it en bloc with the explorations of modern painting. A sort of history by contact, that perhaps does not go beyond the limits of one person, though it owes everything to his frequentation of others. (EM, 139–40)

The essay has five parts. The first sets up an opposition between art and science. The second shows the necessary ontological conditions for a "Visibility"—that "delirium of vision" celebrated by painting. The third is a critique of metaphysics by painting as described by Descartes in *La dioptrique*. The fourth part, from the beginning of which my quotation in the preceding paragraph was taken, evaluates and interprets the work and theoretical statements of several modern painters and sculptors: Cézanne, Matisse, Rodin, Delaunay, and Klee. The fifth part, which is very short, ends with a description of the curious temporality of artistic works. The history of painting does not, strictly speaking, admit of progress, for "in a sense the first painting went to the end of the future." Works are of the order of that which has been acquired—a category to which I shall have occasion to return.

"Science manipulates things and gives up living in them." From that opening statement it is clear that Merleau-Ponty identifies modern science with operational thought, the "cybernetic ideology" that, in his view, bodes ill for the future.

> If this kind of thinking were to extend its dominion over humanity and history, and if, ignoring what we know of them through contact and our own situations, it were to set out to construct them on the basis of a few abstract indices—(as a decadent psychoanalysis and culturalism have done in the United States)—then, since the human being truly becomes the *manipulandum* he thinks he is, we enter into a cultural regimen in which there is neither truth nor falsehood concerning humanity and history, into a sleep or nightmare from which there is no awakening. (Ibid., 122)

This position is comparable to that of Heidegger, who places the spirit of science in technology. But Merleau-Ponty considers it a relatively recent development, and admits that classical science "retained a sense of the opacity of the world." That is why it sought a transcendent or transcendental foundation for its operations. But "science manages without the excursion into metaphysics that Descartes had to make at least once in his life; it begins from the point he ultimately reached" (ibid., 137). That is, the certainty of the external world, which Descartes founded on the cogito and the principle of God's continuous creation, has come to be accepted as self-evident by science, which relegates the problem of the relation of the knowing subject to the world and to itself to the province of psychology.

"Eye and Mind" constitutes, in my view, the fullest expression Merleau-Ponty has given to his aesthetics. To the discursive strength of his arguments must be added the seduction of a style that constantly evokes our factual situation in the lived world, a style whose function is to keep that situation vividly present to the mind during the course of the analysis. It is essential, for example, that we as readers of the text see a world not just spread out before us, as an epistemological object, but surrounding us, containing us, running through us. Vision hatches in the middle of things, in the fault or hollow that has been covered (hidden?) by the term "subjectivity," and that Merleau-Ponty wishes to renew and revitalize as the "dehiscence" of Being—the "bursting open" and the "deflagration" of Being.

Vision cannot be the *intuitus mentis* of idealism, because vision is movement. Therefore it requires a body. What would vision be without movement? It is the intertwining of our sensorimotor projects. The eye explores, questions objects, and to see is to know, in principle at least, how to approach them. Vision is not like the end of a blind person's cane: it precedes itself, is clairvoyant, "tele-vision." Nor does the seeing subject resemble the idealist's epistemological subject.

> It is a self, not by transparency, like thought, which never thinks anything except by assimilating it, constituting it, transforming it into thought—but a self by confusion, narcissism, inherence of the see-er in the seen, the toucher in the touched, the feeler in the felt—a self, then, that is caught up in things, having a front and a back, a past and a future. (EM, 124)

To recapitulate, Merleau-Ponty's aesthetics of painting is grounded in a metaphysics of vision, and vision, in turn, in an ontological description of the body subject as a seeing seenness. Thus everything turns on the validity of the account of the lived body. Such an account is offered to us in the following remarkable passage, which summarizes the ontological overlap of the body, concluding with an evocation of the relationship between contingency and necessity that Merleau-Ponty believed to characterize the human condition.

> A human body is present when, between the see-er and the visible, between touching and touched, between one eye and the other, between hand and hand a kind of crossover occurs, when the spark of the sensing/sensible is lit, when the fire starts to burn that will not cease until some accident befalls the body, undoing what no accident would have sufficed to do. (Ibid., 125)

Once the ipso facto situation has been posited, all the problems of painting are also present. The painting is the visible trace, the icon, the carnal form, the internal equivalent of the world in me. The painting is not a *thing*, but the carnal essence of the thing, a visible to the second power.

Where is the painting, in what space? For its spatiality is not that of the *res extensa*—but it cannot be assigned a place in the Platonic heaven of essences, either, since it must exist for vision.

The animals painted on the walls of Lascaux are not there in
the same way as are the fissure and limestone formations. Nor
are they *elsewhere*. Pushed forward here, held back there, supported by the wall's mass they use so adroitly, they radiate
about the wall without ever breaking their elusive moorings. I
would be hard pressed to say *where* the painting is I am looking
at. For I do not look at it as one looks at a thing, fixing it in its
place. My gaze wanders within it as in the halos of Being.
Rather than seeing it, I see according to, or with it.
(Ibid., 126)

What is the difference between the way we look at things as opposed to pictures? Things are not only visible, but also offer a field of
research to the intellect for analysis and scientific investigation, whereas
the painting is an analogue only in relation to the body. The painting
"does not offer the mind an occasion to rethink the constitutive relations
of things, but rather it offers the gaze traces of vision from the inside,
in order that it may espouse them; it gives vision that which clothes it
within . . . " (ibid.). The painting is the *inside of the outside* (that "imaginary texture of the real," the essence we discover within the thing, all the
facettes of which present themselves as expression).

The "sensitive chiasma" is the locus of reversibility that is, in
Merleau-Ponty's view, the ultimate truth. Its archetype is the human
body, which realizes a kind of natural reflection, being both subject and
object of its own perception. That doctrine of identity in difference owes
much to the Hegelian dialectic. But Merleau-Ponty rejects the synthesis.
There can therefore be no question, in his philosophy, of an end of history. Consequently, if he denies the notion of progress in the conclusion
of "Eye and Mind," it is not simply because "some fate holds us back."

If no painting completes painting, if no work is itself ever absolutely completed, still, each creation changes, alters, clarifies,
deepens, confirms, exalts, re-creates or creates by anticipation
all the others. If creations are not permanent acquisitions, it is
not just that, like all things, they pass away; it is also that they
have almost their entire lives before them. (Ibid., 149)

Let us insist: creations are not *acquisitions* in the sense of deeds done
once and for all, events that have definitively taken place. But they open
up onto a perspective that will never again be closed: they are of the
order of the *advent* rather than of the *event*. This sort of acquisition had

been described by Merleau-Ponty fifteen years earlier in *Phenomenology of Perception*. The influence of Husserl is clear.

> After the construction is drawn, the geometrical relation is acquired. Even if I forgot the details of the proof, the mathematical gesture has founded a tradition. Van Gogh's painting is forever installed within me. A step has been taken from which there is no going back; and even if I have chosen no clear memory of any of the paintings I have seen, my entire aesthetic experience will henceforth be that of someone who has known Van Gogh's painting. . . . We must recognize acquisition as an irreducible phenomenon. (PhP, 393)

The synthesis that destroys while preserving, the Hegelian *Aufhebung*, is unrealizable. There is, it is true, a sort of self-mediation, in which each term breaks open, destroying itself to become itself. Painting, however, is not to be considered as being at the end of the process, but in the middle. It *is* that metamorphosis: "Essence and existence, imaginary and real, visible and invisible—painting scrambles all our categories, spreading out before us its oneiric universe of carnal essences, actualized resemblances, mute meanings" (EM, 130).

Voicing Vision

Merleau-Ponty's aim, in such works as "Cézanne's Doubt" and "Eye and Mind," is clearly not just to collect "sayings" of painters, utterances of an esoteric wisdom known only to practitioners of the visual arts, and then to give them his own philosophical interpretation. True, the philosopher does not dismiss out of hand the self-understanding of novelists and painters.[14] He praises the energetic, artisanal language of Cézanne, but is careful to distinguish the painter's views from the philosophy implicit in his vision. It appears that the painter's theoretical views of what he or she does may make possible or even foster a painterly practice, but they do not (without hermeneutic interpretation at least) necessarily possess much explanatory power. "The painter—any painter, *while he is painting*, practices a magical theory of vision" (EM, 127). Merleau-Ponty also finds philosophically significant elements in the paintings themselves. The ubiquitous "eye" of the mirror in so many Flemish works is as it were an inorganic "digestion" of the world into a spectacle. "In paintings themselves we could seek a figured philosophy of vision—its iconography, perhaps" (ibid., 129). The fundamental bias of painting is that everything, in order to exist, must become visible.

Now the attempt to translate the observation of lived experience into philosophical meaning could be proposed as a characterization of phenomenology as a whole. Specifically, by a return to the "hither side of experience," i.e., to the region that is so close or so familiar to us as to escape attention, the phenomenologist hopes to articulate truths whose authenticity is all the more convincingly assured by a confirmation of intimate echoes, out of the range of normal hearing or so constantly in the background of our consciousness as to be normally inaudible: "unthematized," or "horizontal."

Whence the charge, made by one member of Merleau-Ponty's doctoral committee, of falsifying "direct experience" by an impossible attempt to return to it in full philosophical consciousness, and the suggestion that the candidate might better turn his energies to the writing of novels.[15] But I believe that Merleau-Ponty's subsequent writings contain an adequate answer to this charge; for they tell us that philosophy is a form of motivated creation, and that in this it is not unlike other art forms. It completes, or at least prolongs and keeps open, original experience; it is not a gloss upon a closed, main text.

If that is the case, there may be more than just an etymological continuum relating the (philosophical) *concept* to the (literary) *conceit*. If, in place of the *prise*, the hold of the closed hand, the con-cept (the *Begriff*), we often find in Merleau-Ponty a more slipping grasp—argumentation by persuasion, by evocative suggestion (he finds a *bougé*, a shift, blur, a slippage, even at the heart of the algorithm [*PM*, 128])—it may be because this use of the idea as a cursive, heuristic device is more suitable to the task of eliciting meaning from the vision and action of our perceptual lives. Philosophy, which has tended to employ the idea more frequently in its function as a conceptual container, has sometimes, in Merleau-Ponty's aesthetic meditation, found the fluency to let vision speak—otherwise than through the "voices of silence."

The Aesthetic Dialogue of Sartre and Merleau-Ponty

Marjorie Grene

Merleau-Ponty's discussions of painting, together with his criticisms of Sartre, show up strikingly the contrast of their philosophies.[1] I shall use the comparison of the two philosophers' views on art to illuminate their treatment of four basic existential concepts. These are: first, being-in-a-world; second, the concept of the lived body; third, communication; and fourth, freedom.

Let me first recall the biographical background of the aesthetic dialogue I propose to examine. Sartre and Merleau-Ponty belonged to the same generation of students at the Sorbonne and the same circle of friends; Merleau-Ponty is mentioned occasionally in Simone de Beauvoir's autobiography. He is the only one of this circle (unless Raymond Aron is included) who became an academic: he was professor at the Sorbonne from 1949 and held the Chair of Philosophy at the Collège de France from 1951 until his death in 1961. In 1945 he had joined with Sartre in founding the literary and philosophical review, *Les Temps Modernes*, but resigned a few years later over the issue of Sartre's relation to the Communist party. His attack on Sartre was formulated in a chapter of his *Adventures of the Dialectic* "Sartre and Ultra-Bolshevism,"[2] to which Simone de Beauvoir replied in a counterattack: "Merleau-Ponty and Pseudo-Sartrism." The breach seemed to be complete; but the former friends were in fact reconciled: Sartre recounts their meeting in this connection, in the issue of *Les Temps Modernes* published in memory of

Merleau-Ponty after his death. Indeed, the first essay in Merleau-Ponty's book, *Signs* (1960) is dedicated to Sartre, and the preface to that collection suggests that the renewal of their friendship was at least in part occasioned by Sartre's moving introduction to the posthumous work of a mutual friend, Nizan. In fact, the bitterness of Merleau-Ponty's attack on Sartre was the measure, in my view, of the depth of his admiration for him and for Beauvoir. Merleau-Ponty was a philosopher for whom artistic creation was a central theme, the paradigm, as we shall see, of the human condition, and they were *his* artists: it was they who, in their novels and plays, exhibited concretely the common philosophical concern of all of them. He had said as much publicly and eloquently on a number of occasions. And then they let him down.

The quarrel, on the surface, was political, but, as Merleau-Ponty himself said in the Ultrabolshevism essay, their difference went much deeper: it was, he said, both as personal as possible and as general as possible: it was philosophical.[3] Their quarrel brought to the surface, in other words, a very deep-seated difference in their ways of looking at the world. One can put it briefly by saying that while Sartre is *a man of words,* Merleau-Ponty is *a man of vision.* It is this contrast that I want to elaborate, starting from the problem presented by Sartre's literary criticism and working back to the foundation of the problem in the premises of his philosophy.

The existential approach to literature involves trying to see a writer's work as expressive of his "project," his fundamental way of being human. Every one of us, in his life, is engaged in making of his given situation a composition, an organic whole, that is uniquely his; an artist does this in and through his work, which therefore speaks to us of his particular style of being-in-the-world. Now this approach in criticism can be very illuminating indeed, trying, as it does, to achieve, and to speak from, an understanding of the artist as a whole man, deeply engaged in a human task. An example of successful existentialist criticism, for instance, is Sartre's account of Flaubert in his *Question of Method.*[4] Flaubert's origin in the middle class does not *make* Mme Bovary, neither do his particular circumstances, his domineering father, his brilliant elder brother, his own effeminacy: but all these circumstances, both general and particular, are the conditions upon which, the limits within which, he, freely and uniquely, created his own being in his work. They are, to put it in very un-Sartrean terms, the matter to which he, by his own act, gave unique and significant form. In highlighting this relation between life and work, the remarks on Flaubert scattered through *Question of Method* add a new dimension to one's understanding of *Madame Bovary,* and that is the final test of significant criticism.

Yet if one looks over the pages upon pages of Sartrean critical writing, which proliferate as only a review editor's publications can, such passages as the Flaubert ones seem to represent an unstable equilibrium between two apparently incongruent extremes. On the one hand, Sartre often falls back, in his evaluation of literature, into a perverse *inwardness*, an extreme subjectivism where all relation to the world is vehemently renounced; and on the other hand, in his lengthy and equally vehement pronouncements on committed literature, he evaluates other writers exclusively for their *external* significance, for their "social message." In the former mood he elevates Genet, thief, homosexual, and narcissist, to sainthood; in the latter, Marxist or quasi-Marxist frame of mind, he finds in Richard Wright's *Black Boy* the greatest American literary work, simply, one must suppose, because of the social wrongs with which it is preoccupied. Now of course one might say that these two opposite tendencies, one wholly subjective, the other wholly objective in its critical standards, are at one in their Marxist affiliation: that is, they both express admiration for a literature of rebellion against the emptiness and stupidity of bourgeois society. But this is an indirect and superficial unity. It is not only the fact that Genet is a reject of his society, a prisoner and a pervert that attracts Sartre to him—though that helps; he really wallows in Genet's total isolation, *as such*. For him, Genet represents a last, inverted transformation of the medieval ordered universe. Chesterton said, he reminds us, "that the modern world is full of Christian ideas run wild." And *Our Lady of the Flowers*, he is confident, would have confirmed him in his view: "It is an 'Itinerary of the Soul toward God,' the author of which, run wild, takes himself for the creator of the universe. Every object in it speaks to us of Genet as every being in the cosmos of St. Bonaventura speaks to us of God."[5]

When Sartre wrote, in *Being and Nothingness:* man is a useless passion, he tries to become God and fails, he had not yet met Genet. For Genet has succeeded in precisely this Sartrean task, the task of Sartrean man: and it is the total rejection of the world that enables him to succeed: "This absence of connection with external reality," Sartre says, "is transfigured and becomes the sign of the demiurge's independence of his creation. . . . In the realm of the imaginary, absolute impotence changes sign and becomes omnipotence. Genet plays at inventing the world in order to stand before it in a state of supreme indifference."[6]

And what is this self-created world in which Genet is God? It is the last phase of what Plato in the *Gorgias* calls a plover's life, savoring endlessly the only material left to a human being who has cut off the whole external, human world from any relation to himself: i.e., those physical pleasures devised by the most ingenious devotion to the stimulation of his own body by itself. Such a life has little to do with the concern for social justice that is supposed to characterize "committed literature": indeed, it is its very contrary.

Why this strange see-saw in Sartre's critical writing? The first step on our way to an answer to this question we may find in his theory of the imagination.[7] The imaginary, for Sartre, is pure negation. I stand, as a consciousness, over against the world; to *imagine* is to cut myself off from the objects that confront me, to deny them. Imagination therefore is simply denial, an emptiness. That is why Genet, outcast, imprisoned and denied all instruments but his own ingenuity, so dramatically embodies Sartre's ideal of the imaginative life. But if, out of such an empty inwardness, I project the world again, envisage action in the world, a relation to others, this projection is itself deformed and distorted by the emptiness of its source. The denial of a denial does indeed produce assertion of a sort, but a mechanized, abstract assertion, not an insight into concrete situations. It is literature committed on principle, not immersed in history. What Sartre looks for in committed literature is "totalization," the full swing round from the void of imagination as he sees it. But history is *never* total, and his theory of committed literature remains as unreal, as remote from the feel of concrete action, as the void of imagination itself. So Sartre swings, in his literary theory, as in his ontology, between the two abstractions nothingness and being, being and nothingness. If he does occasionally, as in the passages on Flaubert, halt at a midpoint between the two extremes, it is *despite* his philosophical method, not because of it, that he manages to do so.

But Sartre himself is a novelist and playwright. Why should he hold so strangely abstract a theory of literature? To take the next step in our answer, we must look back briefly at the course of his philosophical development. Sartre spent a year in the early thirties at the French House in Berlin, studying the phenomenology of Husserl. One of Husserl's central concepts, which especially impressed him, is the concept of *intentionality*. Every thought, Husserl had insisted, is by its very nature directed toward an object—not necessarily an external, physically existent object; indeed for the phenomenological study of thought it is irrelevant whether the object in fact exists or not. But what is essential is the *directedness* of thought. The pure "I think" of Descartes is not, as he had thought it self-contained, but turned outward beyond itself to that of which it is a thought. But the conscious mind, the ego, is therefore, Sartre argued, *nothing but* this relation to its object. In itself, it is empty. If *A* consists in a relation to *B*, and *B* is subtracted, what is left is *nothing*. And that is just what happens when I subtract the outward direction of my thought. If I turn inward to myself, if I look for the content of my own subjectivity as such, what I find is just exactly *nothing*.[8] The same message, applied this time explicitly to the visual arts, is conveyed by Sartre's essay on Giacometti, the artist who was obsessed by vacuum—the very contrary, as we shall see, of Merleau-Ponty's Cézanne. Thus Sartre writes:

> Ironic, defiant, ceremonious and tender, Giacometti sees empty space everywhere. Surely not everywhere, you will say, for some objects touch others. But this is exactly the point. Giacometti is certain of nothing, not even that. For weeks on end, he has been fascinated by the legs of a chair that did not *touch* the floor. Between things as between men, the bridges are broken, and emptiness seeps in everywhere, every creature concealing his own.[9]

It is this fascination with emptiness, with nothing, that, for Sartre, marks the imagination and all its work, in the visual arts as well as in the literary. Imagination is the denial of the full, the out-there; what it makes, in here, is—nothing.

Why this all or none attitude? The answer lies yet another step back in Sartre's philosophical history. Beauvoir, in her memoirs, remarks of herself and Sartre in their early days together, "We were Cartesians; we thought we were nothing but pure reason and pure will." This is quite literally true of Sartre's thinking: his Cartesian premises fix irrevocably the limit of his thought.[10]

For Descartes, the mind was wholly self-explicit, luminously aware of each clear and distinct idea in turn, the sum of which taken together composed the totality of knowledge. And over against this area of pure intellectual transparency, the material world was equally explicitly there to be known. Both these, mind and matter, Descartes believed to be substances, independently existent, though dependent at every moment on God to recreate them. Now Sartre has certainly abandoned the seventeenth-century conception of substance, of independent self-existent entities, as well as the conception of an all-powerful, nondeceiving God to support our knowledge of them. All that is left him, then, of the Cartesian heritage, is the demand of total explicitness, the refusal to see any lurking opacity behind what can be clearly formulated, thoroughly apprehended, arbitrarily chosen. Add to this shrunken remnant of Cartesian reason the vector of intentionality, the tie of thought to its object, and you have the truncated dialectic that is Sartre's philosophy, the unending oscillation between a meaningless other out-there and an empty center in-here.

However Sartre has elaborated the relation of the self, and, in particular, of the writer, to society, he has never abandoned or broadened the limits of his philosophy. Take the relation of my consciousness to my body. My body, says Sartre, is the necessity of my contingency, the stubborn flaunting by myself to myself of the limits of my project, of my fancy. We have here subjectivism versus its denial, sheer being versus the subjectivity that is *its* denial. This is but the first stage of the irresoluble conflict that is to follow. Beyond this most intimate otherness, all contact with external things or agencies equally represents their threat to myself. For if my self-consciousness is but the denial of them, they are the denial, the annihilation of my self-consciousness. Thus the chestnut root nauseates Rocquentin. Thus, a fortiori, every other person, himself a denier of the world of which he makes me part, threatens me with extinction. And Sartre's social perspective, finally, the perspective of committed literature, looks out, not on any concrete I-thou relationship, any communion in submission to a common cause: that would be the self-deception of bad faith. On the contrary, his social perspective looks out upon a great web of such I-other conflicts, where each is entangled by the threat of all the others and so, despite themselves, they weave themselves into a society. Union here can be only indirect, through common hatred: "Hell is the others."

All this follows closely and clearly from Sartre's philosophical starting point. In arguing that this is so I have, as I mentioned earlier, been restating in large part Merleau-Ponty's criticism of Sartre. But Merleau-Ponty also reproaches him in another way. He is, he says, too much of a writer.[11] This is at first sight a puzzling statement. What seems to be wrong with Sartre is that he lacks the breadth of starting point needed to allow communication with his fellow men; but surely writers do want to communicate. How is it then *as a writer* that Sartre conceives the self as so isolated, the world of imagination as a dimensionless void? Ironically, Sartre himself, in his first volume of his autobiography, published since Merleau-Ponty's death, has both illuminated and amply justified his friend's reproach. The book, of course, is called *Words* and the title is brilliantly chosen, for he shows us there how from early childhood he lived in a fictional world, a world made by himself in and through romancing, in and through words, taken not as a means of hiding himself from them and building inwardly an imagined kingdom all his own. It was a kingdom where, as Merleau-Ponty said, "all is significance";[12] but luminously, unequivocally significance, where the ambiguities, the silences, the unsayable realities that underly all living speech could be forgotten or denied. This strange unchildlike childhood already expresses the quality of existence Merleau-Ponty was describing by the phrase "too much a writer" or that I was trying to convey in calling Sartre "a man of words."

It is this quality too, that strains and stultifies Sartre's use of existential concepts in philosophy. Consider briefly the four concepts listed above. First, Heidegger's *being-in-a-world* becomes for Sartre not so much being-in as being–over against; it is confrontation, not indwelling, I *against* the other. The *person* as mind and body, secondly, is, as we have seen, but the narrowest arena of this opposition. Third, *communication*, the relation to other persons, remains forever the expression of contradiction and antagonism. Strictly speaking, there are only my words; but no hearer to address them to. And finally, what of Sartrean freedom? Plainly, on Sartre's premises, in terms of the dialectic of being and nothingness, we are *indeed* condemned to be free. Freedom is unqualified and absolute but impotent. The Sartrean hero seeks his own act but, unless in the perverse inversions of a Genet, he can never find it. For like Sartrean imagination, and indeed as the very being of the imaginer, it is essentially denial over against, never within, the world, that world which alone could give it concrete embodiment.

Merleau-Ponty begins, according to his own statement, where Sartre leaves off, not with the imaginary, sundered from the real, but with the union of real and unreal, of affirmation and denial, that marks our living experience.[13] This statement, however, is not quite accurate, since Sartre, starting from the two bare abstracts, being and nothingness, is unable to achieve a viable synthesis between these contraries. What Merleau-Ponty's statement does truthfully convey, however, is, for one thing, the kinship of his thought with Sartre. They both move intellectually within the sphere of influence of the phenomenology of Heidegger and Husserl, and, as I have already suggested, Merleau-Ponty's thought often resonated closely to Sartre's own literary work. But Merleau-Ponty's statement also puts, if not precisely, the very sharp opposition that does in fact separate the two. Merleau-Ponty begins, not where Sartre *does* leave off, but where he ought to arrive and cannot, i.e., with the concrete situation of the individual person, projecting, not an abstraction, but himself. For the phenomenon Merleau-Ponty starts from and remained with as *his* problem is not the emptiness of Sartrean imagination, but the fullness of real, embodied, ongoing perception, perception not over against the world, but in it.

It was visual perception, in particular, that especially concerned him (hence my slogan "man of vision") and for him the paradigm case, the activity that uniquely shows us what perception is, was the activity of the painter. Not the writer making fables for himself, but the artist making a world—*our* world—through eye and hand and canvas: that is the person we should look to to learn both what the world is and what we are. In his earliest book, *The Structure of Behavior,* he had already suggested that it is through art that human transcedence, our way of being-in-the-world, can best be understood.[14] And in an essay, "Eye and Mind," written the year before he died, he was still haunted by this theme. For the painter, he believed, withdraws behind the world to make the world afresh. It is not, Cézanne said, a picture the painter is trying to create but a piece of nature itself. And of Cézanne, who is for him the painter par excellence, Merleau-Ponty says: "His work seems to us inhuman because it is making humanity, going behind the every-day human world, creating the hidden handling of experience through which we make our world the world it is, through which we people it with objects." He does this, Merleau-Ponty says, by using the impressionists' discoveries, and then transcending them to restore the object. Impressionism, he says "was attempting to reproduce in painting the effect objects have as they strike the eye or attack the senses. It represents them in the atmosphere where we perceive them instantaneously with absolute shape bound to each other by light and air." Now to get this effect, it was necessary to use only the seven colors of the prism, eliminating ochre and the earth colors, and also to take into account the reverberation of complementary colors. Thus it it was a question of grass, not only green but its complement red must be hinted at as well. And further, of course, the impressionists conveyed the airiness they wanted by breaking up the local hue itself. So, Merleau-Ponty says, "a canvas which no longer corresponds to nature, point by fine point, restores by the interaction of its parts the general truth of the impression." But Cézanne went further than this. He used not only the seven colors of the prism, but eighteen colors: six reds, five yellows, three blues, three greens, one black. "And this use of warm colors and of black, show," Merleau-Ponty argues, "that Cézanne wishes to represent the *object,* to rediscover it behind the atmosphere." "At the same time," Merleau-Ponty continues, "he renounces the division of hue and replaces it by graduated mixtures, by an unfolding of chromatic shadows on the object, by a colour modulation which follows the form and the light received by the object." But the fact that color dominates the pattern, does not, he says, have the same meaning in Cézanne as in impressionism: "The object is no longer obscured by reflections, lost in its relations with the air and with other objects; *it is as though a secret light glowed within it, light emanates from it, and there results an impression of solidity and matter.*"[15]

Yet if modern painting has wrestled with such problems with new theories and new techniques, the task of the painter through the ages has been a constant one: to reveal and remake the achievement of visual perception which in our routine lives we perform without focal awareness or reflection. "The visible in the layman's sense forgets its premises," he remarks in "Eye and Mind."[16] The painter recalls these premises, and so exhibits them to us explicitly, at a reflective level, as it were, yet immediately, in our perception of the painting, so that we see, not simply the object, but the object *as* we see it: we reenact our seeing. In *Night Watch* the hand pointing at us in the center of the painting is caught again in profile as shadowed on the captain's body. It is this kind of fusion of nonfusible aspects, Merleau-Ponty argues, which make us "see things and a space." But in perception *of* things and space we see *through* such play of contrary aspects: it points *to* the thing, and does so by its own self-concealment. To see the thing, says Merleau-Ponty, it was necessary not to see the very premises on which in fact our vision rests. It is this act of seeing *from* the play of aspects *to* the thing in space that the painter reveals to us.

But in the act of vision so revealed we have found the world not so much over against us as around us. Seeing is not only a confrontation, but an indwelling. It is "having at a distance," and this "bizarre possession" too the painter reveals to us. Merleau-Ponty rebukes Berenson for praising Giotto's "evocation of tactile values"; painting "evokes" nothing, he insists, "least of all the tactile." On the contrary, "it gives visible existence to what lay vision believes invisible, it brings it about that we have no need of a 'muscular sense' to possess the voluminousness of the world." The vision of the painter, doubly mediated—indeed, triply, though our seeing of it—this "devouring vision," as he calls it, "beyond the 'visual data,' opens upon a texture of being whose separate sensory messages are but the punctuation or the cesuras, and which the eye inhabits, as a man inhabits his home."[17]

"The eye inhabits being, as a man inhabits his home": a very tissue of "category mistakes," yet a true, and, for the philosophy of perception, a revolutionary statement. However complex an achievement vision may be—and if we think of its neurological foundation it is immensely complex—in its phenomenological being, in its "what," it is immersion in the world: a distanceless distance, a living *in* that extends the existence of the seer to the outer limits of his seeing, and concentrates the seen in him as its center. Our visual perception is the most striking example of what Plessner calls "mediated immediacy." And this immediacy of the mediated, necessarily forgotten in the pragmatic use of sensory input, is, again, just what the painter is striving to demonstrate. He reverses the ordinary direction of outgoing, practical vision: the world fascinates him, draws him to it. Thus a painter confesses: "In a forest I have sometimes felt that it was not I who was looking at the forest, I have felt on certain days that the trees were looking at me. I was there, listening."[18] Merleau-Ponty inserted in the original edition of "Eye and Mind" a print of Klee's *Park bei Luzern* which vividly exemplifies this mood. Yet at the same time, *through* this receptivity, the painter creates the visible world, and himself, its viewer and inhabitant: "I expect to be inwardly submerged, buried. Perhaps I paint in order to rise up."[19]

Out of this immersion in the world, then, the painter makes the world, and shows us how, through "making" it, we have immersed ourselves in it. This interpretation of the painter's task is illustrated, for example, in Merleau-Ponty's discussion of Cézanne's "return to colour" in his later work. Cézanne himself said of color: "it is the place where our brain and the universe meet." What did he mean by this? It was not, Merleau-Ponty assures us, a question of finding colors "like the colours of nature"; it was a question of seeing, and working, in "the *dimension* of colour, which creates, of itself for itself, identities, differences, a materiality, a something." Not that this gives us a "recipe for the visible": there is no such recipe, not in color any more than in space. But "the return to colour has the merit of leading a little closer to the 'heart of things' "— though it is "beyond the colour envelope as it is beyond the space envelope."[20] The color technique of the *Portrait of Vallier* illustrates Merleau-Ponty's point here: the whites used among the colors, he says, "have . . . the function of shaping, or cutting out a being more general than being-yellow or being-green or being-blue." But the most striking example is that of the late watercolors. Whatever the merits or demerits of Merleau-Ponty's interpretation of Cézanne in general, his description here is perspicuous: "in the water-colours of the last years," he writes, "space, of which one would suppose that it is self-evidence itself and that for it at least the question *where* does not arise, space itself radiates about planes which we cannot assign to any place." We have rather "the superposition of transparent surfaces," the "floating movement of planes of colour which cover each other, advance and retreat."[21] Nor is it a question here, he insists, of adding "another dimension to the two dimensions of the canvas, of organizing an illusion or a perception without an object, the perfection of which would be to resemble as much as possible our empirical vision." "For the depth of a picture (and likewise its height and breadth) comes from we know not where, to present itself, to grow out of the frame. The painter's vision is no longer a looking at an *out-there*, a 'physical-optical' relation, solely with the world. The world is no longer before him through representation: it is rather the painter *who is born in the things* as if by concentration and as the coming to itself of the visible."[22] Thus the painter bodies forth the emergence of the visible as the birth of our being, the emergence of ourselves as seeing beings, and of the world as the colored, spatial sphere in which we are.

We must beware, therefore, of the sort of talk that puts qualities, feelings on the canvas. The painting, once achieved, haunts us as the world does when we have shaped it into a world. The painting is not on the canvas, nor at the place, if there is one, represented by it. It is ambiguously and embracingly here, nowhere and everywhere. Cézanne's *Mont Sainte-Victoire,* transcending the "moment of the world" when he painted it, will be always wherever people have eyes to see. "It is made and remade from one of the world to the other, differently, but no less actually than the hard rock above Aix."[23] To deny this is to misread radically the painter's gift. In this connection Merleau-Ponty made explicit his opposition to Sartre on the theory of visual art. Sartre had written of Tintoretto's *Road to Golgotha:*

> That yellow rending of the sky above Golgotha is an agony
> made into a thing, an agony that has turned into a yellow rend-
> ing of the sky, and is suddenly submerged by . . . the qualities
> of things, their impermeability, their extension, their blind per-
> manence. . . . That is to say, it is no longer legible, it is like an
> immense vain effort, forever stopped halfway between heaven
> and earth, meant to express what the very nature of things pre-
> vents them from expressing.[24]

Thus the painting is, for Sartre, in the last analysis, a thing, over against me, threatening me, like every other thing. What "feeling" it does convey is, he says, a little "haze of heat" hovering about the canvas. To this Merleau-Ponty replied:

> This impression is perhaps inevitable among professionals of
> language, the same thing happens to them that happens to all

of us when we hear a foreign language which we speak badly: we find it monotonous, marked by too strong an accent and flavour, just because it is not ours and we have not made of it the principal instrument of our relation with the world.[25]

But for the painter, he continues, and for us too if we devote ourselves to living in painting,

> the sense of the painting is much more than a little haze on the surface of the canvas, since it was capable of demanding *this* colour and *this* object in preference to any other and since it commands the arrangement of the picture as imperiously as a syntax or a logic. For the whole picture is not in these little local agonies or joys with which it is besprinkled: they are only components in a total sense less pathetic, more *legible* and more enduring.[26]

Merleau-Ponty illustrates his point by retelling the anecdote of the innkeeper of Cassis who was watching Renoir at work. Renoir, intently watching the sea, was painting washerwomen at a stream. "He kept gazing," the puzzled onlooker said, "at I know not what and then changed one little corner." How can one look at the sea in order to paint a freshwater stream? How could the sea tell Renoir about the washerwomen's brook? "The fact is," says Merleau-Ponty, "that every fragment of the world—and in particular the sea, so riddled with eddies and waves, so plumed with spray, so massive and immobile in itself, contains all sorts of shapes of being, and by its manner of reply to the onlooker's attack, evokes a series of possible variants, and teaches beyond itself, a general manner of saying what is."[27] Painting, in short, embodies our openness to being. Even in speech, and more strikingly in the arts that speak through silence, it is the ineffable ground of being itself that the artist seeks to encounter and that addresses us through his work. All meaning means what cannot be said; even the most formal signs carry their significance not in themselves but in what they signify, in what we understand *through* them. And in painting we have, visible and incarnate, the concrete expression of this tension, this reverberation between sign and signified, meaning and what is meant. This is intentionality, not caught between two unattainable abstractions, but at home. The painter shows us our being-in-the-world in its original quality, drawn to being and within it, yet, within it, absent from it in our withdrawal, in our gaze. For this tension of being and distance-from-being, again, is not a see-saw like that of Sartre's being and nothingness, but a living unity-in-separation: ineradicably equivocal, bright and shadowy at once, with the opacity and the luminousness of being itself: "In this circuit," says Merleau-Ponty, "there is no rupture, it is impossible to say where nature ends and man or expression begins. For it is voiceless Being itself which comes to us here, in vision, to show forth its proper meaning."[28] That is why, Merleau-Ponty argues, the dilemma of representative versus abstract art is badly stated: No object is ever *wholly* like its "representation," and at the same time even the most abstract painting "represents" reality: it is in this sense that "the grapes of Caravaggio are the grapes themselves."[29]

Painting, then, shows us paradigmatically the character of our being-in-a-world. It does so, secondly, because, as the art of and through vision, it displays as no other activity can the single equivocal unity of the person, a unity which Merleau-Ponty expresses in the phrase *le corps vécu,* the *lived body,* and which can perhaps be better expressed in English by speaking of embodiment of the person as *embodied.*

The painter, Valéry said, brings his body with him; and indeed, Merleau-Ponty comments, we could not imagine a disembodied spirit *painting.* Nor, for that matter, would speech be possible for a pure mind, detached from tongue or pen. Speech is significance *in* sound or ink or chalk; it is mental and physical *at once.* Even so, a Sartrean life of words, of a pure verbalizing consciousness, is at least a possible illusion. If thought is, as Plato said, the dialogue of the soul with itself, we can at least imagine it running on, cut off from reality, in a kind of ghost world. But every painter, however "abstract" his style, is working, with arm and hand, to shape physical material, colors and lines. The painter at work stands, for Merleau-Ponty, for the bodily rootedness of all creative activity.

But, you may well ask, why only painting? Why not sculpture? Why not music? The sculptor shapes material with his hands, much as we try, in our projection of ourselves into the future, to shape the contingent material of our lives. And even better, perhaps, the composer working with sounds shapes a temporal material, he gives significant form to successive as well as simultaneous events. The shape of a human life, surely, is much more closely mirrored here than in the quiescent two-dimensional surface of a picture. If life itself may be described as *configured time,*[30] then it is music that we should take as the art that can best teach us what we are. The ear is as truly embodied spirit as the eye. And admittedly, Merleau-Ponty did say, in *The Structure of Behavior,* that it is art in general that best reveals the way in which we fashion our biological environment into a human world.[31] But it is certainly the case of painting in particular that haunted him till the end of his life.

For it is painting that is most plainly and purely the art of vision, and for Merleau-Ponty it is visual perception that most clearly expresses the way we live our bodily lives. For one thing, vision is presence in absence: in it our very being is fused with distant objects, we become part of them and they of us. Moreover, the awareness of what is visible embraces at the same time an invisible: when I look at an orange, I see the whole round object even though only one aspect of it is strictly present to my eyes. True, when I hear a passing car, I hear a *car*, not just a noise of which I then proceed to judge: that is a car. My perceptive grasp of things is always already interpretative. That fact remains, whatever sense I use as my example. Indeed, Merleau-Ponty himself insists that perception in its living existence is kinaesthetic: we grasp, through our senses and more than our senses, through the whole complex series of transactions with the world that constitutes experience, the presence about us of other things and other lives. It is only in analysis and reflection that we separate the five senses and learn to understand their distinctive achievements. Despite this common basis of co-operation among the separate or separable channels of sense, however, there *is* a special way in which visual perception illustrates the character of the lived body. Vision exemplifies as no other sense does what we may call the mutuality of subject and object. I not only see, I am in part visible to myself, and I am wholly visible to all others. I can look at other people and they can look at me. This seems so obvious as to need no statement, let alone the tortuous paragraphs and pages that Merleau-Ponty devotes to his theme. But it is, all the same, the kind of obvious truth which has far-reaching philosophical consequences when you look at it more closely. A Sartrean consciousness gazing at another person must either make him an object or succumb to becoming one himself: there is no mutuality of gaze. Even a dumb object, Rocquentin's chestnut root, by its very existence makes my consciousness absurd. But, Merleau-Ponty insists, vision is already *as such* vision *by* a visible body: it is not subject fighting to the death with object, consciousness against body, but always and in its very essence the two in one. So he says, in one of the most pregnant statements of his favorite—indeed, almost his obsessive—theme:

> Visible and mobile, my body is numbered among things, it is one of them, it is caught in the tissue of the world and its cohesion is that of a thing. But because it sees and moves itself, it holds things in a circle around itself, they are an annex and a prolongation of itself, they are encrusted in its flesh, they form part of its full definition and the world is made of the very

stuff of the body. These reversals, these antinomies are different ways of saying that vision takes place or develops out of the
medium of things, there where a visible being sets about seeing, becomes visible for itself and for the vision of all things.[32]

Again, this paradoxical direct-indirectness, this active passivity of vision,
Merleau-Ponty believes, is quintessentially expressed in painting. This
system of exchanges once given, he says, "all the problems of painting
are there. They illustrate the enigma of the body and it justifies them."
Cézanne had said: "Nature is within." Merleau-Ponty comments: "Quality, light, colour, depth, which are out there before us, are so only because they awaken an echo in our body, because it makes them
welcome." And from this inner echo, "this fleshy formula of their presence that things evoke in me," springs the painter's creation: the seen at
one remove, yet immediate, even more immediate, in its reflective reality: "a trace, visible in its turn, where every other eye will rediscover the
motives which support its inspection of the world." The painting, in
short, is "a visible to the second power, fleshy essence or icon of the
first."[33]

Thus painting is far from being an "image" in the sense of an
unreal copy of some prosaic reality: it has its nature in the very "duplicity," as Merleau-Ponty calls it, of perception itself. Now in fact this thesis
of the ambiguity of perception and especially of the interplay of per-
ceiver and perceived, is a favorite motif of painters. They like to present,
for example, that most striking and uniquely human phenomenon: the
mirrored image of ourselves, which shows us ourselves in a kind of half
reality as others see us. A mirrored life is a uniquely human life: no other
animal can live in this strange, ambiguous relation to its own body; consider, for example, the complex mirrorings of Velasquez's famous court
scene, *Las Meninas*. Matisse's fascination with painting himself painting
expresses a kindred theme. The painter is immersed in the visible world,
struggling to express its visibility, yet he himself, doing this, is visible to
himself doing this. Both cases—the mirror, and the painter painting his
own activity of painting—generate an infinite regress which expresses
the very heart of human reflectiveness. Not a still, bright center of consciousness, but an inexhaustible proliferation of level upon level of significance constitutes human thought.

But every level, every shade of meaning, however it may transcend the here and now, is, again, rooted in bodily presence. Modern
philosophy, under the spell of the scientific intellect, has forgotten this
truth, Merleau-Ponty argues, and the insights of modern painting can

show us where philosophy has failed. Modern thought, he says in "Eye and Mind," is dominated by operationalism: that is, by the belief that all problems can be solved by the experimental manipulation of precisely specified variables. But significance never floats freely on the surface of things, as a scientistic philosophy would seem to suppose it does. It is always grounded in the being of the living, embodied individual; but individual life can only be *lived,* not said; in its opacity it eludes the formalisms of science, however powerful. The archetype of an operationalist theory of vision, for Merleau-Ponty, is Descartes's *Dioptrics,* where, as one might expect, vision is a matter of pure geometry, wholly transparent to the clear intellect. Descartes, Merleau-Ponty points out, shows little interest in painting: had he done so, he would have needed a different ontology. But when he does talk about it, what interests him exclusively is line and form. He might work out a theory of engraving, though even this would be, on his view, as it is not in fact, a mere copying of the geometry of the real extended world. But color in its living nature, color as it captures us, as we dwell in it, is wholly alien to a Cartesian mentality. Consider again the play of color which the impressionists have taught us to see. This is a reality of which the Cartesian theory of perception can give no account.

Perspective, too, in its bodily reality, is something different from the pure geometrical perspective of the intellect which interested Descartes. Merleau-Ponty points out, for example, how Cézanne uses the actual distortion of a line as seen. There is a portrait of Mme Cézanne in which the border on both sides of the body fails to make a straight line; "but we know," he writes, "if a line passes under a large band of paper, the two visible segments appear dislocated." Similarly, in the portrait of Gustave Geffroy the table at the front spreads out before us—for when the eye traverses a broad surface, its images are taken from different points of view, and so the total surface is warped. "Cézanne's genius," he says,

> is through the total arrangement of the picture to make the deformations in perspective cease to be visible in themselves when we look at them in the lump; and they only contribute, as they do in natural vision, to give the impression of an order in process of birth, an object in process of appearing, of collecting itself under our eyes. There is nothing less arbitrary than these celebrated deformations.[34]

Indeed they are only in theory deformations; for in fact they restore the living reality which the intellect in its arbitration distorts.

Merleau-Ponty's account of what I have called the mutuality of vision, moreover, exemplifies also my third point of comparison with Sartre. Our being-in-the-world is indwelling as well as confrontation; and the world we dwell in is necessarily inhabited not only by things but by other persons too, by all those who see me, just as I see them. Communication is not an insoluble problem for Merleau-Ponty as it is for Sartre, but the given from which we start: the very emergence of myself as a center of experience reveals me as one among others. However isolated the painter in his struggle with the visible, therefore, he is struggling with, he is bringing into being, a common human world. The innkeeper did not understand what Renoir was doing at the seashore, but still the work Renoir created was there to speak to him and to all of us of the human condition, of the being in which together we are all immersed. So it is, again, that Cézanne's *Mont Sainte-Victoire* can speak to all men always, everywhere.

The painter's place in the history of his art, moreover, Merleau-Ponty believes, shows us, more immediately than the history of literature can do, the nature of tradition. Each generation of painters has to deny the style of its predecessors and at the same time profits by their example; yet for all the painter's efforts to renew his art, the paintings of the past are there, present to us still. The writer, on the other hand, in writing, remakes language, and the literature of the past becomes at least partly obsolete, accessible to us only by an intellectual effort. It needs a verbal as well as imaginative exertion to read Chaucer; Giotto is there still, as near at least as Padua or Florence. Literature is more contemporary but also more temporary. The problem of painting, in contrast, is a quasi-eternal one, embodying, therefore, a single unbroken tradition. It remains, Merleau-Ponty says, "an abortive attempt to do what is always still to be done,"[35] yet an attempt which, in this forever uncompleted endeavor, unites men of each generation mutely but profoundly with the whole human past. "The field of pictorial meanings has been open," he writes, "ever since a man appeared in the world." This is so just because painting so truly mirrors the embodied situation:

> The first drawing on the walls of caves founded a tradition only
> because it inherited another: that of perception. The quasi-
> eternity of art merges with the quasi-eternity of incarnate exis-
> tence and we have in the exercise of our body and of our
> senses, insofar as they insert us in a world, the means of under-
> standing our cultural gesticulation insofar as it inserts us in his-
> tory. . . . The continuous attempt at expression establishes a

single history—as the hold of our body on every possible object establishes a single space.[36]

Here again communication with the past, as with the present, is the very ground out of which human existence springs. Temporally as well as spatially we dwell in and come to individual awareness out of our communal being.

History is a favorite theme of existential philosophers, yet Merleau-Ponty is the first writer in this tradition to found the historical being of man in communal existence. Existentialism is known with some justice as a philosophy of the lonely, alienated individual; but for Merleau-Ponty the dimension of human togetherness, both the communication of one with another and the immersion of the individual in a communal heritage, is a presupposition of human life. The painter speaks to his contemporaries of the world they see and of the way they see it; and he echoes a voice as old as humanity itself. It would be irrelevant here to compare Merleau-Ponty's conception of history or communication in general with that of other philosophers like Jaspers or Heidegger. But let me just look back briefly to compare the lesson Merleau-Ponty draws from painting with Sartre's theory of committed literature. For Sartre, the ego is not only isolated from others, but is itself simply a negation of the objects to which it is, in essence, a relation: it is the amputation by itself of itself from being. In committed literature this nonexistent existent, this empty ego, projects itself outward again to form a program of social action. This produces, however, as Merleau-Ponty rightly insists, not a literature of concrete activity, a reflection of history as lived, but an abstract, and false, equation of art with politics. It produces propaganda.

Here again, Sartre's premises allow him no other issue; and once more, we can express this limitation of his thought by pointing to his fascination with words, words for their own sake, not for their meaning—i.e., for what they point to, but cannot articulate. Speech itself, Merleau-Ponty reminds us, is grounded in silence. Even a novel has to speak, not in words, but through them; it has to signify through speech an unspoken reality, a style of life, that transcends words: "it expresses tacitly, like a painting."[37] But it is this *tacit* ground of speech which makes communication possible. There is no good in speaking if my hearer has ears but hears not and his hearing is silent. That is why painting so usefully exhibits the nature even of speech in its primordial functioning of what Merleau-Ponty calls "speaking speech" rather than mere language. Painting is the struggle for expression through silence, its voice is the voice of silence; and this paradigm, cut off from the abstract explicitness of language, can effectively exhibit, therefore, both the tacit ground of each act of communication, and the communion, through the "voices of silence," of each with all. It breaks the circle of verbalization and brings us face to face with one another in the world. It points toward the resonance of those occasions when we encounter one another, and toward the shared encounter with being, potentially reflective but never wholly reflected, which constitutes our common human destiny.

I listed at the beginning four concepts I wanted to mention in connection with Merleau-Ponty's view of art. So far I have referred to three of these: being-in-the-world, embodiment, and communication. Where for Sartre we have consciousness against the world, we have, for Merleau-Ponty, indwelling as the ground of confrontation. Where for Sartre we have the conflict of mind with body, and the internecine war of self against self, we have, with Merleau-Ponty, on the one hand, the integrity of the lived body and, on the other, the organic participation of the individual in a common cultural world. Finally, there remains the contrast in their conceptions of freedom. It is here that Merleau-Ponty's discussions of paintings and painters come closest to the practice of Sartre in his best literary criticism, yet we can see plainly in this case also how far he stands from Sartre in his basic philosophical beliefs.

In his reflections on painters and their lives, Merleau-Ponty practices what Sartre had christened "existential psychoanalysis," that is, he examines the artist's life as bearing on his work, and expressing it insofar as an artist's life *is* a life becoming expression. But that does not mean that the life, even in its hidden origins, determines the work. It is the man as artist in his whole projection of himself into the world that the existential critic seeks to understand; and that means to understand the work in its intrinsic significance, for the work *is* the artist's project, his freedom realized. When Van Gogh, Merleau-Ponty says, in painting *Crows over a Wheatfield,* sought to "go further," this was not a question of going one step further in a beaded causal sequence; the "further" expresses the tension that always subsists between the one who is not yet and the one who is already.[38] This is the pull of the future, full of significance not yet realized, upon a past waiting to be made significant. It is not a question here either of a one-level series of causal determinants and their effects, nor of a pure "spiritual" meaning, subsisting in a cloud-cuckoo land all on its own. Rather there is an essential polarity between the painter's life as ground and material of his work, and the work as significant expression of and through the life. Thus Cézanne, Merleau-Ponty argues, would appear to an outside observer a schizoid type; even his good

friend and biographer Bernard could fail to see the relevance of his suf-
ferings to his task as a painter, could see them as mere weaknesses or
eccentricities. And yet Cézanne's life has a bearing on the work, and expresses it, since in the last analysis Cézanne's life is the life "which this
work demands."[39] In his practical criticism, in other words, Merleau-
Ponty shows us the same equilibrium between the artist's work and his
world which Sartre also exhibits in his accounts of Flaubert or Baudelaire. For Sartre, however, as I have tried to argue, this delicate balance
of work and life, of significance and sheer happening, is always endan-
gered by the Sartrean demand of *total freedom.* In a Sartrean free act I
must make, not only my decision and my act, but the very standards by
which I must decide. I make the world, singly and suddenly, I become
God. But in fact I do no such thing—and so I become a useless passion,
fallen back from the hopelessness of my infinite demands upon absurdity
and despair. The ontology of being and nothingness, in other words,
cannot in fact provide an adequate theory for the practice of existential
criticism; Sartre's philosophy belies his best critical insights. In contrast,
Merleau-Ponty's theory of freedom is adapted to the needs of his practical criticism, which in turn confirms his theory. First, freedom for him is
not literal and final, as for Sartre, but, like the lived body whose freedom
it is, ambiguous. Cézanne is both schizoid sufferer *and* reshaper of the
visibility of things. These are not two legs of a see-saw, but two aspects of
the inescapable ambivalence, the irridescence of the very texture of our
lives.

Secondly, freedom for Merleau-Ponty is indirect. The painter
wrestling with a problem that grips him, struggling for expression with
the material of line and color, the material of his experience, is displaying human freedom *through* the demands of his determinate situation,
not somewhere else, over against them. Cézanne, says Merleau-Ponty,
struggled and suffered and doubted to the end his power to do what in
fact he was magnificently engaged in doing. "We never see our freedom
fact to face,"[40] not because, like Sartrean freedom, it is an impossible
ideal, but because it is so real, woven into the intricate stuff of life itself.

And finally, freedom is never finished. Indeed, it *is* that openness
to the future which most deeply marks our being-in-the-world. Painting,
we have seen, is always, in Merleau-Ponty's view, an abortive attempt to
say what still remains to be said. It is a continuous grappling with a problem which remains always still to be solved. The intellect, he writes in the
closing paragraphs of "Eye and Mind," is disappointed by this conclusion: Are we to go on always asking the same question, moving in a circle,
in a state of continuous stupor? "But this disappointment," he writes, "is

that of the imaginary in a mistaken sense, which demands a positivity that exactly fills its void. This is the regret at not being everything."[41] This seems to be his final comment on the imaginary of Sartre. But the frustration we face here in our intellectual being is compensated by a broader view: "if we can establish neither in painting nor indeed elsewhere, a hierarchy of civilizations nor speak of progress, this is not because some destiny holds us back; it is rather because in a sense the first painting of all already reached into the depths of the future." Its task was not complete, but open: resonant of the future: "if no painting absolutely achieves the aim of painting, if indeed no work absolutely achieves itself, every creation changes, alters, illuminates, deepens, confirms, exalts, recreates or creates in advance all the others."[42]

In conclusion, I should like to think of the next and final sentence—the last of Merleau-Ponty's last complete work—as a hope also for his own uncompleted task, which may well reverberate in the future in ways unsuspected by himself. "If," he says in conclusion, "creations are not an acquisition, it is not only because, like all things they pass away, it is also because they have almost all their lives before them."[43] This is, as against Sartre, Merleau-Ponty's principal merit. His arguments lack the dialectical rigor of Sartre's, they "circle round and round the same landscape." But it *is* a landscape, not a bundle of abstractions; we can live in it, philosophically, and even build in it, with help from a few like-minded thinkers, a conceptual home.[44] Sartre is the last of the Cartesians. He shows us, brilliantly and maddeningly, the impasse to which in our time the modern mind has come. Merleau-Ponty, groping, obsessed with one paradox—the paradox of visual perception—overrhetorical, yet speaks to us as one of the first truly post-Cartesians. He gives us, if not a philosophy—perhaps not even a philosophy of visual art—a foundation on which we can build, and equally, to echo his own paradox, a view of the horizon toward which we can hope to move. The man of words alone is by profession the man of alienation; his philosophy is uncurably a philosophy of alienation. The man of vision may teach us, in contrast, how to begin to build a philosophy of indwelling. He shows how in our very distance from things we are near them, he recreates conceptually, as, for him, the painter does iconically, our mediated immediacy, our attachment through detachment, the very core of our way of being-in-a-world, the puzzle of our freedom.

11

Merleau-Ponty on the Concept of Style

Linda Singer

M erleau-Ponty's fundamental project was to develop a philosophy that would do justice to the world as lived. Part of that effort involved developing a language that would faithfully evoke the preconceptual character of perceptual experience, an idiom that would speak not the language of the subject or of the project, but of their intertwining. This shift from the dualistic context, which underlies everyday language, often engenders a shift in the domain or scope of meaning of the concepts which are retrieved from ordinary discourse. From a philosophical standpoint, this gap or deformation of significance requires articulation, a retrieval of the commitments which underlie it, in short an interpretation.

My purpose in this essay is to explore one such concept which Merleau-Ponty has taken over from ordinary language—the concept of style. Traditionally, the concept has remained within the purview of the connoisseur, historian, or philosopher of art. In this context, style has served both a categorial and an evaluative function. As a categorial tool, style is that in terms of which such questions as attribution, periodization, and authenticity may be resolved. Style is used to catalog works into genres or schools, and to determine the work's historical origins. As an evaluative concept, style is a distinguishing mark of quality, that which separates the extraordinary work from the pedestrian, and the work of the master from those of his students. Style is an object of discernment, whose final determination rests with the connoisseurs and experts.

In contemporary colloquial usage, the term has expanded to areas beyond the aesthetic. But this broadening of usage has served largely to trivialize the term, by reducing style to a fetish of the commodity market. Style is that which demands that we revamp our wardrobes, trade in our cars—in short, commodity culture has effected a conflation whereby stylistic value has become synonomous with the market value of the item in question.

Merleau-Ponty's concern with style is of a different order. He is not interested in style as a technical matter, or as the object of a judgment of taste. Thus he does not develop an explicit method of stylistics. The references to style in his work occur contextually, within the larger discussions of perception and expression. Merleau-Ponty is reluctant to consider style apart from its objects, and the processes by which it is generated and apprehended. This is because style is not simply a veneer over things which can be extracted and investigated on its own. In its most comprehensive sense, style refers to a generalized structure of being-in-the-world, a fundamental component of all phases of existence. Merleau-Ponty uses style as a way of characterizing that persistent and characteristic manner of appearance that we recognize in things and other people, without having to constitute it explicitly. The importance of this concept for Merleau-Ponty's philosophy as a whole is that style provides a way of characterizing the kind of significance that perception reveals, and a way of describing the qualitative impact of the phenomenon.

The format of my exposition has been dictated by the way the concept of style develops in Merleau-Ponty's thought. Despite his intent to extend the scope of the concept beyond its traditional aesthetic context, the bulk of his exposition of style is concerned with style in painting. The reason is that style appears in painting in a very articulated and accentuated way. On the basis of examining a paradigm case, Merleau-Ponty hopes to be able to locate those aspects of style which are transferable to other dimensions of existence. Therefore I will begin with an examination of style as an aesthetic category, and then go on to suggest the ways this concept informs Merleau-Ponty's larger ontology.

Style as an Aesthetic Category

The concept of style has received considerable attention in contemporary discourses about art. The concept developed as a response to the diversity of the artistic enterprise, the fact that works of art from different times and different cultures look different. Style served as a way of categorizing and evaluating these differences. As the term took hold, however, it began to acquire elitist connotations. Style was treated as something which only the expert or the initiate could discern.

Merleau-Ponty's quarrel with much of what passes as stylistic analysis is that its discourse somehow obscures the work and the processes which engendered it. Despite its intentions to the contrary, stylistic analysis often imposes a false mystery which moves the work farther away, rather than drawing it near. It has negated the painter's labors by encasing him in a cult of genius, and has transformed his efforts into magical emanations. It has transformed a living expression into a message from the dead which must be translated by a cultural intercessor.

Merleau-Ponty's impetus for discussing style is to demystify it—to wrest it from the grasp of experts and return it to general accessibility. This is not simply an aesthetic populism, an availability in principle. It is a fundamental reformulation of the concept, one which emphasizes style as a potent perceptual presence, and its dependence upon and potential for extending our perceptual capacities. Merleau-Ponty's intent is to bring style into the open, that intentional space where the concerned gaze and the work interpenetrate and activate each other. What develops from this is a theory of style that avoids technical problems. What interests Merleau-Ponty about style in painting is that it constitutes a highly articulated instance of the phenomenal self-presentation of meaning—an achievement, an emergence, a hard-won expression. The significant thing about style is that it is never just a series of techniques. Style, by helping to guide our eyes across the work's surfaces, allows for a happening of meaning. Style is thus crucial to understanding the aesthetic impact of the work of art, because it testifies to the human capacity to wrest significances from the world and to transform them into a mode of access and illumination which transcends the particularities of its origins.

The major regulative ideal underlying Merleau-Ponty's work on style is that discourse about style preserves its integrity. In the affective phase, Merleau-Ponty cautions against the temptation to dissolve a style into a series of effects. That, to his mind, would be to see the wrong side of the painter's work and to miss its real purpose. To fetishize the spatial distortions of Cézanne or the brushwork of Poussin, is to obfuscate awareness of that which they make visible. It is to mistake means for ends, and to overlook the fact that when viewed globally, these small-scale features are perceptually incorporated into the motif they were designed to serve. In his discussion of the generative phase, Merleau-Ponty is concerned with describing the processes by which style emerges for the painter, and in capturing the divergence between his standpoint and that of his audience. This means refusing to trivialize the artist's efforts by psychologizing or romanticizing them. In the positive moment, this means emphasizing the worldly and arduous character of the painter's labor.

For the painter, style is a lived and engaged phenomenon, as apparent or unrecognizable to him as his walk or other gestures. When he is working, the artist's style remains largely implicit—inseparable from his way of seeing the world and gesturing with his brush. He tends to recognize his style only retrospectively and at a distance. This, however, is not meant to suggest that an artist's style is natural, intuitive, or unconscious. Merleau-Ponty is quick to remind us, through the words of Malraux, that it takes the artist a long time to find his voice.[1] And one need only look to the work of Rembrandt or Picasso to find powerful evidence of a style's capacity to develop and evolve. When Merleau-Ponty emphasizes the lived character of style for the painter, it is to highlight the fact that the artist's work does not emerge with the same radical relief for him as it does for his audience. For the viewer, the painter's style is an optional way of portraying appearances. For the painter, by contrast, style is that by virtue of which he is or is not able to paint the way he wants to paint. For the painter, the development of a style constitutes the actualization of the possibility of expression.

Expression, Merleau-Ponty points out, is a tenuous process. It is "like a step taken in a fog. No one can say where, if anywhere, it will lead."[2] Thus the development of a style and the awareness of its limitations and possibilities is often a source of anxiety for the painter, an anxiety which is not merely personal, but endemic to the enterprise of painting. This is what made Cézanne so poignant a figure for Merleau-Ponty.

Cézanne was an artist who lived with a thematic awareness of the paradox of vision—that vision seems to be both in me and out there in things. Because he wanted to be faithful to the way the world appeared, Cézanne was often led to doubt his work. He wondered whether his point of view was a source of revelation or dissimulation, and whether his vision could take hold in others. The significance of Cézanne's doubt for Merleau-Ponty is that its grounds lay not in Cézanne's individual psychology but in the nature of his project. Cézanne wanted to establish a new way of painting, capable of portraying the emergent character of perceptual stability. His work was not immediately accessible to others (and in fact was very poorly received initially) because it was unprecedented. The very novelty and import of Cézanne's work made him anxious about its ultimate value. Merleau-Ponty says "Cézanne's difficulties are those of the first word."[3]

Cézanne's situation illumines the situation of the painter in general, because any expression is, in some respects, unprecedented. Whether the artist seeks to accentuate or to repress his point of view, his work appears to him both as perniciously autofigurative and alien. The painter recognizes that once they have reached the canvas, the significative intentions which motivated the work have undergone a transformation. Picasso did not see the world fractured. His works represent not just the things as they appear to him, but those things given general visible accessibility. The work, therefore, inevitably transcends its origins. The painter, therefore, can always wonder whether his work has done justice to his intentions, and whether his work has achieved expression. Because the vindication of his work ultimately rests with the gaze of the Other, the painter's project is fraught with risk, doubt, and anxiety.

The significance of this for understanding the emergence of a style is that it removes the illusion that the painter operates from the privileged position of Malraux's "demiurge" or Ruskin's "transparent eyeball." The painter does not live across an abyss in a realm of instant illumination. It is precisely because the painter's world is continuous with that of his audience that his work can take hold in their vision. It is through the basic human capacities for perception that an exchange of meaning between the artist and his work, and the work and its audience, can take place. Therefore, Merleau-Ponty's analysis of the generative phase emphasizes that it is essentially a perceptual-motor activity of vision and gesture.

What distinguishes the painter's vision is not that it stems from some extra faculty, but that it is moved by a nexus of concerns not present in ordinary seeing. Painterly seeing is distinguished by its interrogative orientation and its commitment of praxis. The interrogative orientation of the painter's seeing is manifested in his greater attention to the visual world and its underlying conditions. He works at developing sensitized modes of discrimination in order to discern the ground phenomena of vision that ordinarily get taken for granted or overlooked. Unlike the ordinary spectator who transcends his seeing toward things seen, the painter cannot take the synthetic products of vision for granted. He is concerned not only with those aspects of vision where things reveal themselves as what they are, but also with the surrounding field, and the interaction of forces which help to constitute the thing's appearance. Because the world is a constant resource to the painter, regardless of whether his work purports to represent it, Merleau-Ponty says that an artist may be said to discover his style in the world.[4]

The painter's commitment to painting the world also informs the manner and objects of his seeing, by transforming the world into a world-to-be-painted. This engenders a vision which tends to suspend common sense in favor of an abandonment to the flow of appearances, the rhythm and melody of which he will try to project before himself in paint. But the painter knows that his project is not completed at the level of vision alone. It must be made visible through the movement of his brush across the canvas. He must learn to use that brush as the blindman uses his cane, to navigate and articulate the world around him. The painter's project is a struggle to find the expressive gestures which will allow him to paint the way he wants to paint.

The concept of expressive gesture is the pivotal one in Merleau-Ponty's account of style, for it is that which provides the link between the generative and affective phases. Briefly stated, style emerges from and appears as an expressive gesture, which is an extension of the body's basic capacities to intentionally intertwine with the world.

The painter, in developing his style, finds that he must adjust his gestures to the demands of things he wants to paint. Far from being an activity of pure conquest, the painter's brushwork often constitutes a response to the motif he has chosen. Like any other movement, the painter's gestures are drawn from him by what he wants to do, and thus occur with a certain intentional spontaneity. The artist is often unsure of just how his work is accomplished. Matisse, for example, was stunned by a film of himself at work.[5] The artist is most aware of his style when it appears as a limitation. When it works he lives it as an existential "I can."

To the viewer, however, style appears as a joyful emanation, a certain manner of modulating appearances which reveals previously unseen aspects of the visible. Style appears to him as a thoroughgoing transformation of the world by which familiar things of the world acquire the power to gather new significances around them. Style establishes a coherent orientation toward the world it portrays. "For each painter style is the system of equivalences that he makes for himself which manifests the world he sees. It is the universal index of coherent deformation by which he concentrates the still scattered meaning of his perception and makes it exist expressly."[6] In this passage, Merleau-Ponty is emphasizing that style is an interpretation, an optional way of depicting the world. Optionality does not imply, however, that stylistic decisions are made in a vacuum, or that they are without factical roots or motivation. A style's optionality is not a function of personal choice. For many painters like those who worked in the workshops of Rembrandt or Rubens, style was not a matter of choice. Learning to paint meant learning the style of the master. Style is an option because there is no preestablished way of presenting the world. All styles constitute the exercise of an option because they are situated responses which do not merely reproduce the visible but also interpret it. A style, therefore, provides a range of practices and sensibilities, but these are not necessarily fixed. They can also be transferred, put to uses other than those for which they were originally intended, and thus can open new possibilities. This is why a da Vinci can emerge from the atelier of Verrocchio, or why an artist like Giotto can change the way the highly conventionalized art of his age looks.

By emphasizing style's interpretative character, Merleau-Ponty reminds us that all the ways of depicting the world are inventions, and that no style has privileged access to presenting the world as it is. The illusionism of Dutch still lifes or Renaissance spatial recession are as near to and as far from the real as Dali's melting clocks or Arp's free-floating forms. Therefore, the painter need not choose between painting the world and expressing himself. No painting can be purely self-referential. A private painting is as unintelligible as a private language. On the other hand, no painting is entirely free from the particularities of its origins. Painting is possible because the artist and his world can engage in a mutual exchange of significance.

The history of style (and the fact that style in painting does have a history) has a dual significance for Merleau-Ponty. On the one hand, style provides powerful testimony to the capacity of human perception to grab meaning from the world, and in so doing, to expand its own capabilities. Style provides a chronicle of the human effort to preserve and capture the meaning of the visible world as it unfolds. On the other hand, the history of style manifests a unity beneath this apparent diversity, and reveals the common ground where the efforts of all painters are united in a common will to portray the visible. The history of painting reveals that there is a unity of human style: "We may speak of a unity of human style which transcends spatial and temporal distances to bring the gestures of all painters together in one single effort to express and the works in a cumulative history—a single art."[7] The art to which Merleau-Ponty refers here extends beyond the realm of painting and toward a human orientation toward expressively appropriating the world. Painting provides a context where style emerges more clearly, because it is an enterprise in which the development of a standpoint and a manner of practice are deliberately cultivated. But for Merleau-Ponty, painting constitutes only one instantiation of a more general phenomenon of style. It is to these other manifestations that we will turn in the next section.

Style as a General Ontological Category

In examining Merleau-Ponty's use of style as an ontological category, one must take into account the larger philosophical purposes it was designed to serve. The concept takes on significance in the context of Merleau-Ponty's efforts to reconstruct the ground of knowledge from within the domain of perception, and to explain how meaning happens in the world for a finite incarnate consciousness. It is my contention that the concept of style is crucial to that undertaking, for it functions as the qualitative correlate of the perspectivalism that is at the heart of Merleau-Ponty's ontology. Style is the affective or modal consequence of being an embodied point of view. Style permeates perception and its objects as the field of lived significance that arises from their intertwining.

In the objective phase of perception, style serves as the phenomenal presence of the thing's identity. Style reveals the thing in its suchness or carnal particularity. It is through its style that the perceptual object is present as what and how it is. Consider Merleau-Ponty's description of a piece of wood:

> Everything appears to us through a medium to which it lends its own fundamental quality; this piece of wood is neither a collection of colors and tactile data nor even their total *Gestalt* but something from which there emanates a woody essence; these "sense data" modulate a certain theme or illustrate a certain style which is the wood itself and which creates round this piece of wood and the perception I have of it a horizon of significance.[8]

In this context, style is employed to emphasize that in originary perception, the wood does not appear to us as a collection of qualities or as a set of necessary features. Essence here is used in the sense of scent or aroma to suggest the distinctive appearance which is the woodiness of the wood. What Merleau-Ponty wants to prove by this example is that even in the case of natural objects (things not explicitly penetrated by human purpose) there is a distinctive appearance which is intrinsic to the thing, a fusion of substance and quality which constitutes the thing in its suchness. The woodiness of the wood is not explicitly constituted. It is sensed or perceived as a field of significance that demands a response. Style's impact is thus most dramatically felt as a perceptual and implied motor response, rather than as a something discriminable to be named. Style is that in the thing which requires a perceptual and motor adequation, an adjustment of our anticipations and needs to those of the thing. This is especially true for objects of use. The style of a musical instrument consists in those particulars to which the musician must adjust when he plays. If we consider the wood as being part of a rail-backed chair, it becomes clearer how style can imply a motor and postural adjustment. The wood's style is now present as a certain kind of rigidity or resilience which allows for a restricted range of postures. The woodiness of the wood here serves to establish an affective space or atmosphere entirely different from that provided by the overstuffed armchair.

Structurally speaking, style serves to effect a kind of perceptual closure on the basis of which the thing is identifiable in its suchness. Style is that which secures the harmonious flow of adumbrations which grounds the movement from the thing-seen-from-a-point-of-view to the thing seen. In this sense style functions in a way analogous to Husserl's concept of a noematic nucleus. Both concepts represent a response to the perspectivalism inherent in perception. Because the perceptual synthesis is always made on the basis of inadequate evidence, there has to be some structure that ensures the coagulation of the flow of appearances. For Husserl, the unity of the perceptual object depended upon the adumbrations hovering about a core of meaning or inward closure. For Merleau-Ponty, however, the synthesis of the thing is entirely practical and perceptual. The thing or the individual can maintain a persistent presence for us because it is a consistent manner of appearing, that is, transferrable over time and space. Style is Merleau-Ponty's way of describing the emergent character of perceptual unification which can never be perfectly reconstituted in thought.

Style is also the way Merleau-Ponty describes the unity of the lived body and the presence of the Other as an incarnate consciousness. Part of his intent is to establish an explicit analogy between the lived body and the work of art on the ground that both are expressive fields which are capable of radiating significances which transcend them, and of intertwining with other significances in the world.

The lived body is unified by its style in a way analogous to the unification that style effects in the painting. Both exist as qualitative affective closures which permit of further unfoldings. The body image has the coherence of a style because, like the work of art, it is the expressive vehicle of a point of view. The lived body is not just an array of parts and functions, but a synergic unity linked by carnal intentional mappings. Style is that by virtue of which human behavior is not just a series of gestures—as Camus suggested, a "dumb show"—but a melodic unfolding of a point of view, a distinctive way of being and being-with. Having a style is, for Merleau-Ponty, a correlate of being a body and having a history: "I am a psychological and historical structure and have received with existence a manner of existing, a style. All my actions and thoughts stand in relation to this structure."[9] Style constitutes the horizons of significance which reveal the Other as an alternative orientation toward existence, a presence to the world analogous with and divergent from my own. This thought takes on special import when considered in the context of what is referred to as the problem of other minds. The existence of the Other was a problem for philosophy as long as reflection was taken as the paradigm of evidence for the presence of a consciousness, since the Other's internal life is not available as such. The concept of style, by contrast, secures the Other's direct accessibility as a distinctive way of inhabiting the world. The Other exists, not behind the flow of his activities and gestures, but through them. His integrity is not that of a conceptual consistency, but of an existential project which is directly present, even if I cannot reconstruct its inner workings.

Personal style is an uncanny admixture of the anonymous and the personal, the inherited and the created. It is lived as an ambiguous exchange of significance between the individual and the world he inhabits. Style emerges as an intertwining of freedom and facticity, as the appropriation of a given situation and the transcendence of it. A personal style is never simply given or simply chosen. It is a response to and founded upon the conditions of existence and embodiment. It constitutes the establishment of a lived coherence which gathers the elements of existence into a life, a project with direction and character. Style ensures my existence of a stability, while allowing for the possibility of growth and change.

The integrative function of a style will become clearer when we contrast it with a pathological situation in which the capacity of a style to link existence into an intentional fluidity is largely absent. Schneider is a man whose body and world are damaged by the schrapnel lodged in his brain. This leaves Schneider with impaired perceptual functioning and a world that is qualitatively impoverished. People hold no sexual or social interest for him. He has difficulty conversing, for he cannot remember a story except by memorizing its facts one by one. He cannot gesture spontaneously, but can do so only by creating a situation that demands that gesture. Schneider is living out a moribund style in a world devoid of the intentional connections that are normally present for the healthy subject. His is a ritualized existence tied to the actual. The fluid exchanges of meaning which occur for the healthy subject are, in Schneider's world, solidified and rigid.

In ordinary perception, however, style permeates the subjective phase. Perception, according to Merleau-Ponty, "already stylizes."[10] Perception stylizes because it cannot help but to constitute and express a point of view at the same time that it is the condition for revealing a world that inevitably transcends it. There is no articulation of the world that is free from perspectival conditions, and there is no standpoint that reveals the thing-in-itself. Style establishes the perceptual field as a sphere of activity by offering a promise of closure which permits of further unfoldings without sacrificing existential stability. In the human dimension, style is that which provides a general horizon of continuity and purpose which gathers the world into a sphere of significance or the promise of it. Style characterizes the nature of existential coherence under the conditions of finitude.

The final context in which Merleau-Ponty appeals to the concept of style is in the realm of cognition and intellection. Style is a component of the process and objects of knowing as the phase of predisclosure or fore-having. The temporality of the knowledge process is such that its objects reveal themselves first as preemptory articulations, promises of significance. As Merleau-Ponty expresses it "every concept is first a horizonal generality, a generality of style."[11]

Before we have penetrated a philosopher's thought through a process of analysis, we sense its meaning, Merleau-Ponty says, by assimilating its style. The work of the philosopher reaches us in a way akin to the impact of the work of art. Both are systems of equivalences which establish a coherent orientation toward the world they articulate. Philosophy is thus considered by Merleau-Ponty to be an essentially interpretative activity which depends on the preconceptual capacities of its style in order to communicate. Thought proceeds not in spite of the affective context it presupposes but instead relies upon this basic level of significance as a background for its thematic assertions. This is why Merleau-Ponty understands philosophy as always involving a retrieval of its context as well as a transcendence of it. When he characterizes phenomenology as a style of philosophizing, he is calling attention to the fact that the meaning of phenomenology is a meaning in genesis.[12] Unlike a doctrine which gathers itself around a common set of tenets or principles, phenomenology's awareness of itself as a movement arose from practice, and a predisclosed sense of its common affective ground and purpose. Its development as a movement testified to the possibility of acting upon a set of significances which become explicit only in retrospect.

The ultimate payoff of style for a philosophy of the lived world is that it makes explicit those structures which secure the possibility of meaning in the world which has not yet become transparent to thought. As the qualitative correlate of human finitude, style constitutes the transformation of facticity and point of view into a mode of access to being. Style offers the prospect of a thoroughgoing perspectivalism that does not fall prey to skepticism. The diversity of style, in art and in the human enterprise at large, provides powerful evidence of the fact that the world will never be reduced to a conceptual transparency from a distance. By appealing to the concept of style in novel contexts, Merleau-Ponty reminds us that the world is an essentially expressive field, and that there will always be something to say about it.

12

Since Lascaux

Olivier Mongin
Translated by Michael B. Smith

esthetics permanently subtends Merleau-Ponty's thought and permeates his entire work, to the point of becoming synonymous with his philosophical reflection. "To the degree that Merleau-Ponty's philosophy is a phenomenology of perception, it may be said to be in its entirety within the domain of aesthetics."[1] "From 'Cézanne's Doubt' to 'Eye and Mind,' from *Phenomenology of Perception* to *The Visible and the Invisible,* Maurice Merleau-Ponty never ceased meditating on vision. In the room in which he suddenly collapsed one evening in May, 1961, an opened book, to which he was never done referring, bespoke his last labors over [Descartes's] *La dioptrique.*"[2]

But it is not enough to recognize the importance of the *aesthetic imperative*: we must also grasp its specific role, so that we do not make the mistake of falsely construing it as a general theme that might take the most varied forms (articles on the novel, cinema, or painting; frequent references to Stendhal, Valéry, Proust . . .), or even of presenting it as that side of Merleau-Ponty's reflections that progressively takes the place of his political thought—whose dialectic adventures would be construed as leading him to the brink of skepticism and aestheticism! But quite to the contrary, the *aesthetic imperative* allows Merleau-Ponty's work to gather its strength for a renewal, a metamorphosis. Restricting my considerations to the area under scrutiny, painting does not follow history— aesthetics does not follow politics. Painting necessitates a different view of history, by initiating a reflection on the event, on primordial historic-

ity—of which the pictorial work is an exemplary figure. Painting, far
from diverting Merleau-Ponty's attention away from history, from the
flesh of the world, brings it back to it constantly, by way of a reflection on
the event.

"We would doubtless rediscover the concept of history if we accustomed ourselves to modeling it after the example of the arts" (S, 91).

"I shall entitle my book *Introduction à la prose du monde* [*Introduction to the Prose of the World*]. In this work I shall elaborate the category
of prose beyond the confines of literature to give it a sociological
meaning."[3]

"This philosophy, yet to be elaborated, is what animates the
painter—not when he expresses his opinions about the world but in that
instant when his vision becomes gesture, when, in Cézanne's words, he
'thinks in painting' " (EM, 139–40).

Cézanne, or the Gesture of Painting

Merleau-Ponty wrote a substantial piece on Cézanne as early as in 1945.
"Cézanne's Doubt," published in the journal *Fontaine*, made its contribution to the debate over the issue of creative freedom, a debate that has
since become one of existentialism's classical themes. Availing himself of
Freud's psychoanalytic interpretation of Leonardo da Vinci in *Leonardo
da Vinci: A Study in Psychosexuality*,[4] Merleau-Ponty reflects on the question of the influence of Cézanne's life on his painting, and does not elude
the usual paradox such a question unavoidably raises: "Two things are
certain about freedom: that we are never determined and yet that we
never change. . . . It is up to us to understand both these things simultaneously, as well as the way freedom dawns in us without breaking our
bonds with the world" (CD, 72).

Yet this text is not to be read as a purple passage of existential
literature: it develops an entire critique of historical determinism, of interpretation by History—which soon becomes inextricably linked with
the movement of the aesthetic reflection. "Cézanne's Doubt" proceeds
by elimination—by a progressive discussion of the usual paradigms. Discourse that consists in reducing the new to the old, the actual to the
inactual, or in seeking the reason of History, is rejected. Why try to understand a given period of Cézanne by the one preceding it, or his *Mont
Sainte-Victoire* by the first sketches? Why relate Cézanne's work exclusively to the impressionist influence? "Left to himself, he was able to look

at nature as only a human being can. The meaning of his work cannot be determined from his life. This meaning will not become any clearer in the light of art history—that is, by considering influences (the Italian school and Tintoretto, Delacroix, Courbet and the impressionists), Cézanne's technique, or even his own pronouncements on his work" (ibid., 61). Thus the history of art and the history of the individual are both artifices, gratuitous constructions that make it impossible to grasp the specificity of the painter's gesture. This is a double critique, that foreshadows the strong case Merleau-Ponty made against Malraux's *Musée imaginare* in "Indirect Language" (chap. 3 of *The Prose of the World*). It is an impassioned polemic that will allow Merleau-Ponty to show that the museographical representation of the history of painting is indissociable from the romantic vision of the Great Individual, and that the Individual and History go hand in hand.

> Malraux is unable to avoid the idea of a "subterranean torrent" of history which reunites the most distant paintings, a Painting which works behind the painter's back, a Reason in history of which he is the instrument. These Hegelian monsters are the antithesis and complement of Malraux's individualism. Once one has shut up art in the most secret reaches of the individual, the convergence of independent works can only be explained by some destiny that rules over them. But when, on the contrary, one puts painting back into the presence of the world, as I am attempting to do, what becomes of Painting in itself or the Spirit of Painting?[5]

What becomes of the Spirit of Painting? To answer such a question involves abandoning the concepts of both History and the individual, and implies less concern for a vague defense and illustration of the freedom of the creator than for leaving the painter face to face with himself or herself—face to face with nature. As in Cézanne's case, the painter par excellence. "Left to himself, he was able to look at nature as only a human being can." Thus, the painting must be seen, perceived, in all its autonomy, in all its singularity above all, inseparably from the gesture of painting, the act of painting. "Because he has returned to the source of silent and solitary experience on which culture and the exchange of ideas have been built in order to take cognizance of it, the artist launches his work just as a man once launched the first word" (CD, 69). As a work that is launched, a simultaneous *launching* of the world and the artist, the painting is a structuring of perception, that coherent deformation of the world that the perceptual act alone can make possible. The painting is, as it were, a supplementary outgrowth of perception, an excrescence of the human gaze. "Pictorial expression takes up and goes beyond the structuring of the world begun in perception" (PW, 61). Painting transforms perception into a gesture that is amplified in the pictorial work. Merleau-Ponty, in his analyses of Renoir's *Les Lavandières*, would again describe the painter's gesture as the prolongation of the work of perception. "Thus perception already stylizes . . . " (PW, 60).

Lascaux

But is it enough to stop here, having established a relationship between the Spirit of Painting and a philosophy of perception, as if the latter were a broadened prolongation of the theme of individual freedom? "Cézanne's Doubt" and "Indirect Language" authorize our further specification of the relationship of painting to History, to temporality. If the gesture of painting stands out separately from History (both the History of the individual and of painting) it is because it is first and foremost an event.[6] It is that event that reappears along the course of time ever since human beings have attempted to reflect, to focus on the experience of perception, that originary experience of his relation to the world. "But indeed only a human being is capable of such a vision, which penetrates right to the root of things beneath the imposed order of humanity. All indications are that animals cannot *look at* things, cannot penetrate them in expectation of nothing but the truth" (CD, 67). "It is the expressive operation of the body, begun in the least perception, that is amplified into painting and art. The field of pictorial significations was opened the moment a human being appeared in the world" (PW, 83). Merleau-Ponty, echoing the prevalent use of Lascaux imagery of the period, also to be found in Georges Bataille and Maurice Blanchot,[7] sees in the painter's gesture the autofiguration of humanity, the structuring of the human. Indissociably the painter's gesture marks an event and gives humanity form. "And the first drawing on a cave wall founded a tradition only because it was the recipient of another: that of perception" (ibid.).

The painter's gesture is that gestation of humanity that will go on completing itself forever improvising, outside all of History's reasons. Humanity, the consciousness of humanity, the realization of the human is not at the end of a History, the last step of a journey; it is present in every painter's gesture "since Lascaux." It is not the privilege of a fraction of the world, an elite, but a universal experience since human beings have been portraying themselves. "The first cave paintings opened a limitless field of exploration, posited the world as something to be painted or drawn, hailed an indefinite future of painting. That is what moves us in them, makes them speak to us, and causes us to respond to them through metamorphoses in which they collaborate with us" (PW, 72).

Painting/Language

The human Universal is not the end, the last note of the Music of History: it resonates the moment the human being performs his perception, that little concerto of humanity. The fact that Merleau-Ponty's aesthetics, his interpretation of the Spirit of Painting, is one with a critique of Hegel's view of History, can be seen even more clearly when, in "Indirect Language," he distinguishes several historical rhythms. Hegelian History bursts apart, splitting into several forms of history, several temporalities. Orchestrating a polyphonic reflection on language and painting, Merleau-Ponty presents *a threefold historicity*.[8]

1. Historicity as event history, synonymous with that experience in which humanity "calls itself back to itself," and the paradigm of which is painting. That history-event is crucial, since it breaks with the representation of the Universal of the philosophies of History.[9]

2. Historicity as an integrating history, synonymous with memory, cultural history, symbolic complexes. An indispensable history, without which humanity would have no memory of itself. An ambiguous, fragile history, that can always lay claim to totalization, to "closing" History, as in the case of philosophical discourse; whereas "[t]he idea of universal painting, of a totalization of painting, of painting's being fully and definitively accomplished is an idea bereft of sense" (EM, 148). Event history *accumulates* pictorial expressions, while advent history tends to *integrate* experiences of language, running the risk of one of them claiming to totalize the others.

3. Historicity as museum history, a pathetic, flat, passive history, "full of traditions," since it juxtaposes works as strangers to one another. That history is forgetfulness, and kills memory by showing nothing but disconnected elements, ignorance and exteriority.

Faced with such historical dissonance, the attitudes of language and of painting toward time will be opposite, as demonstrated in the following textual montage (which contains excerpts from PW, 99–101).

Painting

Event
Each new painting occurs in the world inaugurated by the first painting. It fulfills the vow of the past; it has the past's proxy and acts in its name. But it does not contain the past in a manifest state and is a memory for us only if we also know the history of painting. It is not a memory for itself and does not pretend to totalize all that made it possible.

Each new painting . . . does not pretend to totalize all that made it possible.

Painting is always in suspense; it accumulates; it does not integrate.

The past of language is not only a past that has been overcome, but also understood. Painting is mute.

It is essential to truth to be integral, whereas no valid painting ever claimed to be integral.

Language

Culture, Memory, Traditions
The word, on the other hand . . . claims to recapture, recover, contain the past in substance. . . . [The word is not content to push the past away] in making a place for itself in the world; it wants to conserve it in spirit or in its meaning. The properties of fractions do not falsify those of whole numbers, nor do those of solid geometry falsify those of plane geometry.

It is characteristic of the algorithm to preserve former formulations as it changes them into themselves and their legitimate meanings.

Here sedimentation does not only accumulate one creation on top of another: it integrates.

The writer can conceive of himself only within an established language, whereas every painter recreates his own. . . . The transformations that it [the written work] brings to the language remain recognizable after the writer is gone, whereas the painter's experience, once it has passed into the work of his successors, ceases to be identifiable.

The attitudes of language and painting with regard to time are almost opposite. The painting, despite the costumes of the subjects, the furniture and utensils depicted, and the historical circumstances to which it may allude, establishes its charm immediately within a dreaming eternity we can easily return to

centuries later, even without having been initiated to the history of the civilization that bore it. Writing, however, begins to
communicate its most lasting meaning to us only after having
introduced us to circumstances and arguments long since past.
The *Provincial Letters* would tell us nothing if they did not
bring the theological disputes of the seventeenth century back
to the present. *The Red and the Black* would tell us nothing
without the gloom of the French Revolution. But painting pays
curiously for the immediate access to permanence it allows itself, for it is subject much more than writing to the passage of
time. Leonardo da Vinci's masterpieces make us think of him
rather than of ourselves, and of Italy rather than mankind. Literature, on the contrary, insofar as it gives up the hypocritical
prudence of art and confronts time bravely—displaying it
rather than vaguely evoking it—"grounds it in meaning" forever. Sophocles, Thucydides and Plato do not reflect Greece,
they hold it out for inspection—even for us who are so far
from it. (PW, 101–2)

From that opposition between painting and language there
emerges no radical superiority of painting. "The inferiority of painting is
supposedly due to its being recorded only in works and its inability to
become the foundation of everyday human relations, whereas the life of
language, because it makes use of ready-made words and a sonorous material we all possess in ample supply, nourishes itself through its own
[perceptual?] commentary on speech" (PW, 110). Yet if there is a sense
in which painting has the advantage, it is in its universality, in the experience of humanity from which it is inseparable. One who has forgotten
the painter's gesture may have delusions about the meaning of History,
may want to *integrate* it definitively, while painting reminds us that we will
never possess the ultimate meaning of the painter's gesture.

The Figure of the Universal

Confronted with such conceptual architecture, one might smile. . . . It
seems to me more interesting to point out that its course runs parallel to
the reflection of Claude Lévi-Strauss, and that there is a debate with
structuralism discernable in all this. Merleau-Ponty, building a radical
case against the philosophies of History, has helped us better understand, after the fact, the role of structuralism; its positive spirit, more-

over. What he retained from his reading of Mauss and Lévi-Strauss was the fundamental thought (without which it is idle to claim to have escaped from the domination of History) that the Universal is shared by all humanity since Lascaux—that no fraction of the world-in-becoming can pretend to possess the meaning of Lascaux after the fact. Just as "uncivilized thought" is quite as human as rational thought, the Lascaux cave paintings are just as human as Klee's canvases. Without any forced interpretation, it is easy to grasp that in these pages Merleau-Ponty has pursued a vigorous reflection on the human Universal and, potentially, on the ethical Universal—which was a radical departure from the intellectual preoccupations of his day.[10]

In sum, painting remained the condition of possibility for that entire new approach; it is impossible to separate the domains of reflection (in this case his aesthetics and his reflections on History) in Merleau-Ponty.

Painting/Music

We still must grasp more precisely why painting, the painter's gesture, is an exemplary mode of expression in Merleau-Ponty, and why Lévi-Strauss favors music over painting, and especially over all reflection on history and the event. Most often the interpretation of the relationship between music and painting is carried out in Lévi-Strauss's terms: i.e., the question becomes whether or not *painting* is a *language*, whether it falls under the law of double articulation.[11]

In the opening chapter of *The Raw and the Cooked*, Lévi-Strauss sees this quality of double articulation in painting (the first articulation being colors, the second their arrangement), but he indicates that the second level remains nonetheless a prisoner of the sensible aspect of the colors.[12]

> Painting organizes intellectually, by means of culture, the natural world, which was already present to it as a sensible organization. Music moves in exactly the opposite direction, for culture was already present to it, but in a sensible form, before it organizes it intellectually by means of nature. The fact that the entire manifold upon which music operates is of the cultural order explains why music is born entirely free from the bonds of representation, which keep painting dependent upon the sensible world and its organization into objects.[13]

With painting we do not escape from the sensible. . . . Thus, on
an entirely different level, Lévi-Strauss specifies that painting is dependent upon the sensible in the language of culture, while music attempts
to translate that language directly into meaning, which allows it to avoid
the step of the sensible. But does not such a dependence upon the sensible have a positive side? Is it not that originary experience, ever brought
back, that makes possible the event, that gesture of humanity repeated
by painting—whereas music closes temporality? Further, is it not the de-
preciation of the perceptual and the sensible that leads Lévi-Strauss to
miss the event and draws him into the famous polemic on History with
Sartre in *Savage Mind*?[14] Did the structuralist critique of the subject and
of consciousness have of necessity to lead to a denial of all possible forms
of historicity? At that time, Merleau-Ponty's thought showed great originality, since, despite his having perceived that structuralism could favor
a different approach to the human Universal, he did not break with a
reflection on temporality, the new. . . . That thought, far more complex
than it appears, does not do well when departmentalized, being so much
compounded of interwoven concepts, crossed intelligences.

Here we have a work that boldly faces the modern world, a work
that puzzles over historicity and humanity in the wake of the breakdown
of Reason and History. Once we have recognized this polyphonism (in
Bakhtin's sense), this internal dialogue, this labor of the work, how can
we not read "Eye and Mind," a text devoted to painting and aesthetics,
as a reflection on history—how can we not read its meditation on the
internal dissonance in Rodin's sculpture as an interrogation on temporality? Merleau-Ponty attempts to conceive of an active temporality in
which the one and the other, the Same and the Other, do not cancel one
another out.[15] A temporality in which coexistence would be inseparable
from dissonance: neither submission to the One, nor dispersal, scatter-
ing . . . which always returns to the Same. At which point the painting
takes on a quasihistorical form—becomes a prodigious sound-box, or
rather sight-box for our world!

"Vision alone teaches us that beings that are different, 'exterior,'
foreign to one another, are yet absolutely *together*" (EM, 146). If we were
to continue in this line of thought, we would eventually see that the references to Heideggerian Being (the neutrality and scant ethics of which
are well known since Levinas) are reflected in Merleau-Ponty as simultaneity, coexistence, the Other. Having taken aesthetics as our guideline,
we find that it leads us into a silent dialogue with ethics, with politics—
provided we do not treat words as fetishes.

Music, Painting, Structure: Reflections by Claude Lévi-Strauss[16]

Merleau-Ponty deeply enjoyed music, as the memory of many conversations attests. And yet, from the first pages of "Eye and Mind," it appears that he discounts it, to the benefit of painting alone. He puts on one side the writer and the philosopher, from whom "opinions and advice" are required, and on the other the painter, the only one "entitled to look at everything without being obliged to appraise what he sees" (EM, 123). As for music, he mentions it only briefly, to exclude it. "Too far beyond the world and the designatable to depict anything but certain schemata of Being—its ebb and flow, its growth, its upheavals, its turbulence" (ibid.).

It is already odd to observe that that way of understanding music reappears in *The Visible and the Invisible*, but transferred to science. "The deductive science renders explicit the structures, the pivots, certain traits of the inner framework of the world" (VI, 226). And just as "Eye and Mind" finds drawing somewhat suspect, giving it less status than the depiction of light and color, whereas *The Visible and the Invisible* integrates both aspects into the art of painting and gives them equal importance (VI, 211–12), so it is on the same level that painting and music will henceforth be placed. This is borne out by the very last pages of the text (VI, 149–55), containing a meditation originating in the one Vintevil's sonata prompted in Proust—in which music, far from being a "schema" on the hither side of Being, is said to give us "a carnal experience" of it.

Thus, in pages written almost contemporaneously, two different ways of envisaging music coexist: one that almost denies it the right to Being, the other that sees in it one of Being's purest manifestations. And both are approaches to the same problem, but they are couched, in one case, in phenomenological terms, and in terms of ontology in the other. For, in "Eye and Mind," it is a certain order of perception that is appealed to, to instruct us about Being, which is often described as "vertical," because the knowledge we obtain of it consists in "baring all the roots" (VI, 169). The reasons for the choice of visual perception are clear: people rely essentially on it to assess silent objects, the majority of which at any given moment are beyond our sense of touch. Painters can instruct us on the intimate nature of that constant and common perception, but musicians cannot do so on auditory perception, because music is foreign to articulated language, and because musical sounds and their concatenation, unlike light and color, are cultural works. Seen in this perspective, these works break with the naive experience of pre-objective Being, rather than, like painting, leading toward it. In *The Visible and the Invisible,* on the contrary, the truth of perception taken as a goal is subordinate to the truth of Being, the former being reduced to an approximation of the latter. Mr. Ingres, who it appears was wont to say that a well-drawn picture was by the same token sufficiently well painted, would not easily have found his place in the selection contained in "Eye and Mind," but *The Visible and the Invisible* rehabilitates him. "The line, the stroke of the brush, and the visible work are but the trace of a total movement of Speech, which goes unto Being as a whole, and . . . this movement contains expression through line as well as expression through color" (VI, 217). Hence it is less surprising that music, for which "Eye and Mind," interestingly, uses the term "schema" ["*épure*"],[17] should find its place at the heart of Being, just as the schema itself (taken now in its literal sense) regains its place at the heart of painting understood as constituting a movement toward Being.

Perhaps by looking in this direction we can understand the ambivalence of Merleau-Ponty's position on structuralism, to which he always showed himself sympathetic and encouraging, with some reservations. The notion of structure, like music, could alternatively hold quite distinct status in his thought: sometimes "schema" or "pivot" of Being, and nothing but that, with the risk of that abstract form being used for quasiscientific purposes, to set out to conquer subjectivity. Then, "when it [science] has completely invested what it first put aside as subjective, it will gradually put it back; but it will integrate it as a particular case of the relations and objects that, for itself, define the world. Then the world will close in over itself, and, except for what within us thinks and builds science, that impartial spectator, that inhabits us, we will have become parts or moments of the Great Object" (VI, 15).

13

Eye and Mind

Mikel Dufrenne

E ye and Mind" is one of the last texts of Merleau-Ponty, and perhaps
one of his finest. Sartre wrote of it, " 'Eye and Mind' says all provided one knows how to decipher it."[1] But can this be done? Rather
than risk such an undertaking, I would like principally to comment
on the title itself.

One notices immediately in "Eye and Mind" that the two words
are treated unequally in the text, for "eye" appears repeatedly in the
writing of Merleau-Ponty, while "mind" is rarely mentioned. No doubt
this is due to a certain danger in denominating it in the manner that
delighted "philosophers of mind." For the mind is not an organ like the
eye, nor is it a substance that can be designated by a substantive. If it is
called by name, it is for the purpose of designating certain acts characteristic of what *The Structure of Behavior* called the human order. These
acts demonstrate a cogito that seeks to be transparent to itself. In them is
consummated (*se consomme*) the separation of the subject and the object
that has already taken shape but that is not yet completed in vision: in
brief, thinking as opposed to seeing. My first point of questioning bears
precisely upon the *and*. What is the meaning of this conjunction? It cannot signify a dialectical relation, since there are only two terms; unless we
adhere, as does Adorno, to a negative dialectic, in which case *and* would
designate a relation of opposition as in being and nonbeing. But it can
also mean a relation of priority as in cause and effect, or even a relation
of complementarity as in form and content. Obviously, only a reading of
the text will permit an answer to this question, and if the text stresses one

of these meanings of *and*—namely, opposition—it persuades us perhaps not to exclude the others.

To begin with, the eye is foremost: it is first in the title because it is first in the becoming (*le devenir*) of man. Man sees before he thinks, and no doubt he arrives at thought because it is aroused by vision, although Merleau-Ponty does not describe this advent. In any case, seeing is opposed to thinking, and it is precisely toward this theme that analyses are directed. For example, if these analyses invoke painting at great length, it is in order to show that "we cannot see how a mind would be able to paint." All the difficulty lies here: By hardening the opposition between eye and mind, can we still account for the emergence of thinking, for the movement leading existence to a reflexive life? Between seeing and thinking, contemporary philosophy is given a mediation: *speaking,* which is the contemporary of seeing. Merleau-Ponty, however, does not invoke this mediation, and it is here that Lyotard, for example, raises his principal objection. According to Lyotard, Merleau-Ponty forgets that nothing happens before "entry into language," save the still blind vicissitudes of drives. It is true that Merleau-Ponty does not situate speaking in seeing, for his analysis of painting excludes discourse—and not only that of the expert or semiotician but also that of the painting itself. Poussin wrote to Chanteloup: "Read the story and the painting." Merleau-Ponty does not seem interested in paintings that tell a story, unless it is the fundamental story, that is, the very genesis of appearing. Thus speaking neither kindles nor illuminates seeing. On the contrary, speaking itself might be understood as a type of seeing: the speaking subject (*l'homme parlant*) is in language as he is in the world, he harmonizes with its thickness (*l'épaisseur*) as he does with the flesh of the sensuous, he lives it by inhabiting it. Moreover, speaking can perhaps be equated to seeing for the purpose of disclosing it. This would be the language of "hyperreflection" of which *The Visible and the Invisible* speaks. This language "becomes philosophy itself," endeavoring to "express beyond significations our mute contact with things when they are not yet things said."[2] This is indeed the admirable language with which Merleau-Ponty approaches brute being (*l'être brut*), leaving it to speak within himself as the dream allows desire to speak.

If philosophy requires this effort, it is because seeing, to repeat, is irreducible to thinking and cannot be comprehended by it. But what about the reverse? Can we not comprehend thinking through seeing? Is there not a type of seeing that, far from opposing thinking, would be its auxiliary? When, confronted with a proposition, we respond "I see," are we not in our response equating thought with a type of vision? *Wesen-*

schau is still *Schau*. Besides, thought has willing recourse to a visible of which it avails itself: one has only to think of geometrical figures, linguistic "trees," or the diagrams of graphic semiology. For Descartes, space without hiding places in which these signs are drawn is precisely the in-itself that knowledge masters. We can then ask the following question: Are there not two regimes of vision of which at least one, since it is regulated according to thought, presupposes it while the other precedes it? Merleau-Ponty does not state this explicitly, but it is what Descartes suggests to him. Indeed, if we follow Descartes: "There is no vision without thought. But *it is not enough* to think in order to see. Vision . . . is born 'as occasioned' by what happens in the body."[3] So "the enigma of vision is not eliminated by Descartes; it is relegated from the thought of seeing to vision in act." But Descartes is unwilling to "sound out this abyss." What is important for him is the edification of knowledge; and today science does not even trouble calling for metaphysics.

It can be said that Merleau-Ponty, facing this renunciation of reflection, directs all his attention to the savage regime of vision, and perhaps all the more so because this regime is never obliterated: even when the mind inspects signs of convenience, or, as Alain said, when perception brings judgment into play, the eye remains present and open, to the point of sometimes leading the rational vision astray in the same manner that discourse is distorted once tropes (*figures*) are introduced into it. Perhaps what one calls "totalizing thought" (*la pensée de survol*) is the vocation of thinking, whenever the subject stands at a distance with respect to the object in order to become its "master and possessor." This is precisely the purpose of language whenever it allows for the passage from presence to representation. This thought is, however, never fully realized, as it is always sustained by perceptual faith that anchors us in the truth of the sensuous. The eye, said Breton, exists in a savage state, and it may be that it is never completely tamed, even when it is employed by understanding; no more than when vision, instructed by language, becomes the utilitarian and assuring (*sécurisante*) vision of a prosaic reality.

Merleau-Ponty thinks of the savage in vision according to the Husserlian model of passive synthesis. This vision does not organize the visible, nor does it bestow a meaning upon it or constitute it as readable and expressible in words. It receives the visible, rising from an invisible that still clings to it; one can say at the very most that vision opens itself to the visible which is given to it. This act of giving is an event in the visual field. Lyotard says of this event that "it can only be situated in the vacant space opened by desire."[4] He also states that "it belongs to this giving which releases us." But what about this *us*? To think *id*, one must still think *ego.* And why say release us rather than seize us? We are only released when and because we are seized. If there is an event, something happens to someone. In this case we have an act of giving. It is no doubt correct that the subject does not exist prior to the event, for he is born with and from it. Is this a transcendental subject in a transcendental field? Why not? But for Merleau-Ponty, this transcendental field is not the place of desire, the ephemeral film traversed by anonymous fluxes. Rather, it is brute being, this originary being (*l'originaire*) that the philosopher calls flesh: the "last notion," he says, because it is the first. This event, forever starting anew, which takes place as well as inaugurating place, is the bursting forth of originary being. Consequently we have the upheaval of appearing, for this bursting forth produces a chiasm and institutes a distance between man and things, born simultaneously and continuing to exist for themselves without ever radically separating from each other. In addition, the reversibility of the visible and the seer, this double dehiscence of the visible in the seer and the seer in the visible attests that "things are the secret folds of my flesh."[5] We therefore cannot evade the question of origin. It is not the body that gives access to originary being, it is originary being that gives access to the body. And in the end, such is indeed the enigma of vision: far from the eye explaining vision, as a reductive science would want, vision explains the eye. Bergson has already claimed this, but for Merleau-Ponty this resilience (*le ressort*) of vision is not creative evolution, but rather the bursting forth of originary being.

Merleau-Ponty examines painting in order to think the unthinkable, and in particular he examines the kind of painting instituted by Cézanne. Classical painting can lead us astray, for one is inclined to believe that it originates from and appeals to the mind. On the one hand, in fact, the painters of the Renaissance claim that their art has attained the status of the liberal arts by their use of mathematics in order to substitute an artificial perspective for a natural one. In this manner their drawings are based on a fundamental law. On the other hand, these artists appeal to a spectator who is more concerned with the intelligible than with the sensuous. This can be seen in the perceptual studies of Alberti: in order to entertain a painting constructed through this perspective, the spectator must see with a single eye (monocular perspective), situated at the required distance and which is neither spherical nor mobile. But everything changes once painters abandon this exacting truth in their painting and look for another one that is primary and has no need of justification according to the standards of knowledge.

Truth is an unveiling; once again it is the bursting forth of originary being, the "deflagration of being," or the apparition of what Klee calls the *Urbildliche*. This being is not a different agency, even less a transcendental one. It is born in tearing itself from the invisible at the same moment that vision is awakened. Painting accomplishes what hyper-reflection tries to say. What the painter, through sheer patience, wants to see as well as to present for our seeing, is the very birth of seeing in contact with its newly formed image. He wants to take this moment when "things become things and . . . world becomes world" by surprise.[6] He is not interested in what follows, after language or culture, or in what Adorno calls the administered world, in which fruit bowls are machine-turned and mountains explored by geographers. The painter returns to a pre-real, which is also a sur-real in the sense meant by the surrealists, as their objective chance is but another name for the inaugural event in which man is still very much mingled with things. The painter leads the noumenon back to what is properly the phenomenon, that is, to the manifestation of appearing.

We speak of appearing, and not appearance. Cézanne is not an impressionist, even when he invokes his "little sensation." For him it is not a question of restoring a truth of the seen that would dismiss line while making color vibrate; nor is it a question of the production of a playing field for fantasies brought about by the deconstruction of a system of representation. Cézanne does not deconstruct, he pre-constructs. He does not shatter the fruit bowl, he shows us its genesis, that is, not its production but its coming into the visible. And this space that the fruit bowl comes to inhabit is not a predetermined one in which it is able to take form, it is rather a space that springs from it, a dimension of its flesh. And it is definitely a question of the flesh: it is this texture of the sensuous ordered in this case according to the visible. The mathematical Logos by which the mind informs reality is unable to account for it, and thus this flesh appeals to another Logos, "a system of equivalences, a Logos of lines, of lighting, of colors, of reliefs, of masses,"[7] according to which a face of the world accedes to visibility.

Thus the eye deserves to be mentioned first in the title. It is not, however, for the purpose of designating a determined organ assigned to a precise function, but rather for designating this strange power of opening of the flesh. This flesh, which is not yet a body, is itself reflected once a chiasm is brought about in it. The eye, putting us into the world by opening a world to us, precedes the mind. But was it still necessary then to mention mind? We know that Merleau-Ponty challenges "totalizing thought" and the philosophies of consciousness that consider it as both possible and praiseworthy, and that he also does his best to render thought enigmatic by showing its roots in perception. The philosopher's thinking, forever beginning, as Husserl said, is a thinking about the beginning. It tells us that no thought can be absolutely liberated from this beginning, for mind is grounded in eye. What remains afterward is for the cogito to declare itself and proclaim its rights as well as a science to be developed and a human order instituted. Man forgets that he was born and that he belongs to what gives birth to him. One must therefore mention the mind even if it is only carnal and savage, even if, in order to think, it is necessary to be, and this being is always a being in the world, a seer-visible (un voyant-visible).

In the end, there is still a final question concerning the title: eye, of course, but why not ear or hand, for that matter? We have found in Merleau-Ponty the idea of a primitive Logos, a system of equivalences between elements of the visible. But this system of equivalences is also constituted between diverse sensorial registers, as Phenomenology of Perception has already indicated. Synesthesias are the lot of all perception. The flesh is polymorphous and polyvalent. The sensuous must also allow itself pluralization, for no matter how subtle the discourse of hyperreflection may be, it can only divulge orginary being as having already burst forth. For the language it organizes already designates a constituted world where the body has organs and where the perceived is reduced to distinct objects. In order to remain close to this savage Logos, should Merleau-Ponty have written "the sensuous and mind"? In any case, what "Eye and Mind" says about the visible can also be said of the sonorous and the tactile, since it is linked to them. But it seems that Merleau-Ponty wanted to bestow a radical privilege upon the visible. If he evokes music, it is in order to cast it aside. "It does not depict anything but certain outlines of being."[8] As for the tactile, he excludes it from painting: "When, apropos of Italian painting, the young Berenson spoke of an evocation of tactile values, and he wasn't the only one, he could hardly have been more mistaken; painting evokes nothing, least of all the tactile."[9] But in the absence of evocations there are equivalences attesting to the fact that the whole body is invoked. It is on this condition that the tactile makes itself visible. Vision is not devouring, it is mobilizing.

In the end the eye is still the most important organ for what Descartes called the practice of life. Here there is no need to invoke the symbolism with which psychoanalysis burdens it! I would willingly say that if Merleau-Ponty chose to write "Eye and Mind," it is simply because he loved painting. Others will say that his desire was invested (s'investissait) in paintings rather than in music; and after all, that is not such a bad investment!

14

Cézanne's Mirror Stage

Hugh J. Silverman

S elf-portraiture is the hidden agenda of Maurice Merleau-Ponty's essay "Eye and Mind" (1961).[1] Although he does not mention any particular self-portraits nor does he cite the activity that produces them, the question of self-portraiture serves as the organizing feature of the whole essay. The text is permeated by discussions of painting, the eye, the painter's hands, mirrors, the specular image, and my body as both seeing (*voyant*) and seen (*visible*). All the necessary elements of self-portraiture are available in Merleau-Ponty's account of the relation between eye and mind. Although the text can be (and has been) read without even raising the question of self-portraiture, the complex workings of the essay become clearer once this feature is uncovered.[2] And for an understanding of the meaning and practice of self-portraiture, Merleau-Ponty has a great deal to offer.

A self-portrait is produced in the activity of self-portraiture. The self-portrait results from the painter's practice. The self seeks to render itself visible by painting a picture of itself with the use of a mirror. What appears, what is made visible is the painted self. Working directly from a single mirror without applying any correction in the rendering of what is seen, the painter will appear to be painting with the left hand if the actual procedure was done with the right. Although many self-portraits show only the head and shoulders, the specular image still produces a left-right inversion which is understood only when the function of the mirror is taken into account. Van Gogh's severed ear is indeed on the left side as one might expect for a right-handed person who might be inclined to cut off an ear. However in the various self-portraits which were produced after the self-mutilation took place, it seems as though Van Gogh has lost his right ear. Specific self-portraits of Dürer, Rembrandt, Corot, Pissarro, and De Chirico show them to be painting with their left hand—indicating that they are each in fact right-handed. Other Dürers and Rembrandts, a Reynolds, and a Kokoschka show that the hands and arms have been readjusted to look as though they were not engaged in the act of painting at all. In these cases, both hands are occupied with some other function. A 1971 self-portrait of Max Beckmann shows him painting with his right hand while a 1937 version is indeterminate. What must be noticed however is that the eye is coordinated with the hands. In both Beckmanns the eyes are directed away from the frontal view—suggesting that two mirrors were used. Although some painters have no objection to portraying themselves as holding a brush and palette, most present themselves as if they were a statue bust or as if sitting for a court painter. Often rectifying the self to look like the pose of another, self-portraiture offers a pictorial account of the self. In self-portraiture, the self constitutes itself as other—slightly modifying Rimbaud's dictum: *le je est un autre.*

　　Selbstbildnis—autoportrait—autoritratto—autorretrato—self-portrait. A self-made portrait of oneself—a drawing, picture, image, painting, or some sort of delineation of oneself by oneself. The German term stresses the self's production of an image or likeness of itself. The romance language locutions pick up the Greek prefix *auto-*, meaning "of itself" or more specifically "of oneself"—what is done independently, naturally, and just exactly so, not with the help of others. Understood as an *auto*-portrait, by contrast with what is "natural" in a *"nature morte"* (a dead nature or still life), the self-portrait draws out precisely what is alive. One's self is alive. The reflexive pronoun αὐτός appeals to one's true self, but the self in the Greek (Orphic-Platonic) view that one's true self is the soul and not the body is rendered impossible in the case of an *autoportrait*. The *autoportrait* is precisely a rendition of the painter's body by the very one whose image appears in the painting. Leonardo, Dürer, Rembrandt, Chardin, Delacroix, Cézanne, Van Gogh, Miró, Picasso, and so forth all paint their own bodies. The *autoportrait* offers a plan or image (*protractus* in Medieval Latin) of the self. The plan offered is corporeal. The body is what is seen in the painting. Although the self renders itself—the true self, the very one (*autós*)—it is distinctively embodied, visible, seen. The Italian version provides another feature: the self—the very one—is not simply given there in the painting, on the canvas; in an *autoritratto* there is a drawing out (*ritrarre*), an extracting. On the one hand, the self draws itself out, extracts itself; on the other hand, the self is what is drawn out or extracted. In the Spanish word *autorretrato,* it is not clear whether the prefix is *auto-* or *autor-*. If the latter, then the *autor* or author is portraying-portrayed. The author is agent and patient. The author portrays and is portrayed. To the Spanish way of speaking, the self is an author—the direct connection with autobiography is established—the self originates the painting, the self produces its own picture of itself as a writer might write about his or her own life, as an autobiographer might write his or her own life.

In self-portraiture, the self offers a plan of itself; in painting oneself, one draws oneself out. The self-portrait cannot be a drawing or image of the self understood only as soul (*psychē* or *anima*); it must also involve the body. In the self-portrait, the self is necessarily represented as embodied. Traits of the self—traces of the self—constitute the self-portrait. The traces are bodily shapes, expressions, and glances. The self traces itself and leaves traces of itself in the painting of the self-portrait. Self-portraiture is the self establishing a likeness of itself as a painting. The likeness is a visible trace, extract, sketch, plan, outline of the self. As such, it is not the self. As such, the self-portrait is inadequate as a rendering of the self. Nevertheless, something is appropriated; the trace or extract or image is complete—it delimits itself as self-portraiture and fulfills its task even though it does not capture the self.

Self-portraiture is painting. Merleau-Ponty distinguishes painting from science and philosophy. The three activities intersect in crucial ways. By following Merleau-Ponty's account it will become evident that what painting accomplishes is different—not separate—from the workings of science and philosophy. More particularly, the status of visibility as that which arises in the activity of painting and which is articulated in philosophical interrogation establishes the space in which self-portraiture can and does occur.

"Eye and Mind" opens with the statement "*La science manipule les choses et renonce à les habiter*" (*OE,* 9). Science takes knowing as its enterprise. Scientific activity according to Merleau-Ponty attempts to manipulate things and gives up trying to inhabit or live them. Science keeps its distance from things in their particularity. It offers models for understanding things as objects in general. Variables and indicators provide the mechanisms according to which things are manipulated. Even when science treats forces, fields of energy, chemical reactions, and biological instincts, scientific activity concerns itself with the natural world of things but at a distance. The project of knowing in which science engages refuses to enter into the texture of things, to live the things it studies. The thinking which science involves places great weight upon the various techniques for grasping and obtaining the knowledge of things which it seeks. It introduces experimental conditions according to which things are operated upon, worked over, and transformed. But the specific thing or things in question could be substituted by others. Indeed they lose their interest and significance when they acquire a uniqueness and individuality which does not allow for substitutability and generality. The activity of science is an activity of mind (*l'esprit*). Scientific thought does not want to enter into the visible. It wants to stand back from the visible in order to provide rules, regularities, and models for understanding it.

Descartes's *Dioptrique* offers an example of thinking which gives itself a model and then tries to reconstruct the visible according to that model. Descartes seeks to eliminate the equivocal and the ambiguous in vision. When a Cartesian looks in a mirror, he does not see himself; he sees only a mannequin, an exterior, an outside. For Descartes, scientific thought deals with extension. If a Cartesian were to try to paint, he would offer only a representation of that extended thing. Painting would thereby be only an artificial device for representing extension. In another way, but with similar difficulties, the Renaissance theory of perspective tries to account for every point in space. The famous Dürer woodcut of the painter looking through a grid in order to paint what he sees in each of the little squares provides an example of how a technique can be employed to scientifically reproduce the thing in its spatial multiplicity. In both procedures, the painter makes a science of painting and stands back from the things that are painted. Colors are deemphasized and perhaps even rendered incidental to the representation of or perspective on the object. Scientific thinking in general involves what Merleau-Ponty calls a *pensée de survol*. This overview thinking or bird's-eye view of things tries to grasp the totality from a distance. However, something in space escapes our efforts at *survol* (*OE*, 50). What escapes is precisely what a painter such as Cézanne makes visible in painting.

In distinguishing painting from scientific activity, Merleau-Ponty appeals to a certain type of modern painting which the eye (*l'oeil*) symbolically signifies more than mind (*l'esprit*). Cézanne is paradigmatic; but in the 1964 Gallimard edition of *L'oeil et l'esprit*, one also finds reproductions of work by Giacometti, Matisse, Klee, Nicholas de Stael, Richier, and Rodin. Although a few other artists are cited, including Robet Delaunay, Duchamps, Rouault, and Dubuffet, together they constitute the type of painters and sculptors whom Merleau-Ponty regards as stressing the eye as opposed to the mind. They serve as exemplary of what is in question when he speaks of painting.

"Painting dips into the net of brute sense" (*OE*, 13). Where science stands back from things in order to make sense of them, painting dips into the very texture of the sense of things. Where science (under the Cartesian model) succeeds in a particular domain and tries to apply its achievement to all others, painting enters into the field of sense in its specificity. Painting limits itself to the visible of the here and now. As Merleau-Ponty puts it, "the eye inhabits as one lives in one's house" (*OE*, 27). And earlier in the text:

> The eye sees the world and what is lacking in the world in order to be a painting; the eye sees what is lacking in the painting in order to be itself, and once achieved, the eye sees the painting which answers to all these lacks and it sees other people's paintings as other responses to other lacks. (*OE*, 25–26)

The eye sees lacks and rectifies them in painting because the painter enters into the texture of the world with its multiplicity of sense. The painter can fulfill these lacks because he notices them as precisely that which is to be made visible on the canvas. To everyday seeing, the lacks remain invisible. The painter makes them visible by painting them. "Painting gives visible existence to what profane vision believes to be invisible" (*OE*, 27). Painting establishes what Merleau-Ponty calls "visibility." Visibility arises out of the conjuncture of the visible and the invisible, out of the making visible of what is invisible to everyday seeing. The thing seen is the same whether to everyday seeing or to the painter's eye. The thing embodies a network of brute sense (or meaning), a sensuousness which is invisible to everyday seeing and which is unimportant to scientific thought. To the painter, the primary task is to make the network of brute sense visible as the visibility of the painting.

In Merleau-Ponty's later ontology, visibility arises out of the seeing-seen (*voyant-visible*). In everyday experience, the locus of this visibility is the body. The crossing-over (back and again)—*recroisement*—of touching touched, seeing seen, one eye and the other, one hand and the other establishes the intertwining, chiasm, or bodily space. Merleau-Ponty, the philosopher, calls this intertwining visibility. He speaks of the body as a "curious system of exchanges" (*OE*, 21). He cites Valéry as claiming that the painter "brings along his body." "In lending his body to the world, the painter changes the world into painting" (*OE*, 16). By establishing the visibility that delineates the space of his body and by lending that visibility to the world of things, the painter is able to translate his own visibility into a new visibility—the visibility of the painting. By directing his mobile body into the visible world, the painter transforms that visibility into a painting.

Visible things and my body double each other with a secret visibility (*OE*, 22). The secret visibility involves a tracing (*un tracé*) which arises out of the concatenation of things and my body. This tracing is what is left over in the double crossing of the inside and the outside, the outside and the inside. The tracing is a marking out of the secret visibility which is neither outside nor inside, neither thing nor body, neither visible nor invisible. This tracing is what makes painting possible. The tracing of the secret visibility is rendered in a particular way on a particular canvas. It could have been otherwise. When the secret visibility is rendered in a particular way in a particular painting, a transubstantiation has taken place. The visibility is no longer the visibility of a painter's body confronting a mountain or a bowl of fruit. The visibility is now the visibility of a visible painting. The mountain or the bowl of fruit is no longer visibly there; it has been replaced by the painting of a mountain or a bowl of fruit as what is visibly there. The substance of the visibility has been radically transformed: transubstantiated. The tracing of the painter lending his body to the mountain or to the bowl of fruit has become the tracing of the viewer looking at a painting of the mountain or bowl of fruit. The new tracing is indeed a tracing of the old. The secret visibility of the painter's body given over to the mountain is not the same secret visibility as that of the viewer looking at the painting. The tracing continues; the visibility is continually reborn. The painterly seeing-seen (*voyant-visible*) is transformed for the viewer. Painting celebrates the enigma of visibility and offers a restitution of the visible while scientific thought provides a model for the control and transformation of the things themselves. The only way science can accomplish its task is by ignoring visibility and by providing an intelligible construction of what is there—visible or not.

The task of the philosopher is to interrogate. The philosopher can interrogate the relation between eye and mind, body and things, science and painting. Interrogation for Merleau-Ponty is an asking in the between (*inter-rogare*). By situating the inquiry between body and things, the philosopher can articulate the character and meaning of visibility. By interrogating the relation between science and painting, the philosopher can establish the place of philosophy itself. By interrogating painting, the philosopher asks about the particular type of visibility that arises in the practice of painting. The philosopher delineates the single network of Being and particularly its various "branches" as manifested in painting, notably: depth, color, form, line, movement, contour, and physiognomy. These "branches of Being" constitute the special visibility of painting and give it its specificity. The philosopher does not provide an account of how these branches or ramifications of Being are produced, nor does the philosopher qua philosopher engage in the producing of them. The philosopher does not offer a history of their occurrence in particular paintings nor does the philosopher analyze how the various branches interrelate in a particular painting. The philosopher remarks them as branches of Being and interrogates their function, meaning, status, and location in the production of the visibility of painting.

II

Self-portraiture is a kind of painting—a rather special kind. To interrogate the differences in the thing painted is to ask about painting itself. When the thing painted is a mountain, a mirror, or oneself, fundamental differences occur in the type of visibility produced. Consider the case of Paul Cézanne.

During the last nine years of his life, Cézanne often painted the Montagne Sainte-Victoire near Aix-en-Provence. In 1894, after the death of his mother, Cézanne decided definitely to abandon his special sites near Estaque on the Mediterranean. Although he continued to spend some of his time in Paris, he returned to his natal city of Aix-en-Provence, perhaps with the idea that he would find a new subject to paint. The Montagne Sainte-Victoire served his purposes admirably. He painted the mountain from the quarry in Bibemus, from the north of Aix, from the Tholonet road, from the Château-Noir terrace, from the Lauves heights, from Saint-Marc, from Gardanne, from Beaurecueil, and so on. Each constituted a different view of the mountain. He would paint the mountain at different times of day (perhaps not with the meticulousness with which Monet rendered versions of the Rouen cathedral, but nevertheless with extensive variety). He chose different seasons. He used oil on canvas, and some watercolors on white paper. He painted the mountain year in and year out during his later life. Again and again he brought his body to a site from which he could see the mountain. Even the last time he went out to paint it in 1906, he was caught in a storm and died soon thereafter. He regularly lent his body to the mountain in the act of painting it. Visible, ominous, "imperious and melancholy" (he described it in his youth), the Montagne Sainte-Victoire was as invisible to the inhabitants of Aix as the Eiffel Tower is to Parisians and the Empire State Building is to New Yorkers: always there, but hardly noticed. Even today driving along the Autoroute du Sud, if it were not for a landmark sign along the road, many automobile drivers would find the mountain invisible to their everyday gaze. By lending his body to it, standing before it with his easel and palette, Cézanne would lean forward toward his canvas and render visible what the profane eye would not see. Through both vision and movement, Cézanne would transpose the visibility of his own body in its relation to the mountain into the secret visibility of his canvas. The tracing of the invisible in the visible mountain would be inscribed onto the canvas and the new visibility would appear. Painting with his eyes and his hands, he attends to the depth of Being there in the mountain; he establishes that depth along with color, form, line, movement, and contour in the painting.

It would not suffice for Cézanne to simply reproduce external forms. He would have to paint pure forms which follow their own internal laws of construction. His practice was to paint traces or slices of things by attending to the solidity of Being on the one hand and its diversity on the other. The domain in which he operates is the space of difference between Being as a fullness and Being as sheer multiplicity. What he paints specifically are the traces of the difference—the network of sense. In order to paint the traces, he paints color. But there is no recipe for painting the visible. No predeterminations are available as to *which* colors are to be used. Indeed, the vast array of colors used to render the mountain at different times and from different views is quite extraordinary. Yet in each case, the Montagne Sainte-Victoire is distinctively visible in the painting; the tracings of the actual mountain are carried into the visibility of the painting.

The painter does not paint a world displayed before him as in the representation of things. The representational account no longer holds. The painting becomes "autofigurative" in that it establishes its own figuration—through the ramifications of Being. The painting determines itself as a trace, fabric, cloth, texture. This network constitutes the field of difference in which visibility arises.

Although the painter must stand back a considerable distance from the mountain in order to paint it, Cézanne paints the Montagne

Sainte-Victoire in its particularity. He is interested in *this* very mountain. And the visibility of his painted mountain is that of this specific mountain in the painting. As Cézanne says, "the painter thinks in paint." Rendering the visible as visibility is thinking in paint. Thinking in paint is not an activity of mind (*l'esprit*) as it is for scientific thought. Oddly the geologist, botanist, or zoologist must move much closer to the mountain than Cézanne does. However, what the scientist who is concerned with rock formation, vegetation, and animal life wants is not this particular case of the thing, but this particular one as an instance of many (for which other examples would probably be equally suitable). The scientist's thinking is calculative and generalizing. The thinking the painter engages in is interpretive and specifying. As Merleau-Ponty remarks in "Cézanne's Doubt": the painter interprets.[3] However, "this interpretation must not be thought [*une pensée*] separate from vision" (*Doute*, 27). The thinking in which the painter engages is noncalculative, but as Cézanne said "a painter is not an imbecile" (*Doute*, 27). "The mountain makes itself seen by the painter and the painter interrogates it with his gaze" (*OE*, 28). The painter thinks in paint—utilizing but transforming the activity of the scientist. The painter interrogates with his gaze—employing the activity of the philosopher but charging it with the sensuous. Although Cézanne stands back from the Montagne Sainte-Victoire, he also makes it visible—each time with a novel visibility as he interrogates, thinks, and interprets it.

Suppose now that the thing in question, the object to be painted is no longer a mountain, but rather a mirror—a mirror placed in front of the painter so that the same sort of triangle that occurs when painting the mountain is reproduced, i.e., the painter, the canvas, and the thing. This time, however, the thing, the mirror incorporates an image of the painter painting. The object is not just the mountain over there, but the mirror with the painter's image right here. What is visible is not the mountain, but rather the painter's image. Usually the frame of the mirror is omitted in the painting—only the image of the painter is rendered visible. In painting the mountain, Cézanne renders visible what is invisible to the profane eye. In self-portraiture, he makes the mirror invisible and his specular image visible.

Unlike the Montagne Sainte-Victoire, which became a motif in Cézanne's later years, he produced self-portraits throughout his lifetime. In 1858–61, he is young clean-shaven (except for a trim moustache), short-haired and scowling. In 1865–68, he is bearded, balding at the forehead looking back from his apparent right with a somewhat pensive air. In 1873–75, he is wearing a cap with a long full beard, hair falling over his ears and a drawn look. At about the same time, another self-portrait shows him quite bald with a trimmed beard and what Rilke called "an incredible intensity." In 1877–79, his beard is shorter, more carefully cut, and he is wearing a white malleable folding hat. His look is that of a storekeeper caught unaware that someone is looking at him. And so the self-portraits go, his hair and beard length change, usually he directs his attention off to his apparent left suggesting that he painted with his actual right hand. In a couple of paintings, he has a melon hat. Once in 1885–87, he portrays himself holding a palette in his apparent right hand facing an easel concealing his apparent left hand, indicating that he was in fact painting with his right hand. In 1898–1900, the last of the available self-portraits, he is wearing a beret, a goatee and moustache with a rather concentrated look. This time, although still facing toward his apparent left, if one covers the lower arms, it is evident that the painting was performed with the apparent right. But then if one looks at the eyes, unlike the earlier self-portraits, they are oriented off to the apparent left. Coordinating the hand and the eyes in reading the painting, it is now clear that two mirrors were employed. The apparent right is the actual right—the double mirroring corrects the inversion.

Unless two mirrors are employed, the eyes in the self-portrait are centered—oriented directly forward. The viewer has the sense of being caught in a face-to-face stare. The eyes are looking at me, one might think. It is as if he is trying to tell me something. Yet he is only looking at himself in the mirror. The viewer who is duped into believing that a staring match is underway is in fact an intruder. Cézanne is simply looking at himself in the mirror. But the mirror is invisible. Cézanne the *voyant-visible* produces a visible self with an invisible mirror. Cézanne's visibility is traced in the visible of the self-portrait producing a new visibility as it is seen by a viewer. When Cézanne sees himself in the mirror, a single visibility is produced. When Cézanne looks at his own self-portrait a double visibility occurs. The new visibility becomes equivocal to Cézanne's gaze and unequivocal to that of another viewer. For Cézanne, the self-portrait is the self as other reflecting itself as the same. What is invisible to Cézanne the man is made visible in the visibility of the self-portrait and offered as posterity in the painting. What is now visible in the painted self like the painted mountain is a new visibility at most tracing out the old. Cézanne's many self-portraits offer a chronicle of his self-images but they will always leave behind the *voyant-visible* of Cézanne's actual life. They are at most the traces of that life made visible in paint.

III

Jacques Lacan reintroduced his conception of the "mirror stage" in 1949 at the Sixteenth International Congress of Psychoanalysis under the title *"Le stade du miroir comme formateur de la fonction du Je."* In that same year, Merleau-Ponty gave his lectures on "Consciousness and the Acquisition of Language" as Professor of Child Psychology and Pedagogy at the Sorbonne. In those lectures, he cites Lacan's notion of "prematuration" in the child's psychological development. Although Lacan was seven years Merleau-Ponty's senior, they knew each other's work and were acquainted personally. Lacan for instance provided an article for the special number of *Les Temps Modernes* devoted to Merleau-Ponty after his death in 1961. The notion of "prematuration" arises particularly in the "Mirror Stage" essay, which had been presented in earlier form at the Fourteenth International Congress of Psychoanalysis in 1936.

The mirror stage, which apparently occurs anywhere between the ages of six months and eighteen months, involves basically three levels. At the first level, the child reacts to the image presented by the mirror as a reality or at least as the image of someone else. Then the child stops treating the image as a real object, and no longer tries to take possession of the other hiding behind the mirror. But subsequently the child sees this other as the child's own image. At this last level, identification begins to take place: the child progressively takes on the identity of the subject.

Identification with the specular image only occurs after the child has treated the image as an image of another and after that assumption of alterity breaks down and a radical distancing from the image as other takes place. Thus when the child sees the image as an image of him or herself, it is not so much that it is the self as that it is *not other*. The "I" (*"je"*) is formed out of a dialectic in which the image is postulated as other, denied, and then affirmed as the self. One could say that it is a process of incorporation of otherness into the self. Naturally this occurs only in the case of the recognition of self in the mirror. Objects and other people remain other.

For Lacan, the mirror stage involves the self or subject becoming a subject. When the child assumes an image of him or herself as other, a transformation in the self takes place. The mirror catalyzes a discordance between the self (*le "je"*) and its own reality. The mirror stage accomplishes a relation between the organism and its reality or between the *Innenwelt* (personal world) and the *Umwelt* (environment). Thus "the specular image seems to be the threshold onto the visible world."[4] The

mirror itself brings about the recognition of otherness in order to identify with the image it sees. What is other in the mirror is determined at
the third level as precisely the same as the self (and not, in fact, other).

In Merleau-Ponty's account, the mirror in what is here called Cézanne's mirror stage reverses the transformations Lacan describes.
When painting the mountain, Cézanne stands back from it in order to
lend his body to it (unlike the scientist who moves closer to it in order to
stand back from it). When painting the mirror, Cézanne knows that the
specular image is himself. Cézanne identifies with the image in the mirror; but in self-portraiture he undertakes to make himself other, to paint
a portrait of himself as other than himself. Indeed, as Lacan claims, the
specular image seems to be the threshold onto the visible world. But in
the case of Cézanne, the door opens the other way: the specular image is
a threshold onto the visible world of the painting and not the world from
which the painting arises. The specular image is a threshold onto the
visible world of the self-portrait and its visibility. With the help of the
mirror, the tracings of the relation between the *Innenwelt* (inner world)
and the *Umwelt* (external world) established from childhood are transposed by an inversion of the intertwining. The effect is to produce tracings of the *Innenwelt* in the *Umwelt* of the self-portrait.

Instead of painting the mountain, Cézanne is painting himself,
making himself other, making his body visible. In this case, he literally
lends his body to the world of things in order to transform them into
paint. Cézanne takes the visibility of his body as the visibility of a *voyant-
visible* and transposes it onto the canvas. In the case of self-portraiture,
Cézanne doubles the invisible. When looking at a mountain, one does
not see oneself seeing; one sees only the visible. When painting the
mountain, the painter makes visible what is invisible in his experience of
the mountain. When looking at himself in the mirror, Cézanne sees what
is typically invisible to him: he sees his nose, his eyes, his chin, his beard,
etc. The mirror makes what is invisible visible. When painting himself
from the image in the mirror, Cézanne takes what is typically invisible to
him and brings another invisible—the one that accompanies all his seeing—and produces another visible which is the self-portrait. The self-
displaying visibility of the mirror is reproduced in the self-displaying visibility of the self-portrait. But self-portraiture is not representational any
more than painting the Montagne Sainte-Victoire is representational.
The self-displaying visibility of the mirror is not duplicated in the self-
displaying visibility of the self-portrait. They are not identical, although
there is a tracing of one onto the other. Cézanne produces the self-
portrait by bringing out (making visible) what would be invisible to some-

one else looking at Cézanne and painting a portrait of him (as Pissarro did in 1874 and Renoir in 1880). Hence in painting the visible specular image, Cézanne doubles both the invisible of the self and the image and the visibility of the image and the painting. Cézanne's seeing fills in the visible of the specular image with a plan (*protractus*). The visible is filled in with the invisible which Cézanne makes visible in paint. Cézanne draws out or extracts features of himself and renders them visible by means of what Merleau-Ponty calls the branches of Being—the tools of painting. The self-portrait leaves traces of the specular image and hence of the self. But the traces are not the visible self. The traces are the self as other, as self-portrait.

Self-portraiture almost invariably requires a special tool: the mirror. This everyday instrument establishes the painter's visibility in its most salient respects. The mirror locates the place of the eye (*l'oeil*)—the very feature which Merleau-Ponty symbolically associates with the painter. The mirror pinpoints the *voyant-visible* as visibility, as the place of freeplay (*Spielraum* or *enjeu*), as the repeated tracing, marking out, the difference between visible and invisible, seer and seen. The place of the freeplay, the visibility, the difference is the place of the "*je,*" the place of the self, the "I"—centered where the eye is located. Self-portraiture appropriates what is appropriate to the visibility of the painter, makes visible what is invisible in the specular image, and appropriates the canvas producing a new visibility. The mirror stage makes the new visibility of the self-portrait possible.

The mirror makes it possible for the self which paints itself to disclose the flesh (*la chair*) of the painter. The mirror functions as an instrument of disclosure (*dévoilement*). It uncovers the painter's painterly embodiment. Since, according to Merleau-Ponty, every technique is a technique of the body, the mirror also operates in that way. In this case, rather than concealing its function as a technique, the mirror discloses itself. The mirror operates as a dispositive. It discloses itself because of the orientation of the subject's eyes and because of the tending toward painting that one arm indicates. But at the same time, it conceals its identity as a mirror in all of Cézanne's self-portraits. Because the mirror acts as a dispositive, the visibility that arises in self-portraiture both discloses and conceals, makes visible and invisible at the same time. The mirror marks the ambiguity of the painterly experience while also structuring that experience according to depth, color, form, line, movement, contour, and physiognomy—the branches of Being (*les rameaux de l'Etre*).

Although the mirror is always hidden in Cézanne self-portraits, not all painters require that the mirror be invisible. A 1787 Gainsborough shows the painter looking forward, elegantly attired, with an oval shape around the bustlike pose that could well be the frame of a mirror. Furthermore, not all painters use only one mirror. A 1917 Max Beckmann shows him painting himself. His eyes are directed away from the frontal view and he is painting with his right hand. Similarly, a 1484 Albrecht Dürer has the young man looking off to the left. A view of his right cheek is provided. Only the right hand is seen and it could well be holding a brush. Once again, it is quite plain that both Beckmann and Dürer in these instances made use of two mirrors in order to correct the mirror image effect. Only Beckmann would have had access to photography, whereby the appropriate double impression effect could be produced. A 1980 Francis Bacon tryptich entitled *Three Studies for Self-Portrait* discloses three views of his face in Bacon's habitually distorted fashion. In the center view, the eyes face forward as in traditional self-portraits. The two side panels are oriented about 45 degrees toward the center, indicating that he painted from three mirrors with the two side ones angled inward about the same on each side. Thus the one on the right shows his apparent left cheek and the one on the left shows his apparent right cheek. Since only the head is displayed, it would be difficult to determine whether the actual sides of their mirror images are seen. And the distorted visibility accentuates the difficulty of such a determination.

Some self-portraits conceal not only the mirror, but also the sense of the painter painting. When only the head or bust is shown, the question of deception does not arise. But when Dürer in 1493 holds a plant in both hands or in 1498 sits with his hands folded on a table in front of him; when a later Rembrandt shows the artist plumply and ornately seated holding a scepter in his apparent left and his apparent right placed firmly on a hazy chair arm; when Reynolds in 1780 grasps a document in one hand and places the other at his hip; or when Max Beckmann in 1937 holds both of his hands in front of him encircled with prisoner's chains, the painter orients the visibility of the painting away from its status as a mirrored self-portrait in order to establish the self in an alternative role. Many painters have no objection to portraying themselves with brush and palette in hand. They disclose their painterly embodiment as visible, but the differences in the particular manner and style of Henri Rousseau, Corot, Monet, Kokoschka, Modigliani, and Picasso—to cite some examples—are quite extreme. In each case, the mirror operates as a dispositive (as the locus of visibility with its concomitant ambiguity) establishing its uniqueness and vitality of function.

IV

Many autobiographers have characterized their enterprise as self-portraiture. The celebrated report by Montaigne to his reader in the *Essais* is indicative: "I want to be seen here in my simple, natural, ordinary fashion, without pose or artifice; for it is myself that I portray."[5] Montaigne understands his writing project as self-portrayal. Almost two centuries later, Rousseau begins his *Confessions* with the statement: "Here is the only portrait of a man painted exactly according to nature and in the fullest truth that exists or will probably ever exist."[6] Montaigne and Rousseau borrow from painting what they seek to accomplish with words. In writing their own lives, they offer a verbal picture of who they are and what they have done. Their picture is in fact a narrative. The traces are not visible tracings but rather the writing of their lives as text. The intertwining that produces visibility with respect to self-portraiture results in textuality in the case of autobiography.[7] Visibility is perceptual textuality and textuality is written visibility.

Because of the mirror stage, in self-portraiture the eye is centered. When a single mirror is employed, the eye is oriented in a directly frontal view. The forces of the painting tend to draw toward and concentrate upon the place of the eyes. In autobiography, the self is dispersed, disseminated throughout the narrative. The eye is substituted typically by a first-person singular "I" which speaks and narrates its own life. The eye in self-portraiture is coordinated with the hand, for both are instruments of visibility. In the autobiographical text, the self speaks and is spoken in terms of the "I," but the hand that writes remains invisible.[8]

The case of photographic self-portraiture more closely approximates painting because it is visual and also involves vision. However, the differences are notable. Just as there is no mirror in autobiography—the brush corresponds to the pen, the paper to the canvas, the ink to the paint—in photographic self-portraiture, the camera forces the elimination of the mirror stage. In self-portraiture, there are two moments of self-displaying visibility: that of the specular image and that of the painting. The painter lends his body to the mirror which provides a self-displaying visibility. The painter reiterates that self-displaying visibility by tracing it in paint and thereby providing another self-displaying visibility. In the case of photography, where the photographer takes the picture of him or herself with a cable, the camera does not operate like the mirror—it is a type of non–self-displaying visibility. Unlike the painter who sees what he or she paints and hence paints from the visible, the photographer has to set the scene with him or herself as markedly invisible. The context is arranged and the photographer must look through the camera in order to determine where to sit or stand when the picture is taken. Hence before and while the picture is taken, a specifically non–self-displaying visibility is at work. The photographer lends his body to the photographical procedure by placing it before the camera. The painter is situated in front of the mirror, but what is painted is the specular image. The photographer takes a picture of the actual body and not an image of it. The photograph itself is a kind of fixed image of the self and its body.[9] Hence although the photographer lends his body to the photographic procedure, only the photograph itself offers a self-displaying visibility.

In self-portraiture, the self is displayed, made visible, drawn out, extracted, projected, and rendered as a version of itself. The mirror stage offers a unique feature to the activity of portraying oneself. The traces of the portrayal constitute the frame out of which the self in its corporeality is rendered visible. The painter's visibility is the painter's identity as other. The painter's life—captured at a moment, in a phase— is identified in the space of difference that the mirror as dispositive marks in its visibility. This specular self-displaying visibility is appropriated and reiterated in the self-portrait. Self-portraiture forms an enterprise in which a new self-displaying visibility comes into being by tracing the ex-appropriated self of the mirror into the texture of painting.[10]

The Thinker and the Painter

Jacques Taminiaux

Translated by Michael Gendre

T he title of my presentation, "The Thinker and the Painter," is intended to suggest that in Merleau-Ponty's eyes there was a link between the activity to which, as a philosopher, he had devoted his
life and the activity to which painters devote theirs.

Such a proximity calls for a clarification and an explanation. It
needs to be both clarified and explained because it does not go without
saying. I need only to recall that for the founder of the Western philosophical tradition those two activities are antithetical. Plato, one recalls,
strongly maintains in the *Republic* that to paint amounts to refuse to
think and that the activity of thinking requires a sort of detachment from
perception and the perceived, which is the very element to which the
painter is attached. To paint is to refuse to think because for Plato the
painter is par excellence the one who takes sides with appearances,
which are labeled adverse to Being. He copies appearances without ever
taking into consideration the essence (or he deals with copies without
ever being concerned with their models). He celebrates the shadowy
lights—the *clair obscur*—of the sensible realm as well as the equivocities
that surface throughout it, and he fails to recognize that, beyond this
confused area, it is possible for the eyes of the mind to have access to the
clear and peaceful ordering of intelligible Ideas provided that the mind
be detached from the sensible realm. This access to Being beyond Appearance, or more precisely this access to appearances devoid of the ambiguities of the sensible, is reserved for the thinker. It allows him to

understand with total clarity that what the painter prides himself on is worthy only of disdain: the work to which he devotes so much effort is in vain as, at the time when the painter believes he captures what truly is, he lets something that is nonbeing lead him astray. Although he wants to raise sensible things to the glory of a pictorial radiance, he achieves only the flimsy fabrication of nonreal copies of entities that are themselves devoid of being and truth because the sensible realm is not the medium within which the true aspect (*eidos*) of things is apprehended. The sensible aspects of things are nothing but the distorted reflection of their true physiognomies. Fascinated by the sensible appearances of things, the painter therefore produces only reflections of reflections.

Now is not the time to question the transformations undergone by the Platonic conceptions throughout the history of philosophy, nor even to evoke their persistence, under different forms, in the writings of philosophers of painting.

Those writings are relatively scarce, because only at the beginning of the nineteenth century, with Hegel and Schopenhauer, does one find philosophers of the first rank producing elaborate analyses of pictorial works.

Let me restrict myself to mentioning that, even when those analyses grant considerable attention to painting and seem to bestow upon it the privileged status of a form of thought, they continue to function within the space of those bimillennial oppositions elaborated by Plato: the thing itself and its copy, the real and the imaginary, the sensible diversity and the intelligible unity, the body and the mind. In other words, what those analyses seem to give to painting with one hand, they take back with the other. Thus Hegel, in contrast to Plato, entertains the notion that art is the manifestation of the Idea. But he immediately adds, in perfect accord with the Platonic distinction between the sensible and the intelligible, that the element within which art produces its works, the sensible, is not adequate for a genuine manifestation of the Idea.

Likewise Schopenhauer, also in contrast to Plato, maintains that the Idea is manifested by art, which does not mean that art manifests the rational character of the Idea as Hegel thinks, but instead manifests the profoundly absurd character of the thing-in-itself, the insatiable will. Yet there is also a profound agreement between Schopenhauer and Plato. This agreement emerges when Schopenhauer specifies his general thesis with the claim that art—even though it is an eminent form of thought because it exhibits the truth of reality; that is, the truth that reality is absurd—still is not adequate to think what it attempts to grasp. The reason for this inadequacy is simple: art continues to entangle us in sensible phenomena (and therefore in the emanations of the will to live) at the very moment when it shows the absurdity of these emanations.

Schopenhauer, in spite of the abyss that separates him from Hegel, agrees with the latter, and finds himself in profound agreement with Plato when he says that the flaw of art is that it rivets us to the sensible. And both continue to maintain with Plato that, in the final analysis, thinking and being attached to the sensible are antithetical attitudes and terms.

Such an antinomy is precisely what Merleau-Ponty, from the beginning until the end of his work, never stopped denouncing. To think, for Merleau-Ponty, does not mean to turn away from the perceived; rather it means to grant it the status of a first ground, to dwell within its boundaries, to listen to its echoes, to interrogate it, to always go back to it. Now it is precisely because thinking for him was fundamentally attracted to the perceived that thought, in the sense he gave to it in his own work, has to free itself from the dichotomies in which the philosophical tradition was trapped.

Perception

To what degree does the perceived invite thought to rid itself of those dichotomies if thought takes the perceived as its privileged theme of meditation? Exactly to the degree that the dualistic oppositions that originated in Plato are not applied to the perceived. Already the Husserlian descriptions, whose importance and innovative character Merleau-Ponty had been quick to acknowledge, stood for him in contrast to the Platonic heritage carried along and transformed by Descartes to fashion the scientific project of the modern *mathesis*; those Husserlian descriptions were able to show that the phenomenal character specific to the perceived brings about a constant overlapping of those terms deemed antithetical and heterogeneous in the tradition. The tradition of modern philosophy, whether it be rationalistic, empiricist, or Kantian, finally relegated the perceived to the realm of pure multiplicity and diversity. Such a tradition maintained that the perceived as such is recalcitrant to unity and identity.

It is against this notion that Husserl reacts. He shows that it is not beyond the diversity of its aspects—the famous Husserlian profiles—or above them, that the perceived thing acquires its unity and its identity. These two features do not occur to the thing from the exterior and after the fact by virtue of a synthetic act of the understanding or an associating repetition. It is at the very core of the diversity of those profiles that, from the outset, the unity of the perceived thing emerges. In the perceived realm, the unity is not heterogeneous to multiplicity, rather it is folded within the multiplicity of the thing and is even required by it. Likewise the identity of the thing is not the antithesis of a difference. The perceived entity would lose its perceptual density, its incarnated existence, and would cease to be perceived if the aspects that are presented by it did not announce other aspects, which are not yet offered to sight. These latent sides form the horizon hidden by the first ones. A thing perceived from all sides would not be a perceived thing. In a rather similar manner, the realm of perceived entities does not fall prey to the classical antinomy between the particular and the general.

The perceived never presents itself as some strictly individual feature, some singular form, some incomparable color. At the outset, as the Gestalt psychologists discovered at the beginning of the century, perception generalizes: we do not see this particular white as strictly particular but as an example of whiteness. At the outset, too, perception stylizes: we see at the same time this singular tree as singular and as a token of the type "tree"; together with its singular form, we apprehend the type that connects it to all other trees.

In addition to an overlapping of the particular and the general, the perceived attests to a surprising overlapping of our fellow beings and the "I," a pluralistic interweaving of subjects. From the start, I am aware that the profiles of a thing—which remain latent for me so long as I remain within a given vantage point—are manifest to others who see the thing from another point of view. And even the aspects given to me do not present themselves as private images that occur within the solipsistic theater of my states of consciousness, but as aspects of the thing that bear witness to the thing's constitution and that cannot be denied by the person next to me. On this point, the descriptions given by Merleau-Ponty can claim as theirs Husserl's motto: "We see and we understand not simply as an individual among other individuals, but as individuals along with others [*miteinander*]."

To those various overlappings that allow the perceived to overcome the classical dichotomies, one should also add analogous overlappings on the side of the perceiving subject and in the very relation which this subject maintains with the perceived.

According to a traditional and established way of looking at things, vision and movement are heterogeneous: it is one thing to see, it is another thing to be in motion. As a consequence, the perceiving subject is more or less spontaneously interpreted as a spectator who, in addition to the capacity for seeing, has the unrelated capacity to move around. But such a distinction is shattered by phenomenology. Phenomenology requires that one recognize in the one who sees—qua seeing, and not by virtue of some extrinsic accident—"an intertwining of vision and movement,"[1] such that to see is, at the outset, to be able to come within proximity of what is seen, to hold it at arm's length and to come within closer range. As Merleau-Ponty says so well, "the map of the visible overlaps that of my intended motions" and "this extraordinary overlapping . . . makes it impossible to consider vision as an operation of the mind that erects in front of it a representation of the world" (PrP, 162; OE, 17; EM, 124). But this overlapping of vision and motion, which blurs the traditional opposition of contemplation and action, goes hand in hand with another "interwining," the one between vision and visibility. What such an intertwining of vision and visibility calls in question is another traditional distinction that has always been taken for granted: the distinction of activity and passivity, more precisely of spontaneity and receptivity. The point is that the being who enjoys both vision and movement is an integral part of the visible: while seeing the visible, the perceiving being is at the same time visible and in the act of seeing. Moreover, that being's moving body, which is itself part of the visible, is at the same time moved and self-moving, in the same manner as it touches things and is touched by them. By virtue of that fact, the body is at the same time decentered and centralizing. It is paradoxically the same thing to say that, "as visible and self-moving, my body is to be counted among things, is one of them" and, in apparent conflict, also to say, "Since [the body] can see itself and move itself around, things are maintained in a circle around it, are encrusted within its flesh as part of its full-fledged definition, and the world is made of the very stuff from which the body is made" (PrP, 163; OE, 19; EM, 125). Those intertwinings, those overlappings, have the effect of dismantling a great many traditional oppositions; furthermore, they move as a barrage against the classical notion of reflection as *cogito me cogitare*, as the presence to itself of the *cogitatio* within its *cogitatum*. The teaching of the phenomenological analysis of perception is that, in contrast to the classical notion, a reflective capacity exists at the very core of perception, but this reflection does not allow us to see perception as a "thought of seeing" in the sense that Descartes used to give to the expression. Because it is linked to "the impossibility of dividing the being who sees from the seen entity," the reflexivity that arises at the very core of perception is one of a flesh caught by fleshly ramifications at the very same time it becomes a self.

In all this, there is an interiority that, as Merleau-Ponty says, "does not precede the material arrangement of the human body" (PrP, 163; *OE*, 20; EM, 125) because the interiority occurs thanks to that arrangement, yet does not result from assembling various parts for the sake of an intended sum total. To say that the interiority precedes the arrangement of the body would make it as enigmatic as a spirit descending into some automaton and would be equivalent to saying that "the body itself is without inside or 'self.' " To say that the interiority results from the arrangement of the body is to conceive that this interiority is the aftereffect of the disposition of the parts of the body. It would be necessary therefore to conceive this arrangement as *partes extra partes* without granting to the body itself—taken as parts, whole, and interaction of parts and whole—the possibility of reflecting upon itself. It is true that,

> if our eyes were made so that not one part of our body could fall within our purview, or if some tricky arrangement made it impossible for us to touch our own bodies without affecting how we move about things—or simply if we had lateral eyes that do not produce an overlapping of the visual fields as some animals do—such a body, unable to reflect upon itself, would then be incapable of feeling itself; such a body almost as rigid as stone, which would not quite be flesh, could not be the body of a man, and would be devoid of humanity. (PrP, 163; *OE*, 20; EM, 125)

But this does not mean that corporeal reflexivity is produced by the spatial disposition of organs in which each has a strictly determined function, because that disposition as such, precisely because it would be *partes extra partes*, would also be without overlappings, without intertwinings, without the interwoven reality of fleshly existence. One must therefore grant that it is an interweaving, an intertwining which must count as the basic datum for which no mechanical theory of the body will ever give a proper account.

Thought

The phenomenal features specific to the perceived and to perception cast a light on the activity of thinking, inasmuch as the account of thinking that seeks to give them full justice and follow them closely is very different from the account of thinking that emerged from the Platonic tradition or the tradition of modern classical philosophy. This contrast is highlighted in the preface to *Signs*,[2] which dates back to the same period as the essay on "Eye and Mind."

According to the Cartesian tradition, thought is a pure activity that penetrates with light anything that appears to it and that is revealed to itself free of any shadows in the mode of a pure presence to itself. Such a notion is rejected by a thought that takes the primacy of perception so seriously as to define itself in terms of the phenomenal features already present in perception. "The philosophy of the overview," Merleau-Ponty says in memorable words, "was an episode, and it is now over" (S, 14; S, 20). To the question "What is thinking?" one who has turned the world of perception into his dwelling place cannot answer in the manner of Descartes or Plato. Valéry somewhere in his work uses the expression "flesh of the spirit."[3] Two themes allow Merleau-Ponty to stress the appropriateness of this remark: time and language. It is the intrinsic link between thought and both time and language that compels thought to be defined, as perception was defined, in terms of intertwinings and overlappings. To think, in the Cartesian sense, means to intuit a clear and distinct idea at the present time: thought is performed exclusively in the present. And as that thought is pure intuition, language is not essential to it; it is nothing more than an instrumental means destined to preserve some former intuitions that, as such, transcend language.

In contrast to the Cartesian perspective, Merleau-Ponty stresses the intrinsic link, not between thought and the present, but between thought and the nonpresent, the nonactual. If thought is alive, he says, it is "by virtue of the sliding motion which pushes it outside of the present into the non-actual" (S, 14; S, 21). Thinking indeed always means to rest on some previously acquired thought that by definition is always a past, but that, instead of being just obsolete, opens "a future for thinking, a cycle, a field" (S, 14; S, 21). In the activity of thinking thus understood, what is successive and what is simultaneous are not contradictory terms as they would be for Descartes. They overlap. Thus Merleau-Ponty writes: "If I think, it is not because I step outside of time into an intelligible world, nor is it because I recreate meaning out of nothing, but rather it is because the arrow of time pulls everything else along with it and causes my successive thoughts to emerge, in a sense, as simultaneous or at least as legitimately overlapping each other" (S, 14; S, 21). On a closer inspection, what takes place here is a double overlapping: that of the successive over the simultaneous and also that of the past (the acquired) over the future (the field of thought that calls for an exploration). And on even closer inspection, to those two overlappings several others are linked. The time to which the activity of thinking is linked is not constituted by the thinker who would rule over it: the thinker is affected by the push, the onrush of time; the thinker receives it, is receptive and sensible to it. To say that "my thought is nothing but the other side of my time [*l'envers de mon temps*]" amounts therefore to saying that it is "the other side of my passive and sensible being" (S, 15; *S*, 22). But to acknowledge that is also to acknowledge that I cannot think without remaining assigned, affixed to the sensible at the very time I distance myself from it to reflect on it. It is to acknowledge also that the solipsism of the *ego cogito* is nothing but an abstraction. It is true that one must isolate oneself to think, but within that very isolation others remain included. There is therefore both an overlapping of the sensible on thinking and of the others on the one who thinks. Merleau-Ponty condenses these overlappings in a superb formula: "But if it is true that my thought is nothing but the reverse of my time, of my passive and sensible being, then whenever I try to understand myself, the whole fabric of the perceptible world comes too, and with it come the others who are caught in it" (S, 15; *S*, 22).

Thinking does not require that one leave the sensible to move to the intellectual, it requires that the individual reflect and retrieve the intertwining structures that are the very ones at work in the sensible. Just as to see is already to have seen and yet to remain open to what remains to be seen, likewise to think is always already to have thought and to be open to what remains to be thought. In both cases the same connection with time comes into play. Spontaneously we have the tendency to believe that perception is nothing but a spatial relationship of a "here" that is perceiving to a "there" that is perceived. But time is secretly involved in that relationship. The thing that I perceive, I see as being already there, before my eyes set down upon it, and in that sense it is past. But at the same time, it offers itself as belonging to the future, as a "hoped-for thing" ("*la chose espérée*" in Merleau-Ponty's expression); that is, as arousing the power I have of exploring it, of investigating it from all sides. My perception is therefore the overlapping of two dimensions: the present and actual with the nonpresent and nonactual, or in other words, *the visible and the invisible*. Other individuals are involved in such an overlapping, because what is invisible for me is from the outset apprehended by me as visible to those who face the perceived things from another side. To appear perceptually is at the outset to appear, not only to one single being, but to several beings. And just as the most insignificant perception bears witness to the plurality of human beings, the most unpretentious thought bears witness to the presence of other thinking individuals. Indeed, what is it to think but to be in a dialogue with oneself? In such a dialogue we are carried along by words of which we are not the authors and that others have transmitted to us.

The connecting bond of time, the bond weaving thought to language, confirms the appropriateness of Valéry's phrase of "the flesh of the spirit." Similarly, the fact that one cannot think without talking to oneself, albeit silently, the fact that words give rise to thoughts, constitutes an overlapping that makes us suspicious of the appropriateness of the Cartesian idea of thought that in its own solitude gains and retains the position of a universal legislator.

This overlapping is something quite different from a parallelism between two levels of reality, both of which are construed as complete and comprehensive, the level of ideas and meanings and the level of the code that expresses them. On this subject, Merleau-Ponty writes: "The weakness of every brand of parallelism is that it takes for granted correspondences between the two levels and masks from us those operations which produced them in their overlapping" (S, 18; S, 26). Just as my vision of the object at a distance finds in my body a correspondence in my ability to acquire a closer vision of it, in the same way it is my being immersed within the existing body of concrete words—upon which I depend when I speak and that I received from a tradition of speakers of the same language—that connects me with the art of thinking what still remains to be thought. But in these conditions, the position of the thinker has nothing in common with the regal condescension of Plato's philosopher or with the solitude of the Cartesian cogito. Just as to perceive is first and foremost to be caught by the visible, that is, to be included in it, in the same way, to think is first and foremost to be caught "by a Speech and a Thought which we do not own, but which own us" (S, 19; S, 27). Whereas the thought of the overview "held the world subdued at its feet" (S, 22; S, 31), in contrast the thought that takes root in the various overlappings just recalled is capable of accounting for what Merleau-Ponty calls the "verticality" of the world.

Painting

I trust that I have provided enough context that we may now turn our attention to painting.

But before doing so, because the notion of overlapping has played a major role in my exposition, I would like to be allowed a few words to illustrate that notion with an example familiar to everybody, which will clearly indicate the deficiency of the classical alternatives. What I have in mind is the intersection of two gazes. When two gazes, two pairs of eyes, intersect and meet, there is an overlapping of the one who looks and the one who is seen. The philosophy of reflection—which first posited the "I think" as a principle—cannot take this into account, as it moves within the asserted duality of the same and the other, of the cogito and extension, or, as Sartre, a Cartesian, puts it, of Nothingness and Being. For the philosophy of reflection, what is at stake here is a juxtaposition such that either one of the two conscious beings relegates the other to the status of being an object, or is so relegated by the other, in such a way that there is "only one *cogito* at any given time" (S, 17; S, 24). The alternative postulated by reflection is simple: either I cast my gaze on the other individual and then I am the subject and the other is the object; or else it is the other's gaze that is cast on me and then I am the object and the other person the subject. What this reflection fails to understand is that the crossing of the two gazes surmounts that antinomy: what happens is that there is indeed an adjustment of one individual to the other, or as Merleau-Ponty says, "two gazes, one inside the other [*deux regards l'un dans l'autre*]."

The idea central to Merleau-Ponty's meditation on painting, in particular in the essay "Indirect Language and the Voices of Silence"[4] and in "Eye and Mind," is that all the problems of painting concern the overlappings that, as I have suggested, led Merleau-Ponty to define thought itself in terms of overlappings.

Painters, for example Dürer, have often said that the outline of their paintings had been derived by them from an inspection of the things in nature, out there; but no less frequently they would say conversely that this outline had been found within themselves. Thus I may invoke Cézanne, who used to say that "nature is inside,"[5] but I could also mention the classical advice of a Chinese painter who used to say that to paint a bamboo, one must first be able to grow it inside oneself. Taken together, these suggestions indicate that the painter paints not only what is visible, but the intertwining of the visible with the seeing. I proposed the view that the dimensions of the visible are inseparable from the seeing individual, from the echos that they provoke in our bodies inasmuch as it is our bodies that gather those dimensions. Such echos are what each painting makes noticeable. In this regard, Merleau-Ponty asks: "That internal equivalent, the carnal formula for their presence which things spark in me, why in turn wouldn't they give rise to an outline, still in the visible realm, inside of which any other seeing eyes will uncover the motifs which sustain their own inspection of the world?"[6] And then he answers: "Thus emerges something visible to the second degree, the carnal essence or the icon of the first" (PrP, 164; *OE*, 22; EM, 126). There is an aphorism of Paul Valéry's that Merleau-Ponty used to like: "The painter brings in his own body." This seems a trivial point: one cannot conceive of an individual as capable of seeing a motif, of mixing colors, of handling a brush, unless that individual had a body. But the aphorism ceases to be trivial if it is taken to mean that the painter is the one who expresses on his canvas the schema of one of the manifold relationships of overlapping that the sensible realm weaves with our body.

If this analysis gives us a faithful description of the phenomenon of painting, a picture is never a *trompe l'oeil*, a fake of a thing, or a double, or a copy; painting is never a system of elements, or fragments, or "visual data" borrowed from the world, the so-called real world, to envisage reality in its absence, as Plato used to think in antiquity or Descartes and Pascal at the beginning of modernity.

The picture is not an unreal double of reality; it manifests to our gaze the unmistakable schema of the life of things within our bodies. Even Giacometti, one of those artists whose works might seem at first to be only remotely related to common perception, can write: "What I am interested in when I look at any painting is the resemblance." And he adds as if to emphasize that this resemblance has nothing to do with the phenomenon of *trompe l'oeil:* "that is to say what for me is resemblance: what allows me to discover a little bit of the external world" (PrP, 165; *OE*, 24; EM, 126).

Under these conditions, the work of the painter comes to disrupt the standard distinction between the real and the imaginary (the latter being conceived as unreal or fictional). What the artist's work brings under our gaze is not the unreal double, the fictional copy of the real, but what Merleau-Ponty calls without contradiction "the imaginary texture of the real." Hence the overlapping of the visible world and the seeing individual must now be associated with a second overlapping: the one between the real and the imaginary. This overlapping is often expressed by the creators who apparently are most prone to giving free rein to fantasy. The words of Max Ernst, for example, might well stand as a manifesto for all surrealists: "The role of the painter," he said, "is to project what is visible and seen within himself" (PrP, 168; *OE*, 30–31; EM, 129). Color also attests to this overlapping, if it is true that, already in the everyday visual field and to a greater extent in painting, each color is inseparable from the symbolic or cultural significance invested in it and is never ultimately a pure "sensorial datum," except in the laboratory of the psychologist.

It might be objected that this schema which things evoke in the body of the painter belongs strictly speaking to him or her alone, that it is the artist's private world and therefore has no reality. But the paradox is precisely that this supposedly private world, as soon as it is expressed, becomes constitutive of a common world. Thus the schema that became a picture and a painting elicits echoes in different individuals and imposes upon each one a specific way of looking at the world. In his novel, *Remembrance of Things Past*, Marcel Proust notices that shortly after the time when Renoir's paintings of women were the targets of sarcasm and reprobation because of their supposed failure to look like real women, people began to look at women in light of Renoir. One could say almost the same thing concerning Modigliani's paintings or the drawings and cutouts of Matisse. Strange though they were when they were first released, those works were quickly seen as awakening echoes in all of us and eliciting carnal recollections, thus allowing us to recognize a collective schema of femininity.

Thus the intertwining of the visible and seeing blends the overlapping between real and imaginary together with the intertwining of the private and the shared. It is as if painting attested to a generalized overlapping function. But let us return to the intertwining of the visible and the one who sees. It works indeed in two directions: the visible, as we just said, elicits in the seeing individual a carnal schema of what the visible realm is; but in addition, the seeing individual is part of the visible realm, too. This notion was expressed by a variety of painters who, as Merleau-Ponty observed with regard to Paul Klee, liked to say that they felt "looked at by things" (PrP, 167; *OE*, 31; EM, 129). This is also what, as early as the classical period, painters expressed in an iconographic manner either by depicting themselves in the process of painting (Matisse does this in some drawings) or, as in many Flemish and Dutch interiors, by installing some sort of onlooker in the form of a mirror in which the entire scene is reflected. The mirror, as Merleau-Ponty says, functions "as a pre-human gaze that is the symbol of the gaze of the painter." And he adds: "The mirror appears because I am seeing-visible, because there is a reflexivity of the sensible; the mirror translates this reflexivity and redoubles it." And further on: "It is the instrument of a universal magic which transforms things into spectacles, spectacles into things, myself into someone else and someone else into myself" (PrP, 168; *OE*, 33–34; EM, 129–30). If Merleau-Ponty speaks here of magic, it is not of course because of some exotic taste for the irrational, but instead because he wants to highlight the contrast between the actual vision and its reconstruction by analytical thinking in a philosopher of reflection such as Descartes, for example. Such a reflection in principle refuses the promiscuous contact of the seeing individual and of the visible to such an extent that "a Cartesian does not see *himself* in the mirror: he sees a mannequin, the 'outside' of a being" which for him is not the carnal appearance of his flesh, rather it is a simple "image"—upon which his thought makes the judgment that it is the mechanical reflection of his own body, a reflection to which his thought in a second move grants, in the same way as to an effect, some resemblance to its cause (PrP, 170; *OE*, 38–39; EM, 131).

These intertwinings are far from being the only ones expressed by painting. Indeed, what painting expresses most forcefully is the reciprocal overlapping of all the dimensions of the sensible—light, shadows, colors, reflections, lines. For a thought of the Cartesian type, it goes without saying that line and color are distinct just as much as form and content are different: the line determines the contour of a thing, or its envelope, which color then fills up. But a distinction of that kind, which is not problematic for the understanding, is precisely what painting brings into question. A few lines, and only lines, are sufficient for the prehistorical painters of the cave of Teruel in Spain to make us see a group of hunters. Merleau-Ponty recalls that Leonardo da Vinci in the *Treatise on Painting* proposed as a task for each painter to discover within each object "the unique and specific curve woven in it which permeates throughout its extension as its generating axis" (PrP, 183; *OE*, 72; EM, 142). To take a more contemporary example, Paul Klee is a painter for whom one single line is enough to set up in front of us the character of a "Timid Brute" and more generally to make visible a kind of genesis of things. This shows that, instead of being a limit, a line can express the entire thing and paradoxically function as a "total part." What is true of line is also true of color: it, too, functions as a total part capable by itself, without any lines, of presenting the object in its specific form and voluminous character as in Cézanne who used to say, "When color is at a perfection, form is at its fullest."

No less indicative of the overlappings that I am talking about is the fact that often good painters—I am thinking of Degas, Picasso, and Matisse—also turn into good sculptors, in spite of the fact that the manipulations and processes required to be a sculptor are very different from those required by painting. In this, Merleau-Ponty sees "the proof that there is a system of equivalences, a *Logos* of the lines, of lights, of reliefs, of masses, a presentation without any concept of universal Being" (PrP, 182; *OE*, 71; EM, 142). Painting shows, he says somewhere else, "a polymorphism of Being."

It is again the notion of overlapping that guides Merleau-Ponty's meditation on style in his essay on André Malraux's book on art, *The Voices of Silence*.

One meaning of style is the structural cohesion achieved by an individual work, a cohesion with which the spectator quickly becomes familiar and that allows him or her to recognize as works of painter X or Y paintings he or she has never seen before. On this topic, Malraux mentions a "coherent deformation" and he talks as if the shaping into a form effected by the artist was purely arbitrary with regard to the visible in the sense that style creates its own system. More precisely, he speaks as though styles were imposed from the top by the artist, without any prior anticipation in the visible. "The plastic arts," he writes, "are never born out of a way of looking at the world, but of shaping it." It is this voluntarist stand, this idea of a sovereignty, this acosmic attitude, to which Merleau-Ponty objects. And what he objects to in those notions is the fact that they are based on the previous dichotomies and dualities. In sum, Malraux confronts us with a choice between the visible world and the spiritual world of the creator; and as the artistic world has no antecedent in the visible one, the victory of a style seems to imply the abdication of the many who live in the visible in favor of the sovereign genius of the creator. There is no abdication, Merleau-Ponty objects, but only recognition. Recognition here is based on the fact that a style imposes itself simply because it adheres to the visible and somehow or other finds in the sensible its own antecedents; precisely because of this, a style is accessible to others, it is interindividual and does not emerge *ex nihilo* from the stormy solitude of the genius (S, 53–55, 57–59; S, 67–68, 72–73). From the perspective of others, the painter can sometimes appear as the creator of a counterworld, but for the painter at work there is but one world, and this world is what beckons him or her to work in a call to which the work will never stop responding.

One last mode of intertwining remains to be investigated. Not only do painters respond to what the visible world elicits in them, rather than merely continuing the task instituted by their own beginnings, they also inscribe themselves within a tradition of painting that overlaps on their work, just as their work is intertwined within the tradition. Here again the debate with Malraux is instructive. Malraux insists that painting forms a unique temporal adventure such that there is an affiliation among past and present painters, some kinship of present and past in the pictorial problems and solutions, in short, a sort of unity of painting as such. But that unity is expressed by him in such terms that it appears to be only retrospective, that is, made present and visible, and constituted after the fact, only by virtue of the modern phenomenon of the museum. In this view, the unity of painting seems to be transhistorical, and in the actual history Malraux sees nothing but scattered disunity, the struggle of each painter against others, forgetfulness, failure to be acknowledged.[7] It is to such a duality —the unity created by the museum, on the one hand, and historical dispersion, on the other—that Merleau-Ponty objects. To say that the unity of painting is retrospective amounts to failing to recognize that, just as to see is always to see more than one sees (for it provides access to a fringe of invisible features that have no place within the totality of strictly visual data), in the same way to paint is always to paint more than one paints. As soon as there was painting, it was in excess of itself. At the same time as it offers a field of visibility that goes beyond the given picture, the perceptual power of the painter is doubled with a prospective power. So, rather than oppose the nontemporal unity of the museum to the scattered character of actual history, the point is to understand actual history in terms of temporal overlappings. By virtue of these overlappings, neither the acquired nor the new can be regarded as entirely acquired or entirely new, and "the idea . . . of a totalization of painting . . . is meaningless" (PrP, 189; *OE*, 90; EM, 148).[8]

If it is true that such overlappings constitute the roots and the resourcefulness of thought, and if it is true on the other hand that painting itself has its roots and its resourcefulness in analogous overlappings, then one understands why Merleau-Ponty could speak of a "mute thought of painting" (PrP, 189; *OE*, 91; EM, 149).

But by the same token it is evident that Merleau-Ponty stands oceans apart from the philosophers who, ever since Plato, have been proclaiming in one guise or another that there must be an overcoming of painting—whether this be in the name of Platonic or Cartesian ideas, in the name of the history of the Spirit, in the name of material praxis, in the name of the absurdity of the will, or in the name of the history of Being. The reason for this notion of an end of art is that the attention of those philosophers, when they happen to be concerned with things pictorial, never dwells on the specificity of the visible. If one grants the visible realm its own full rights, then—against the pronouncements made by those grand narratives which, starting with the myth of the cave, proclaimed the death of art—one should be able to maintain: "Should the world still last millions of years, for painters, if some are still left, that world would still remain to be painted and will end before being completely captured" (PrP, 189; *OE*, 90; EM, 148).

16

The Dimension of Color

Véronique M. Fóti

She walked ahead of me along a dusty road on the outskirts of Jaipur, a labouring woman tired from her day's work. Her lavender veil was draped over a mustard-yellow *ghagra* (skirt); and balancing a basket on her head, she revealed the half-sleeve of her magenta-pink *choli* (blouse). A profusion of clear-green bangles adorned her arms; and heavy silver ornaments gleamed on her ankles. As in a waking dream, she walked on with measured pace, past men with their lemon-yellow, orange, and red turbans, past camel-carts, her eyes on the desert colors of the horizon.[1]

"**P**hilosophy," Merleau-Ponty notes, "paints without colors in black and white, like copperplate engravings."[2] Colors, which rank high among the essentials of life for the Rajasthani woman described above, are suspected by philosophy of frivolity, excess, abandon, and are exorcised, like other "supplements" (in the Derridian sense), with mixed alarm and disdain. Albeit an intellectually attuned ear might catch the music of the spheres, the light of reason, supposedly, is achromatic.

Apart from suggesting the abstract and oppositional character of metaphysical reason, Merleau-Ponty's remark also calls to mind a classical philosophical and scientific text which he will address explicitly only in "Eye and Mind":[3] Descartes's *Optics.*[4]

Descartes, Merleau-Ponty observes in "Eye and Mind," preferred the graphic art of engraving to painting, an art preoccupied with color

(PrP, 171f.; *OE,* 42; EM, 132). A discussion of engravings anchors the analysis of pictorial representation in the *Optics;* and they already make an enigmatic appearance in Descartes's significant dream sequence of 1619.[5]

As concerns representation, Descartes argues, in the *Optics,* against the scholastic theory of vision which is representational in that it postulates *phantasmata* emitted by the object and received by the eye.[6] The phantasmal representatives function by virtue of resemblance; yet Descartes points out, engravings can represent "forests, towns, people, and even battles and storms" with mere black ink marks on paper, showing that the perfection of a representing image "often depends on its not resembling its object as much as it might" (*CMS,* 165; *AT* VI, 113). Color belongs, for him, among the simulacra unnecessary for or detrimental to representation. Descartes, noting that we would need "yet other eyes within our brain" to register the resemblance between object and phantasm (*CMS,* 167; *AT* VI, 130), and that the proponents of *phantasmata* have nothing to say concerning their actual formation, bodily nature, or transmission, dismisses the scholastic theory which Merleau-Ponty refers to as "the magic of intentional species, the old idea of efficacious resemblance" (PrP, 171; *OE,* 40; EM, 132). What is unacceptable to Descartes is precisely this quasimagical aspect for which color plays an important part; and he proceeds, indeed, to relinquish the entire sensory and qualitative manifold in which colors have their being, reducing it, as "a text offered for our reading" (ibid.), to a schematic model of the purely quantitative determinations of material nature.

Merleau-Ponty, noting that painting, for Descartes, can obviously in no way define our access to being, speculates that an attentive study of painting would inaugurate another philosophy, one no longer enthralled by the ideals of conceptual grasp, intellectual mastery, and technical manipulation, but willing to interrogate the unmotivated and irreducibly complex upsurge of a world "which is not matter or in-itself" (PrP, 171; *OE,* 40; EM, 132). Since painting, unlike the graphic arts, is centrally concerned with problems of color, it can no more treat color as a "secondary quality" than it can relegate voluminosity or depth to the derivative status of a "third dimension":

> what is in question here is the dimension of color which creates
> of itself and for itself identities, differentiations, a texture, a
> materiality, a something. . . . The return to color has the merit
> of leading us somewhat closer to "the heart of things" . . . but

this lies beyond the color-envelope as well as beyond the space-envelope. (PrP, 181; *OE,* 67f.; EM, 141).

Merleau-Ponty's critical focus is not trained, ultimately, on the "classical" constructivism of Descartes—an operationalist thought which knows itself to be such and which derives its assurance precisely from its explicit self-limitation over against the enigmas of embodied existence and of the divine creative intellect. It is trained on contemporary technoscience which, as a somnambulent operationalism, lacks lucid awareness of its own limitations, its artifices, its belonging to the historicity of manifestation. Ironically, Merleau-Ponty suggests, such rampant operationalism may mark the consummate reign of a Cartesian nightmare (i.e., of pervasive and undetectable distortion) from which there is no longer any awakening. One can observe a certain kinship between Merleau-Ponty's critique of "operationalism" and Heidegger's thematic of technicity as the closure of metaphysics; but in keeping with Merleau-Ponty's claim that "the perceptual world is . . . Being in Heidegger's sense,"[7] the whole issue is transposed, somewhat incongruously, upon the register of perception.

Even leaving aside the incongruities of this fundamental problematic, it is unsurprising—given the complexities of the history of philosophical discourse on vision, light, and color, and given Merleau-Ponty's utterly innovative effort to bring this discourse up against the "evidences" of painting—that the analyses of "Eye and Mind" are both provocatively insightful and tantalizingly inconclusive. Neither the character (i.e., the historico-philosophical situation) of the Cartesian project and discourse on color, nor yet the philosophical scope and import of thematizing "the dimension of color" are fully worked out.

The present paper is a response to the fascination as well as frustration of Merleau-Ponty's text. I propose to ask how and why, on the basis of Cartesian optics, the light of reason metaphorically divests itself of phenomenal color; to explore, as a partial effort at philosophical situation, Greek discourses on light and color; and to assess the import of Merleau-Ponty's attempt to vindicate "that other and more profound opening unto things given to us by the secondary qualities, notably color" (PrP, 172; *OE,* 43; EM, 133). Given the scope and complexity of the issues, however, this effort can accomplish no more than a first foray into what is, for philosophical discussion, still to a large extent *terra incognita.*

Descartes: Color as Natural Sign

I don't *see* that the colors of bodies reflect light into my eye.
—Wittgenstein, *Remarks on Colour*[8]

Descartes insists on the inessentiality of color and other sensory qualities to *res extensa* which can be described equally as matter or space.[9] Although he finds that sight, the "noblest" and "most comprehensive" of our senses, depends on color to achieve optimal discrimination, he treats color-judgments as the very prototype of judgments tending to error; for the percipient, unaware of what produces "the very clear and vivid sensation," tends to regard color as an inherent property of things. The problem here is that "we cannot find any intelligible resemblance between the color which we suppose to be in the objects and that which we experience in our sensation."[10]

The intelligible laws of color are, for Descartes, inaccessible to vision; they pertain to the geometry of reflection and refraction, and to the microstructure and defining "action" of light. Specifically, Descartes points to the ratio between the rates of axial spin and rectilinear motion of the spherical particles of "subtle matter" which permeates the universal plenum and is agitated by light.[11] This theory of differential motion is invoked not only to account for the spectral hues of the rainbow, but also for the characteristic color of certain material objects, such as the red hue of blood. The latter, Descartes explains, is due to the fact that the microstructure of blood is such as to cause an acceleration in the axial spin of the globules of subtle matter in its interstices.[12] Descartes, of course, did not clearly grasp the distinction between spectral or prismatic colors (discovered by Newton in 1660), which form the additive color system, and colors produced by light reflection, forming the subtractive color system, nor could he have understood the utter dependence of reflected color on the illumining wavelength of the spectrum. Had he illuminated the blood, which in white light reflects chiefly the red part of the spectrum, with a beam of green light, it would have appeared a deep black, whereas the supposedly blackish "color of shadows" can change to red, yellow, violet, blue, or green with certain changes in illumination.

These relationships, however, cannot be set forth without reference to vision, since it is the human eye which, for instance, seeks to restore the completeness of the spectrum when presented with any one of the three primary colors, or with one of a pair of complementary colors, giving rise to the astonishing phenomena of simultaneous, successive, or reversed contrast.[13] Descartes's mechanistic physiology of vision, consisting in a theory of the formation and coded neural transmission of retinal images to the brain and ultimately to the pineal gland (the seat of the soul), relegates vision to passivity and cannot begin to account for the optical laws of color perception. The supposed breakdown of resemblance in color perception—the fact that we see hues rather than the geometry of reflection—is explained only in terms of the purported biological advantage which vivid sensory qualities offer to the percipient. For Descartes, light and color, as we perceive them, are signs instituted by nature, in accordance with a secret code, to convey to us certain motions and relationships in an efficient and useful manner:

> Now if words, which signify nothing except by human convention, suffice to make us think of things to which they bear no resemblance, then why should nature not also have established some sign to make us have the sensation of light, even if the sign contained nothing in itself which is similar to this sensation? . . . [I]t is our mind which represents to us the idea of light each time our eye is affected by the action which signifies it.[14]

It is the task of the intellect to decipher the code. Given that perceived color, for Descartes, is entirely explicable in terms of mechanical causes and the sign relationship (so that he can model his schematization of vision, in the *Optics*, on the blind man's touch), and given that the mechanics of vision registers (without resemblance) configurations present in the object, the notion of an autonomous domain of color vision governed by its own laws had to remain strictly alien to him. Had Descartes become aware of the utter dependence of perceived color on chromatic context and other contextual factors, he would probably have stressed the derivative and untrustworthy character of the phenomenon, rather than searching for either the visual laws of the interaction of colors or, beyond these, for the "matrix of vision" which David M. Levin describes as "an intertwining play of radiant energies."[15] Given Descartes's reduction of color to a natural sign, it is not surprising that painting seemed to him devoid of philosophical interest. The Royal Academy, founded less than two decades after Descartes's death, remained thoroughly Cartesian in its conviction that, in painting, color, as a purely sensory element, must be subordinated to rational considerations. It was not until the beginning of the eighteenth century that French art theory, through the work of Roger de Piles, came to acknowledge the primacy and cardinal importance of color in painting.[16]

Greek Discourses on Color

> There are many subjects that can be painted in contrast of hue.
> The significance of this contrast involves the interplay of pri-
> meval luminous forces. The undiluted primaries and seconda-
> ries always have a character of aboriginal cosmic splendor, as
> well as of concrete actuality.
>
> —Johannes Itten, *The Elements of Color*[17]

It has been observed that Homeric color vocabulary, while highly sensitive to the varied phenomena of luminosity and darkness, is impoverished with respect to hue.[18] Later Greek poetry similarly has been shown
to lack vocabulary for certain hues, notably for blues and greens. In her
study of ancient Greek poetic color terminology, Alice E. Kober concludes that "there is no doubt that the Greek poets did not distinguish
colors carefully"—a fact which, amusingly, she is inclined to excuse
since "even today men as a sex are notorious for their inability to distinguish greens and blues, violets and purples."[19]

The question as to possible connections between this emphasis, in
Greek poetic diction, on luminosity at the expense of hue, and the prominence which Heraclitus and Parmenides, in ushering in the philosophical light metaphorics, give to fire and night, the kindling and extinction
of light, luminosity and darkness, presents a complex and challenging
issue which cannot be taken up here.

A different approach to color, however, characterizes the plural-
ist Presocratics who showed an interest in color perception and pigmentary mixture. Anaxagoras's argument that perception requires contrast
(reaffirmed by Aristotle, *De Sensu*, 445b 20), was, according to Sextus
Empiricus, embedded in a discussion of imperceptible color gradations.[20] Because of the contrariety involved, Anaxagoras took all sensory
discernment to be painful (ibid.). Empedocles's theory of color perception as involving effluvia is familiar from the caricature in Plato's *Meno*
(76c, d), and from Aristotle's more extensive discussion in *De Sensu*
(437b 12–488a 5). Interestingly, Empedocles compares the generation
of mortals to the way in which painters, blending their pigments
(*pharmaka*) create, as if by magic, the semblances of many diverse things
(Fr. B23). Democritus, finally, ascribes color, like other sensory qualities,
to "convention and obscure knowledge" (Frs. B9, B125); yet he is known
to have composed a lost treatise on color perception and pigmentary
mixture.[21]

Plato, in the *Timaeus,* endeavors to give a probable and reasonable account of colors—an account belonging to the domain of *anangké*

or necessity, and lying, in Gadamer's words, "somewhere between an ongoing *story* of the premeditated actions of the demiurge and a logically consistent explanation of the cosmic order in rational terms."[22] The account of vision which precedes this analysis of color belongs, by contrast, to the teleological domain, although it considers the "auxiliary" rather than the primary, ideal causes of phenomena (46c 9–46d 3).

Whereas Cartesian vision is essentially dualistic and passive (Descartes acknowledges that the eyes can take the active role of emitting light, but only in the case of "creatures which can see in the dark, such as cats" [*CMS* I, 154; *AT* VI, 86]), Plato insists on the luminary power of the eyes and on a bond of affinity between seer and seen. The eyes continually send forth a stream of gentle, nonburning fire or light which coalesces with the light reflected from visible objects, engendering, in the line of vision, phenomenal appearances which are bodies of light (45b, d). In the darkness of night, this same ocular fire may give rise to dream images (46a).

Although Aristotle, with explicit reference to the *Timaeus*, rejects the theory that vision involves the issuance of light from the eyes (*De Sensu*, 437b 13–24), the theory contains an important insight, expressed by Merleau-Ponty in the acknowledgment that the positions of seer and seen "inevitably invert themselves" (PrP, 167; *OE*, 31; EM, 129), and by David M. Levin as the realization that "I am by nature a body of light, that I and the phenomenal displays of light are really one" (*The Opening of Vision*, 480). Levin achieved this insight into what he calls the nondualistic, nonegological character of vision through his practice of the Dzogchen Dark Retreat. This practice culminated, for him, in a visionary experience characterized not only by extraordinary luminosity, vividity, and distinctness, but also by "colours of incredible, 'supernatural' purity, intensity, aliveness, and clarity" (481). Somewhat surprisingly, however, color remains a minor theme in Levin's study, being largely confined to a marginal discussion in the notes.[23]

How then does color fare in Plato's nondualistic account of vision? Plato's analysis is probabilistic and schematic; he explicitly acknowledges the impossibility of giving a fully reliable explanation, given that the proportions involved lack proper measure, and that only God can change the one into many, and the many again into one (68d). The proportions involved are those between different kinds of flame or light which, although akin in their pyramidally articulated microstructure, differ as to the size and swiftness of their particles. If the fiery particles issuing from a visible body are equal to those of the visual fire, an effect of transparency results, whereas impinging flame with larger or smaller particles will, respectively, expand or contract the visual stream, yielding the appearance of white or black color. Rapidly impinging particles, on the other hand, cause tears to flow, which Plato describes as a mixture of fire and water (68a 2). These effractions and the resultant interactions of flame and moisture gives rise to a plethora of dazzling colors, whereas, if the impinging flame is intermediary (presumably in swiftness), a red glow is produced in the ocular moisture (68a, b). The redness or brilliance which are thus created enter into the visual genesis of other chromatic hues, such as yellow, blue, or leek-green, granting, however, that the proportions cannot be specified (68c).

It is evident that Plato bases his explanation neither on the spectrum nor on pigmentary mixture; its intelligibility seems to derive from the visual dynamics of colors, i.e., from the fact that some colors are seen as expansive, others contractive, aggressive or receding, dynamic or stable. Plato, in other words, focuses on the spatial and dynamic effects created by colors and color relationships. Plato's interest in these phenomena, however, seems limited to the geometric expressibility of spatial relationships which allows him to construct schematic models in the first place, and which promises to overcome the resistance of color to intellectual analysis. While it is not possible, within the confines of this essay, to explore the relation of the spatiality of color in the *Timaeus* to the *khora*, it is clear that Plato's understanding of this spatiality is phenomenologically impoverished.

The discrepancy between Plato's nondualistic theory of vision and his attempt—perpetually threatened with frustration—to schematize color announces itself more strongly in the derogatory treatment of color in other dialogues. Thus Plato remarks in the *Theaetetus* that color, arising out of ongoing processes of interaction, lacks stability and will not appear the same to different percipients or even to the same percipient at different times (153e–154b). While color shares such instability with other sensory qualities, it exercises, in addition, an almost magical fascination upon the soul (*Rep*, 602c 9–d 5), a fascination exploited by the illusionary techniques of *skiagraphia*.[24] Plato, in the *Republic*, likens a licentious democratic constitution to a gaily colored garment laden with embroidery in every imaginable hue and admired by those who are immature, impressionable, and lacking in taste (*Rep*, 557c). Color appears divorced here from the revelatory splendor of light exalted in Plato's heliotropic metaphors; it has become the emblem of multiplicity and transience, and thus of what is merely phenomenal. Its modern relegation to a secondary status is well prepared for.

In the concluding myth of the *Phaedo*, however, Socrates portrays the "true earth" as resplendent in the pure radiance of its twelve hues and their many gradations and variants, of which, he remarks, the pigments of the painter barely afford an adumbration (*Phaedo*, 110b 6–13). These colors of the true earth (of which Socrates names only three: radiant white, gold, and sea-purple) are not perceived by the living, nor yet by those who have died in the practice of philosophy (for they go to indescribably pure abodes), but by the unphilosophic dead who have led just and holy lives (114b 7–c 7). Perhaps these visionary and extraordinarily beautiful colors take the place of an intellectual vision of the *eidē* for nonphilosophic souls. If so, their affirmation forms a fitting conclusion to a dialogue in which Socrates, at the threshold of death, tells of having been divinely admonished to practice the arts (60e–61a). It marks also the emergence of a symbolic understanding of colors such as is characteristic of Hindu and Buddhist iconography as well as, to some extent and with more fluidity, of symbolist painters such as Redon or Gauguin, who described colors as mysterious spiritual forces.[25]

Whereas Descartes attributes the grasp of the basic, quantitatively expressible determinations of material nature, such as size, shape, position, motion, and number, to the pure intellect, Aristotle (excluding position from the list) considers them "common sensibles." Vision has privileged access to these common sensibles; for the proper object of vision is color, in which all bodies share, and in and through which they are revealed (*De Sensu*, 437a 4–8).

Aristotle rejects the Empedoclean and Platonic theory of fiery effluences from the eyes as incoherent and as constituting, moreover, only a roundabout way of explaining vision as he thinks it should be explained: on the basis of touch, which is to say, through the motion of a medium linking object and eye (*De Sensu*, 437a 23f.; 438a 26–28; 440a 16–20). He agrees with Democritus as concerns the watery constitution of the eye; for water is naturally transparent. Transparent bodies are receptive to light; and light actualizes the potentiality of transparence (*De Anima*, 448b 10). As Aristotle puts the point in the *De Anima*: "Light . . . is neither fire nor, generally speaking, a body, nor an effluence from a body . . . but the coming-to-presence (*parousia*) of fire or something like it in the transparent" (418b 14–17).

This *parousia* creates light as the actualization of transparence; and since light is *energeia*, Aristotle rejects the Empedoclean theory that it is motion (418b 22). However, precisely because it involves no motion, actualized transparency as such is not seen. Vision requires not only light but color, either in the actualized transparence itself or in surrounding bodies. Color is *dynamis* or potency; it is "the power to produce motion in actualized transparence," thus rendering it visible (*De Sensu,* 418a 31–419b 2; 419a 10–20).

It should be noted, parenthetically, that Aristotle also recognizes a form of visibility which depends on darkness rather than illumination, namely the phenomena of phosphorescence or bioluminescence (*De Anima,* 419a 1–8). He remarks that, whereas light renders visible the proper color of things, in these phenomena, proper color is not seen (ibid.). Bioluminescence, however, is not colorless but shows an unearthly spectrum of glowing, phosphorescent hues. Perhaps Aristotle is referring to these phenomena in his preceding cryptic remark that the visible is either color or something expressible in words which happens, however, to have remained nameless (418a 22f.). He offers, in any case, no further discussion of phosphorescence.

Aristotle postulates, in *De Sensu,* that the potentiality of transparence is found, to some extent, in all bodies, accounting for their visibility, albeit only diaphanous bodies such as air, water, or crystals exhibit it in its purity (439a 22–25). Radiance or brightness is the proper color of illumined air or water (439b 1f.), whereas, in nondiaphanous bodies, the luminous actualization of transparence or its nonactualization are manifest, respectively, as white or black color (439b 15–18). Aristotle's entire account of color has so far been given, with striking conformity to Homeric sensibility, in terms of luminosity and darkness. Thus he faces the vexing question of how to account for the genesis of chromatic hues.

In response, Aristotle puts forward three hypothetical explanations which constitute a progression from optical to quasichemical analysis, of which he inclines to accept the third. The first hypothesis postulates a combination or alternation of invisibly minute black and white particles according to various proportions, resulting in what is now called optical mixture. The theory allows for the expression of at least some colors as numerical ratios and promises a quasimusical harmonics of color; but Aristotle rejects it since he cannot countenance its presupposition of invisible magnitudes (*De Sensu,* 439b 19–440a 6; 440a 21–30).

The second hypothesis takes as its model the painterly technique of overlay, with the overlays presumably restricted, at least initially, to films of white and black. The model has the advantage of presupposing neither invisible magnitudes nor imperceptible time intervals (which are also required by the first hypothesis); and it still allows for proportional analysis (440a 7–15, 25–30). Aristotle, however, favors the third hypothesis of continuous material mixture or blending, noting that some blends may be expressible as numerical ratios, with many depending, however, on mere preponderance (440b 1–25). Given that, on all these theories, the chromatic hues are intermediate between the achromatic extremes of black and white, Aristotle concludes that their number is definite or limited (445b 20–28).

It is evident that Aristotle is unable to account for the genesis of the chromatic hues, since hue cannot be assimilated to brightness, and since he lacks the spectrum or the refraction of light in water (tears) which functioned like a prism. Notwithstanding his careful observation of phenomena such as the vanishing of color when the colored object is brought into contact with eye (*De Anima,* 418b 20–30), his study of color is at a greater remove from the phenomenology of vision than Plato's. His rejection of the Empedoclean and Platonic theory of the fiery eye, moreover, leaves him—whatever its scientific merit—with a dualistic schema of seer and seen connected by a transparent medium which can be set in motion. It is not far from this conception to Descartes's model of the blind man's stick. Seer and seen are incapable here of interchanging their places; and Aristotle states explicitly in the *De Anima* that "sensible objects are individuals external to man" and that sensation, for this reason, differs from knowledge (417b 19–28).

Unlike Plato, Aristotle acknowledges certain lawlike and mathematically expressible properties of color, as shown by his concern with numerical proportion. His choice of the material blending hypothesis tends, nevertheless, to frustrate proportional analysis. This analysis is confined, moreover, to the optical or chemical constitution of individual colors and accounts for whether or not they are pleasing to the eye. The assumption is—quite erroneously—that everyone will have the same color preferences. Aristotle does not think of extending mathematical analysis to color relationships and shows, in fact, no awareness of the utterly relational character of color.

The Logos of Color

The various "colours" do not all have the same connection
with spatial vision.
—Wittgenstein, *Remarks on Colour* (35)

The preceding discussion of philosophical discourses on color has been highly selective, with the selection guided by Merleau-Ponty's own engagement with the tradition. His chief dialogue, however, is not with the Greeks, but with Descartes and with the rationalist effort to think representation nonmimetically, which culminates in the Leibnizian understanding of representation as geometric projection. The rationalist slighting of color is tied up with this rethinking of representation. Merleau-Ponty, in his dialogue with the tradition, makes no reference to the rich nineteenth-century context of discussion, stimulated by Goethe's anti-Newtonianism, which includes the contributions of Schopenhauer and Hegel.[26]

Already in the *Phenomenology of Perception*, Merleau-Ponty insists that color is not an isolable and simple quale or sensory datum which might function as a component of the as yet unorganized perception of infants.[27] As concerns the infant, Merleau-Ponty points to a gradual evolution from indeterminate and "physiognomic" color awareness to the "change in the structure of consciousness" which marks the perception of distinct colors (PhP, 29f.; *PP,* 38.). The notion of the quale springs from a refusal "to recognize any colours other than those fixed qualities which make their appearance in a reflexive attitude" (PhP, 305; *PP,* 352). This refusal ignores the perceptual genesis of color constancy and local color, as well as the disciplined, abstractive fixation of the gaze needed to isolate areas of pure surface color from the perceptual field. Physics and physiology, Merleau-Ponty notes, "give an arbitrary definition of colour which, in reality, fits only one of its modes of appearance and has for long masked the rest" (PhP, 306f.; *PP,* 252). This arbitrariness reflects the circumscription of the phenomenon in philosophical discourse, particularly that of Descartes and of his efforts to come to terms with the scholastic Aristotle. Descartes, nevertheless, is a master of disguises and masks, so that, as Merleau-Ponty remarks in "Eye and Mind," constructivist science and philosophy do not spring from Cartesianism by direct filiation, but are "two monsters born of its dismemberment" (PrP, 177; *OE,* 58; EM, 138).

In the *Phenomenology*, Merleau-Ponty stresses, in particular, the integration of color perception into the complexities of sensory-motor organization, and thus into lived spatiality. A study of these interconnections shows not only the insertion of the sentient body into the perceptible world, but, more fundamentally, the breakdown of the subject-object schema of metaphysical discourse. Vision resists the subject's efforts at intellectual appropriation; for, as "a thought subordinated to a certain field" (PhP, 217; *PP,* 251), it is marked by dispossession and anonymity.

Whereas the *Phenomenology*, with its theme that "my body is the fabric into which all objects are woven [*mon cops est la texture commune de tous les objects*]" (PhP, 235; *PP,* 272), emphasizes simultaneous participations, such as the intersensory, sensory-motor, contextual, and sentient-sensible interconnections, *The Visible and the Invisible* elaborates, in particular, temporally structured participations which engage the historico-cultural, archetypal, libidinal, oneiric, and imaginal dimensions. Through these "simultaneous and successive" participations, an ephemerally perceived color becomes an articulating knot in a many-layered, interlaced netting which captures the "invisibles" of ideality and meaning in its meshes. The chiasmatic intercalation of these articulations of what Merleau-Ponty terms "vertical genesis" indicates a structure of persistent divergence in connectedness, a resistance to completion and totalization.[28]

Color functions here as a dimension not only in that it is a modality of the enveloping presence of the sensory field, but also in that, as a matrix of crystallization, it has the anonymous generality of an element: "Now this particularity of the color, of the yellow, and this universality are not a *contradiction*, are *together* sensoriality itself: it is by the same virtue that the color, the yellow, at the same time gives itself as a *certain* being and as a *dimension*, the expression of every *possible* being" (VI, 218; *VI*, 271f.).

Merleau-Ponty's notion of a sensory universality which is dimensionally organized and not amenable to conceptual grasp comes into sharper focus in "Eye and Mind." He speaks here of the *"logos* of equivalences" which interlinks different registers of visibility, such as form, depth, line, or color, as "a conceptless presentation of universal Being" (PrP, 182; *OE,* 71; EM, 142). In the ontological reworking of his phenomenological problematic in *The Visible and the Invisible* (a reworking which, in the end, undermines his own notions of "ontology" and "perception"), Merleau-Ponty understands dimensionality as ideality. This ideality, however, cannot be dissevered from the sensory domain but is its articulating "lining," the invisible of the visible, or even—in Heideggerian terms—"the Being of this being" (VI, *151; VI,* 198). Being reveals itself as an acausal and a-telic proliferating dimensionality which Merleau-Ponty calls dehiscence (VI, *227, 265;* VI, 280, 318f.); and perception participates in this differential proliferation by virtue of the percipient's "being set up on a universal diacritical system" (VI, *233; VI,* 287).

Color functions thus as "a concretion of visibility" organizing the differential latency which Merleau-Ponty calls "flesh." In his phenomenological ontology, a reciprocal "precession" interconnects ideality (structure, order, meaning, intelligibility) and sensoriality. This thoroughgoing interpenetration without coalescence undercuts both the "positivistic" causal or epistemological analyses of color and the Goethean-romantic repudiation of its mathematical study,[29] allowing for philosophical approaches which do not foreclose the phenomenon. For Merleau-Ponty, such approaches are prepared for in the history of modern painting which shows, for instance, the possibility of modulating space out of the instability of color and which refuses to recognize the classical privilege of the "form-spectacle" without, for all that, seeking in color another privileged "key" to the visible. Merleau-Ponty notes thus that the confrontation of the universe of classical thought with the researches of modern painting generates an awareness of "a profound discordance, of a mutation in the relationships between man and Being" (PrP, 179; OE, 63; EM, 139).

Notwithstanding his important insight concerning this interpenetration, however, Merleau-Ponty's focus is trained on one side or one direction of this reciprocal movement, to the neglect of the other. He emphasizes the cohesion of ideality with the strata of perceptual articulation and experience but tends to neglect the possibility of an "ideal," e.g., mathematical, analysis of these strata. He therefore slights the lawlike and, to some extent, mathematically expressible traits which characterize not only the physical infrastructure of color but also its phenomenal manifestations, preferring an almost mystical discourse of "exhalations" and—in a cryptic quotation from Hermes Trismegistus—of "the inarticulate cry which seemed to be the voice of light" (PrP, 182; OE, 70; EM, 142).

The phenomena of color and color-vision, far from being inarticulate, exhibit lawlike traits of astonishing intricacy. By way of example, one can consider here the laws of complementarity as they operate in spectral and material color, the ordered geometrical expressibility of harmonious relationships on the twelve-hue color-circle, or Itten's discovery that "the six fundamental hues on a black ground conform to the Golden Section in their gradations of depth" (The Elements of Color, 77). E. H. Land's experimental work, moreover, has shown that full-color photographic images are generated when two black and white transparencies, obtained by photographing color objects on black and white film with the use of complementary color filters, are superimposed on a projector. Full-color images resulted even though, apart from not using color film, a color filter admitting only a narrow band of the spectrum (e.g., a segment of its yellow part) was placed on the lens of the projector.[30]

Despite their Newtonian basis, these experiments show an intriguing affinity to Aristotle's hypothesis of the generation of chromatic hues from black and white overlays, with the difference that the laws of such generation are no longer sought in the physico-mathematical or (in the case of pigments) chemical constitution of colors alone, but also in vision itself. Whereas Merleau-Ponty would probably agree with Itten's statement that it is the concern of painting to liberate the spiritual essence of form and color, releasing it from imprisonment in the world of objects (*The Elements of Color*, 95), he neglects the painter's complementary concern with structural laws. As Itten expresses it, in the language of the workshop: "If we can find objective laws of general validity in the realm of color, then it is our duty to study them" (ibid., 26).

The importance of Cézanne's painting for Merleau-Ponty's researches into the phenomenology of vision reflects, in part, the fact that, as Merleau-Ponty puts it, Cézanne "did not think he had to choose between feeling and thought, between order and chaos," but strove, rather, "to put intelligence, ideas, science, perspective, and tradition back in touch with the world of nature which they must comprehend."[31] Cézanne, during his painterly career, moved increasingly toward letting color function as what (with reference to depth or voluminosity) Merleau-Ponty calls a first dimension, showing that "the world is a mass without gaps, a system of colors across which the receding perspectives, the outlines, angles, and curves are inscribed like lines of force; the spatial structure vibrates as it is formed" (SNS, 15; CD, 65). Writing to Émile Bernard in 1905, the year before his death, Cézanne observed that, in his old age, "the sensations of color, which give light" prevented him from filling his canvasses and from "continuing the delimitation of objects when their points of contact are fine and delicate, " thus leaving his paintings in irremediable incompletion.[32]

Merleau-Ponty, in his perceptive discussions of Cézanne's art, stresses the painter's "intuitive science," his ability to recapture, in his visual meditations upon the luminous landscapes in the vicinity of Aix, "the vibration of appearances which is the cradle of things" (SNS, 18; CD, 68). What he neglects, however, is what Itten called "Cézanne's logically derived color construction" resting upon "formal and chromatic principles" (*The Elements of Color*, 11). Albers similarly points out that Cézanne's ability to modulate depth out of color depended importantly on his discovery of the curious spatializing properties of "middle mixtures" (pigmentary mixtures equidistant from their "parent" colors in both brightness and hue) which are due to a neutralizing of color boundaries. Cézanne, Albers observes, "was the first to develop color areas which produce both distinct and indistinct endings—areas connected and unconnected—areas with and without boundaries—as a means of plastic organization."[33]

Such attention to the lawlike characteristics of color as they articulate themselves in and for vision (rather than in a putative ideal substratum inaccessible to vision) is an important way in which modern painting prepares for the phenomenological ontology or ontology of the flesh which Merleau-Ponty begins to work out in *The Visible and the Invisible*. This ontology, as already indicated, is structured in terms of dimensionality and dehiscence rather than in terms of levels of reality interlinked by formal or causal relationships. At the same time, Merleau-Ponty's insistence on a reciprocal precession of ideality and sensoriality allows him to mediate between the empiricist and "intellectualist" strands of the metaphysical tradition. In stressing not only the carrying-over of the "style" of sensory or perceptual experience into the entire range of ideality, but also—at least in principle—the permeation of sensoriality by ideality, he reconnects phenomenology with the rationalist tradition which emphasizes the mathematical structure of the real. At the same time—as has here been argued with respect to the dimension of color— he undertakes an important and daring resituation of intelligibility and analytical reason. To the extent, however, that he veers away from tracing the precession of mathematical "ideality" upon the sensory domain, he tends to frustrate the consummation of a guiding insight.

From *Discours, Figure*

Jean-François Lyotard
Translated by Michael B. Smith

Favoring the Figural

. . . if the truth does not appear where it is expected, and if no discourse can exhibit it in its full signification because it does not belong to the domain of discourse, then this book is not true, to the extent that it obviously attempts to produce articulated significations. But it is not a scholarly book either, since it makes no attempt to construct a unified theory, even to function as a background. It is rather a dislocated body, in which speech inscribes fragments that can, in principle, be stuck together in various ways, but which must, because of constraints of typographical composition (which are those of signification and ratio), be presented in an immutable order. Even though this order is determined, and determinate, it is . . . surely not arbitrary, but arbitrarily privileged (by the constraints just mentioned) as compared with others. A good book, in order to let truth be in its aberrancy, would be a book in which linguistic time itself (the time in which signification unfolds, the reading time) would be deconstructed; a book the reader could start anywhere, and read in any order. A book to graze in (and one that would also be free from the literary genre of the aphorism: I say this in thinking of Nietzsche, who was still too inclined to that genre). This present book is not that good book. It remains within signification. It is not the book of an artist: deconstruction does not operate directly within it, but is *signified*. It remains a book of philosophy, in that respect. True, the signification is fragmentary; there are gaps, and, I hope, some riddles. But that only means that the object it produces is uncertain, intermediary—something I would like to be able to call (by way of excuse) an interworld, after Klee, or a transitional object, à la Winnicott. But it is not really that, because such a status belongs only to the figural objects of games, of painting. Here, I repeat, I shall not let the figure turn into words in accordance with its own game. I want the words to *say* the preeminence of the figure; I want to *signify* signification's other. I still want. I want too much. I am still but the least of men, and the space of this book is no more than baroque. But still, it must be said in my defense, this "too much" is little.

I have renounced the folly of unity, the folly of supplying the ultimate cause in a unitary discourse, the fantasy of the origin. The Freudian utopia keeps us within the purview of the rule dictated by the so-called death drive, which is that the unification of the diverse, even in the unity of a discourse (even in the unity of the Freudian discourse), is always rejected, always forbidden. Just as, on the basis of the consideration of that rule, the ego, as a unitary constituted psychic order, must be rejected, similarly it is time philosophers abandoned the project of producing a unitary theory as if it were the last word on things. There is no *arche*,[1] but neither is there the Good as a unitary horizon. We never touch the thing itself except metaphorically, but that laterality is not, as Merleau-Ponty thought, that of existence, which is far too close to the unity of the subject, as he himself recognized in the end;[2] it is that of the unconscious or of expression, which in one and the same moment gives and withholds all content. That laterality is difference, or depth. But while Merleau-Ponty posited it as the possible movement of going off into the distance while at the same time remaining here, as ubiquitous openness, continuous mobility, and saw as its model the sensible chiasma, thus falling prey to the illusion of unitary discourse,[3] I shall surrender to figural space—along with Cézanne and Mallarmé, Freud and Frege. Depth still far exceeds the power of a reflection that would signify it, place it within its language—not as a thing, but as a definition. Meaning is present as absence of signification; however, the latter takes hold of the former (which it can do: one can say anything), and meaning is exiled to the margin of the new act of speech. There we have the death drive, ever intertwined with Eros-Logos. To construct meaning is never anything other than to deconstruct signification. There is no model assignable to that evasive configuration. It will be said that violence is at the beginning as castration, and that the silence or death that our words would like to flush out from their cover is the descendent of that initial terror that gave rise to desire. So be it, but the locus of that desire being utopia, it should be understood that we must give up the attempt to ascribe a place to it.

The preceding is very important for practice—for the practical critique of ideology. This book itself is but a detour, leading to that practice. If I have had to wait a long time to overcome my resistance to writing it, that is surely (among other reasons) for fear of being seduced, turned aside from that goal, paralyzed by language. As for its usefulness, and how much of it has remained active, warm—that is not for me to judge.

A word in retrospect. There is a falling away as the sections advance. The reader will notice this. He or she will complain that my thinking is uncertain. What diminishes progressively from beginning to end is the importance given to perception. First, the order of discourse is explored, in order to isolate signification properly so-called from designation. Thus a phenomenological space, or a space of vision is set apart. Its properties are assumed to be quite distinct from those of linguistic signification, although they are not actually analyzed, since Merleau-Ponty's phenomenology of the visible is adopted wholesale. Then we move from sight to vision, from the world to the phantasm; and the responsibility for the constitution of the object, of what confronts us directly, which was originally assigned to the discursive gaze, is shifted over and entrusted to wish-fulfillment. The figure is correspondingly dispaced. It is no longer the image of presence or representation, but the form of the mise-en-scène, the form of discourse itself, and, at a still deeper level, the phantasmal matrix. The lesson of Freud takes precedence over that of Husserl.

The key moment of transition is the greatest of pitfalls: the category of continuity. If it is true that gesture is meaning, it must be so by opposition to linguistic signification. The latter is only constituted as a network of discontinuities; it gives rise to an immobile dialectic in which thinker and thought never intermingle, and in which the elements of the latter never overlap. The gesture, on the contrary, as Merleau-Ponty understood it, is the experience of a meaning in which the sensed and the sensing make up a common rhythm, like the two sides of the same furrow, and in which the constituents of the sensible form one organic, diachronic whole. The difficulty is that the gesture is relative if not to a subject, at least to a kind of subjectivity, be it an anonymous one, or be it nature, as Mikel Dufrenne says. It is experienced, lived, or in any event it structures the lived; it is based upon an unconscious that is not the object of repression, but the subject of constitution.

At first sight, the meaning psychoanalysis speaks of also appears as continuity. It can legitimately be contrasted with linguistic signification, as the plastic expanse of condensation, displacement and distortion stands in contrast to the discrete, transparent space in which signifiers are formed by regulated differentiation. Libidinal and sensible meaning [*sens sensible*] seem to coincide, to stand together in opposition to the signification of language. It is this coincidence that is eventually undone in this book, as the phenomenological mask slips down to reveal . . . not the face of the unconscious that no one has seen nor will see . . . but the mask of desire. The falling away is that of phenomenology.

The turning of the tide is the reflection on difference, on the organization of sensible space. The fact that the latter cannot be reduced to a geometrical organization entirely thinkable in concepts—it was precisely phenomenology itself that emphasized this. "Eye and Mind" went as far as it was possible to go in the direction I have indicated through its description of *passivity*, the passivity of the perceptual synthesis, which was already in Husserl. What Merleau-Ponty meant to show in contrasting Cézanne's space with that of *La dioptrique* was that an articulated, discontinuist, active, logical conception of meaning and space could not but miss the datum or rather the donation of the visible. This latter event was precisely invisible to Cartesian thought, as it is in our constituted experience of extended objects. Merleau-Ponty demonstrated that it took Cézanne's enormous immobility to clear away the rationalization of perceptual space and to perceive the primary donation in its obliqueness, it ubiquity, its lateral transgression of the rules of geometrical optics. What Cézanne desired was Mount Sainte-Victoire to cease being a visual object and become an event in the visual field; and that is what the phenomenologist hopes to—and in my opinion cannot—understand.

His ultimate concept, his most delicate concept for the apprehension of the event-like quality of the datum, is surely not intentionality: it is passivity. But this concept can only function in the field set up by phenomenology, as the opposite or correlate of intentional activity, as its underlying support. The intention as act rests upon a passive synthesis which is the very donation of that which is intended. That passivity is therefore still thought of as a *supposition* of the intending subject, as a presupposed immanence in the subject's transcendent relation to the object. The subject is in a sense deposited (dispossessed), but also posited within that relation. It is in this manner that Merleau-Ponty wishes to move from the "I" to the "One" [*du Je au On*]. But consider the distance remaining between "One" and "That" [*entre On et Ça*].[4]

The "One" is not event-producing in relation to the "I"; on the contrary. Following that direction toward anonymity, what would we find? At best the organization of the forms of sensibility, a space-time hidden deeper than the one that is lived, and less tributary to the properties of physics than the one Kant described, but nevertheless a space and time that form a *framework* within which the given is given, in which events arise, but not serving as the principle of any event. It may be as preconceptual a system as you please, but like all systems, it will be one capable of accounting not for the fact that there are events (in the visual field or elsewhere), but precisely for the fact of the event's (or donation's) being reabsorbed, received, perceived, integrated into a world (or history, etc.). The enigma of the event will remain intact even after having tried to descend to the level of the "One." It is not the search for the conditions, anonymous or otherwise, of the data that immobilized Cézanne before his mountain; it was the search for the donation. Phenomenology cannot reach the donation because, faithful to the philosophical tradition of the West it remains a reflection on knowledge, and the function of such a reflection is to reabsorb the event, to retrieve the Other in the Same.

The event in its initial alterity cannot come from the world, to which we are attuned in sense.[5] The discordance cannot come from speech, which to the degree it is understood is articulated signification and the object of knowledge. It is equally impossible for it to come from a world with which the lived body cooperates to produce the sensoria that are its element. True, the body-in-the-world can be event-producing in the order of discourse, since it is obvious that meaning is not deposited in it as is signification in language. And this is why the presence of figures in discourse can be understood as the insertion of gestures, which normally occur against a background of continuous space, within a field such as language, which does not in principle tolerate transformations except among discrete elements. This is the proper context for Merleau-Ponty's notions of "encroachment" and "laterality." These effects are pertinent in defining the poetic order or rhetoric in general. But to what should they be attributed?

On this question we should allow our thinking to be oriented by the fact that these disturbances in the order of signification have always been presented in myth, tragedy, and philosophy as guilty. It is impossible to impute that culpability to the lived body alone. That body is not a place of predilection for disturbance and the event. There is a silent infrastructure in the life of the flesh, its ὑγίεια, and it is true, as Merleau-Ponty thought, that it [the *hygieia* of the flesh] is but a chiasma in the milieu of the world, encompassed within it, and encompassing it. On the basis of that euphoria Merleau-Ponty has attempted to build a pagan philosophy. But his paganism remains caught up in a problematic of knowledge; this produces a philosophy of intelligent flesh, which is a happy philosophy, but which misses the significance of dispossession. The event qua disturbance is always what defies knowledge: it may defy the knowledge that is articulated in discourse, but it may also disrupt the quasi-understanding of the lived body and destroy its harmony with itself and with its objects—as in the case of emotion. There can be as much guilt and impropriety contained in a look or a blush as in a slip of the tongue. It is not the body that disturbs language, but something other that can disturb both language and the body. To accept the body as the locus of the event is to accept the burden of the defensive displacement, the vast rationalization carried out by the Platonic-Christian tradition for the purpose of disguising desire.

The event cannot be posited elsewhere than in the vacant space opened up by desire. That vacuum is precisely donation's place of predilection. This can be seen directly in the anguish that underlies all the emotions,[6] but also in the presence, within discourse, of words and expressions indicating the troubled regions in which the speaker receives. Such a vacuum is not an "attitude" to be recommended, an ethical stance, such as exemplified in the paradox of Kierkegaard's knight of faith or Levinas's an-archy.[7] The will to become the enthusiast of the event, or to be at the service of the event, is still an illusion—an ethical temptation. It is for the donation to dispossess us, not for us to appoint ourselves for dispossession. The event does not occur where expected: even a lack of expectation will be disappointed. It is not possible to pass over to the side of the primary process: that is a secondary illusion. Desire has its rejection within itself—which is the principle of dispossession of its objects. Desire is truly unacceptable; we cannot pretend to accept it. To accept is still to reject it. It will erupt as event elsewhere.

The event cannot be situated truly if we begin by removing it from the empty space left by repression or at least rejection in general. Neither discourse nor the body have, within themselves, that crossed out, twisted disposition that *allows* donation precisely because it *forbids* the recognition or understanding of the datum. Cézanne's prayer: May the familiar mountain dispossess him, may it appear elsewhere from where the eye awaits it, and thus seduce him. It is a prayer of *deconciliation*—an antiprayer. A prayer that connects the visible neither with the I-Thou of language nor the [anonymous] One of perception, but with the That of desire; and not with the immediate figures of desire, but with its operations.

Such is the displacement or angle of rotation that will be perceived in this book. It may be more precisely circumscribed in the course of the reflections on opposition and difference. It may be asked: Since you say that the order of the [anonymous] perceptival One masks the order of the That, why did we not throw off the mask, obliterate the former? I would answer that this displacement is precisely what counts for me as event in this book. By virtue of what order, what supposed function of the book, or what prestige of discourse, should it be obliterated?

Recessus and Hyperreflection

Reflection, which believed itself comfortably installed within the negative as upon a high mountain peak from which it could look down over both sides of language, now finds itself, after the structural critique of showing [*du montrer*], and the dialectical-phenomenological critique of the system, expelled from its position and apparently condemned to nomadism. It learns that it is besieged on two sides (by the unconsciousness of language and of sight), and that it cannot take possession of these two sorts of elementary intervals—one constituting signification and the other referentiality. The prisoner of a language, without which it would only be sight, but chained to the distanciation of seeing, outside of which that language would be a mere thing, unable to be spoken, reflection must tread the boundary line at which the first silence, that of structure, meets the second, that of the phenomenon, to produce speech. It runs the risk of falling into either the positivism of the system or the intuitionism of the gaze's object. It is denied the dialectic "solution" of a synthesis of the two negative axes, and condemned to advance only in keeping its imbalance, as the sole witness of its existence, intact.

The exclusion of dialectic prompts other directions. The philosopher, as long as he does not also become a painter, must remain within the orbit of language, of structural unconsciousness. But what speech can still accomplish is to exert upon its own language that transgression over separate spaces—that mobility, that depth that characterize the referentiality of discourse, which structuralism omits. It is not to draw or paint in themselves—it is to paint and draw with and in words. Merleau-Ponty called this "hyperreflection."[8]

What philosophy "finds in thus returning to the sources, it says,"[9] obviously, but that saying, according to Merleau-Ponty, could be of such a texture as to respect that source-like quality within itself, that ontogenesis it seeks to signify. Discourse, in his view, by an operation upon itself, attempts to equal the "origin" it wishes to say. A discourse on origin, an original discourse: in his eyes, a discourse of openness as opposed to a language of "eloquence," which would be a discourse of closure. "[T]he words most charged with philosophy are not necessarily those that contain what they say, but rather those that most energetically open upon Being, because they more closely convey the life of the whole and make our habitual evidences vibrate until they disjoin."[10] And after that affirmation—by a sort of retreat to be interpreted neither as modesty nor as a kind of admission in the form of a denial, but rather as a way of warding off the contraction of that hope into a "thesis," the avoidance of another alienation of language along the lines of the one he has just exposed in Sartre's problematic of nothingness—the philosopher immediately adds: "Hence it is a *question* whether philosophy as reconquest of brute or wild being can be accomplished by the resources of the eloquent language, or whether it would not be necessary for philosophy to use language in a way that takes from it its power of immediate or direct signification in order to equal it with what it wishes all the same to say."[11] As for the "answer" to that "question," we thought we already knew it. It appears to be restated throughout the book. "As the world is behind my body, the operative essence is behind the operative speech also, the speech that possesses the signification less than it is possessed by it, that does not speak *of it*, but speaks *it*, or speaks *according to it*, or lets it speak and be spoken within me, breaks through my present."[12] "As the nervure bears the leaf from within, from the depths of its flesh, the ideas are the texture of experience; its style, first mute, then uttered. Like every style, they are elaborated within the thickness of being."[13] And if we must attempt to characterize this "style," this is how it should be done.

> [T]here is or could be a language of coincidence, a manner of making the things themselves speak—and this is what he seeks. It would be a language of which he would not be the organizer, words he would not assemble, that would combine through him by virtue of a natural intertwining of their meaning, through the occult trading of the metaphor—where what

counts is no longer the manifest meaning of each word and of each image, but the lateral relations, the kinships that are implicated in their transfers and their exchanges.[14]

"There could be . . . ," "It would be a language . . . ": a daydream, conducted in the mood and tense of the unreal present. But it is also a glimpse at the style of hyperreflection, which is thereby related, assimilated to the style of the dream. This reverie on language joins the "language" of the dream; the "natural intertwining" of meanings, the "occult trading of the metaphor," the "lateral" relations of words and of images: it is all there—displacement, figurability, all the operations that make up the "style" of the dream and also of poetry. All their "work," as Freud would say.

Surely Merleau-Ponty did not contemplate *replacing* philosophy with reverie. He thought that a model of discourse, closed or obsessed with closure—the model of "rational" philosophy—has to be dispossessed of the interrogation of the originary if it wants to allow something to say itself within it that otherwise, armed with its eloquence, it does not succeed in saying. But by what shall that model be replaced? Can one philosophize outside discourse, and conduct a discourse without ratio? It may be arrogant to declare that what I am seeking here is, in the same direction as that indicated in Merleau-Ponty's last writing, why and how poetry and dreams are related to hyperreflection—why and how language can, by giving up the framework of the scientific logos, if not *approach* the "origin" more closely, at least produce, in its very texture, an approximation of what it [language] is not. This may seem unfaithful to the spirit of *The Visible and the Invisible*, if it is true that the exhibition of the rationality of the clandestine cannot help but entail what may seem to be the restauration of a philosophy of the negative; and it is precisely from such a philosophy that Merleau-Ponty unceasingly differentiates and frees himself. But the negative I propose to bring out by moving in this direction is not that of Sartre, nor of a Hegelian dialectic. It unfolds, as I have indicated, into an invariant interval of the system and the mobile spacing of sight. And this dual development is so essential that, if hyperreflection can tend toward poetry or dreams, it is because they both obviously presuppose language, but a language undone. They both obviously presuppose the table, but an invariant interval of the table— that interval worked and submitted to distortion, "vibrating to the point of disjoining."

To undo the code without destroying the message, but rather, on the contrary, in freeing the meaning, the lateral semantic reserves that are hidden beneath the main frame of the word—this is the performance of a set of operatives that Freud called dream work. I shall attempt to show that this work consists entirely in the transgression of regular divergences [*écarts*] that compose the weave of language, and that it is thus "wish-fulfillment." Such a description requires at least two negativities: that of the structure of language and that of visual experience, both included in our use of discourse. The former is included as an invariant code, common to the speakers and to all the words spoken in that language; it is, if not sufficient to explain how it is possible for two people to communicate, at least the condition of communication. The latter [the negativity of visual experience] is included in our use of discourse as distance to be crossed, as distance indicating the place where what I say goes, as an open horizon ahead of the words and drawing them toward it—a negativity that is at the root of our spatial existence, a mobility constituting depth. That mobility of the gesture in which the energetics and the flash of desire are concealed—that is what appears to come swooping down (once the censure is lifted) upon the "ratio" of language, upon what Merleau-Ponty called *"parole parlée"* [spoken—as opposed to speaking—language].[15] In doing so, it produces the "disorder" of the dream, of poetry, of the figure, and in fact reveals the unstable, impossible "order" of a being divided between Eros-Death and Eros-Reality, between variant and invariant, between figure and discourse.

With this dissociation of the two negativities we can follow the same path as that of Merleau-Ponty—but in the other direction, our back turned to him. He wanted to prolong the gesture, the mobility of the sensible, extending it to reach even into the domain of the invariability that characterizes the linguistic system, in order to express what is constitutive of verbal expression, to restore the act that opens up the possibility of speech. A final attempt on the part of transcendental reflection. But unavoidably the system is always already there, and the gesture of the spoken word that is presumed to create signification can never be grasped in its constituting function—a function in which it is always grasped (and in no other way can be) in the form of *deconstruction*. What can be shown in order to reach the order sought by Merleau-Ponty is how the trans-Logos [*outre-Logos*] resides within language—how it invades language to transgress the invariants, the keys to signification, and awaken within it that lateral meaning that is surreality. But if this meaning is surreality, then the energy to deconstruct is not just on the hither side of the Logos, but on the hither side of the real as well—or of the perceptual. It is further entailed that this sensible or rather the *visible* with which we shall be dealing is not the visible that is given to the utilitarian or scientific eye of the hurried observer, the Westerner; it is not even the visible captured by the eye trained to be patient, to see the invisible, such as that of Merleau-Ponty's Cézanne. It is the visible of a vision without subject, the object of the eye of no one. And it will not do to try to descend with the phenomenologist into the hither side of the realist view of the constituted, the data: we must make up our minds to stop phenomenologizing, if we wish to reach that something that resembles phenomenological constitution. It is something that cannot be constituted, but is graspable only through a totally different method—deconstruction—and based on the totally unexpected results of recessus.

It has always been necessary for phenomenology to overcome or be purged of its naivete qua philosophy of consciousness. As for perception, Merleau-Ponty energetically put it through the school of the body, showing that there is structure before signification, that the former supports the latter, and that nihilation by the for-itself is a fantasy. But as for language, the importance granted to the linguistic gesture seems to have turned the philosopher away from considering that other structural preconscious in which this gesture is carried out, and without which it would be impossible. It makes up the anonymity and transitivity in which every speech act is immersed, and that regulate it more or less in the same way that the natural harmony between chromatism and movement, in which the body is steeped, can regulate its positions and gestures. The *ratio* of language must be given its due, at the risk of being antiphenomenological—just as Merleau-Ponty did for the *Gestalt* and *Aufbau* [construction] of the body. It is the need for that reestablishment of a balanced view that prompts me to withdraw my trust in the art of writing, and to actualize in the philosopher's own discourse the movement, distortion, osmosis and association that are the speaking word [*parole parlante*]. There is no exclusion to be declared between the latter and the spoken word [*parole parlée*]. To say that discourse is a gesture is in any case a metaphor, and the distance between the two terms of that metaphor—movement and statement—is entirely dependent upon the fact of language.

We must cease conceiving of language as inertia, a dead letter, through a Manichaeanism inherited from Bergson. The dichotomy must be revised. At the very moment in which we describe transgressions of the linguistic order, we say them, we signify them, we communicate them, and in so doing we incorporate them within the order transgressed. The infinite power of the system is the ability to say even what reduces it to silence—to make possible commentary on the very thing (the work of condensation, shifts, figuration) that defies it. Even the silences that, in language, are not linguistic ones, even the blanks that are not coded, even the intervals that are not regulated, even the twists that are not syntactic turns, can be described—signified, transmitted. Articulated language carries its limitation within itself: the inability to place outside itself—take as an object and signify—its present intentional act. But every intention can be taken as an object, can fall beneath the power of language, once it is placed outside. It is upon this limitless power that artistic commentary is based, that Freud's interpretations were based; I will take it as my basis as well. The silent look, the gesture of desire, condensation and displacement, the entering of the figure into the text via the rebus—in short, the confusion of spaces, can be uttered, articulated in a discourse. This discourse does not give us the possession of seeing, desiring, moving: but no discourse possesses its object. If we restrict ourselves to the range of this concept of possession, it must be said that language can at most let itself be possessed by its object—which is what Merleau-Ponty desired. That is the discourse of the artist. But the philosopher's discourse must renounce possession in one sense or the other, because philosophy is born at the moment when the word is no longer inhabited by the world or the gods. It is philosophy's destiny to speak soberly, at a distance, never to be "of it" entirely. It is for us to take up that particular distancing [*écartement*] in contact that is the lot of the philosophical mode of expression, that is neither an art nor a science. Its justification and prototype is the linguistic order, because language, by its constraints, which can all be reduced to invariants, to constant intervals, establishes that arbitrary *word at a distance* from the order of things, opposing the free movements presupposed by perceptual extension with the sine qua non limits of linguistic "space."

The pertinent opposition here is not between the spoken word [*parole parlée*] and the speaking word [*parole parlante*], the former being assimilated to language, the latter to gesture and movement. Rather, in every statement, there are two dimensions. There is the one in which the units used by the speaker are connected by opposition and correlation, at the various levels distinguished by linguists (in André Martinet's functionalism, the first and second articulations); and there is another dimension, in which the signifying intention surges forth. On one hand there is the dimension of the language, which is not simply the spoken word but also the matrix of countless propositions, and on the other the dimension of the intention, the linguistic gesture, which "speaks" through its expression, but first and foremost because it observes the constraints of language. A statement may be more inclined to observe the constraints established by the language and to mould its signifying intention to it respectfully, or it may undo the constraints and force the elements of the language to yield to the vector of desire. In this latter case, it may distort the code, inserting unexpected intervals between words, or even within words—the same sort of spaces that separate or regroup imaginary entities; it may introduce the motility of desire, built on the polarity of near and far, within the spatiality of language. But even then it must respect certain conditions of meaning if it wishes to avoid chaos pure and simple. This is the moment I would like not to mimic in my own writing, but to take by surprise at the end of my gaze; this work of the poet, the writer, the dream, that puts the figural into the abstract, the "real" into the "arbitrary," giving discourse almost the same flesh as that of the sensible. This work of regression, as Freud called it, leads to the discovery that the truly pertinent opposition is only between variant and invariant, between mobile and rigid negativity, and that the order of language is to the order of expression as what is twice articulated to what is once articulated.

What is invariance? It is variance, plus the negation of variance. And what is variance? It is distance [*écartement*] denied as being unbridgeable, distance transgressed. And what is, yet again, invariance? The negation of that negation that is in mobility.

But the relation between these two negations is *not dialectic*; one is not a moment of the other. If we wish to articulate them together in truth, i.e., while keeping them in their exteriority, in their irrevocable inequality, in what may be called their *difference*, it becomes necessary to conceive of them in relation to the destiny of desire. For it is only the consideration of desire that allows us to hold reflection *aside* from the dialectical reconciliation of the two negations, and to keep a space open to show (through hyperreflection) how invariance and variance, i.e., the secondary and primary processes, are both always given together and can never form a unity. What guarantees signification is the observance of the oppositions between the terms of a system. It is by virtue of the same respect for instituted differentiations [*écarts*] (by the prohibition against incest) that the mother must withdraw before the subject's demand, thus opening up for the latter, by her retreat, the space of seeing-imagining. This concatenation of the Father-negation with the Mother-negation, far from promising the reconciliation of signification and meaning, obliges us never to be able to conceive of one except as the breaking and entering of the other. To want to coincide with the imaginary interworld by a pure representational and ineffable intuition is a wish-fulfillment conditioned by the repression of desire's interdiction: "There is no law." To presume to coincide with the law in a formally

closed and totally signifying discourse is also a wish-fulfillment, dependent upon the foreclosure [*Verwerfung*]¹⁶ of desire: "There is nothing
but the law." There is no Father in Merleau-Ponty's philosophy, or else
there is too much; in short, this throws his discourse into an insatiable
demand for the Mother.¹⁷

Philosophy and Painting in the Age of Their Experimentation: Contribution to an Idea of Postmodernity

Jean-François Lyotard

Translated by Mária Minich Brewer and Daniel Brewer

I imagine you are asking for my system on the arts today, and how it compares with those of my colleagues. I quake, feeling that I've been caught, since I don't have anything worthy of being called a system, and I know only a little about two or three of them, just enough to know they hardly constitute a system: the Freudian reading of the arts, the Marxist reading, and the semiotic reading. Perhaps what we should do is change the idea that has been dressed up with the name "system."

By wanting something systematic we believe we are real contemporaries of the "system theory" age and the age of the virtue of performativity. Do you have something to say about the arts? Let's look at how you say it, at the set of language-based operators you use to work on your material, the works of art. And let's look at your results. That's the system being asked for: the set of word tools that are applied to given aspects of music, painting, film, words, and other things, and that produce a work of words—commentary. The time is past when we can plant ourselves in front of a Vernet and sigh along with Diderot, "How beautiful, grand, varied, noble, wise, harmonious, rigorously coloured this is!"[1] Don't think we don't regret it. We are philosophers though, and it's not for us to lay down how you should understand what artists do. Recently in France, philosophers have made enough of an incursion into art to prove pretty irritating to critics, gallery directors, curators, and occasionally artists;[2] so it is futile now for us and those like us to flaunt pretended innocence in front of works of art. If something systematic is what is wanted, doesn't the fault lie with those philosophers who, by getting involved in commentary on art, transformed it into something of a theoretical treatise and dared the specialists to do the same?

This is only an illusion though. If you look just a little closer you will see that when the philosophers you have in mind decided to talk about the arts, it was not in order to explain works or interpret them. They wanted even less to make them fit into a system or build a system based on them. What then was their purpose? I'm not quite sure, and this is what we must try to grasp. But in any case these philosophers have had almost no part in the request for a system, except inadvertently. More often than not, they have purposely thwarted it as best they could. The request emanates instead from a new stratum: the managerial staff of the art professions, the reading engineers, the maintenance crews for the big explanatory machines patented under the name of Ideology, Fantasy, Structure. The less unscrupulous of these specialists have stopped at what offers resistance in the work, seems to be badly coded, badly ciphered, in a word, really deceptive because it cannot be converted easily into system words. To explain the work's elusiveness, these specialists have worked out a system for the necessity of these asystematic zones. Homage is paid indirectly, by using terms like the symbolic, the Other, the text.

This is the way philosophers enter the stage of "criticism," by way of this gap through which the work escapes being converted into meaning. The work is evasive? That's what they like. Isn't the commentary machine working very well? Does a given work make it malfunction? This is a good sign, indicating that the work cannot be transformed wholesale into signification, that its destination is uncertain and its relevance with respect to certain systematic features is undecidable.

But doesn't this quite simply amount to reestablishing the ineffable in aesthetics? "How beautiful, grand, etc."? Now, we should know that the exclamatory and the vocative are outmoded games or figures, that the genres in which they were accepted are completely out-of-date today, namely the ode, dithyramb, entreaty, and address; we should know that the progress of "philosophy" according to Diderot,[3] of history according to Nietzsche,[4] and of industrial society according to Benjamin,[5] stifles style's verve, exhausts artists' energy, and tarnishes the work's aura. And we should know that we're supposed to mourn this loss. We no longer converse with works of art, says Benjamin, or at least they no longer return our gaze when we look at them,[6] which shows just how deep-seated the crisis of perception is. You may think this crisis is over, but hasn't it got even worse? Forty years after Benjamin's diagnosis, isn't there a crisis of communication in which today's works are relegated to the limits of not only the visible but also the intelligible? Wasn't this turn for the worse really the cause for the request for a system, the request being quite simply to understand apparently senseless works?

Things could be put this way. But let's go back a bit to Diderot's vocative. When he exclaims, "O nature, how great you are! O nature, how imposing, majestic, and beautiful you are!,"[7] he is actually speaking to nature, he believes himself able to speak to it. Is he crazy? Is this the eloquence that Bataille referred to when he said that eloquence ended with Manet?[8] Does Diderot believe that nature is a person endowed with language, a goddess? And is this where we differ from him, in the fact that for us, spectacles of nature and of the arts are objects to be made into systems, and for him they are to be adored?

We should pay attention to Diderot's style. In the same 1767 *Salon,* while discussing Vernet's painting, he describes Vernet's landscapes without any warning as natural sites he is passing through in the company of a tutor-abbot, his two young pupils, and two servants carrying picnic baskets; he also relates to Grimm the conversations he had with this abbot and with himself concerning nature, the sublime, art, worldliness, and politics, all the while scaling these pretend mountains and setting out on these lakes painted with oils. What is Diderot doing with this contrivance, which prefigures the manner of *Jacques the Fatalist?* He leads one to confuse, or rather to make permutable, reality and fiction, history and narrative, as they used to say, diegesis and metadiegesis as Gérard Genette calls it.[9] In other words he leads one to treat the interlocutor we are told about (the abbot) the same way as the interlocutor to whom "Diderot" speaks (Grimm, the reader); he leads one to situate in the same realm, both the story's hero, the actor of assumed reality, the object of narration (*he*, the abbot) and this narrative's addressee, the spectator of this reality, the listener of this story (*you*, reader). The two scenes, the one involving Vernet's painting, where the dialogue with the abbot occurs, and the one involving Diderot's text, where the philosopher's address to his reader occurs (and perhaps where the present commentary is taking place), are thus placed on a par. They are not mixed together, but they are also not hierarchized, neither of them entitled to be called exclusively real or exclusively fictional.

Under such conditions even the "I" is subject to the principle of permutability. By staging himself in his own name during these conversations with the abbot which pepper their meandering strolls through Vernet's landscapes, Diderot, too, ends up on the side of third persons and nature.

Another consequence of this style is that you and I, Diderot's readers, can be counted among his characters. According to the reciprocity of the principle whereby his hero, the abbot of the 1767 *Salon*, becomes his interlocutor, he has only to speak to us and thereby make us his addressees for it to become reasonable, due to this mechanism, to assume that we can just as well be counted among his heroes.

This same principle is applied, even though the effect seems extremely paradoxical, when the philosopher, having described a corner of a Vernet painting as if it were a real landscape, turns with amazement to the painter and urges him to begin drawing. "Vernet, my friend, take up your pencils and enrich your portfolio as quickly as you can with this group of women."[10]

There is no eloquence in this style. Eloquence is the rhetoric of the irreversible. It is not "I" speaking, but rather what "I" speak about that speaks through me. This rhetoric is based also on a movement of substitution: the referent of my discourse is, in a way, the latter's addressor. "Nature" is speaking, if you wish. Fine, but this style can go no further. It must not be implied that the inverse is possible, that I and also *you*, the addressee, can occupy the place of referent; there must be no suggestion that instead of being destined exclusively to speaking and listening to the evanescent meaning of being, our phrases might be the referent of other phrases, our works the referent of other works, our names the referent of other names and that we might be written just as much as we are writers. Eloquence is a manner of speaking or writing that suggests the permutation's irreversibility: it, the divine, speaks in me, never do I speak in it. The univocal movement in which the referent is called to occupy the place of the addressor seems inevitable, if what is at stake is speaking truthfully. This seems to be the only way to attest to the faithfulness of what is said to what is.

If, like Diderot, you accept the reversal, if you show that what is can present itself "in person" only because it is presented in this mode or according to this voice, as the referent of another "poem" which also has its addressor and addressee, if you show that these interlocutors in turn are never original but are instead themselves the possible characters of one or more games that are played out on other stages and related by and to other interlocutors, and, finally, if you state that nothing is off-stage or that what is off-stage is a component of the stage, and that no eye can know all theaters at once, then in your rhetoric the words occupying the various instances will have to be able to switch among these instances. Thus the addressee of your work will be led to call *being* or *nature* not this instance that is assumed to speak through your work, but the very circle of metamorphoses your work displays and of which it is an episode.

Diderot's manner is made up of these movements of permutation. What is spoken about can indeed begin to speak and address itself to whomever is speaking. There can be no eloquence in this, and the effect is always, as Schlegel wrote regarding Diderot's style, one of "impudence" and an "incomparable impertinence."[11] Why? Because the referent has no monopoly on the *"I,"* or, inversely, because what speaks has no privilege to speak the being of the referent. The *"I"* position is occupied by a succession of proper nouns, as is the case with two other instances, that of the referent and the addressee. Allow me to call this metamorphic manner *satire*.[12]

What is really important is not even the impertinence Schlegel mentions. "More than once," he writes, "[Diderot] surprised nature in a charming state of undress, sometimes he also saw her relieve herself."[13] Whether or not in satire nature shows her rear is not the most interesting thing for the philosopher, rightly or wrongly. What is interesting is first of all that nature shows something and hence that it addresses itself to us, and second that nature shows us not one, but many things. And so it is very hard for us to know what it wants to signify to us; it is as if nature were unaware of us. Nature never says to the artist, "that's the way to show it," or to the critic, "that's the right commentary," or to the philosopher, "you've got it, speak to me."

Nature is a "site" machine, to use Diderot's term; we would call it a "situation" machine, just as Horace Vernet or a *Salon* exhibition is a picture machine. Unlike the systematic or scientific thinker, the philosopher is interested in this machine not because its products repeat themselves as equivalencies (multiple copies), but because they repeat themselves as events (singularities, originals). Nature is judged to be artistic when it is not induced by laziness to produce regularities, when the series of its "tableaux" does not form continuous calculable curves that can be ascribed to divine providence, to divine proportion, to the universality of structure and taste, that authorize us to "read" its works. In satire there is greater artfulness if the theaters aren't alike, if in passing from one to another the "author" is not constricted by the necessity of a unity that lies in wait for him like his sepulchre, so that instead of conquering his identity through working, he dissipates it. Rather than foster in the addressee a lamentable turning back to self or in the commentator the morbid jubilation of having proved with examples that his system "works" in every case, he instead breaks his discourse, and those to whom it is directed, into the discipline of incommensurables, which is the discipline of the infinite.

Are we to take this nice speech to mean that this is the present situation of the arts and commentary on them, that nothing has changed since Diderot? Do you think that the pages of Diderot's *Essay on Painting* devoted to divinities made flesh and flesh made divinities—I can't quote them, just go read them, you know: "The poet consecrated Thetis's two beautiful feet, and these feet were true to life, Venus's ravishing bosom, and this bosom was true to life, etc."; you know the passage that ends with, "In the tribute of admiration that they [the ancients] paid to beauty, there was some strange mixture of dissoluteness and devotion"[14]—well, do you think this praise of paganism, this indulgence for an art that "had an effect on nature itself" and could be said to turn reality into theater, can still be applied at the present time? Isn't it to be feared that nothing could be less present-day than this paganism, in this the age of systems, telecommunications, and profitability matrixes?

As you know, one can debate a lot about what is contemporary and what is not. As far as I'm concerned paganism can be extended to include even time: there is no one single time; a society (or a soul) is not synchronous with itself, nor is a sector of society, or an institution like art, or even (if this still has any reality today) a segment of the institution like sculpture or film. There are only parachronisms all around; it is the observer's timepiece that judges what is present-day, just as in the universe, except that one wonders what in human history, and especially in the history of the arts, functions as the speed of light.

One must account for the fact that certain descriptions from the 1767 *Salon*, despite the genre's obsolescence, are more current than certain axioms from Kandinsky's *Point, Line, Plane*, dated 1926; certain aspects of Duchamp's *Bride*, which has already passed fifty, are fresher than the latest Balthus. According to my timepiece, at least. By this I mean, without wanting to impose my own time, that examples of parachrony such as these are possible and are possible for everyone. Thus we must admit a multiplicity of current times, which necessarily gives rise to paradox.

Now, if today's artworks can be identified and commented on, it is at the price of the paganism or the satire that deifies the multiple to the point of including even the computation of time. Reread the text Kojève wrote for Kandinsky which, chronologically speaking, isn't all that old.[15] It is a model of what is not present-day. Figurative painting is put into four classes, all of which are declared to be abstract, and all subjective, since figures are taken from nature by the subject, the painter. With the watercolor of 1910,[16] however, Kojève maintains that an objective and concrete type of painting is born which draws nothing from nature, which reproduces nothing. This type of painting is an object that possesses its own self-sufficiency and does not derive it from its model. Thus it is itself nature. Kojève can go on to conclude that this is "*total* painting, as opposed to *abstract* and *subjective* [read figurative] painting, which is necessarily *fragmentary*." This is obviously the Hegelian speaking, a man of the nineteenth century, because he believes in a univocal, albeit complex movement of natural, cultural, and spiritual realities toward their perfect elucidation. He is seeking to persuade you that with Kandinsky, the art of painting, by abandoning representation, passes from the subjective to the objective, and from the part to the whole, and that it is passing through a moment in its development as decisive as the one that brought about the transition from Kantian subjective criticism to Hegel's absolute idealism. I am saying that this way of placing things in perspective is out-of-date, even though it is of today and aims at extolling what is currently most up-to-date.

If our French philosophers take some interest in these aspects of art, it is to the extent that they come looking for this experience of the perceptible, or rather these experiments on the perceptible, which help them pursue their own experiments on philosophical language. Merleau-Ponty certainly would not have been a great commentator on Cézanne if "Céanne's doubt" hadn't been his own. As for Diderot, he off-handedly places the philosopher's task under the authority of the dictum of *Ut pictura poesis*. "I have got into the habit of arranging my figures in my head as if they were on canvas; it may be that I transfer them there, and that I am looking at a huge wall when I write." This is how he excuses his connivance with the works of his friends, Greuze, Lagrenée, and Chardin.[17] Thus commentary will be made to conform to figures, and figural work will take place in language analogous to what painters do on canvas.[18]

There is a name for this successfully completed work—"the most beautiful colour in the world," and "unctuous white, even, without being either pale of matte," a "mixture of red and blue that transpires imperceptibly," "blood and life that make the colourist lose heart." It must be rendered if you are to have anything more than "a simple and limited little technique, which among ourselves we call a protocol." In a word, the flower of chromatics is called "flesh," and if Chardin's limitations are taken for nature itself, "it is because he makes flesh whenever he wants," even with peaches and grapes.[19]

I am not saying that Merleau-Ponty was looking at a huge wall when he wrote "Eye and Mind," or that the "flesh" he attempts to describe in the feline prose of *The Visible and the Invisible,* the silent spoken word dwelling in the chiasma of the perceptible, has anything to do with the rears and bosoms of Greuze that Diderot hallucinated while writing. Merleau-Ponty implies as much when he says, "This flesh that one sees and one touches [when the body claps another body] is not all there is to flesh, nor this massive corporeality all there is to the body."[20] But how can one keep from seeing that with the chiasma of the perceptible, the reversibility of the seer and that which is seen, of the speaker and that which is spoken, of the thinker and that which is thought, he pursues the same shift of positions that gives our satire its style?

"It is first of all by the world that I am seen or thought." The seer is seen while he sees, and thus there is vision in things. If the philosopher's phrases never stop beginning anew and folding back on themselves, leaving nothing, certainly not concepts, in his reader's mind, only the trail of a passing, it is because the philosopher's phrases must themselves make it perceptible in their form that they are a work. As a work these phrases seek out another work (that of the artist), and are displayed before other works (those of commentaries) which in turn seek them out. Actaeon can pursue Artemis only being pursued; painting looks at you, music hears you, etc. The three positions of sensing and of using language—*who, about whom,* and *to whom*—must be able to be occupied by the same word: I who am speaking, but also *I* am the one to whom *one* is speaking, and someone about whom *one* is speaking.

You're protesting, raising the objection that Merleau-Ponty is no satirist (even though his model, Proust, was not too bad a one). Yet just reread the following passage from "The Intertwining—The Chiasma" and you'll see that in attempting to say what kind of speech it is that he calls "operative," he designates the very reversibility of language-based instances we have just mentioned as one of satire's basic traits. "As the visible takes hold of the look which has unveiled it and which forms a part of it," he writes, "no locutor speaks without making himself in advance allocutary, *be it only for himself;* because with one sole gesture he closes the circuit of his relation to himself and that of his relation to the others and, with this same stroke, also sets himself up as *delocutary,* speech of which one speaks: he offers himself and offers every word to a universal Word."[21]

No, I assure you that the following argument can be put forth without too much paradox: there is a double requirement for satire. On the one hand there must be the reversibility of what is visible with what sees, of what can be said with what speaks. This establishes the isomorphism of the one group with the other. On the other hand, there must be a lack of referentiality for the whole set of experiences, an impossibility of making them topographically contingent and synchronous, a necessity for the contingency of points of view and/or speech, or the infiniteness of the system of stages. This twofold requirement governs "the prose of the world" no less than it does "satire," and it finds its double basis in the experience of the arts, which are polytheistic.

Here I'll admit my disadvantage and grant you that Merleau-Ponty fails in the satirical task, and it is because he remains monotheistic. Once again a matter of style. Even if the treatise assumes the modern form of the meditation or the inquiry, it is a genre and nothing but a genre, unable to match the multiplicity it treats. With satire, however, you have free rein, and according to the occasion you can turn pedagogical, dissertational, narrative, conversational, lyrical, epic, or dry as an auditor at the Government Accounting Office; and so you can give yourself the means to enjoy the most heterogeneous of experimentations, to have them be enjoyed, and to be enjoyed by them. In satire, genres are mixed because the persons speaking are varied, and each speaks according to his or her own genre. The treatise, however, is a genre that incites arrogance, and the arrogance of philosophers is metaphysics. Merleau-Ponty, one of the least arrogant of philosophers, still is unable to say that the eye's relation to the visible which is the relation of Being to itself in its primordial "enfolding," finds expression in Cézanne or Giacometti, without immediately devalorizing other experimentations, such as Marey's, the cubists', or Duchamp's.[22] He does so because they are unaware, he believes, of "the paradoxical arrangement," the dischrony of elements as they relate to the whole, which alone, according to Rodin whom the philosopher follows here, can restore the being of movement or being as movement. This peculiar intolerance causes Merleau-Ponty to misjudge experiments on the perceptible and the speakable in works that require the commentator to exert just as strong a pressure on language as the pressure exerted by a Cézanne. Such inflexibility in the name of Being. . . . But being didn't choose Cézanne to express itself, now did it? Nor Merleau-Ponty, nor anyone. Don't try to reestablish these ponderous elections, poetic institution, Heideggerian preaching.

"Being" chose Rameau's Nephew—in other words, everyone and no one, a late watercolor of Mont Sainte-Victoire, but also a certain photograph of a hand touching a mouth taken by Man Ray around 1930.[23] This bypasses the banalities the philosophers of the decline of the *aura* or of the institution of being have managed to peddle concerning photographic art.[24]

You're wondering what connection these reflections could have with the situation of the arts and their commentary, in this the beginning of the eighties, since you're convinced of their obsolescence. Here's my answer. Take the catalog of a fairly important international exhibition, Documenta 5 for instance, which isn't recent but was strong enough to remain in people's minds. Then tell me whether the arts today—not even including music, dance, theater, and film (which were not represented at Krefeld), to say nothing of literature—whether the current plastic arts do not by themselves form a world according to the previously mentioned twofold requirement. Don't they form both a satire through the immense diversity of the genres, and at the same time a field where the whole point is always to try out whether that situation, that event, that hole in the ground, that wrapping of a building, those pebbles placed on the ground, that cut made on a body, that illustrated diary of a schizophrenic, those *trompe l'oeil* sculptures, and all the rest— whether that too says something to us. The powers of sensing the phrasing are being probed on the limits of what is possible, and thus the domain of the perceptible-sensing and the speakable-speaking is being extended. Experiments are made. This is our postmodernity's entire vocation, and commentary has infinite possibilities open to it.

Today's art consists in exploring things unsayable and things invisible. Strange machines are assembled, where what we didn't have the idea of saying or the matter to feel can make itself heard and experienced. The diversity of artistic "propositions" is dizzying. What philosopher can control it from above and unify it? Yet it is through this dispersion that today's art is the equal of being as the power of things possible, or the equal of language as the power of plays.

It should not be said that each of these experimentations is merely a subjective perspective on a Being that is its single totality or its single kingdom, and that Leibniz after all expressed the truth of perspectivism in metaphysical discourse.[25] The unity of what is involved in each artistic proposition today is included in the proposition itself in its singularity; no one singularity is more "subjective" than another, since none of them has the privilege of objectivity. These essays, like these phrases, are made "within being" and not before its eyes. Each work presents a micro-universe; each time, Being is nothing but each one of these presentations.

No one knows what "language" Being understands, which it speaks or to which it can be referred. No one even knows whether there is only one Being or many, and whether there is only one language of Being or many. The arrogance of the philosophical treatise, implicit in its form, is saying at least, "There is one single Being." This arrogance increases when it asserts, "And it speaks only one language." It is fulfilled by assuming, "I am going to speak it to you." But what do innumerable artists do? They are careful not to make pronouncements on the matter. Instead they essay. And so through them we glimpse the importance that must be given to the essay. Being or beings do not reveal themselves; they present tiny universes with each work. They essay and make micrologies that babble, huff and puff, and are envious of one another. And these essays together constitute satire.

The possibility of a classical aesthetics is called into question once again. What such an aesthetics requires is an architectonics of the faculties, or a logic of the concrete universal, be it only an idea of Nature as a priori.[26] But these must be invariants occurring as a rule. Now, the only invariable criterion with which today's work complies is whether or not some untried possibility of sensation or language is revealed in the work, something still without rules. Aesthetics becomes a paraesthetics, and commentary a paralogy, just as the work is parapoetics. Being or beings only let themselves be tempted indirectly, seduced, like the gods.

This leads to experimentation, which is poles apart from experience. Remember the words of Benjamin: "The replacement of the older narration by information, of information by sensation, reflects the increasing atrophy of experience."[27] What would he have to say today about the works of music, photography, film, and video, but also painting or dance, theater, and literature, that explicitly take the usable information unit in the relevant sensorial field as their experimental material, striving to construct syntaxes as scarcely "human" as possible!

I see no decline in this at all, except that of an aesthetics stemming from Hegel, for whom what was at stake was indeed "experience" in the sense of passion of the spirit traversing perceptible forms in order to arrive at the total expression of self in the discourse of the philosopher. This is an aesthetics grounded on the "absolute" genre of the speculative narrative, on the form of finality, and on metaphysical arrogance. "It is not the object of the story," Benjamin wrote, "to convey a happening *per se*, which is the purpose of information; rather it embeds it in the life of the storyteller in order to pass it on as experience to those listening."[28] It can indeed be said that there is no longer any experience in this sense, which is that of the Phenomenology of Spirit. Today what subject would the great metaphysical narrative tell about? Would it be the odyssey, and for what narratee? The direction artistic research is taking consists precisely in producing with experimentations something that does not give rise to this sort of experience and in which it is not essential that a subject objectivize its suffering and know it as meaning. Adorno sees this mutation much more clearly than Benjamin (thirty years later, to be sure), and he discerns the sort of peril the postmodern work incurs. "The real reason for the risk of all these works of art [today] is not their contingent element, instead it is the fact that all of them have to follow the will-o'-the-wisp of their immanent objectivity with no guarantee that the productive forces, the artist's mind and his technical process, will be equal to this objectivity." At least the transition to experimentation is not immediately rejected here as an aestheticism that blocks out the somber obviousness of the end of history and experience after Hegel. "What can be called the seriousness of art," Adorno adds, "without any musty idealism, is the pathos of objectivity which presents the contingent individual with something more and something other than he is in his historically necessary insufficiency."[29]

The break with the thought of decline is not complete, however. Adorno has to restrict experimentation's effect. Its "seriousness" must also be a manner of maintaining art "outside suffering," in a state of relative irresponsibility. This judgement shows that an aesthetics of the passion of meaning still persists even in the very intuition of the "pathos of objectivity," which was announced by the satire of micrological presentations.

In Milwaukee, I remember, there was a meeting on performance in postmodern culture organized by Michel Benamou. Raymond Federman had made his contribution, which was an audiovisual montage of eleven texts, each marked by the suspension of meaning, deported, orphaned, refugee, stateless.[30] John Cage, who was with us there, stood up afterwards and, with uncharacteristic vehemence, withdrew his support from the work, protesting that, despite its clever deconstructive apparatus, it remained dedicated to expressing the lack of meaning for a subject. In short it was modern, in other words, romantic. The gap between the pathos of objectivity and the passion of meaning depends on very small details. Even the project of Benjamin's The Arcades, or Adorno's "micrologies" is probably not enough to maintain this gap.[31]

Perhaps the passion of meaning "must" continue to dwell in works, and so Hegel must continue to outlive himself in them. Who can decide that such is surely the case, or whether the opposite is? But we must come to a decision. It is not the same thing to stress invariants, the persistence of the nostalgia of meaning and romanticism in contemporary works, as it is to emphasize the minuscule but immense conversion that causes them to cease bearing the responsibility of continuing speculative metaphysics and be answerable to an ontology and a politics that are satirical. If you side with the second course, the first judges you to be ignorant and frivolous, not very up on the traps of representation. But be that as it may, we still want, and the question is: What do we want of art today? Well, for it to experiment, to stop being only modern. By saying this, we're experimenting.

And what do we want of philosophy? For it to analyze these experimentations by means of reflexive experimentations. Thus philosophy heads not toward the unity of meaning or the unity of Being, not toward transcendence, but toward multiplicity and the incommensurability of works. A philosophical task doubtless exists, which is to reflect according to opacity.

One more remark. Why say satirical "politics"? Because what is tried in each artistic proposition and in the satire they make up collectively is also social being. You multiply manners of speaking and sensing, but how will you communicate? The contemporary artist knows that this difficulty in communicating happens. Along with Baudelaire he tries to transform it into experience.[32] Cézanne, who conveniently legitimated his experimentations by calling them innate "sensations," appears to have given up the idea already. Sounding like one of Zola's heroes, he repeats and accepts the undermining of consensus that his work instigates and reflects when he writes to his son just before his death, "Connections (*relations*) can help us slip in, but sooner or later the public can tell that it's being hoodwinked."[33]

How can generalized satire and the social bond be made compatible? This question anticipates the possibility of a satirical "politics."

Letter to Alphonse de Waelhens (28 April 1962)

Rene Magritte

Merleau-Ponty's very brilliant thesis is very pleasant to read, but it hardly makes one think of painting—which he nevertheless appears to be dealing with. I should even say that . . . the way he talks about painting is like discussing a philosophical work by studying the author's penholder and paper. (He talks about "painters of matter" as though "matter" aroused new interest, had some new existence by virtue of being manipulated by a painter! [EM, 124]) Descartes dealt with drawing, but thought primarily of copperplate engraving. He had a hard time seeing the drawing through the copperplate engraving, which is actually a process and not the drawing.

I think Merleau-Ponty's essay would be more illuminating if it were limited to the "question" of the visible world and man. Painting is not inseparable from this "question," of course, but it is not interesting unless it is conceived as an evocation of mystery. The only kind of painting Merleau-Ponty deals with is a variety of serious but futile divertissement, of value only to well-intentioned humbugs. The only painting worth looking at has the same raison d'être as the raison d'être of the world—mystery.

Action Painting and the World-as-Picture

Wayne J. Froman

> N'est-ce pas la peinture la moins figurative qui a le plus de chance de changer notre vision du monde?
>
> —Paul Ricoeur (*Temps et récit III, Le temps raconté*)

> Heidegger made clear that with respect to the disputed "objectlessness" [of modern art] it was not a question of an historical novelty, but it was rather a question of something essentially different in the fulfillment of Western destiny.
>
> —From a report of presentations made by Heidegger in Bühler Höhe[1]

In his essay "Die Zeit des Weltbildes," Martin Heidegger describes how a mode of world-apprehension, specifically, the apprehension of world-as-picture, is integral to modern science. This mode of world-apprehension is essential to the metaphysical foundations of the modern age, which Heidegger observes, were worked out philosophically by René Descartes. In his essay "L'oeil et l'esprit," Maurice Merleau-Ponty describes the congruity between Descartes's investigation of sight in *The Dioptric* and Descartes's understanding of Renaissance painting. Merleau-Ponty observes that Descartes was right in taking inspiration from Renaissance painting. The inspiration available to Descartes in Renaissance painting reaches beyond his investigation of sight, to the metaphysical foundations of the modern epoch as worked out philosophically by Descartes. I will demonstrate how Renaissance painting displays the mode of world-apprehension that is essential to the metaphysical foundations of the modern epoch.

Heidegger finds that what takes place in Descartes's work that lays the metaphysical foundations of the modern age, is the establishment of the subject as "ground of Being," in a way that indicates, at the same time, the limited or finite character of this metaphysical ground. Merleau-Ponty points out how Descartes's work defines the mode of world-apprehension that is essential to the metaphysical foundations of the modern age, while, at the same time, that work indicates the limited or finite character of this mode of world-apprehension. In this way, Descartes's thought holds open possibilities for modes of world-apprehension that differ from the apprehension of world-as-picture. I will describe how outstanding achievements in Renaissance painting both display the modern mode of world-apprehension and hold open possibilities for other modes of world-apprehension. On this basis, I will propose that these achievements are foundational art. That is to say, they are akin to foundational thought as understood by Martin Heidegger, thought in which the metaphysical foundations of an epoch are worked out in a manner that entails, essentially, a mode of world-apprehension.

I will then propose that mid–twentieth-century abstract expressionist painting, or action painting, is foundational in the sense determined in my discussion of the relation between Descartes's thought and Renaissance painting. Action painting accedes to the dynamic that produces modes of world-apprehension, and in so doing, displaces the apprehension of world-as-picture and opens possibilities for different modes of world apprehension.

Foundational Thinking and Art

In "Die Zeit des Weltbildes," Heidegger describes how experimentation in modern science, the characteristic methodology of modern science, adheres to a rigor that is guaranteed by a fixed "ground-breaking" schema that is projected in advance of the setting up and execution of experimentation. Experimentation is guided by a set of rules or principles that are determined to be applicable to the diversity of facts even as they change, and by laws that are determined to hold change constant in a necessary course or direction. An example of the type of principle Heidegger describes is the principle of inertia. Experimentation thus integrates the manifold of facts in flux within the "ground-breaking" schema that is projected in advance. Explanation of what is already known is provided by facts that are displayed in the course of experimentation, and explanation of facts that are displayed in the course of experimentation is provided by facts that have already been brought under the purview of the principles and laws at work in the "ground-breaking" schema. This methodology is continually adapted to results of experimentation. This constitutes the "driven activity" (*Betrieb*) characteristic of modern science. Heidegger provides clear illustration: "Within the complex machinery that is necessary to physics in order to carry out the smashing of the atom lies hidden the whole of physics up to now."[2]

The projected "ground-breaking" schema guarantees the rigor of scientific methodology insofar as it becomes identified with nature as such. Heidegger describes this schema:

> the self-contained system of motion of units of mass related spatiotemporally. Into this ground plan of nature as supplied in keeping with its prior stipulation, the following definitions among others have been incorporated: Motion means change of place. No motion or direction of motion is superior to any other. Every place is equal to every other. Every force is defined according to—i.e., is only—its consequences in motion, and that means in magnitude or change of place in the unity of time.[3]

Rather than a "discovery of nature," modern science, with its methodology of experimentation and explanation, announces the institution and establishment of the already projected "ground-breaking" schema as nature per se. This identification is inseparable from a mode of world-apprehension whereby world is apprehended as picture.

Anything and everything is "brought to stand before oneself as standing over against oneself"—is *pro*posed, or *re*presented, to oneself. World is apprehended as picture. Once this takes place, the existence of any and every entity is identified with the position that it holds exclusively. That position is dependent upon a subject that apprehends the world-as-picture. The subject takes over the identity of the essential nature of a human being. The order or arrangement of entities in the picture is one that involves, essentially, the possibility of being totally deployed or exhibited as a system. These features of the apprehension of world-as-picture are indispensable for the scientific operation of bringing the diversity of facts in flux under the purview of principles and laws at work in the projected "ground-breaking" schema, and thereby rendering the sphere of research, opened by that schema, thoroughly accessible to scientific methodology.

Heidegger observes, in "Die Zeit des Weltbildes," that Descartes was the philosopher who worked out the metaphysical foundations of the modern age. The apprehension of world-as-picture is essential to those foundations. In Descartes's *Meditations on First Philosophy*, nature is identified as a self-contained system of entities, the spatial and temporal features of which are functions of position within the system as apprehended by a subject. Errors in judgment such as the one that Descartes reports at the outset of the *Meditations*, regarding the height of a tower seen from a distance, are essentially errors pertaining to position, and they can be rectified by the scientific procedure to which nature is thoroughly accessible. Apart from the identification and rectification of such errors, the very apprehension of world-as-picture is beyond doubt. This implicates the existence of the *subject*. This is the identity of the essential nature of Descartes as a human being whose existence Descartes cannot doubt.

Merleau-Ponty observes, in "L'oeil et l'esprit," where he discusses Descartes's understanding of Renaissance art, that in his investigation of sight in *The Dioptric* Descartes "was right . . . in taking his inspiration from the perspectival techniques of the Renaissance [in that] they encouraged painting to freely produce experiences of depth and, in general, presentations of Being."[4] What one sees when one looks at a Renaissance painting is an extracted segment from the world-as-picture, as the segment is seen in two dimensions, on the scale of the canvas. The versatility of the painter in rendering such scenes in two dimensions on the scale of the canvas is suggestive of the versatility of the ego, which, for Descartes, is responsible for the spatial dimensionality, the depth of the self-contained system of entities that constitutes nature.

Merleau-Ponty's elucidation of the inspiration available to Descartes from Renaissance art reaches beyond Descartes's investigation of sight to the working out of the metaphysical foundations of the modern age that entail the apprehension of world-as-picture. The fact that Renaissance paintings exhibit primary features of the apprehension of world-as-picture is not a mere coincidence. Renaissance perspective, brought to the high level of mastery achieved by Italian painters of the Renaissance, involves the composition of a fully equilibrated canvas that is first made possible by the "bringing to stand before oneself as standing over against oneself" of world-as-picture that is self-contained. This perspective is achieved in relation to a "vanishing point" that determines

what can be painted in within the scene, as well as the positions of whatever appears, and that "vanishing point" corresponds with the point that
is optimum for viewing the painting. It is when a viewer occupies that
optimum point that the viewer sees an extracted segment from the
world-as-picture, as that segment is seen in two dimensions on the scale
of the canvas. This is first made possible by the positioning of anything
and everything in relation to a subject that takes over the identity of the
essential nature of a human being when world is apprehended as picture.

Detail in Renaissance painting, raised to a height characteristic of
the work of Dutch master painters, where anything and everything that
lies within the scope of sight defined by the position of the viewing subject can be painted in within the scene with detail that seeks to be exhaustive, regardless of the dimensions of the canvas, exhibits that feature of
world apprehended as picture whereby the order or arrangement of entities in the picture is one that involves, essentially, the possibility of being totally deployed or exhibited as a system.

The *re*presentation of anything and everything that appears
within the scenes of Renaissance painting, the *re*presentation essential to
the apprehension of world-as-picture, is prior to the finished Renaissance painting and is not accomplished by it. The appearance in painting
of Renaissance perspective and detail does not mark—any more than
does the establishment of modern science with its methodology of experimentation and explanation—a "discovery of nature," but rather announces a mode of world-apprehension whereby world is apprehended
as picture.

Heidegger identifies Descartes as a foundational thinker. The laying of the metaphysical foundations of the modern epoch that takes
place in Descartes's work is guided by the fundamental question that first
gave rise to philosophy, the question concerning the meaning of Being.
It is with his identification of the subject as the ground of Being that
Descartes loses sight of the question concerning Being—loses sight of
the question concerning the Being of the ground—and so exemplifies
the forgetfulness of Being inherent in the metaphysical tradition. In
"L'oeil et l'esprit" Merleau-Ponty points out how Descartes's work,
while defining the mode of world-apprehension characteristic of the
modern epoch, indicates the limited or finite character of the establishment of the subject as a metaphysical ground. Merleau-Ponty observes
that notwithstanding the positioning of entities by the subject, with respect to the subject, which is responsible for the spatial arrangement of a
world in depth, Descartes, at the same time, recognized

the vision that really takes place, an honorary or instituted
thought, squeezed into a body—its own body, of which we can
have no idea except in the exercise of it and which introduces,
between space and thought, the autonomous order of the compound of soul and body. The enigma of vision is not done away
with; it is delegated from the "thought of seeing" to vision in
act.[5]

For Descartes, the exercise of this vision that introduces the autonomous
order of the compound of the soul and body is not to be thought.
Merleau-Ponty writes:

> We have to push Descartes this far to find in him something
> like a metaphysics of depth. For we do not attend the birth of
> this truth; God's being for us is an abyss. An anxious trembling
> quickly mastered; for Descartes it is just as vain to plumb that
> abyss as it is to think the space of the soul and depth of the
> visible. Our very position, he would say, disqualifies us from
> looking into such things. Here is the Cartesian secret of equi-
> librium: a metaphysics which gives us decisive reasons to be
> no longer involved with metaphysics, which validates our
> evidences while limiting them, which opens up our thinking
> without rending it.[6]

In identifying Descartes as a foundational thinker, Heidegger identifies
Descartes's work as thought that holds open possibilities for a "retrieval" of the question concerning the meaning of Being. In pointing
out the indications in Descartes's work of the limited or finite character
of the identification of the subject as metaphysical ground, Merleau-
Ponty points out how Descartes's work holds open possibilities of modes
of world-apprehension other than that which is essential to the metaphysical foundations of the modern epoch.

Outstanding achievements in Renaissance painting similarly hold
open possibilities for other modes of world-apprehension. For example,
the manner in which the faces and figures in paintings by Rembrandt are
wrested from a darkness in which they would be obscured, holds open
possibilities of acceding to the exercise of that vision that introduces the
autonomous order of the compound of soul and body, the dynamic that
produces different modes of world-apprehension. In a different way,
the luminous atmosphere through which human figures and landscapes
modulate through gradations on the threshold of vision in paintings by
Leonardo da Vinci, holds open possibilities for modes of world-

apprehension other than the apprehension of world-as-picture. In that
these works are equilibrated compositions, displaying extracted segments of a self-contained world apprehended as picture—as that segment is seen in two dimensions on the scale of the canvas—while, at the
same time, they hold open possibilities for modes of world-apprehension
other than the one that is essential to the metaphysical foundations of
the modern epoch, these works may be identified as foundational works
of art, akin to foundational thinking, as described by Heidegger, such as
is found in the work of René Descartes. These works of art are precur-
sors of innovations in painting that will take place later, such as the explorations of light in work that will mark the start of "modern painting,"
work by Cézanne and by the impressionists.

To say this about works of art is not to say that the possibilities for
modes of world-apprehension that are held open in the works are indistinguishable from those held open in foundational thought, but is to say
of the most far-reaching achievements in art and thinking what Heidegger does say about poetry and thinking in the essay, "Dichterisch wohnet
der Mensch": "Poetry and thinking meet each other in one and the same
only when, and only as long as, they remain distinctly in the distinctness
of their nature." [7]

Action Painting

In mid–twentieth-century action painting, also named, somewhat mis-
leadingly, abstract expressionist painting, a shift takes place in painting,
from painting where a prior image is rendered on a canvas by the artist,
or where the artist paints toward the goal of an image engendered on the
canvas, to painting where the artist comes to the canvas as a site for acting, so that the painting displays the event that takes place when the
artist paints, rather than conceal this event in favor of an equilibrated
composition that displays an extracted segment of a self-contained world
apprehended as picture.

In that action painting does not render a prior image on a canvas,
a precursor of action painting was Paul Klee, about whom Merleau-
Ponty says the following, in "L'oeil et l'esprit," citing from Henri
Michaux's *Aventures de lignes*: he was perhaps the first to

> "let a line muse." [The line] making its way in space . . . cor-
> rodes prosaic space and the *partes extra partes*; it develops a way

of extending itself actively into that space which sub-tends the spatiality of a thing quite as much as that of a man or an apple tree. This is so simply because, as Klee said, to give the generating axis of a man the painter "would have to have a network of lines so entangled that it could no longer be a question of a truly elementary representation."[8]

The picture that takes shape results from the association of traces left on the canvas of an overlap between the field of vision and the field of motor projects. It is in this overlap that Merleau-Ponty discovers what he calls the "reversibility" at work in vision. This is a dynamic whereby the content of vision is what it is by virtue of the seer's location in the field of the visible, that is, the seer's visibility. The traces on the canvas of the overlap of the field of vision and field of motor projects introduce the viewer to that space which sub-tends the spatiality of a thing, a man, or an apple tree, the site of reversibility in vision. Merleau-Ponty observes that Klee, when painting "[held] rigorously to the principle of the *genesis of the visible*, the principle of fundamental, indirect, or—as Klee used to say—absolute painting."[9]

In action painting, the dynamic of painting, the motion that leaves traces on the canvas, which, in Klee's paintings, introduces the viewer to that space that sub-tends the spatiality of a thing, a man, or an apple tree, and which, in Renaissance painting, had succeeded in displaying an extracted segment of a self-contained world apprehended as picture, becomes the very subject of painting. In *Phenomenology of Perception* Merleau-Ponty described the motion of *"le corps vécu,"* the lived body—prior to, and sub-tending locomotion in a world that is represented by a subject to that subject—as, in effect, a resolution of strains or tensions in the perceptual field. This motion effects a synthesis of the sectors of bodily experience, including the field of vision and the field of motor projects. Resolution gives rise to other strains or tensions in the perceptual field. Later, in the course of his investigations of the act performed by the artist, particularly the painter, Merleau-Ponty came to understand this as the dynamic of "reversibility."[10] It is this dynamic that becomes the very subject for action painting. The way in which the action painter paints with this dynamic as the subject for painting is described by Harold Rosenberg, whose studies of action painting remain a standard: "From his first gesture on the canvas, be it a sweep of yellow or the figure 4, he establishes a tension upon the surface—that is to say, outside himself—and he counts upon this abstract force to animate his next move."[11]

Early on, action painters sought to adhere to this motion, which is not guided by any prior image, by introducing "automatic painting" that would be as strictly automatic as the early experiments by the surrealist poets. This approach stands out in the paintings where Jackson Pollock substituted pouring or dripping paint on the canvas for applications of paint with a brush. From a random beginning, the subsequent impulsive application of paint would be precipitated by what happened on the canvas in such a way that, to use Pollack's own word, "contact" with the painting could remain unbroken. As did surrealist poets, action painters soon found that "automatic art" was a rather limited means of access to the dynamic in which their art originates. It excludes whatever might accidentally interrupt an impulsive reaction to what takes place in the work of art. This becomes an extremely restrictive effect. In fact, these experiments resulted in a crisis that nearly marked a breakdown of the artistic effort of action painting. But ways toward adhering to the dynamic that effects a synthesis of the visual and motor sectors of bodily experience were discovered by action painters in the limitations encountered by "automatic painting." Willem de Kooning and Hans Hofmann, for example, left "automatic painting" as an exclusive approach behind before their major contributions to action painting. Pollack began, in his final canvasses, to incorporate other approaches. What "automatic painting" had effected was the change from coming to the canvas as a place to render a prior image, to coming to the canvas as a site for acting.

In addition to departing from procedures for rendering a prior image on a canvas, action painting departs from procedures for working toward the aim of engendering an image on the canvas. Because of this, action painting more radically discomposes the world-as-picture displayed by premodern painting than does work by Klee or by other progeny of Klee. This step is apparent in a shift that takes place in de Kooning's work. At first, shapes resulting from a disjoining, in two dimensions, of figures that as whole figures would render three-dimensional subjects, would be recombined in a manner directed toward the production of a symbolist configuration on the canvas. This recombination of shapes gave way in de Kooning's work, in favor of paintings where the features of the painting that appear in the course of painting it are no longer apprehended as elements in a configuration that is taking shape, but rather are temporary resolutions of strains or tensions in the painter's perceptual field, resolutions that give way to other strains or tensions. Harold Rosenberg describes a result of this shift: "dozens of paintings disappear" into a major work by de Kooning.[12]

De Kooning did not at this point impose the restrictions characteristic of "automatic painting." He began to mark particular tensive points in the specifically visual schema of the field of overlap between the visual and motor fields. In his series of "Woman" paintings, he marked particular tensive points, which, when associated, became a figure of a woman. Harold Rosenberg describes this as a paradoxical effort to make the figure of a woman appear on the canvas while specifically not rendering a prior image on the canvas, nor painting toward the goal of an image engendered on the canvas in the course of painting. These paintings apparently did mark a crisis point for de Kooning. In recent years, exhibited paintings, "land and seascapes" and successions of untitled canvasses, introduce the viewer, by way of traces of the overlap between the visual and motor fields, only to other such traces—and the effect is to discompose the apprehension of the painting as, itself, a region of a world apprehended as picture. A simple delineation between the painting and the exterior of the painting is no longer fixed within a self-contained context of world apprehended as picture.

Conclusion

Heidegger, in his 1955 essay "The Question Concerning Technology," indicates that art may yet hold out the possibility of extricating civilization from the extreme danger inherent in the "technicity" that characterizes our world-historical situation. The extreme danger is that of an oblivion where the poetic nature of our existence is, in effect, paralyzed by "the measurable" and "the calculable" in such a way that we can no longer avail ourselves of the dynamic of the poetic nature of our existence. The mode of world-apprehension characteristic of the modern epoch accelerates this extreme debilitation insofar as it seizes and submits any and every entity to a systematic order that is thoroughly accessible to measure and to calculation. "Technicity" establishes a network within which any and every entity is already integrated into "the measurable" and "the calculable." That is a given. This supports the research methodology characteristic of modern science. This also results in the relegation of art to the status of the "merely aesthetic." These are two of the fundamental features of the modern epoch identified by Heidegger in "Die Zeit des Weltbildes." In order that art may succeed in providing a possibility for extricating civilization from the extreme danger of our world-historical situation, the relegation of art to the status of the "merely aesthetic" must be brought to an end. When asked where matters stand with regard to modern art, Heidegger, in his 1966 *Der Spiegel* interview says that "whatever modern art portends is obscure to [him], nor [does he] see what it's looking for or what it considers art to be."[13]

Action painting "looks for" the dynamic in which the art of painting originates. Action painting proceeds by making the motion of painting the subject of painting. The open-ended movements of the painter, animated by strains or tensions in the traces left on the canvas of the overlap of the visual and motor fields, discompose the apprehension of world-as-picture. In the oscillation of those traces between associations out of which images emerge and a sheer interplay with other such traces, action paintings hold open possibilities for modes of world-apprehension other than the apprehension of world-as-picture essential to the metaphysical foundations of the modern epoch. This makes action painting, foundational art.

After having made the motion of painting the subject of painting, action painting radically unsettles the apprehension of world-as-picture by discomposing the prior delimitation between the painting and exterior of the painting. There are paintings by de Kooning where the oscillation between associations out of which images emerge and a sheer interplay between the traces left on the canvas of the overlap of the visual and motor fields, is interchangeable with the oscillation of the surface of the sea, and vice versa. What action painting portends is an end to the fixed boundaries of art that has been relegated to the status of the "merely aesthetic." A "feeling of mutation within the relations of man and Being," which is how Merleau-Ponty describes seeing the achievements of earlier modern painters, is evoked by action paintings.

On the Topic of Art and Truth: Merleau-Ponty, Heidegger, and the Transcendental Turn

Robert Burch

I

My purpose in the following discussion[1] is to initiate what in Heideggerian terms might be called a "lover's quarrel" (*liebende Streit*)[2] over the question of art and truth. It is truth, however, and not art that is the focal issue. I am not concerned to solve a specific problem in the philosophy of art or art criticism, nor to outline the elements of a phenomenology of purely aesthetic experience. Besides, if one doubts the ready division of philosophy into discrete domains and permanent problems, and the concomitant invention of aesthetics as one such study unto itself, then the very delineation of such concerns would from the start be questionable. In any case, my topic has ostensibly a different compass. It centers upon Merleau-Ponty's and Heidegger's respective researches into the relation of philosophical, or what is the same, ontological truth to art and to the domain of the aesthetic.[3] Yet it also situates these discussions more generally in relation to an aporia intrinsic to the transcendental viewpoint. Stated in broad terms, the aporetic issue is: How are transcendence and

its philosophical comprehension possible for a being who in its very being is limited to the bounds of experience? Here the theme "art and
truth" is an aesthetic issue first as part of, so to speak, a reworked transcendental aesthetic (an "*aestheisologie*" in Merleau-Ponty's terms),
wherein the possibility of experience and the possibility of artistic creation coincide at their root. In exploring this topic, my intent is not simply to catalog similarities and differences between Merleau-Ponty and
Heidegger as a contribution to impartial scholarship, nor to set one
against the other for the sake of some definitive "refutation." Rather, by
highlighting and contrasting certain themes and tendencies in their respective versions of the art/truth relation, focusing chiefly upon their
later writings where this relation is most fully developed, I hope to open
a way toward reconsideration of the transcendental project as such. In
proposing this, it is not my assumption that either Merleau-Ponty or Heidegger ought straightforwardly to be read as a transcendental philosopher, nor even that they situate themselves in relation to the overall
sense of that orientation in precisely the same way. Nevertheless, by
seeking to subvert the aporia and tensions implicit in the transcendental
project, each in his own way comes to disclose the essence of that project
at its limit. These disclosures, especially in their contrast, merit consideration on their own terms.

II

A brief reminder of some basics of the transcendental project will serve
to orient us. The *locus classicus* is of course Kant's "Copernican" hypothesis: "We must . . . make trial whether we may not have more success in
the tasks of metaphysics, if we suppose that objects must conform to our
knowledge."[4] This is first and foremost an ontological rather than strictly
an epistemological thesis. The transcendental inquiry into the mode of
our knowledge of objects a priori is an inquiry into the manifold ways
that beings as beings can appear; and this *is* ontology.[5] Of course, to
understand ontology in this way is to place the question of Being itself on
a radically new plane. Instead of the quest for "reality-in-itself" to whose
inherent principles and categories the mind must simply conform, or the
search for the highest and most general necessary "cause" *meta ta physika*
responsible for all that is, at its inception transcendental philosophy
seeks the Being of beings in the subjective roots of the transcendental
horizons of consciousness, that is, in how a priori beings as beings can

become objects of possible experience and hence in how they must always already be understood as such. That being(s) *are* in themselves is not doubted; but the question of how they are in themselves pure and simple is supplanted by the inquiry into how they can come to be for us with significance. Being itself is thus not adjacent to human experience, hither or yon, but is its horizonal essence, "the first, internal principle of that which belongs to the possibility of a thing," where "possibility" is itself a modality of experience.[6] The ontological task of transcendental philosophy is to illumine this "horizon" *ab intra* in order to grasp the ultimate englobing sense of what can appear within it.

In at least two respects, the Cartesian lineage of this project should be evident, however oedipal that relation has come to be. First, transcendental philosophy appropriates the connection, at once established and obscured in Descartes's thinking, between ontological truth as the goal of *prima philosophia* and the selfhood of the self. With Descartes, the self-certainty of the subject is the "Archimedean" point in terms of which human thinking gives its measure to the real, determines its own divine grounding, and upon which it then reconstructs the whole system of ontological knowledge. Though in its explicit formulations transcendental philosophy straightway rejects Descartes's inference from *ego cogito* to a substantial ground (*res*), and later challenges the identification of ontological knowledge with what the subject posits objectively and secures in self-certainty, it nonetheless affirms an essential connection between the essence of the self as self-defining and ontological truth. Second, at its inception, transcendental philosophy appropriates Descartes's tacit characterization of the *cogitare* as *re-praesentare*, yet proposes to reverse the commonsense relation of priority whereby the subject would conform to the object as given. Yet, in reversing this relation, the true focus of attention is neither simply subjects nor objects, but the subject/object relation itself. To reflect on this relation, moreover, is ipso facto to transcend it. There are three tensions that inhere in the attempt.

The first tension is already clearly apparent in Kant. Though transcendental philosophy begins by locating the Being of beings in the consciousness of the subject, this does not warrant an immediate and unconditional reduction of the otherness of the object to the subject. That "*esse est percipi*" is a thesis in need of specific demonstration in relation to the whole of experience, not an immediately self-evident truth. To be sure, by means of such demonstration transcendental philosophy seeks to exorcise any shadow of a "thing-in-itself" as an actual, elusive reality that is both for, yet wholly beyond, our constitutive knowledge. Still, it cannot simply dismiss the contribution of what is in itself, even within a radically "intentionalized" or mediated givenness, to the coming to be of the knowing self and to the sense of what appears to it. Yet how this "contribution" is to be assessed remains, to say the least, highly questionable.

The second tension is also apparent in Kant, and arises from an issue that concerns the very possibility of transcendental philosophy as a quest for essential self-knowledge. Kant limits genuine knowledge to the range of possible experience, and the question of the Being of beings to the objectivity of objects that can appear within that range. We know ourselves theoretically under the same limits, that is, either by empirical intuition, which is inadequate to philosophy, or simply by reason's a priori reflection upon the self as the essential limit of the object-world. Yet there is a tension in this thesis. On the one hand, the theoretical task, as Kant puts it, is to provide an "inventory of all our possessions through pure reason."[7] In this regard, however, we are also told that transcendent knowledge of the self through intellectual intuition is beyond the powers of human reason, and that a pure consciousness of self is "a completely empty representation"[8] and "very far from being a knowledge of the self."[9] The reflective inventory has therefore to be of a different order. What we come upon by means of it, Kant claims, is knowledge of ourselves precisely as the universal condition a priori of things becoming objects of our knowledge in general. Though not transcendent, this discovery amounts to genuine transcendental, hence ontological, self-knowledge. On the other hand, Kant's "Copernican" principle is that "reason has insight only into that which it produces [hervorbringt] after a plan of its own"[10] and "puts into [hineinlegt]"[11] objects a priori. Even with respect to the self, we are concerned only with "what reason produces entirely out of itself."[12] But the human self "does not, as it were, make itself,"[13] and what is more, it is dependent upon external objects, in relation to which alone it becomes conscious of itself and hence is a self in the first place.[14] There is in this thesis, then, a tension between the self's transcendental/ontological knowledge of objects of experience as such in virtue of what it "produces out of itself" as the a priori condition of objects, and the self's transcendental/ontological self-knowledge, which is limited to the range of possible objects of experience, yet requires a cognition that transcends the subject/object relation and hence all object-knowledge. This tension may be focused in Kantian terms by asking: How is the essential inventory of self possible, when what is to be disclosed from it are the very limits which precede and make possible all inventories, that is, all designation of items within a limit? Stated in more general terms, the question is: How is the self which is a self only in the midst of experience, its whole thinking included, capable of philosophical self-knowledge that transcends all experience?

The third tension is implied by the first two. Although, historically, transcendental philosophy begins with the subject/object dichotomy as a specific cognitive relation, it moves by the force of its own insights beyond this limitation toward a concept of "experience" that has more encompassing connotations. Its proper fulfillment is not to replace realist "objectivism" with idealist "subjectivism," but to overcome the subject/object opposition in all of its Cartesian formulations, and so to preclude all of the realism/idealism aporias that attend that opposition. In that event, the focal issue is less that of the a priori conformity of objects to the knowing subject than it is the coming to be of transcendence itself, which human being as such sustains and carries forward through all of its experience. On these terms, for transcendental philosophy to account in principle for its own possibility, it must affirm and demonstrate an original twofold mediation: that experience as such is originally mediated through thought and that thinking, even at its highest level, is mediated through experience. For this resolution to be intelligible and defensible in principle, two conditions must hold. A transcending dimension must always already be constituted in experience, a transcendence that belongs together essentially with the self's own self-constitution. Thus would transcendental philosophy be possible. Yet, within experience, that transcendence, though always already tacitly or vaguely understood, is as such and as a whole concealed. Thus would transcendental philosophy be necessary.

III

None of the foregoing sketch, even though crudely and tendentiously drawn, should be all that surprising. Still, one might well ask what it has to do with the question of art and truth. In the immediate post-Kantian tradition, this connection is made directly. In that tradition, the effort to comprehend a transcendence encompassing the subject/object relation leads to an "aestheticism," that is, to an affirmation of the primacy of the act of "aesthetic" creation as at once bringing forth the beautiful object as the self's own essential product and as realizing a truth which always already transcends the subject/object dichotomy. The aesthetic act in the usual sense, that is, as having to do with the production of works of art, comes thereby to assume a decisive "aesthetic" importance in the transcendental sense, that is, as a cipher for the manner in which a priori experience in general is "made." Though not the only one to hit upon this possibility, Schelling is the first to take it up and to develop it in a "*system* of transcendental idealism."

"If aesthetic intuition is simply intellectual intuition become objective," Schelling writes, "it is self-evident that art is the only true and eternal organon and document of philosophy."[15] In the theoretical and practical spheres, consciousness works against a recalcitrant otherness in order to reduce it ever more to the self. In aesthetic consciousness, the conflict falls *within* the creative act per se. Aesthetic creation, so Schelling claims, necessarily unites self and world as two essential moments of the one *self*-productive process, a process that comes to fulfillment in the individual product. The work of art is a free creation of self become objective to itself, that is, "a synthesis of nature and freedom."[16] In the "genius" of artistic creation, then, "a contradiction is solved which is absolute, and solvable by no other means."[17] Aesthetic intuition realizes experientially the self-identity of self and world in the product of art, and only those products which exhibit this identity, "either directly or at least by reflection," count truly as "works of art." "Art," Schelling concludes, "is the eternal and the only revelation that there is."[18]

In thus affirming for human cognition an intuition that at once knows and creates, Schelling ostensibly resolves at least one of the tensions implicit in the Kantian project. In order to be a self, the self must be its own essential product. It is in virtue of this production that it is capable of genuine ontological knowledge that is at once knowledge of self and of world. Thus, whereas Kant had denied to human knowledge a creative intuition that would constitute an absolute synthesis of freedom and nature, and whereas Fichte had posited such an intuition but had failed to show how it could be attained by an empirical self, Schelling affirms its evident actuality in the work of art. Yet, in explaining the possibility of such intuition in terms of artistic production and aesthetic intuition, other tensions emerge that are not so easily resolved.

First, there is an implicit tension in Schelling's "solution" regarding the relative status of art and philosophy, one that would inhere in any *radical* appeal to aesthetic creation. It is art *itself* that is the only revelation and the organon of philosophy. "Grant objectivity to philosophy," Schelling claims, "and it ceases to be philosophy, and becomes art."[19] Yet this risks making philosophical reflection either inadequate, or itself simply a mode of art. In deference to the primacy of philosophy, Schelling wavers on his own thesis. "The universal organ of philosophy," he also writes, "is the *philosophy* of art."[20]

Second, at this stage of Schelling's aesthetic idealism, the artistic realization of truth is limited to the experience of particular and disparate epiphanies, each having in themselves absolute significance for surmounting the subject/object dichotomy. Art is an "eternal" revelation not cumulatively, but in each individual work. "There is properly speaking one absolute work of art which may exist in many versions."[21] Each revelation is complete in itself, the manifestation of self-sufficient truth. Still, outside this privileged revelation, the rest of actual, finite experience remains in all of its fragmentation and opposition.

These unresolved tensions lead Schelling quickly to abandon the transcendental approach in favor of an *absolute* aesthetic idealism.[22] His basic concern is still to "overcome" the subject/object split by showing how that is already accomplished in aesthetic creation, but the strategy is to relocate and exalt even higher the productive power that gives rise to art. Instead of being limited to an essential capacity of the transcendental self, whose highest self-realization is the work of art, the creative power is now declared by Schelling to be the fundamental determination (i.e., the "highest potency") of what truly is (i.e., of the "absolute"). Thus, the ontological task is no longer simply to show how, despite appearances, the non-self is in truth a product of, or reduces to, the self, but to show how both self and non-self are complementary aspects of the one self-developing reality. The nexus of this system is still the creative power that gives rise to art, but now reinterpreted as that power which defines what truly is in itself, and which artistic production truly enacts and philosophy comprehends.

By the measure of a nondogmatic transcendental thinking bound to the limits of experience, Schelling's new attempt suffers from a dual weakness. First, the starting point of absolute identity is likely to seem little more than a bare assertion, a claim to "absolute knowledge" that comes, as it were, "shot from the pistol" and which "makes short work of other standpoints simply by declaring that it takes no notice of them."[23] Yet this belies its very claim to absoluteness, since the proof of that claim would require the complete, systematically demonstrated self-detachment of knowledge from all limiting relations to its object. Second, the assertion of absolute identity is also apt to seem rather barren, an empty assurance that "all is one" serving, one might say, "to palm off its absolute as the night in which . . . all cows are black."[24] In contrast, a successful post-Kantian ontology would have to demonstrate the fully articulated system of knowledge, not just in opposition to the experience of this-worldly fragmentation, but in the very midst of and *through* all the forms of experience. It is Hegel, not Schelling, who gives this project its most complete and convincing expression.

Hegel seeks to disclose an all-encompassing transcendence, the englobing whole of experience beyond the subject/object opposition. His language is that of *Aufhebung* and "overreaching," and his task is to provide a "ladder" to absolute knowledge by demonstrating systematically and cumulatively the transcendence that inheres in all the essential *Gestalten* of experience. There are two aspects of his attempt that are especially relevant to the present discussion. First, in Hegel's system art still has an exalted status. It is *a* form of absolute experience, that is, of experience in which subject and object, idea and reality, are realized as one. "Beauty and truth are in one way the same. . . . The beautiful is determined as the sensuous appearance [*sinnliche Scheinen*] of the idea."[25] So regarded, art constitutes an *essential* moment in the self-realization of truth, that is, the moment of "knowing, in the form and shape of the objective itself, in which the absolute comes to intuition and sensibility."[26] As such, it constitutes the "first [*nächste*] and immediate satisfaction [*Selbstbefriedigung*] of absolute spirit."[27] Yet "the manifestation of truth in sensuous form is not truly appropriate to spirit."[28] To be brought into its most proper element, the truth as embodied in art must be reenacted and so encompassed and transformed in philosophical concepts. Yet when that is accomplished, "art is no longer the highest mode in which truth acquires existence."[29] The relation of art and philosophy is thus decided: Art is a necessary stage in the realization of absolute truth, a stage presupposed by philosophy. But philosophy "sublates" the truth that art fashions; that is to say, it both "preserves" what is essential in that truth and yet "removes it from its immediacy and so from a determinate existence open to external influences."[30]

This thesis leads to the second, relevant point. Within the Hegelian circle of reflection, art cannot in the end have a decisive claim against conceptual thought, since that thought is absolute and subsumes all other forms of experience. Indeed, in principle, however much Hegelian thought claims to be open to all experience (and to presume absoluteness, it must be radically open), its fulfillment lies in a system of identity in which nothing essential is excluded or uncomprehended. On the one hand, without *real* contingency, singularity, and the visceral otherness of finite beings as encountered by embodied, finite selves, there would be to begin with no human experience at all. "Spirit is spirit only insofar as it is mediated by nature."[31] On the other hand, however, in reenacting the "logic" in virtue of which alone contingent and necessary, singular and universal, self and not-self come to be, Hegelian idealism presumes to comprehend these realities *absolutely*. On this score, Hegel does admit that "the unlimited wealth and variety of forms, and the utterly irrational contingency which mixes with the external order of natural forms, . . . sets limits to philosophy."[32] Though in principle the systematic place—indeed the necessity—of contingency and singularity is grasped, the contingent particular in its very contingency and particularity is not. Yet acknowledging this limit does not elicit from Hegel a corollary admission that the contingent particular stands as a reality "in itself" beyond conceptual thought. Of all of nature, he claims, "its characteristic is positedness, the negative, in the same way as the ancients conceived matter in general as *non-ens*."[33] Within the circle of reflection, not all reality is simply identical to the idea; but the idea "overreaches everything finite."[34] The difference between beings and Being as Idea is thus ultimately, absolutely no essential difference at all. And when that thought is realized, no important disclosure can remain for art itself.

It is at this point that both Merleau-Ponty and Heidegger would object in the name of the independence (*Selbstständigkeit*) of beings in their difference from the truth of Being, or of the visceral presence of the world and of brute Being itself, against the absolutely all-mediating Concept. In doing so, each reinstates a privileged role for artistic creation in relation to ontological truth. As with idealism, the task is still to disclose a transcendence beyond any assumed preeminence of the subject/object dichotomy. Yet both Merleau-Ponty and Heidegger reject in principle the goal of a complete, exhaustive conceptual exposition of Being that would have the clarity and self-possession of the absolute Idea. What for early Schelling, and for Hegel, was a short-coming, namely, that each aesthetic epiphany and each finite claim to truth falls short of absolute comprehension, is evidence for Merleau-Ponty and Heidegger of an inescapable, positive limit—an essential, ontological finitude and historicity that pertains to the very possibility of transcendence and openness to the world. Their respective appeals to art thus bring into question more forcefully the scope and limits of reflective thought, as well as the tensions within Being of *sens et non-sens*, of disclosure and concealment. Their task is to undercut or subvert the originality of the subject/object split, and their language is that of "origin" and "stepping back." They seek to uncover a transcendence that is the "concealed source" of experience, prior to all mere "beginnings." Thus, whereas idealism wishes to gather up (*er-innern*) without essential remainder all of the already implicitly accomplished meanings into a closed system of absolute knowledge, Merleau-Ponty and Heidegger seek a more radical recovery (*retrouver, Wiederholung*) of the origin of such meanings in the creative communion of self and world. It is to the details of their respective attempts that I want now to turn.

IV

Merleau-Ponty himself gives the best summary account of his fundamental project in the text he provided for his candidacy to the Collège de France. He writes:

> I found in the experience of the perceived world a new type of relation between the mind [*esprit*] and truth. The evidence of the perceived thing lies in its concrete aspect, in the very texture of its qualities, and in the equivalence among all its sensible properties—which caused Cézanne to say that one should be able to paint even odors. Before our undivided existence the world is true; it exists. The unity, the articulations of both are intermingled. . . . We experience in it a truth which shows through and envelops us rather than being held and circumscribed by our mind.[35]

It would neither be feasible nor appropriate here to attempt to sort out in detail the implications of this discovery. Yet, for the purposes of understanding Merleau-Ponty's "aesthetics" as an "ontology of art" (in both senses of the genitive), the relevant theses may be stated as follows.

1. The touchstone of philosophical inquiry, the *terminus a quo et ad quem* of its investigations, is the original perceptual world of lived experience, the "sensible and opened world such as it is for our life and our body"[36] and the silent foundation for all our interactions, practices, and meaning accomplishments. "All efforts," Merleau-Ponty writes, "are concentrated upon recovering [*retrouver*] a naive contact with this world, and endowing that contact with philosophical status."[37]

2. The goal of this "recovery" is the elucidation of the essence or the origin of the world. The world is not a "fact or sum of facts," but the "locus [*lieu*] of an inscription of truth."[38] Its essence is not a fixed "what" captured in a single direct insight, nor a separate ground beyond the world. It is an "active and living" essence, the full way of being (*Wesen*) of the world,[39] the origin of truth as an occurrence of Being itself. It is "an event of the order of brute or wild being," Merleau-Ponty writes, "which, ontologically, is primary."[40]

3. As the "horizonal" occurrence of ontological truth, the world is the *fond* against which self and things are installed as reciprocal dimensions of the same Being, Being lived as *la chair*. This reciprocity is a "pre-intentional present," an original unity of embodied self and sensed things as "total parts" of the same carnal, corporeal world.[41] "The world is made of body's own stuff,"[42] the "flesh" that envelops the sensing and

the sensed, that is constitutive for both, yet is more than their sum, and is the means of their encounter and communication. Between the sensing and the sensed something of a "pre-established harmony" exists, an original resonance within the world at the origin of experience. "My body is the model of things, and things are the model of my body."[43]

Yet this is not a simple and given reciprocity. On the one hand, the embodied self is the center of initiative in the giving of sense, that "remarkable variant"[44] in Being itself without which there would be no world or truth. On the other hand, the things of the world are not simply reducible to the covering that is our creative projection of sense. They are "beings in depth," pregnant with textures and articulations "under the human mask."[45]

4. In its origin, the "world" has its "λόγος ἐνδιάθετος," a sense (λόγος) already disposed and articulated (διάθετος) within itself (ἐν).[46] But as "fond," this meaning is invisible and silent in favor of what is visible and expressed. Giving creative expression to this fond, "philosophy is the reconversion of silence and speech into one another."[47] It is a "λόγος προφορικός," a gebildet sense brought forward from the essence of the lifeworld and giving explicit expression to its silent meaning. It is a "conversion," for it seeks to give a "pure expression" of the world's own implicit meaning (i.e., to render "silence" into "speech"), and yet in the event to be faithful to that meaning itself (i.e., to let "speech" be informed by "silence"). This is also a "reconversion," since already in lived experience there is the nonthematic interplay of expression and silence, of figure et fond.

The implicit silent λόγος "calls for" (appelle) its own explicit expression in a twofold sense. It "requires" our "logic" (or other expression) to bring it forward, a requirement variously felt in human culture and history. "Being is what requires creation of us for us to experience it."[48] It also "evokes" in us the explicit formulation (Gebilde) of its own sense, yet which as an evocation admits of different resonances and responses, the deepest sense of which we do not command. "The λόγος . . . as realized in human being [is] nowise our property."[49]

5. Philosophy dis-covers the world: It is the thematic "study of the Vorhabe of Being,"[50] of the "place" (lieu) of the inscription of truth where Being is originally disclosed in itself. In the deepest sense, then, philosophy is Being's explicit self-interpretation in and through humanity, our creative figuration of original sense that seeks its own origin. "Philosophy, precisely as 'Being speaking within us,' expression of the mute experience itself, is creation. A creation which is at the same time a reintegration of Being. . . . It is creation in a radical sense: a creation

that is at the same time an adequation [to its origin], the only way to obtain adequation."[51]

6. So conceived, philosophy is, as it were, a craft of ontological place, the "creative" expression of the origin of the essential time/space in which we always already dwell. As such it is essentially finite, bound to the historicity and horizons of "place," and to the elusive "silence" and "invisibility" of Being's disclosure. Yet it is also conditioned by the openness of "place," to the fact that we always already belong to the origin of truth which is to be recovered, and thus to an ontological *fond* with ever more to be revealed. Every philosophical disclosure is thus inevitably tentative and perspectival; yet it is not simply relative, nor merely one partial product of the lifeworld among others. Philosophy is a privileged product, for it not only seeks the *typique*, the general schema in the individual example, but it also *is* an expression of Being as such. "Between the *Lebenswelt* as universal Being and philosophy as the extreme product of the world, there is no rivalry or antinomy: It is philosophy that discloses it [i.e., the world as universal Being]."[52]

Merleau-Ponty accords a parallel function to art. "Art" he writes, "especially painting, draws upon this brute fabric of meaning which activism would prefer to ignore. Art and only art does this in full innocence."[53] The privilege of art over philosophy is its "innocence," its effective "suspension" of the world, its achievement, tantamount to a "pure reduction," of expressing essence in the very act of creative origination. It reenacts, as it were, the very coming to be of the world. Of course art may be didactic or *engagé* or attempt to state explicit truths about the human condition, but that is beyond its exclusive ποίησις. In contrast, however, philosophy is by its nature obliged to "appraise" what it sees, to offer "opinions and advice"; and it is obliged self-consciously to justify and legitimate its own procedures and grounds, and thus to "render its own support manageable."[54]

The privilege of painting over the other arts lies in its peculiar "distance." It holds the world "at a distance" for the sake simply of vision. Yet it must translate the three-dimensional map of vision onto the two-dimensional canvas, and thus go beyond the visible objects to their origin, to the heart of visibility itself. In contrast, music offers too little, for it presents no figure circumscribable enough to allow Being to become truly visible in the work. It "is too far on the hither side of the world and the designatable to depict anything but certain outlines of Being—its ebb and flow, its growth, its upheavals, its turbulence."[55] Literature and sculpture in their peculiar ways offer too much. The sculpture as work is too figured, too much itself a perceptual object. Written art, like philosophy, is "contact with Being precisely as creation."[56] Yet neither philosophy nor literature achieves the direct and primitive contact with Being intrinsic to painting. They are too much removed from lived experience itself, too much founded activities. If music is too close, then writing is *too* distant.

According to this account, then, painting and philosophy concern the same thing in a different fashion. They overlap, but their scope is not simply congruent. The peculiar virtue of painting is its potential to disclose the essence of original perception, "to make express the encounter and conflict between one's look and the things which solicit it, between the body and the world it inhabits."[57] The elements of the fabric of painting—depth, color, line, movement, contour and physiognomy are all "branches" of Being, that is, interrelated aspects of the invisible ontological "network," "the inward tapestry, the imaginary texture of the real" on the threshold of profane vision, that makes such vision possible.[58] These elements are not the properties of things, not their "skin," so to speak, but a "system of equivalences" immersed in the flesh, the inward traces of vision that inhere in the "indivision" of sensing and sensed. "There is no break in this circuit; it is impossible to say that nature ends here and that man or expression starts here. It is mute Being which itself comes to show forth its own meaning."[59]

Even in their adequation, philosophical statements do not represent things in their carnal presence. They attempt rather to translate into speech the unseen origin of that presence. Against common opinion, Merleau-Ponty claims an analogous function for painting. It does not present a copy of visible things, something more or less true to what I see. It is in fact "autofigurative," presenting itself as spectacle before all representation.[60] "No worthwhile painting [*aucune peinture valable*] has ever consisted in simple representation," nor could it.[61] Even high realism must decipher rather than merely copy the visible. Painters, as it were, "throw away the fish and keep the net."[62] They offer "a carnal essence or icon," the "secret ciphers" of the visible, something true to how I see.[63] In short, painting "gives visual existence to that which profane vision believes invisible."[64]

The end of painting, so conceived, is not to capture the thing itself nor to objectify the ego, but "to attend internally [*assister du dedans à*] at the fission of Being," that is, to observe and foster the event of vision, the internal reciprocity and conversion that is the origin of all sense.[65] Philosophy too "attends at the fission of Being," but as "speaking thought" it attends differently. Two aspects of this difference have already been indicated. Philosophy gives Being a conceptual rendering, bringing it into discourse; and it is self-reflexive, that is, obliged to demonstrate its own essence, to speak on behalf of itself as well as of Being. Painting is a "mute thinking" that renders Being visible, and speaks for itself only in this. But philosophy at all times seeks ultimate integration and a presumptive universality. The perceived world that painting expresses, the world of color and form, although fundamental, is not the "totality of our universe," nor does our perception of it have a "monopoly on truth."[66] There is a whole range of founded activities (to be sure, ones whose domain of final application is the perceived world), and levels of Being and truth beyond the scope of painting, that philosophy, as "the extreme product of the world," must consider and situate.

Yet this imports a paradox at the very heart of the inscriptions of truth. On the one hand, all attempts at expression, painting included, are enmeshed in a primordial historicity, in an interplay of sedimentation and re-activation. Any expression can easily become a fixed possession with a conventional meaning attached, for example, the "work" as an "object" in the history of art, or a "doctrine" in the history of philosophy. But although such sedimented meanings can be thoughtlessly passed along, each is open to re-activation and reinterpretations that enliven, develop and deploy sense. Each, then, is more than what was "contained" in it. Moreover, the ontological *fond* that evokes and sustains expressive creation is at the same time "beyond the means and goals at hand,"[67] for these are directed to expressing a reality in set figures that of its nature eludes absolute expression and circumscription. "The idea of a universal painting, of a totalization of painting, of a fully and definitively achieved painting is an idea bereft of sense."[68] There is no straightforward progress, no accumulation of a "stable treasure." And "no painting ever comes to be *the* painting."[69]

On the other hand, the origin of expression, that is, the ontological *fond*, "contains everything in advance,"[70] as one might say that *langue* contains all the possibilities of *parole*. Yet it is left for us to realize the possibilities in ever new expressions. "The very first painting in some sense went to the farthest reaches of the future. . . . Each creation changes, alters, enlightens, deepens, confirms, exalts, re-creates, or creates in advance all the others."[71] In a sense, then, every creation is "ever new" and yet "always the same."[72] To specify just what that "sense" is, however, is no easy task.

Merleau-Ponty emphasizes, overall, the unity and completeness of Being's original "dehiscence" and unfolding. "The question," he writes, "is to grasp the nexus, . . . the simultaneous *Urstiftung* of time

and space, which makes it possible for there to be an historical landscape
and an almost geographical inscription of history."[73] Beneath "history"
and "geography" as inscribed by human beings, there is an original geography, "the Earth as *Ur-Arche*," a unity of time-space ("endotime" and
"endospace") which "brings out [*met en évidence*] the carnal *Ur-historie*,"
that is, the history of Being's own self-revelation and its dehiscence
into the unity and tensions of visible-invisible, sensing-sensed, *corps
propre*–things. This suggests, however, that there is no essential otherness nor real essential development within Being.

> I bring into doubt the evolutionist perspective. I replace it with
> a cosmology of the visible in the sense that, considering the en-
> dotime and endospace, for me it is no longer a question of ori-
> gins nor of limits, nor of series of events reaching toward a
> first cause, but a single explosion of Being which is forever [*un
> seul éclatement d'Etre qui est à jamais*]. . . . The past and present
> are *Ineinander*, each enveloping-enveloped—and that itself is
> the flesh.[74]

There is the dehiscence of Being whose essential possibilities are all contained in advance, and "no positive production."[75] This bars all apparent
anthropologisms, all readings of Being and its history that are rooted in
the primacy of "individual praxis" and the encounter with the inertia of
the "worked over matter."[76] Ultimately, then, we are on a plane where
there is only the "universal dimensionality that is Being."[77]

V

Such considerations lead directly to the confrontation with Heidegger.
In this regard, Merleau-Ponty writes: "The 'amorphous' perceptual
world of which I spoke in relation to painting . . . is at bottom Being in
Heidegger's sense."[78] It requires only a minimal sketch of Heidegger's
Seinsdenken to call this claim to equivalence into doubt. We need first to
see what might make it plausible.

    1. *Sein* for Heidegger (like *la chair* for Merleau-Ponty), is neither
subject-being, nor object-being. It is rather the whole process of origina-
tive disclosure, unveiling, or clearing, with its inseparable function of
revealing/concealing, that makes possible as such the presence together
of human beings and beings. It constitutes the most fundamental interpretive context which, by illumining the mass of phenomena in a charac-

teristic way, accounts for the existence of a "world." And it is its own self generating source (*Abgrund*), having no other ground than its own activity and "emmitance."

2. The occurrence of Being has its own intrinsic λόγος, which philosophy expresses (*auslegt*). Language and Being are equiprimordial. That this "expression" is always preparatory is a consequence not of the inadequacies of language, but of the finite and esentially ambiguous character of Being's disclosure. Being opens essentially to a "place" (*Da*, *Lichtung*, *topos*) whose measure can never be exhaustively taken or whose source be plumbed.

3. Human being is itself the locus and medium of this disclosure. The thinking of Being is not an epistemological effort to secure certain knowledge of a universal "object." It is a question of Being's own self-interpretation in and through the human essence, one that is granted and vouchsafed from Being itself.

4. For Heidegger, too, art plays a central role in relation to this disclosure. "Art," he says, "is the becoming and happening of truth."[79] As such, all art is essentially ποίησις, an illuminating projection of sense in the midst of beings, which opens a world in which beings are significantly disclosed. The "poetic" in this sense characterizes the event of Being itself, the process of its disclosure and historical occurrence. Each work of art centers and reveals this ontological ποίησις. It is the "setting-itself-unto-work of truth [*Ins-Werk-Setzen der Wahrheit*]," an event of the disclosure of Being in and through the work.

These, tersely stated, are the relevant parallels. Merleau-Ponty, however, explicitly denies the basic Heideggerian insight that would make them valid. He writes: "There is no absolute difference . . . between the transcendental and the empirical, (it is better to say, between the ontological and the ontic)."[80] What is at stake for Merleau-Ponty is not Being as the "*transcendens* pure and simple,"[81] nor reality *aufgehoben* in the absolute Concept, but "dimensions, articulation, level, hinges, pivots, configuration" in the one and same carnal Being.[82] It is a question of how the one reality unfolds itself and gives self expression to its own mute sense. The *Sache des Denkens* for Heidegger—the inquiry into the concealed source that opens the difference of Being and beings, that is, the *Es* in the *Es gibt Sein*, the *Ereignis* that grants the epochal revelations of Being itself—is only obliquely Merleau-Ponty's concern. In his thought there is still the mystery of the *Urstiftung*, the essence of Being's original self-revelation, but there is *au fond* no ontological difference. Or rather, there is a difference that from the perspective of "endotime and endospace" is ultimately no difference at all.

VI

By tracing the plurality of the world to an *"éclatement"* in the amorphous unity of the one Being, Merleau-Ponty ostensibly subverts the tensions in the transcendental project at their point of origin. Encounter and conflict, body and things, visible and invisible, mute and expressed emerge not as inexorably given oppositions, but as "folds" or "leaves" of the original "fission" of Being. Insofar as the central tropes in play here—"flesh," "fission," "chiasm"—stand opposed to the principle of the "ideality of the finite" such that truth is absolute being-for-self,[83] this recovery of origins can hardly be called idealist. Still, in Merleau-Ponty's strategy there is something reminiscent of Schelling's absolute idealism. Schelling begins from the absolute self-identity of Being as the source from which all oppositions, dualisms, and pluralities derive in and through a self-diremptive, self-articulating, and self-realizing process. Between art as the highest concrete expression of truth and what truly is in itself, there is only a difference of "aspect," that is, a difference between the complete presentations of truth in objective form (*"Gegenbild"*) and the original being of truth in itself as unexpressed idea or ἀρχή (*"Urbild"*).[84] The absolute is not then a third thing invoked to join subject and object, as if these were already fatally severed, but the original reality from which the relation of subject and object derives, an absolute identity that is presupposed by the subject and object's apparent severance. Likewise, with Merleau-Ponty, Being as "flesh" is not a third thing invoked to ground original and thus irreparable oppositions. Rather the oppositions themselves belong to an original internal "interlacing" (*entrelacs*) and "conversion" (*chiasme*) within Being and of Being. "Every relation in Being is *simultaneously* a taking and a being taken, the hold is held, it is *inscribed* in the same Being of which it takes hold."[85] In this "simultaneity" there is no radical disjunction, but a "system of equivalences," of internal resonances. Merleau-Ponty thus subverts the transcendental problem at its root by not admitting the dualism aporia that animates it. "The distinction of two planes (natural and cultural) is abstract: everything is cultural in us (our *Lebenswelt* is "subjective") (our perception is cultural-historical), and everything is natural in us (even the cultural rests on the polymorphism of brute Being)."[86] At the original level, the fissions and folds would be undecidable.

Yet an uncharitable reader might well wonder whether this "dissolves" rather than truly solves the problem. His solution rules out as "abstract" any attempt to distinguish effectively the perceptive activity of constitution and expression, and whatever newness is engendered therein, from the inert density and inexhaustibility of the encountered thing. And this leaves largely unquestioned at the level of our work-a-day experience, the whole dimension of "otherness" and innovation that do not seem easily dissolved into dimensions of Being.

In contrast, by insisting on the ontological difference, Heidegger keeps open the tension in the transcendental perspective. Being itself does not unfold into an "abstract" distinction of ontological and ontic. Rather "beings are in themselves the beings which they are and as they are" independently of their being for us.[87] Yet this thesis is subject to a crucial qualification. Although it posits the existence of beings "in themselves," this is only possible and intelligible in terms of the prior context of Being's disclosure, which is presupposed in all understanding and access to beings. And although the disclosure of Being is prior to ontic truth, this truth itself is not simply reduced to this disclosure. In the light of the ontological difference, Heidegger presumes then to be able to open the question of Being in a genuine way, precisely because he calls into question a naive absolutization of the ontic "in itself."

It remains doubtful, however, whether on these terms Heidegger can indeed give the ontic its due. It is a debased Heideggerianism that in the light of the ontological difference dismisses all concern and involvement with the ontic as *zu metaphysich*. In re-opening the question of Being, Heidegger's *Seinsdenken* presumes to sunder the hegemony of all subjectivist-metaphysical thought, and its "technological" offspring, for the sake not only of a new prevailing revelation of Being, but also a deeper sense of beings themselves, a *Gelassenheit zu dem Dingen*. Still, the concern implied in the *Gelassenheit* cannot dissolve the transcendental problem by dissolving the ontological difference itself. The *Gelassenheit* lets things emerge in their human significance, that is, it seeks to foster and preserve all those creative, nurturing, sustaining possibilities in things themselves that enhance human dwelling, but this is wholly unintelligible other than in terms of the primacy of the disclosure of Being itself.

There are three points in particular at which this confrontation between Heidegger and Merleau-Ponty is most clearly reflected, all relating to a contrast in their basic foci. First, Heidegger is concerned with the origination of truth as meaning, but a meaning which from the start is commensurate with human aims and projects, one that opens a world of human building, dwelling, and thinking. The "thing's thinging" is an in-gathering of the constitutive meaningful elements of such a world. Merleau-Ponty is also concerned with the origination of truth as meaning, but a meaning rooted in the essential elements of visibility itself. The "thing's thinging" is the in-gathering of all that in virtue of which the thing makes itself seen.

Thus, when it comes time to select the artistic examples that best illustrate their ontological theses, illustrations which serve in effect to valorize particular sorts of works,[88] Heidegger and Merleau-Ponty tend to make rather different choices. Heidegger will point to a Van Gogh, that is, to a painting which centers and reveals both an epoch in the history of Being and a virtually timeless *Gestalt* of human significance, of laboring in the fields and treading wearily home. Merleau-Ponty in turn will point to a Klee, a painting that plays more explicitly upon the elements of painting itself, and thus shows us less of things and more of the carnal "network" that brings things to sight.

Second, this difference is reflected also in the relative priority that each thinker accords the various arts. For Merleau-Ponty, painting has priority for the reasons I have suggested. For Heidegger, "the linguistic work, the poem in the narrower sense, has a privileged position in the domain of the arts."[89] Heidegger affirms this on two grounds: that language itself is an essential "saying-showing" that brings beings originally into the "open" as something, that is, as meaningful objects and not merely as visible things present to hand; and that poetry itself best reflects this original ποιησις, the equiprimordiality of Being and language.

Third, Merleau-Ponty, it seems, places more emphasis upon the poetic act than the poetic product. The invisible network of visibility that the painter expresses is given voice in the act of painting itself, but then can easily recede into the *fond* in favor of the painting as itself simply a thing viewed. In order to see the product as an expression of how we see, the viewer in a sense must reenact the process of creation, and not merely look. With Heidegger, the work more directly evokes a resonance of meaning, for it is more directly bound to the "earth," not as traces of the visible, but as lived meanings.

VII

From a Heideggerian perspective, Merleau-Ponty's attempt to subvert the dualisms and "differences" that haunt the transcendental project suffers two faults. First, the invocation of *la chair* as the one Being from which both human being and beings unfold says "too little" about the peculiar, essential correlation of Being and human being in its difference from beings themselves and their properties. It says too little about this, since it reads both that difference and that correlation simply as articulations in the one Being. "But we say too much if we mean Being as the all-encompassing and thereby represent human being only as a special being among others (plants, animals) and put both in the relationship."[90] Second, by seeking an original *non-sens*, *invisible*, *silence*, as the *fond* of what comes to presence, Merleau-Ponty discloses a "network" which is no intelligible dimension of anyone's ordinary, actual lived experience. He thus gives us the essence, not of the perceived world *as it is lived*, that is, in its full richness of meaning as the context of my projects, but a world of visible "things," albeit one congruent with the world of my motor projects and, according to the analysis at least, more fundamental. What this avowedly amounts to is tantamount to a "pure reduction," one found by Merleau-Ponty most properly at work in painting. Yet this is a reduction whose validity Heidegger would in principle deny. By affirming it, Heidegger would likely add, Merleau-Ponty leaves the status of our everyday express meaning accomplishments uncertain. This would be evident in both diachronic and synchronic terms.

One might ask if, at the synchronic level, the original constitution of the visible can indeed be separated from the whole range of projects and meaning accomplishments that constitute my everyday being-in-the-world. If indeed "seeing" is fundamentally "embodied seeing," and the world of vision and the world of my motor projects are one and the same, can a phenomenological wedge be inserted successfully between the constitution of these two worlds? If it can, then how can the bridge between them be rebuilt, that is, how can a meaningful human world be constituted out of pure visibility? Moreover, if one grants this separation of levels of meaning, then the problem of the relative status of philosophical and artistic expression as revelations of truth becomes more pressing. If the wedge cannot be inserted, then what becomes of the "reductive purity" of the disclosures of painting, beyond an empty and founded abstraction?

Corresponding problems might be posed in diachronic terms. One might ask: How, from the perspective of human concerns, expressions, and projects, does the original "explosion" of Being, its *Urstiftung*, relate to the whole suite of subsequent founding moments, its *Stiftungen*, its ongoing institution? This is really a question about how the *Urhistorie* that follows from the original "explosion" relates to mundane history and to all our mundane projects and meaning accomplishments. If from the exalted vantage point of Being's own dehiscence, everything is at once "ever new" and "always the same," then there is no problem of "continuity" and "conservation," of sedimentation and re-activation.

Time itself is a "chiasm"; past and present, *Ineinander*. But from the mundane perspective, in a world where we must continue to make sense of the multitude of structures and meanings that articulate the context of exigent action, such problems do exist. The philosophy of the flesh does not really rescue from mystery how these two perspectives mesh. In this regard, its appeal to ultimate undecidability may look like little more than another "night in which all cows are black."

But converse objections could be directed against Heidegger. By insisting upon the ontological difference, it might be said, Heidegger never reaches the level of Being where one could discover the actual coming to be of a visible world in its visceral presence; in short, he is not radical enough. In direct contrast to Merleau-Ponty, Heidegger seeks a nonsensuous concept of sensibility.[91] The essence of sensibility lies for him not in the internal resonances and equivalences of the "flesh," but in the finitude of Being's disclosure. But a strict Merleau-Pontian would reject the idealism seemingly implicit in this turn. Heidegger, it might be said, dissolves too much of the origin of the visible and the *Seinsstiftungen* into *Verstehen* and *Verständlichkeit*, however much that is evoked from a prior concealment. His insistence upon the ontological difference might thus be taken as a sleight-of-hand, granting beings independence but (not unlike Hegel, from whom he claims to be so far)[92] reducing them to *sens* that belies it. For Heidegger subsumes the thesis that "beings *are* independently of the experience, prehension and comprehension through which they are disclosed and determined" wholly under the thesis that "Being 'is' only in the understanding of those beings to whose Being something like an understanding of Being belongs."[93] Insofar as it proceeds from and indeed entrenches the ontological difference, Heidegger's final resolution simply "to think Being without beings"[94] would only seem to take us further from the origin of our encounter with things *in the flesh*.[95]

VIII

On the face of it, Merleau-Ponty and Heidegger would appear to resolve the third tension in the Kantian project on a like basis, that is, in terms of a fundamental ontological interplay, respectively, of *sens et non-sens, visible et invisible*, and of *Entborgenheit und Verborgenheit, Sagte und Ungesagte*. Moreover, insofar as each thinker does decide this original interplay, they ostensibly privilege the second term. For both of them, the privative prefixes are not intended in this context to denote mere negation, but to signify, as Heidegger puts it, "a pre-essential essence [*vor-wesende Wesen*]"[96] that predetermines the possibilities of whatever can get expressly presented. Yet it is only by means of what is expressly presented that we can ever truly discover this preessential essence. This appearance of similarity between the two thinkers begins to break down, however, when we consider how they interpret the process of this discovery and what it is supposed to reveal. The real question for Heidegger is "not in what way Being can be understood, but in what way Being *is* understanding."[97] Human being as existing, *verständliches Dasein* is the locus and medium for the essential occurrence of Being itself. Though the projective understanding that is our essence "does not create [*schafft*] Being,"[98] this "essence itself belongs to the very constitution [*mitausmacht*] of Being."[99] In this way, Heidegger dissolves the first tension in the Kantian project by effectively resolving the second. Yet, in the event, nothing seems to remain of Being itself other than the self-concealing/self-revealing λόγος that comes to pass in and through our essence, and nothing of beings in themselves in their difference from Being than what is attested to (*bekundet*) in that λόγος. On the face of it, Merleau-Ponty's thesis of the *Vorhabe* of Being and of the relation of λόγος ἐνδιάθετος and λόγος προφορικός would seem to unfold in the same terms. He affirms an essential "creation" on our part called for in Being and without which there would be no experience or comprehension of Being at all. In this "creation" lies our transcendence of the world as a whole and the possibility of our encounter with other things. It is on this basis that Merleau-Ponty could respond to the second tension in Kant's project. Yet in the end he subsumes this thesis under the broader claim that both we ourselves and the things we encounter are essentially "folds" or "leaves" in the original "fission" of the one *être sauvage*. The difference required to account for our evident encounter with an external world of other things is thereby deprived of its decisive originality. The issue of an "in itself" beyond our grasp—Kant's first tension—is thereby resolved insofar as we ourselves are originally of Being-in-itself.

IX

Of course, it might well be that the real difficulty in all of this lies not in the respective projects of Heidegger and Merleau-Ponty per se but in *our* impulse to decide correlations which these thinkers themselves wish, in one facet of their thinking at least, to keep entirely in play. The *Zusammengehörigkeit* of Being, beings, and *Dasein*, or the *entrelacs* and *chiasme* within Being, may simply be undecidable; and it would be a metaphysical prejudice to expect otherwise. Yet in another facet of their thinking, Merleau-Ponty and Heidegger do still privilege one term, and in that measure at least they in effect reinvoke the demand for a decidable center or ground. On that score, so it would seem, neither thinker can so easily have his cake and eat it too. The current fashion is to deride any attempt to designate a privileged domain of transcendence, suggesting that inevitably all such attempts occlude what are the effectively complex and heterologous contexts of their own inscription and so are able to maintain themselves as *philosophy* only through a systematic self-effacement. What is currently offered in the place of such attempts is a play of signification both without limits and without a center that would ground its infinite substitutions. By comparison, any seemingly positive invocation of the themes of transcendental philosophy, and hence any attempt to determine art exactly from a relation to ontological truth, is apt to appear dated and retrogressive, the new fashion—as always—presenting itself in the form of a needed liberation from the narrow-minded styles of the past. And well it might be. Yet, if following that fashion leads us simply to abandon the whole range of transcendental concerns as just one discourse among others, which would mean abandoning in the same way the questions of selfhood, Being, and transcendence, then we might yet be wary of a purchase *trop bon marché*. "That the human spirit should ever wholly abandon metaphysical investigations is as little to be expected as that human beings, in order not to breathe impure air, should ever prefer not to breathe at all."[100]

Notes on Contributors

Editors

Galen A. Johnson is Professor of Philosophy and chairman of the department at the University of Rhode Island, author of *Earth and Sky, History and Philosophy: Island Images Inspired by Husserl and Merleau-Ponty* (1989) and a number of articles on Merleau-Ponty, Piaget, Husserl, and Nietzsche, and coeditor of *Ontology and Alterity in Merleau-Ponty* (1990).

Michael B. Smith is Associate Professor of French at Berry College, Georgia, author of a number of articles on Merleau-Ponty's philosophy, translator of Michel de Certeau's *La fable mystique*, and coeditor of *Ontology and Alterity in Merleau-Ponty* (1990).

Contributors

Robert Burch is Associate Professor of Philosophy at University of Alberta (Canada) and publishes in the areas of German idealism, phenomenology, and philosophy of technology, in addition to his work on Heidegger and Merleau-Ponty.

Mikel Dufrenne is Professor of Philosophy (Emeritus) at University of Paris-XIII (Nanterre). He is the editor of the Klincksiek Collection *Esthétique et Philosophie*. Known for his early work on Karl Jaspers, he is author of *The Notion of the A Priori* (1959, 1966), *The Phenomenology of Aesthetic Experience* (1953, 1973), *Language and Philosophy* (1963), and *Le poétique* (1963). A collection of his essays on aesthetics entitled *In the Presence of the Sensuous* recently appeared from Humanities Press (1987).

Véronique M. Fóti, a native of Hungary, taught at the New School for Social Research and is currently Associate Professor of Philosophy at Pennsylvania State University. She is author of numerous articles on Plato, Spinoza, Merleau-Ponty, Heidegger, and Freud, as well as *Heidegger, and the Poets* (1992). Her translation of Mikel Dufrenne's *Le poétique* is forthcoming.

Wayne J. Froman is Professor of Philosophy and chairman of the Department of Philosophy and Religious Studies at George Mason University. In addition to numerous articles on Heidegger and Merleau-Ponty, he is author of *Merleau-Ponty: Language and the Act of Speech* (1982).

Marjorie Grene is Professor of Philosophy (Emeritus) at University of California–Davis, and is author of *Heidegger* (1958), *A Portrait of Aristotle* (1964), *The Knower and the Known* (1966), and *Approaches to a Philosophical Biology* (1969).

Jean-François Lyotard is Professor of Philosophy at the University of Paris-VIII and Professor of French and Italian at the University of California at Irvine. He is author of *Phenomenology* (1954, 1991), *Discours, figure* (1971), *The Postmodern Condition* (1979, 1984), *The Differend* (1983), and *Peregrinations: Law, Form, Event* (1988). A collection of his essays entitled *The Lyotard Reader* has recently appeared from Basil Blackwell Publishers (1990), and another entitled *Toward the Postmodern* from Humanities Press (1992).

Rene Magritte (1898–1967), a native of Belgium, is known for his surreal and conceptual art work. His paintings at the boundary of image and word are featured in Michel Foucault's *This is Not a Pipe* (1973, 1983). Magritte's engagements with philosophy are found in *Magritte: Signs and Images* (1977) and *Magritte: correspondence et souvenirs* (1993), both edited by Harry Torczyner.

Olivier Mongin is the director of the French journal *Esprit*, and the literary director of the press Editions de Seuil. He has published *La peur du vide* (Paris: Seuil, 1991) and is preparing a study on Paul Ricoeur, to appear in 1993. A former student of Paul Ricoeur, Claude Lefort, and Michel de Certeau, Mongin has published numerous articles on Merleau-Ponty.

Linda Singer was Associate Professor of Philosophy at Miami University (Ohio). She wrote her doctoral thesis on Merleau-Ponty's philosophy of painting at SUNY-Binghamton, and authored a number of articles in continental philosophy and feminist philosophy before her death in 1990. Her book *Erotic Welfare: Sexual Theory and Politics in the Age of Epidemic* has appeared posthumously from Routledge (1993).

Hugh J. Silverman is Professor of Philosophy and Comparative Literature at State University of New York at Stony Brook and is author of *Inscriptions: Between Phenomenology and Structuralism*, and translator of Merleau-Ponty's lecture courses entitled *Consciousness and the Acquisition of Language* (1973) and "Philosophy and Non-Philosophy Since Hegel." He is the editor of numerous collections in continental philosophy including *Philosophy and Non-Philosophy Since Merleau-Ponty*, and his book *Textualities: Between Hermeneutics and Deconstruction* is forthcoming.

Jacques Taminiaux, a native of Belgium, is Professor of Philosophy at Université de Louvain at Louvain-la-Neuve, Belgium and Boston College. He was a student of Merleau-Ponty and is director of the Centre d'études phénoménologiques at Louvain and secretary of *Phaenomenologica* (Nijhoff). He is author of *Heidegger*

and the Project of Fundamental Ontology (1991), and a collection of his essays entitled *Dialectic and Difference: Finitude in Modern Thought* appeared in 1985.

Alphonse de Waelhens (1911–81), a Belgian phenomenologist associated with
Jean Wahl's Collège Philosophique in Paris after World War II, wrote careful
interpretations of the works of Husserl, Heidegger, and Merleau-Ponty (*Une
philosophie de l'ambiguïté*, 1951; *Phénoménologie et vérité*, 1953; *Existence et signification*, 1958). Increasingly interested in psychiatry, his later thought focused on
the relationship between philosophical reflection and nonphilosophical experience, specifically on the experiential body (*La philosophie et les expériences naturel-
les*, 1961; *La psychose*, 1971).

Forrest Williams, a native of Paris, France, is Professor of Philosophy at the
University of Colorado at Boulder. He was a student of Merleau-Ponty at the
Sorbonne whose notes contributed to the résumés of Merleau-Ponty's courses
published in *Bulletin de Psychologie* (November 1964). He is author of numerous
articles on Merleau-Ponty and French philosophy, and translator of Jean-Paul
Sartre's *Transcendence of the Ego* and *Imagination.*

Notes

Preface

1. "Cézanne's Doubt" appeared in *Sense and Non-Sense*, trans. Hubert Dreyfus and Patricia Allen Dreyfus (Evanston: Northwestern University Press, 1964); "Indirect Language and the Voices of Silence" appeared in *Signs*, trans. Richard C. McCleary (Evanston: Northwestern University Press, 1964); and "Eye and Mind" appeared in *The Primary of Perception*, trans. James M. Edie (Evanston: Northwestern University Press, 1964).

Chapter 1
Galen A. Johnson, Phenomenology and Painting: "Cézanne's Doubt"

1. Cf. *Fontaine: Revue mensuelle de la poésie et des lettres françaises* 6, no. 47, Tome 9 (December 1945), 80–100. The director of the review was Max-Fol Fouchet.

   This number of the review also included essays by Roger Caillos on Bossuet and Pascal, by Georges Blin on Gabriel Marcel, by Paul Eluard entitled "Je n'ai pas de regrets," and a piece by Paul Claudel titled "La perle." It also contained the announcement of the first volume number of *Les Temps Modernes*, the political and philosophical journal edited by Sartre with Merleau-Ponty, citing essays by Sartre, Merleau-Ponty, Francis Ponge, and Raymond Aron.

2. We do find in *The Structure of Behavior* brief references to Cézanne and Goya, as well as a discussion of El Greco's astigmatism and rejection by Merleau-Ponty of a reductionist physiological explanation of the meaning of El Greco's work in terms of "visual anomaly" (SB, 203; *SC*, 219). This anticipates one of the themes of "Cézanne's Doubt."

3. Though *La structure du comportement* was published by Presses Universitaires de France in 1942, Merleau-Ponty had completed its writing in 1938. Cf. *SC*, 3d edition, 241, as well as the discussion by Theodore F. Gèraets, *Vers une nouvelle philosophie transcendentale: La genese de la philosophie de Maurice Merleau-Ponty jusqu'à la "Phénoménologie de la Perception"* (The Hague: Martinus Nijhoff, 1971), 1–2, 28–29.

4. Merleau-Ponty made a trip to the Husserl Archives at the University of Louvain, Belgium, from 1–6 or 7 April 1939 to consult Husserl's unpublished manuscripts, and worked successfully from 1942 to 1950, with the assistance of H. L. Van Breda in Louvain and Jean-Paul Sartre, Jean Hyppolite, and Tran Duc Thao in Paris, to establish a deposit for the Husserl Archives at University of Paris, Sorbonne. The details of these events, including copies of Merleau-Ponty's correspondence with Father Van Breda at Louvain, may be found in H. L. Van Breda, "Maurice Merleau-Ponty et les Archives-Husserl à Louvain," *Revue de Métaphysique et de Morale* 67 (Oct.–Dec. 1962), 411–30. This essay has recently been translated in *Texts and Dialogues: Maurice Merleau-Ponty*, ed. Hugh J. Silverman and James Barry, Jr. (Atlantic Highlands, N.J.: Humanities Press, 1991), 150–61.

5. Freud's controversial study of Leonardo and the origins of homosexuality had been published in German in 1910. Paul Valéry's work, "Introduction à la méthode de Leonard de Vinci," had originally been published in *La Nouvelle Revue* (15 Aug. 1895) and was reprinted by Gallimard with "Note et digressions" in 1919. In "Cézanne's Doubt," Merleau-Ponty cites the version of the essay that appeared subsequently in Paul Valéry, *Variété*, vol. 1 (1924).

6. J. K. Huysmans, "Cézanne," *Certains* (Paris, 1889), 42–43. Quoted as collected in *Cézanne in Perspective*, ed. Judith Wechsler (Englewood Cliffs, N.J.: Prentice-Hall, 1975), 31.

7. Statements from Cézanne's art critics, including these by Marcel Fouquier and Georges Lecomte, may be found in Ambroise Vollard, *Cézanne* (New York: Dover Publications, 1984), 115ff.

8. Cf. John Rewald, preface to *Joachim Gasquet's Cézanne*, trans. Christopher Pemberton (London: Thames and Hudson, 1991), 12–13.

9. Fritz Novotny was an Austrian art historian who published the first serious studies of spatial structure in Cézanne's works, and defended the thesis that "a radical rejection of scientific perspective only comes about in the wake of Cézanne's work" with post-Cézanne cubism, but that Cézanne was instrumental in "the breakdown of the laws of perspective as having any value for modern painting." Cf. Fritz Novotny, "Cézanne and the End of Scientific Perspective" (1938), in *Cézanne in Perspective*, 98. The 1932 work by Novotny that Merleau-Ponty studied was entitled "Das Problem des Menschen Cézanne im Verhaltnis zu seiner Kunst," *Zeitschrift fur Aesthetik und allgemeine Kunstwissenschaft* (1932).

10. Cf. Roger Fry, *Cézanne: A Study of His Development* (New York: Macmillan, 1927). Clive Bell and Desmond McCarthy also contributed to the construction of a formalist school of Cézanne interpretation, both by their writings and by organizing an important exhibit in London in 1910 which exhibited twenty-one Cézanne paintings together with works by Gauguin, Van Gogh, Seurat, Matisse, and Picasso. Cf. the editor's introduction, "Roger Fry and Formalist Criticism," by Judith Wechsler, ed., *Cézanne in Perspective*, 9–12.

11. Cf. Meyer Shapiro, *Paul Cézanne* (New York: Harry N. Abrams, Inc.,

1952). To indicate affinities between Merleau-Ponty and Meyer Shapiro is a somewhat dangerous conjunction in the light of Shapiro's more recent critique of Heidegger's "The Origin of the Work of Art." Merleau-Ponty's last essay on painting, "Eye and Mind," was written in quite sympathetic dialogue with Heidegger. Nevertheless, what I have in mind are certain specific features of both Merleau-Ponty's and Shapiro's readings of Cézanne: attention to the subject matter of Cézanne's paintings, attention to color over formal design, attention to Cézanne's experience in the fusion of nature and self, and taking seriously Cézanne's own interpretations of his work in his letters and conversations reporting his sensations and emotions while at work on a painting.

12. Edmund Husserl, *Ideas I: General Introduction to Pure Phenomenology*, trans. W. R. Boyce Gibson (New York: Macmillan, 1931), section 24.

13. The French may be found in "Le primat de la perception et ses conséquences philosophiques," *Bulletin de la Société Française de Philosophie* 41, no. 4 (Oct.–Dec., 1947), 133.

14. "The Origin of Geometry" was an unpublished manuscript of Husserl's written in 1936 that was edited and published posthumously by Eugen Fink in the *Revue Internationale de Philosophie* 1, no. 2 (1939) under the title "Der Ursprung der Geometrie als intentional-historisches Problem." This is where Merleau-Ponty read it, and it became a formative part of his intensive research into Husserlian phenomenology, including his visit to the Husserl Archives at Louvain, Belgium. "The Origin of Geometry" appears in English as appendix 6 in Edmund Husserl, *The Crisis of European Sciences and Transcendental Phenomenology: An Introduction to Phenomenological Philosophy*, trans. David Carr (Evanston: Northwestern University Press, 1970). For further elucidation of Merleau-Ponty's reading and deformation of Husserl's philosophy of tradition in "The Origin of Geometry," cf. Galen A. Johnson, "Husserl and Merleau-Ponty: History, Language and Truth," in *Merleau-Ponty: Critical Essays*, ed. Henry Pietersma (Washington, D. C.: University Press of America, 1990), 197–217.

15. Cf. Maurice Merleau-Ponty, "The Experience of Others (1951–52)," trans. Fred Evans and Hugh J. Silverman, *Review of Existential Psychology and Psychiatry* 18, nos. 1, 2, and 3: "Merleau-Ponty and Psychology" (1982–83), 40. These are the lecture notes from Merleau-Ponty's 1951–52 lecture course, "L'experience d'autrui," given at the University of Paris, Sorbonne.

16. Cf. Edmund Husserl, *Logical Investigations*, vol. 1, trans. J. N. Findlay (New York: Humanities Press, 1970), 275. For further elaboration of Husserl's philosophy of language, cf. J. N. Mohanty, "Husserl's Theory of Meaning," in *Husserl: Expositions and Appraisals*, ed. Frederick Elliston and Peter McCormick (Notre Dame: University of Notre Dame Press, 1977), 18–20.

17. Cf. Paul Ricoeur, "Hommage à Merleau-Ponty," *Esprit* 296 (1961), 1115–20, and "New Developments in Phenomenology in France: The

Phenomenology of Language," *Social Research* 34, no. 1 (1967), 1–30; Jean-François Lyotard, "Philosophy and Painting in the Age of Their Experimentation: Contribution to an Idea of Postmodernity," in *The Lyotard Reader*, ed. Andrew Benjamin (Oxford: Basil Blackwell, 1989), 181–95; and Jacques Derrida, "The Time of a Thesis: Punctuations," in *Philosophy in France Today*, ed. Alan Montefiore (Cambridge: Cambridge University Press, 1983), 34-50.

18. Among other sources, cf. Rodolphe Gasche, "Deconstruction as Criticism," *Glyph* 6 (Baltimore: The Johns Hopkins University Press, 1979), 177–215; Gary Madison, "Merleau-Ponty and Postmodernity," in *The Hermeneutics of Postmodernity: Figures and Themes* (Bloomington: Indiana University Press, 1988); Bernard Charles Flynn, "Textuality and the Flesh: Derrida and Merleau-Ponty," *Journal of the British Society for Phenomenology* 15, no. 2 (May 1984), 164–77; Hugh J. Silverman, "Merleau-Ponty and Derrida: Writing on Writing," in *Ontology and Alterity in Merleau-Ponty*, ed. Galen A. Johnson and Michael B. Smith (Evanston: Northwestern University Press, 1990), 130–41.

Chapter 2
Galen A. Johnson, Structures and Painting: "Indirect Language and the Voices of Silence"

1. *The Prose of the World* was edited by Claude Lefort and published posthumously in 1969. The 170-page manuscript was found among Merleau-Ponty's papers after his death. According to Lefort's chronology, Merleau-Ponty worked on what we have of *The Prose of the World* during the space of one year, 1951, and interrupted his writing in the fall or winter of that year.

There is a wide range of speculation regarding why Merleau-Ponty broke off his work on *The Prose of the World*. Lefort himself believes that the interruption was philosophical, indicating a "profound overhaul" of the problematic of the *Phenomenology of Perception* anticipating the revised ontology of *The Visible and the Invisible* and philosophy of art in "Eye and Mind." Cf. editor's preface to *The Prose of the World*, xiv–xxi.

Sartre contents himself with the psychological speculation that the interruption was caused by the death of Merleau-Ponty's mother in December 1952 and the philosopher's transformed attitude toward his work. Cf. "Merleau-Ponty," in *Situations*, trans. Benita Eisler (Greenwich, Conn.: Fawcett Publications, 1965), 207–9. For my part, this hardly seems plausible in light of the chronology: Merleau-Ponty broke off *The Prose of the World* in the fall or winter of 1951, and he did not lose his mother until December 1953. Sartre incorrectly gives 1952 as the date of death for Merleau-Ponty's mother. Cf. Sartre, *Situations*, 208.

Anna Boschetti contends that the break occurred due to the appearance of Sartre's *The Communists and Peace* in 1952, and the urgency for

Merleau-Ponty to make a response to Sartre, which subsequently he published as *Adventures of the Dialectic* in 1955. Cf. Anna Boschetti, *The Intellectual Enterprise: Sartre and "Les Temps Modernes,"* trans. Richard C. McCleary (Evanston: Northwestern University Press, 1988), 215.

Nevertheless, however we decide the question of motivation, the interruption of *The Prose of the World* cautions us that "Indirect Language and the Voices of Silence" is a transitional essay, and we will read it in that way, noting the lines that come into the essay from Husserl's phenomenology and the lines leading beyond the essay toward the indirect ontology of "Eye and Mind."

2. Now that we have the posthumous edition of *The Prose of the World*, the chapters that surround the third chapter entitled "The Indirect Language" provide valuable context for interpreting the published essay. The two preceding chapters are entitled "The Specter of a Pure Language" and "Science and the Experience of Expression." The three subsequent chapters are "The Algorithm and the Mystery of Language," "Dialogue and the Perception of the Other," and "Expression and the Child's Drawing."

3. Throughout the text, we find sentences altered or rearranged, and some sentences and paragraphs omitted. The concluding two paragraphs of the essay are also rewritten. It would be a considerable and worthwhile scholarly task to catalog these changes, but much beyond what is required here to understand the progress of Merleau-Ponty's philosophy of painting.

4. Résumés from these courses prepared by students and approved by Merleau-Ponty were published in an issue of the *Bulletin de Psychologie*, no. 236, Tome 18 (November 1964), 3–6. These three particular courses have appeared in English translation. "The Child's Relations with Others" and "Phenomenology and the Sciences of Man" are collected in *The Primacy of Perception*, and *Consciousness and the Acquisition of Language*, trans. Hugh J. Silverman, is published as a separate volume from Northwestern University Press (1973).

5. There were four candidates for the Chair of Philosophy at the Collège de France: Gaston Berger, Stéphane Lupasco, Etienne Souriau, and Merleau-Ponty. On the first ballot, there was no absolute majority, though Merleau-Ponty was in first place. On the second ballot, Merleau-Ponty received the majority and was placed "en premier ligne." On the third ballot, Souriau placed highest and was recommended "en deuxieme ligne."

In an unprecedented action on 18 March 1952, the Academy of Moral and Political Sciences overturned the recommendation of the Assembly of Professors and recommended Gaston Berger in first line to the Minister of Education, with Souriau in second line (Cf. *Le Figaro*, 18 March 1952). On 19 March 1952, Merleau-Ponty wrote a letter of protest to the Administrator of the Collège de France, Edmond Faral, who protested to the Minister of Education, Andre Marie. Merleau-Ponty's appointment was decreed on 21 March 1952.

6. The three additional members of the original editorial committee were Michel Leiris, Jean Paulhan, and Albert Ollivier. Aron, Paulhan, and Ollivier left the review within the first year, and Leiris remained only in a diminished role. Cf. Boschetti, *The Intellectual Enterprise*, 173–83.

7. Koestler was a close friend of Albert Camus, and Merleau-Ponty's attack on Koestler was the occasion for the rupture in friendship between Camus and Merleau-Ponty. Cf. Germaine Bree, *Camus and Sartre: Crisis and Commitment* (New York: Dell Publishing, 1972), 204–212. Sartre also gives an account of these events in *Situations*, 253–54. These events marked the end of friendly relations between *Les Temps Modernes* and Camus's review, *Combat*.

8. Merleau-Ponty resigned from *Les Temps Modernes* in December 1952. The occasion was Sartre's insistence on withdrawing a preface Merleau-Ponty had written qualifying an article by Naville, "Etats-Unis et contradictions capitalistes," *Les Temps Modernes* 86 (December 1952). Cf. Barry Cooper, *Merleau-Ponty and Marxism: From Terror to Reform* (Toronto: University of Toronto Press, 1979).

9. The first reply to Sartre's *The Communists and Peace* was made by Merleau-Ponty's friend, Claude Lefort, the only colleague Merleau-Ponty had himself brought into the editorial structure of *Les Temps Modernes*. Cf. Claude Lefort, "Le Marxisme et Sartre," *Les Temps Modernes* 89 (April 1953), 1541–70. Sartre made a reply to Lefort in the same issue of the review, now translated in Jean-Paul Sartre, *The Communists and Peace, with a Reply to Claude Lefort*, trans. Philip R. Berk (New York: George Braziller, 1969), 233–96.

10. Sartre, *Situations*, 156. The original French essay was entitled "Merleau-Ponty Vivant," and appeared in *Les Temps Modernes* 183–85 (October 1961), 304–76. This was a special number of *Les Temps Modernes* devoted to Merleau-Ponty and personally directed by Sartre. In addition to Sartre's homage, it contains important essays on the life and thought of Merleau-Ponty by Jean Hyppolite, Jacques Lacan, Claude Lefort, J. B. Pontalis, Alphonse de Waelhens, and Jean Wahl.

There is a new version of Sartre's homage based not on the published text from *Les Temps Modernes*, but on the original handwritten manuscript found among Sartre's papers following his death in 1980, prepared for publication by Michel Rybalka and translated by William Hamrick in *Journal of the British Society for Phenomenology* 15, no. 2 (May 1984), 1–31.

11. Andre Malraux, *The Voices of Silence*, trans. Stuart Gilbert (Princeton: Princeton University Press, 1978), 280. The French may be found in *Les voix du silence* (Paris: Pléiade, 1951), 278.

12. The attentive reader will find in Merleau-Ponty's Sorbonne lecture course entitled "The Child's Relations with Others" one reference to Picasso to the effect that "it is altogether startling to see certain children much more apt to understand this drawing or that painting by Picasso than the adults around them." Cf. PrP, 150.

13. Malraux, *The Voices of Silence*, 119 (French, 116).

14. Merleau-Ponty's footnotes to the published essay indicate that he worked from the three separate volumes of Malraux's work *Psychologie de l'art*, published in Switzerland by Albert Skira. The volumes were respectively subtitled: *Le musée imaginaire* (1947), *La création esthétique* (1948), and *La monnaie de l'absolu* (1949). Merleau-Ponty considered principally the first two volumes, *Le musée imaginaire* and *La création esthétique*.

15. Malraux, *The Voices of Silence*, 19 (French, 17).

16. Ibid., 345 (French, 346).

17. E. H. Gombrich, "Malraux's Philosophy of Art in Historical Perspective," in *Malraux: Life and Work*, ed. Marine de Courcel (New York: Harcourt, Brace, Jovanovich, 1976), 176.

18. Malraux, *The Voices of Silence*, 356 (French, 354). Merleau-Ponty quotes this text in "Indirect Language and the Voices of Silence" (S, 58; *S*, 73).

19. Cf. Alfred H. Barr, *Matisse: His Art and His Public* (New York: The Museum of Modern Art, 1951), 260. The original interview by Rosamond Bernier with Matisse took place near the completion of Matisse's work on the design of the chapel in Vence named Sainte Marie du Rosaire, and was published as "Matisse Designs a New Church," in *Vogue* (15 February 1949), 76–77 and 131–32.

20. Cf. Lyotard, "Philosophy and Painting in the Age of Their Experimentation: Contribution to an Idea of Postmodernity."

21. Cf. "The Film and the New Psychology," in *Sense and Non-Sense*, 54–59.

22. Cf. Malraux, *The Voices of Silence*, 17–46 (French, 15–44).

23. Maurice Blanchot, "Le musée, l'art et le temps," *Critique* 43 (Dec. 1950), 195–208.

24. Jean-Paul Sartre, *Literature and Existentialism*, trans. Bernard Frechtman (Secaucus: The Citadel Press, 1980), 10. This is the English translation of Sartre's "Qu'est-ce que la littérature?," *Les Temps Modernes* 17–22 (Feb.–July 1947).

25. In a communication to Martial Guéroult of the Collège de France at the time of Merleau-Ponty's candidacy for the chair of philosophy, Merleau-Ponty described his effort in *The Prose of the World*, then in progress:

> Hegel said that the Roman state was the prose of the world. I shall entitle my book *Introduction à la prose du monde*. In this work I shall elaborate the category of prose beyond the confines of literature to give it a sociological meaning. . . . The linguistic relations among men should help us understand the more general order of symbolic relations and of institutions, which assure the exchange not only of thoughts but of all types of values, the co-existence of men within a culture, and beyond it, within a single history. (PrP, 9–10)

26. Malraux, *The Voices of Silence*, 14 (French, 12).

27. Cf. de Courcel, ed., *Malraux: Life and Work*, 266.

28. Matisse purchased this small painting from Ambroise Vollard in 1899 for 1300 francs, an amount Matisse really could not afford. Several times during periods of financial crisis, Matisse was urged by friends to sell the

painting, but he always refused. In 1936, he consigned it to the Petit Palais, Musée de la Ville de Paris. In his letter of transmittal written from Nice on 10 November 1936, he wrote: "I have owned this canvas for thirty-seven years and I know it fairly well, I hope, though not entirely; it has sustained me spiritually in the critical moments of my career as an artist; I have drawn from it my faith and my perseverance." Cf. Barr, *Matisse: His Art and His Public*, 40.

29. All three of Malraux's formulations of the meaning of "style" are taken from volume 2 of *The Voices of Silence* entitled *La création esthétque*, 206, 321, and 323 (French, 204, 319, and 321).

30. Cf. Hugh J. Silverman, "Cézanne's Mirror Stage," *Journal of Aesthetics and Art Criticism* 40, no. 4 (Summer 1982), 374–75, and 271 in the present volume.

31. The term is that of Edward S. Casey in his essay entitled "Sartre on Imagination," in *The Philosophy of Jean-Paul Sartre*, The Library of Living Philosophers, vol. 16, ed. Paul Arthur Schilpp (La Salle: Open Court, 1981), 157.

32. Sartre's theory of imagination has been given an informative exposition and critique by Edward S. Casey, "Sartre on Imagination," 139–66.

33. Cf. Merleau-Ponty, "L'imagination," *Journal de Psychologie Normale et Pathologique* 33, nos. 9–10 (Nov.–Dec. 1936), 756–61. This review has recently been translated by Michael B. Smith in *Texts and Dialogues: Merleau-Ponty*, ed. Hugh J. Silverman and James Barry, Jr. (Atlantic Highlands: Humanities Press, 1991), 108–14.

34. This point is established by Glen A. Mazis, "*La chair et l'imaginaire*: The Developing Role of Imagination in Merleau-Ponty's Philosophy," *Philosophy Today* 32, no. 4 (Spring 1988), 30–42.

35. Sartre, *Literature and Existentialism*, 11.

36. Jean-Paul Sartre, *The Psychology of Imagination*, trans. Bernard Frechtman (New York: Philosophical Library, 1948), 248–52. Cf. Casey, "Sartre on Imagination," 152.

37. According to Roland Barthes in *Elements of Semiology*, Merleau-Ponty was the first of the leading French philosophers to study the work of Swiss linguist, Ferdinand de Saussure. Saussure's linguistics is found in his work entitled *Cours de linguistique générale* (1916). Saussure's influence may have already been at work in *Phenomenology of Perception* in the chapter on "Body as Expression, and Speech" in the form of the distinction between *langue* and *parole*. Nevertheless, Merleau-Ponty explicitly introduced themes from Saussure's linguistics into his reflections on language during the period from 1949 to 1953, particularly in his lecture course at the Sorbonne called "Consciousness and the Acquisition of Language," and his essays "On Phenomenology of Language" (1951) and "Indirect Language and the Voices of Silence," both collected in *Signs*.

For further elaboration of the relation of Merleau-Ponty's philosophy of language to Saussure's linguistics, cf. Stephen H. Watson, "Merleau-Ponty's Involvement with Saussure," in *Continental Philosophy in America*, ed. Hugh J. Silverman (Pittsburgh: Duquesne University Press, 1983), esp. 209–12, as well as James Schmidt, *Maurice Merleau-Ponty: Between Phenomenology and Structuralism* (New York: St. Martin's Press, 1985), chapter 4, especially "Reading (and misreading) Saussure," 105–11.

38. Cf. Roman Ingarden, *The Cognition of the Literary Work of Art*, trans. R. A. Crowley and K. R. Olson (Evanston: Northwestern University Press, 1973). A somewhat less sharp distinction between the artwork and the aesthetic object is drawn by Mikel Dufrenne in *The Phenomenology of Aesthetic Experience*, trans. Edward S. Casey (Evanston: Northwestern University Press, 1973). It should be pointed out that we could wish for a more definitive treatment of this relationship by Merleau-Ponty. For another text in which Merleau-Ponty deals with this question, cf. PhP, "The Cogito," 390–92; *PP*, "Le cogito," 447–50.

39. Cf. Paul Claudel, *Art poétique*, in *Oeuvre poétique* (Paris: Gallimard, 1957), 145. Among other places, the passage is quoted by Merleau-Ponty in VI, 179; *VI*, 233.

Chapter 3
Galen A. Johnson, Ontology and Painting: "Eye and Mind"

1. Rene Magritte, "Letter to Alphonse de Waelhens (April 28, 1962)," in *Magritte: Ideas and Images*, ed. Harry Torczyner, trans. Richard Miller (New York: Harry N. Abrams, Inc., 1977), 55, and reprinted as chapter 19 in the present volume.

2. During most years, two courses were offered on Mondays and Thursdays, except in 1958–59 when Merleau-Ponty offered only one abridged course in order to pursue his writing on the ontology of nature. Merleau-Ponty wrote résumés for each of the courses, and all but the last two were published in the *Annuaire du Collège de France* and collected in the posthumous publication edited by Claude Lefort entitled *Résumés de cours: Collège de France, 1952–60* (Paris: Gallimard, 1968), trans. John O'Neill as *Themes from the Lectures at Collège de France* (Evanston: Northwestern University Press, 1970).

   Since Merleau-Ponty died in May 1961, he did not publish résumés of his 1960–61 courses. His two courses for this last year were entitled "Philosophy and Non-Philosophy Since Hegel" and "Cartesian Ontology and Ontology Today." The notes from the first of these courses were published posthumously by Claude Lefort in *Textures*, nos. 8 and 9 (1974) and nos. 10 and 11 (1975), subsequently translated by Hugh J. Silverman in *Telos* 29 (1976), 43–105. The notes from the second course were edited and partially published by Alexandre Metraux in his essay "Vision and Being in the Last Lectures of Maurice Merleau-Ponty," in *Life-World and Consciousness: Essays for Aron Gurwitsch*, ed. Lester E. Embree (Evanston: Northwestern University Press, 1972), 323–36.

3. Maurice Merleau-Ponty, *Les philosophes célèbres* (Paris: Editions d'Art, Lucien Mazenod, 1956). This work has not been translated into English, except the introductions by Merleau-Ponty collected in *Signs* in the chapter entitled "Everywhere and Nowhere." The two introductions omitted from *Signs* entitled "The Founders of Philosophy" and "The Discovery of History" have recently been translated by Michael B. Smith in *Texts and Dialogues: Maurice Merleau-Ponty.*

4. This chronology is enumerated by Claude Lefort in his "Editorial Note" to *The Visible and the Invisible.* Cf. VI, xxxiv; *VI*, 9.

5. Heidegger wrote: "Language is the house of Being. In its home man dwells." Cf. Martin Heidegger, "Letter on Humanism," in *Martin Heidegger: Basic Writings*, ed. David Farrell Krell (New York: Harper and Row, 1977), 193.

6. In this 1960–61 course, Merleau-Ponty concentrated on the "Introduction" to Hegel's *Phenomenology of Spirit*, and worked from Heidegger's long commentary on Hegel's "Introduction" now translated under the title *Hegel's Concept of Experience*, trans. Kenly Royce Dove (New York: Harper and Row, 1970). Thus, though the course does not give us a direct dialogue between Merleau-Ponty and Heidegger, it does offer us a tacit engagement by Merleau-Ponty with Heidegger. Cf. Maurice Merleau-Ponty, "Philosophy and Non-Philosophy Since Hegel."

7. One of Nicholas de Stael's last works entitled *Les Mouettes* (1955) recalls Van Gogh's *Paysage aux Corbeaux*, and Stael's life ended in a tragic suicide as mysterious as that of Van Gogh. Cf. Michael Seuphor, *Dictionary of Abstract Painting*, trans. Lionel Izod, John Montague, and Francis Scarfe (New York: Paris Book Center, 1958), 267.

8. Cf. Gotz Adriani, *Cézanne Watercolors*, trans. Russell M. Stockman (New York: Harry N. Abrams, Inc., 1983), 81–94. To my knowledge, the only commentator who has discussed Merleau-Ponty's choice of a Cézanne watercolor rather than an oil painting is John M. Carvalho in his essay entitled "The Visible and the Invisible in Merleau-Ponty and Foucault," forthcoming in *International Studies in Philosophy.* I am grateful to Professor Carvalho for sending me an advance copy of this essay.

9. Cf. Samuel B. Mallin, "Chiasm, Line and Art," in *Merleau-Ponty: Critical Essays*, ed. Henry Pietersma (Washington, D. C.: The University Press of America, 1990), 219–51; and Michael Munchow, "Painting and Invisibility—Merleau-Ponty's Line," *Journal of the British Society for Phenomenology* (forthcoming, 1993).

10. Cf. *New Dictionary of Sculpture*, ed. Robert Maillard (New York: Tudor Publishing Company, 1971), 262. Remarkably, the article on Richier concludes: "We owe to this art of beyond the beginning, or beyond the end, one of the most enthralling attempts to sculpture the invisible" (264).

11. Merleau-Ponty does not comment on the reasons that might underly the connection between so apparently disparate sculptors, but one possibility is suggested by the fact that Richier's first teacher, Guigues, had been a studio assistant to Rodin. Cf. *New Dictionary of Sculpture*, 262.

12. Cf. Giuseppe Marchiori, *Modern French Sculpture*, trans. John Ross (New York: Harry N. Abrams, Inc., 1963), 52.
13. In "Eye and Mind," Merleau-Ponty cites Klee's *Journal*, translated by P. Klossowski in 1959. The German edition that appeared in 1956 was edited by Ralph Mannheim and subsequently translated into English in 1961 as *Paul Klee: The Thinking Eye* (New York: George Wittenborn, 1961).
14. Cf. Emile Bernard, *Souvenirs sur Paul Cézanne*, quoted in *Cézanne in Perspective*, ed. Judith Wechsler (Englewood Cliffs, N.J.: Prentice-Hall), 42.
15. Merleau-Ponty simply lists the author and title, Henri Michaux, "Aventures de lignes," without further citation. The work was published as the preface to the French translation of Will Grohmann, *Paul Klee*, trans. Jean Descoullayes and Jean Philippon (Paris: Librairie Flinker, 1954), 5–8.
16. Cf. Paul Klee, *The Thinking Eye*, vol. 1 of Klee's *Journals* (New York: George Wittenborn, 1961), part 4. Also cf. Andres Kagan, *Paul Klee/Art and Music* (Ithaca: Cornell University Press, 1983), 46–47.
17. Cf. Claude Lévi-Strauss, "De quelques rencontres," *L'Arc* (Aix en Provence) 46 (1971), 43–47. This essay by Lévi-Strauss is partially translated in the present volume at the end of Olivier Mongin's essay "Since Lascaux."
18. Cf. Elizabeth A. Behnke, "At the Service of the Sonata: Music Lessons with Merleau-Ponty," *Somatics* 4, no. 2 (1984–85), 32–34. This essay has been reprinted in Pietersma, ed., *Merleau-Ponty: Critical Essays*, 23–29.
19. On reversibility in phonation, see Wayne J. Froman, "Alterity and the Paradox of Being," in *Ontology and Alterity in Merleau-Ponty*, ed. Galen A. Johnson and Michael B. Smith (Evanston: Northwestern University Press, 1990), 98–110.
20. Jean-François Lyotard writes that Merleau-Ponty's method of hyperreflection anticipates his own and Derrida's deconstruction. Cf. *Discours, figure*, 4th ed. (Paris: Klincksieck, 1971, 1985), 56. The same opinion is developed by Rodolphe Gasche in his essay "Deconstruction as Criticism," *Glyph* 6 (Baltimore: The Johns Hopkins University Press, 1979), 188. Regarding Merleau-Ponty and postmodernism, cf. Gary Madison, "Merleau-Ponty and Postmodernity," in *The Hermeneutics of Postmodernity: Figures and Themes* (Bloomington: Indiana University Press, 1988); *Philosophy and Non-Philosophy Since Merleau-Ponty*, ed. Hugh J. Silverman (New York: Routledge, 1988); and Bernard Charles Flynn, "Textuality and the Flesh: Derrida and Merleau-Ponty," *Journal of the British Society for Phenomenology* 15, no. 2 (May 1984), 164–77.
21. Michel de Certeau, "The Madness of Vision," trans. Michael B. Smith, *Enclitic* 3, no. 1 (Spring 1983), 24. Cf. "La folie de vision," *Esprit* 66 (June 1982), 89.
22. Sartre, "Merleau-Ponty," in *Situations*, trans. Benita Eisler (Greenwich, Conn.: Fawcett Publishers, 1965), 222.
23. In a working note from *The Visible and the Invisible* dated July 1959 and entitled "Dualism—Philosophy," Merleau-Ponty wrote: "The problems

posed in *Phenomenology of Perception* are insoluble because I start there from the 'consciousness'-'object' distinction" (VI, 200; *VI*, 253).

24. Cf. Gary Madison, *The Phenomenology of Merleau-Ponty: A Search for the Limits of Consciousness* (Athens: Ohio University Press, 1981), 98–99.

25. Quoted by Sartre from a conversation with Merleau-Ponty in Sartre, *Situations*, 214.

26. Cf. Paul Klee, 1924 lecture at Jena, in *Paul Klee: His Life and Work in Documents*, ed. Felix Klee (New York: George Braziller, 1962), 176–77.

27. For further clarification of Merleau-Ponty's views on the nature of ontological desire, cf. Dorothea Olkowski, "Merleau-Ponty's Freudianism: From the Body of Consciousness to the Body of Flesh," in *Review of Existential Psychology and Psychiatry* 18, nos. 1, 2, and 3: "Merleau-Ponty and Psychology" (1982–83), 97–116, as well as my essay "The Colors of Fire: Depth and Desire in Merleau-Ponty's 'Eye and Mind,'" forthcoming in *The Journal of the British Society for Phenomenology*.

28. This point is developed with great care by Martin Dillon, *Merleau-Ponty's Ontology* (Bloomington: Indiana University Press, 1988), chapter 9: "The Reversibility Thesis."

29. Cf. my essay "Generosity and Forgetting in the History of Being: Merleau-Ponty and Nietzsche," in *Continental Philosophy*, vol. 5, *Questioning Foundations*, ed. Hugh J. Silverman (New York: Routledge, 1993), 196–212. Some portions of the following comments on desire and invisibility are found and further elaborated in my essay "Desire and Invisibility in the Ontology of *Eye and Mind*: Some Remarks on Merleau-Ponty's Spirituality," in *Merleau-Ponty in Contemporary Perspective*, edited by P. Burke and J. Van der ver Veken (Dordrecht: Kluwer Academic Publishers, 1993), 85–96.

30. For an account of Merleau-Ponty's involvement with the "friends of *Esprit*," cf. Theodore F. Geraets, *Vers une nouvelle philosophie transcendentale: La genése de la philosophie de Maurice Merleau-Ponty jusqu'à la "Phénoménologie de la Perception"* (The Hague: Martinus Nijhoff, 1971), 25–27.

Chapter 4
Maurice Merleau-Ponty, Cézanne's Doubt

1. Cézanne's conversations with Bernard are recorded in *Souveneirs sur Paul Cézanne* (Paris, 1912).—*Trans.*

2. "Introduction à la méthode de Léonard da Vinci," *Variété*, 185. [English translation by Thomas McGreevey, *Introduction to the Method of Leonardo da Vinci* (London, 1929).]

3. Sigmund Freud, *Un souvenir d'enfance de Léonard de Vinci*, 65. [English translation by A. A. Brill, *Leonardo da Vinci: A Study in Psychosexuality* (New York, 1947).]

4. Ibid., 189.

5. Merleau-Ponty's expression, "restes d'une fête inconnue," referring to Cézanne's canvasses, appears to echo Marcel Proust's "la fête inconnue et

colorée" (cf. *A la recherche du temps perdu*, vol. 3 [Paris: Gallimard, 1954], 375), describing Vinteuil's music.—*Trans.*

Chapter 5
Maurice Merleau-Ponty, Indirect Language and the Voices of Silence

1. Pierre Francastel, *Peinture et société*, 17ff.
2. Ibid.
3. Henri Wallon, French professor of child psychology—until retirement at the Collège de France.—*Trans.*
4. André Malraux, *Le musée imaginaire*, 59. These pages were already written when the definitive edition of the *Psychologie de l'art* (*The Voices of Silence*, published by Gallimard) appeared. We quote from Albert Skira's edition.
5. Ibid., 79.
6. Ibid., 83.
7. *La monnaie de l'absolu*, 118.
8. *La création esthétique*, 144.
9. *Le musée imaginaire*, 63.
10. *La création esthétique*, 51.
11. Ibid., 154.
12. Ibid.
13. Ibid., 158.
14. Ibid., 152.
15. Sartre, *Situations*, vol. 2, 61.
16. Ibid., 60.
17. *La création esthétique*, 113.
18. Ibid., 142.
19. *La monnaie de l'absolu*, 125.
20. Gaston Bachelard, French philosopher, whose several works on the "psychoanalysis of the elements" had some influence on Merleau-Ponty and Sartre in the forties.—*Trans.*
21. *La création esthétique*, 150.
22. Raymond Aron, French political philosopher, perhaps best known in the United States for his *The Century of Total War*, but also one of the first to make German phenomenology known in France.—*Trans.*
23. Jules Vuillemin, French philosopher of science, successor to Merleau-Ponty in the chair of philosophy at the Collège de France.—*Trans.*
24. Besides, Freud never said that he explained da Vinci by the vulture; he said in effect that analysis stops where painting begins.
25. *Le musée imaginaire*, 52.
26. The expression is Paul Ricoeur's. [Paul Ricoeur, younger and extremely versatile contemporary of Merleau-Ponty and perhaps the leading phenomenologist in France, has probably done as much as any other man to make phenomenology known there and in the United States.—*Trans.*]
27. *Principles of the Philosophy of Right*, para. 118.

28. Ibid.

29. Ibid.

30. Francis Ponge, contemporary French poet and essayist.—*Trans.*

Chapter 6
Maurice Merleau-Ponty, Eye and Mind

1. "L'oeil et l'esprit" was the last work Merleau-Ponty saw published. It appeared in the inaugural issue of *Art de France* 1, no. 1 (January 1961). After his death it was reprinted in *Les Temps Modernes* 184–85, along with seven articles devoted to him. It has now been published, in book form, by Gallimard (1964). Both the *Art de France* article and the book contain illustrations chosen by Merleau-Ponty. According to Professor Claude Lefort, "L'oeil et l'esprit" is a preliminary statement of ideas that were to be developed in the second part of the book Merleau-Ponty was writing at the time of his death—*Le visible et l'invisible* (part of which was published posthumously by Gallimard in February 1964). The translator wishes to acknowledge his immense debt to George Downing, who spent many long hours working over the final revisions of the translation. Also, thanks are due to Michel Beaujour, Arleen B. Dallery, and Robert Reitter for their advice and encouragement.—*Trans.*

2. [Il est là, fort ou faible dans la vie, mais souverain sans conteste dans sa rumination du monde, sans autre "technique" que celle que ses yeux et ses mains se donnent à force de voir, à force de peindre, acharné à tirer de ce monde où sonnent les scandales et les gloires de l'histoire des *toiles* qui n'ajouteront guère aux colères ni aux espoirs des hommes, et personne ne murmure.]

3. Cf. *Le visible et l'invisible* (Paris: Gallimard, 1964), 273, 308–11.—*Trans.*

4. See *Signes* (Paris: Gallimard, 1960), 210, 222–23, especially the footnotes, for a clarification of the "circularity" at issue here.—*Trans.*

5. [Cet équivalent interne, cette formule charnelle de leur présence que les choses suscitent en moi, pourquoi à leur tour ne susciteraient-ils pas un tracé, visible encore, où tout autre regard retrouvera les motifs qui soutiennent son inspection du monde?]

6. G. Charbonnier, *Le monologue du peintre* (Paris, 1959), 172.

7. [Beaucoup plus loin, puisque le tableau n'est un analogue que selon le corps, qu'il n'offre pas à l'esprit une occasion de repenser les rapports constitutifs des choses, mais au regard, pour qu'il les épouse, les traces de la vision du dedans, à la vision ce qui la tapisse intérieurement, la texture imaginaire du réel.]

8. Charbonnier, *Le monologue*, 34.

9. Ibid., 143–45.

10. " . . . une philosophie figurée." Cf. Bergson (Ravaisson), note 46 below.—*Trans.*

11. P. Claudel, *Introduction à la peinture hollandaise* (Paris, 1935).

12. P. Schilder, *The Image and Appearance of the Human Body* (London, 1935; New York, 1950), 223–24. ["the body-image is not confined to the borderlines of one's own body. It transgresses them in the mirror. There is a body-image outside ourselves, and it is remarkable that primitive peoples even ascribe a substantial existence to the picture in the mirror" (278). Schilder's earlier, shorter study, *Das Körperschema* (Berlin, 1923), is cited several times in *The Structure of Behavior* and in *Phenomenology of Perception*. Schilder's later work is of especial interest with regard to Merleau-Ponty's own elaborations of the meaning of the human body; it is worth examining for that reason, as well as for the chance it provides to discern some fundamental coincidences between Merleau-Ponty and certain American pragmatists.]

13. Cf. Schilder, *Image*, 281–82.—*Trans.*

14. Robert Delaunay, *Du cubisme à l'art abstrait* (Paris, 1957).

15. "A minute in the world's life passes! to paint it in its reality! and forget everything for that. To become that minute, be the sensitive plate, . . . give the image of what we see, forgetting everything that has appeared before our time." Cézanne, quoted in B. Dorival, *Paul Cézanne*, trans. H. H. A. Thackthwaite (London, 1948), 101.—*Trans.*

16. Descartes, *La Dioptrique*, Discours VII [conclusion]. Edition Adam et Tannery, VI, 165.

17. Ibid., Discours I. Adam et Tannery, 83. [*Oeuvres et lettres de Descartes*, ed. André Bridoux, Edition Pléiade, 181. Page references from the Bridoux selections have been added in the belief that this volume is more widely accessible today than the Adam and Tannery complete edition.]

18. Ibid., Adam et Tannery, 84. [Bridoux, 182].

19. This paragraph continues the exposition of the *Dioptrics*.—*Trans.*

20. Ibid., Discours IV. Adam et Tannery, 112–14. [Bridoux, 203–4; in English, *Descartes: Philosophical Writings*, ed. and trans. N. Kemp Smith (Modern Library Edition), 145–47.]

21. Ibid., 130. [Bridoux, 217; Smith, 148.]

22. The system of means by which painting makes us see is a scientific matter. Why, then, do we not methodically produce perfect images of the world, arriving at a universal art purged of personal art, just as the universal language would free us of all the confused relationships that lurk in existent languages?

23. *Dioptrique*, Discours IV. [Note 20 above.]

24. Discours V of the *Dioptrique*, especially Descartes's diagrams, helps considerably to clarify this compressed passage.—*Trans.*

25. That is, the painting.—*Trans.*

26. E. Panofsky, *Die Perspektive als symbolische Form*, in *Vorträge der Bibliotek Warburg*, vol. 4 (1924–25).

27. Ibid. [The *Stilmoment*, or moment of an instituted style, does not dispense with the *Wermoment*, or moment of the individual perception.—*Trans.*]

28. Descartes, Discours IV, Adam et Tannery, 135. [Bridoux, 220; Smith, 154.] [Here is N. Kemp Smith's translation of the passage under discus-

sion: "Our knowledge of it (the situation of an object) does not depend on any image or action which comes to us from the object, but solely on the situation of the small parts of the brain whence the nerves take their origin. For this situation—a situation which changes with every change however small in the points at which these nerve-fibers are located—is instituted by nature in order to secure, not only that the mind be aware of the location of each part of the body which it animates, relatively to all the others, but also that it be able to transfer its attention to all the positions contained in the straight line that can be imaged as drawn from the extremity of each of these parts, and as prolonged to infinity."]

29. Ibid., Adam et Tannery, 137. [Bridoux, 222; Smith, 155. N. Kemp Smith's translation is given here.]

30. No doubt Merleau-Ponty is speaking of Princess Elizabeth, Descartes's correspondent. Cf. *Phénoménologie de la perception*, 230–32 (C. Smith translation, 198–99), and Descartes's letter to Elizabeth of 28 June 1643 (Bridoux, 1157–61).—*Trans.*

31. That is, the obscurity of the "existential" order is just as necessary, just as grounded in God, as is the clarity of true thoughts ("nos lumières").—*Trans.*

32. Cf. note 18, above.—*Trans.*

33. B. Dorival, *Paul Cézanne* (Paris, 1948), 103ff. [H. H. A. Thackthwaite's translation (London, 1948), 101–3.]

34. Charbonnier, *Le monologue*, 176.

35. Delaunay, *Du cubisme*, 109.

36. F. Novotny, *Cézanne und das Ende der wissenschaftlichen Perspective* (Vienna, 1938).

37. W. Grohmann, *Paul Klee* (Paris, 1954), 141. [New York, 1956.]

38. Delaunay, *Du cubisme*, 118.

39. Klee, *Journal*. French trans. P. Klossowski (Paris, 1959).

40. George Schmidt, *Les aquarelles de Cézanne*, 21. [*The Watercolors of Cézanne* (New York, 1953).]

41. Klee, *Journal*.

42. "The spectacle is first of all a spectacle of itself before it is a spectacle of something outside of it."—*Translator's note from Merleau-Ponty's 1961 lectures.*

43. C. P. Bru, *Esthétique de l'abstraction* (Paris, 1959), 99, 86.

44. Henri Michaux, *Aventures de lignes*.

45. Ibid.

46. Ravaisson, cited by Bergson, "La vie et l'oeuvre de Ravaisson," in *La pensée et le mouvant* (Paris, 1934), 264–65. [The passage quoted here is from M. L. Andison's translation of that work, *The Creative Mind* (New York, 1946), 229. It remains moot whether these are Ravaisson's or da Vinci's words.]

47. Bergson, ibid.

48. Michaux, *Aventures de lignes*. ["laissé rêver une ligne."]

49. Ibid. ["d'aller ligne."]

50. Grohmann, *Paul Klee*, 192.

51. Rodin, *L'art*. Interviews collected by Paul Gsell (Paris, 1911).
52. Ibid., 86. Rodin uses the word "metamorphosis," quoted below.
53. Michaux, *Aventures de lignes*.
54. Cited by Delaunay, *Du cubisme*, 175.
55. Rilke, *Auguste Rodin*, French translation by Maurice Betz (Paris, 1928), 150. [English translation by Jessie Lamont and Hans Trausil (New York, 1919; republished 1945).]
56. Delaunay, *Du cubisme*, 115, 110.
57. Ibid.
58. Ibid.
59. Klee, *Conférence d'Iena* (1924), according to Grohmann, *Paul Klee*, 365.
60. Klee, *Wege des Naturstudiums* (1923), as found in G. di San Lazzaro, *Klee*.
61. Klee, cited by Grohmann, *Paul Klee*, 99.
62. A. Berne-Joffroy, *Le dossier Caravage* (Paris, 1959), and Michel Butor, "La Corbeille de l'Ambrosienne," *Nouvelle Revue Française* (1959), 969–89.
63. Klee, *Journal*. ["Je suis insaisissable dans l'immanence."]
64. G. Limbour, *Tableau bon levain à vous de cuire la pâte: L'art brut de Jean Dubuffet* (Paris, 1953), 54–55.
65. "Mais cette déception est celle du faux imaginaire, qui . . . "

Chapter 7
Forrest Williams, Cézanne, Phenomenology, and Merleau-Ponty

1. This is a revised version of "Cézanne and French Phenomenology," originally published in the *Journal of Aesthetics and Art Criticism* 12, no. 4 (June 1954), 481–92. At that time, almost forty years ago, none of Maurice Merleau-Ponty's writings had appeared in English, his work was virtually unknown in English-speaking countries, and the phenomenological movement that originated in the work of Edmund Husserl was much less familiar here than it is today. I have not attempted to remove all the signs of the original date of its composition, counting instead on the reader's awareness of the lapse of time. ("Eye and Mind," which of course was not published until 1961, seems to bear out the importance of the link suggested here.)—F. W.
2. In Maurice Merleau-Ponty, *Sens et non-sens* (Paris: Nagel, 1948), 15–49.
3. Here and subsequently we follow the title and data furnished by Lionello Venture in *Cézanne*, 2 vols. (Paris, 1936). See nos. 121 and 84, respectively.
4. See Bernard Bosanquet, *A History of Aesthetics*, 2d ed. (London, 1922), 229.
5. Quoted by Bosanquet, ibid.
6. Ibid.
7. See Venturi, *Cézanne*, nos. 51 and 457, respectively.
8. "Monet is only an eye, but, good Lord, what an eye!" (Quoted from Ambroise Vollard's *Paul Cézanne*, by Erle Loran, in *Cézanne's Composition* [Berkeley, 1946], 28.)
9. Herbert Read, *History of Modern Painting* (Geneva, 1949), xiii.

10. Ibid., xix.

11. Ibid.

12. Read noted correctly that for all his superior intelligence, Cézanne's efforts to explain in words his own intuitive processes as a painter were not always very clear. Read himself attempted to clarify the theoretical issues on Cézanne's behalf by invoking the concept of the "good Gestalt" (see ibid.). As will appear shortly, Read thereby had sensed correctly what Merleau-Ponty took to be central to both Cézanne's artistic project and phenomenological philosophy.

13. Ibid., xviii. (Italics added for emphasis.)

14. Ibid., 20. (Italics in text.)

15. Ibid., xxii.

16. Roger Fry, *Cézanne* (New York, 1927), 77.

17. Ibid., 57.

18. Ibid., 70.

19. Ibid., 35.

20. See M. D. H. Norton, *Translations from the Poetry of Rainer Maria Rilke* (New York, 1938), notes, 242.

21. Rainer Maria Rilke, *Letters of Rainer Maria Rilke, 1892–1919*, trans. J. B. Greene and M. D. H. Horton (New York, 1938), vol. 1, 305 (letter to Clara Rilke, dated 9 Oct. 1907).

22. Ibid., vol. 2, 304 (letter dated 18 Oct. 1907).

23. Ibid., vol. 2, 304 (letter dated 8 Oct. 1907).

24. Ibid., vol. 1, 316 (letter dated 21 Oct. 1907).

25. Cf. *Le Golfe de Marseille, Vu de l'Estaque* (Chicago Art Institute, 1886–90). See Venturi, *Cézanne*, no. 403.

26. Maurice Merleau-Ponty, *Phénoménologie de la perception* (Paris: Gallimard, 1945), 62, n. 1. (My translation from the French.)

27. See Merleau-Ponty, *Sens et non-sens*, 19–22.

28. See ibid., 22.

29. Ibid., 23, 25, 29.

30. Merleau-Ponty, *Phénoménologie de la perception*, chapter 3, and passim.

31. Merleau-Ponty, *Sens et non-sens*, 24.

32. Ibid., 26–27.

33. Ibid., 28.

34. Merleau-Ponty, *Phénoménologie de la perception*, 74.

35. Merleau-Ponty, *Sens et non-sens*, 28.

36. Ibid., 30.

37. Ibid.

Chapter 8
Alphonse de Waelhens, Merleau-Ponty: Philosopher of Painting

1. "Essence and existence, imaginary and real, visible and invisible—painting scrambles all our categories, spreading out before us its oneiric uni-

verse of carnal essences, actualized resemblances, mute meanings" (EM, 130). And also: "Let us begin by understanding that there is a tacit language, and that painting speaks in its own way" (ILVS, 84).

2. A most equivocal expression, but one that it is particularly important for a philosophy of painting to clarify. Let us therefore use it, but put it in quotation marks, to indicate its function as a point of departure "proximally and for the most part" (Heidegger).

3. The painter—Cézanne in particular—is the person "of such a vision, which penetrates right to the root of things, beneath the imposed order of humanity" (CD, 67). "The landscape thinks itself in me," he would say, "and I am its consciousness" (ibid.). This is also why one writer on Cézanne comments rather oddly (but I understand his thought) that the landscapes of that painter are "those of a pre-world in which as yet no men existed." F. Novotny, "Das Problem des Menschen Cézanne im Verhältnis zu seiner Kunst," *Zeitschrift für Aesthetik und allgemeine Kunstwissenschaft* 26 (1932), 275. Quoted in Merleau-Ponty, PhP, 322.

4. But we shall see that the notion of likeness is open to an entirely different interpretation.

5.
> The very significance of the thing is built up before our eyes, a significance which no verbal analysis can exhaust, and which merges with the exhibiting of the thing in its self-evidence. Every touch of colour applied by Cézanne must, as E. Bernard says, "contain the atmosphere, the light, the object, the relief, the character, the outline and the style." Each fragment of a visible spectacle satisfies an infinite number of conditions, and it is of the nature of the real to compress into each of its instants an infinity of relations. Like the thing, the picture has to be seen and not defined. (PhP, 323)

6. Perhaps what comes closest to the meaning attributed to "invention" here is the phenomenological notion of *constitution*.

7. For example: "[I]t is possible to speak about speech whereas it is impossible to paint about painting" (PhP, 190).

8. And that is precisely why "it is Cézanne's genius that when the overall composition of the picture is seen globally, perspectival distortions are no longer visible in their own right but rather contribute, as they do in natural vision, to the impression of an emerging order, an object in the act of appearing, organizing itself before our eyes" (CD, 65). "Nothing could be less arbitrary than these famous distortions" (ibid.).

9. Again, it is Cézanne who confirms this: "They [the classical artists] created pictures; we are attempting a piece of nature" (ibid., 62). "Of nature, he said: 'The artist must conform to this perfect work of art. Everything comes to us from nature; we exist through it; nothing else is worth remembering' " (ibid.).

10. Again let us listen to Cézanne. "Cézanne used to say of a portrait: If I paint in all the little blue and brown touches, I make him gaze as he does gaze. . . . Never mind if they suspect how, by bringing together a green

of various shades and a red, we sadden a mouth or bring a smile to a cheek' " (PhP, 197). And this, which is even more significant:

> In his *Peau de Chagrin* Balzac describes a "white tablecloth, like a covering of snow newly fallen, from which rose symmetrically the plates and napkins crowned with light-coloured rolls." "Throughout my youth," Cézanne said, "I wanted to paint that table-cloth like freshly fallen snow. . . . I know now that one must try to paint only: 'the plates and napkins rose symmetrically,' and 'the light-coloured rolls.' If I paint: 'crowned,' I'm finished, you see. And if I really balance and shade my napkins and rolls as they really are, you may be sure that the crowning, the snow and all the rest of it will be there." (PhP, 197–98)

11. "When I see the bright green of one of Cézanne's vases, it does not make me *think* of pottery, it presents it to me. The pottery is there, with its thin, smooth outer surface and its porous inside, in the particular way in which the green varies in shade" (PhP, 330).

12. Descartes, *La dioptrique*, Discours IV, 112–14. In English, *Descartes: Philosophical Writings*, ed. and trans. N. Kemp Smith (Modern Library Edition), 145–47.

13. It is along these lines that we should interpret the affirmations of a Giacometti (quoted by Merleau-Ponty) or a Magritte to the effect that *likeness* is the object of painting. "The art of painting (which is truly worthy of being called the art of the likeness) makes it possible to describe, through painting, a thought capable of becoming *apparent*." R. Magritte, *L'art de la ressemblance* (London: Catalog of the Obelisk Gallery, 1961), 6.

14. Martin Heidegger, *Being and Time* (New York: Harper and Row, 1962), 55–56; *Einführung in die Metaphysik* (Tübingen: Max Niemeyer Verlag, 1953), 95ff. [In English, see *An Introduction to Metaphysics*, trans. Ralph Manheim (New Haven: Yale University Press, 1959), 124ff.—*Trans.*]

15. Cézanne said: "The outline and the colour are no longer distinct; in proportion as one paints, one outlines, and the more the colour is harmonized, the more definite the outline becomes complete." Gasquet, *Cézanne* (Paris: Bernheim Jeune, 1926), 123. Quoted by Merleau-Ponty, PhP, 323.

16. See W. Grohmann, *Paul Klee* (Paris, 1954), 192.

17. "Because depth, color, form, line, movement, contour, physiognomy are all branches of Being and because each entwines the tufts of all the rest, there are no separate, distinct 'problems' in painting, no really opposed paths, no partial 'solutions,' no cumulative progress, no irretrievable options. There is nothing to prevent the painter from going back to one of the emblems he has shied away from—making it, of course, speak differently" (EM, 148).

18. In fact the previous quote from Heidegger at the beginning of this essay—and the more accurate one—was *"Wozu Dichter?"* I.e., "To what purpose the poet (or writer)?" De Waelhens has adapted Heidegger's phrase to the present context: "To what purpose the painter?"—*Trans.*

19. This was clearly demonstrated in the example, quoted earlier, of the

pool's water and tiling. "In whatever civilization it is born, from whatever beliefs, motives, or thoughts, no matter what ceremonies surround it—and even when it appears devoted to something else—from Lascaux to our time, pure or impure, figurative or not, painting celebrates no other enigma but that of visibility" (EM, 127).

20. "It is no more possible to make a restrictive inventory of the visible than it is to catalog the possible expressions of a language or even its vocabulary and turns of phrase" (ibid.).

21. "Cézanne declared that a picture contains within itself even the smell of the landscape. He meant that the arrangement of colour on the thing (and in the work of art, if it catches the thing in its entirety) signifies by itself all the responses which would be elicited through an examination by the remaining senses" (PhP, 318–19). Or yet again: "Cézanne was always seeking to avoid the ready-made alternatives suggested to him: sensation versus judgment; the painter who sees against the painter who thinks; nature versus composition; primitivism as opposed to tradition" (CD, 63). "Cézanne did not think he had to choose between feeling and thought, as if he were deciding between chaos and order. He did not want to separate the stable things which we see and the shifting way in which they appear" (ibid.).

22. Like the poet who said: "La fille de Minos et de Pasiphaé," or "Amère, sombre et sonore citerne." ["The daughter of Minos and Pasiphae," or "Bitter, sombre and sonorous cistern." Two lines from Racine, often quoted as examples of "pure poetry" before the letter (i.e., before the nineteenth-century ascendancy of "Art for Art's Sake."—*Trans.*]

23. Van Gogh's style "is legible *for Van Gogh* neither in his first works, nor even in his 'inner life' (for in this case Van Gogh would not need painting in order to be reconciled with himself; he would stop painting). It *is* that very life, to the extent that it emerges from its inherence, ceases to be in possession of itself and becomes a universal means of understanding and of making something understood, of seeing and of presenting something to see—and is thus not shut up in the depths of the mute individual but diffused throughout all he sees" (ILVS, 90).

24. "The accomplished work is thus not the work which exists in itself like a thing, but the work which reaches its viewer and invites him to take up the gesture which created it and, skipping the intermediaries, to rejoin, without any guide other than a movement of the invented line (an almost incorporeal trace), the silent world of the painter, henceforth uttered and accessible" (ibid., 88).

25. This again raises the alternative of figurative versus nonfigurative painting. There can be no question of either avoiding being, understood as the unity of nature, humanity and its expressive power, nor of asserting that painting is about objects such as they are "in the real world," as they say. For viewed in this latter manner, things are mere pragmatic abstractions, removed from the expressive encounter, the better to subject them to a different type of encounter; one that as a matter of fact is also expressive,

but in a more impoverished way. The exemplary models for this diminished encounter are calculation and prehension.

26. This is even true of science. For science's progress can be measured unequivocally only in the domain of effectiveness, which is not really the domain of science, but only that of one of the results of science. As far as underlying principles are concerned, the current view is that a science's maturity is to be assessed on the basis of its ability to undergo a "crisis of its foundations."

Chapter 9
Michael B. Smith, Merleau-Ponty's Aesthetics

1. Alphonse de Waelhens, *Une philosophie de l'ambiguité*, 4th ed. (Louvain: Nauwelaerts, 1970), 170.

2. Rémy Kwant, *From Phenomenology to Metaphysics* (Pittsburgh: Duquesne University Press, 1966), 15ff.

3. Merleau-Ponty finished writing *The Structure of Behavior* in 1938. See Theodore Geraets, *Vers une nouvelle philosophie transcendantale* (The Hague: Martinus Nijhoff, 1971), 1.

4. James J. Gibson's term, "affordances," aptly designates the organism's subject/world elaboration of perception and is strikingly consonant with Merleau-Ponty's account. See Gibson's *The Ecological Approach to Visual Perception* (Hillsdale: L. Erlbaum Assocs., 1986), 127. Quoted by J. T. Sanders in "Merleau-Ponty, Gibson and the Materiality of Meaning," an unpublished paper delivered at the Seventeenth Annual International Conference of the Merleau-Ponty Circle, 24 Sept. 1992, at St. Joseph College, Hartford, Conn.

5. Gabriel Marcel's *Being and Having* (1935) must have had considerable influence on the young Merleau-Ponty, judging from a review written by the latter in 1936. The following excerpt from it, which summarizes Marcel's reflection on the lived body, foreshadows the thesis of *Phenomenology of Perception*. "My body does not appear to me as an object, a set of qualities and characteristics to be linked up with one another and thus understood. My relation to it is not that of the *cogito* to the *cogitatum*, the 'epistemological subject' to the object. I and it form a common cause, and in a sense I *am* my body" (*Merleau-Ponty: Texts and Dialogues*, ed. Hugh J. Silverman and J. Barry [Atlantic Highlands: Humanities Press, 1990], 102).

6. This expression, taken from the first chapter of H. Bergson's *The Creative Mind* (*La pensée et le mouvant*), appears in Merleau-Ponty's working notes to *The Visible and the Invisible* (VI, 189).

7. The materialism and idealism referred to here are the products of an atrophied Cartesianism. "Cartesianism, whether it intended to do so or not, did inspire a science of the human body that decomposes that body also into a network of objective processes and, with the notion of sensation,

prolongs this analysis unto the 'psychism.' These two idealizations are bound up with one another and must be undone together" (VI, 26). For a more detailed analysis of Merleau-Ponty's critique of neo-Cartesian "reflective thought," see F. Olafson, "Merleau-Ponty's Philosophy," in *Phenomenology and Existentialism* (Baltimore: The Johns Hopkins University Press, 1967), 179–205, passim.

8. The expression is borrowed from the last stanza of Paul Valéry's poem *La Pythie*.

9. Merleau-Ponty leaves the door open to a theory of the unconscious in *Phenomenology of Perception* when he writes of the hallucination that "we must refuse to attribute to perceptual consciousness the full possession of itself, and that immanence which would rule out any possible illusion" (VI, 344). And in a lecture given in Geneva in 1951, he points out that the unconscious, "that osmosis between the body's anonymous life and the person's official life which is Freud's great discovery" (S, 229), is one of the most significant discoveries of the twentieth century. He defends the notion of the unconscious from Sartre's main objection (for whom the unconscious represented a "third-person" process), giving it the philosophical status of an "ambiguous perception," i.e., "not *un-knowing* but rather an unrecognized and unformulated knowing that we do not want to assume" (ibid.). In the last years of his life, Merleau-Ponty attributed to the unconscious a major role in the elaboration of the perceived object (see VI, 189, 270). Despite Husserl's and Sartre's objections to the notion of the unconscious, it is obvious that the former's *Motivierung, fungierende Intentionalität* and especially *Horizonthaftigkeit*, and the latter's analyses of bad faith represent alternative treatments of closely related phenomena.

10. Claude Lefort, in his editor's preface to *The Prose of the World*, specifies the relationship between the two works.

11. Historian Michel de Certeau identifies some specific effects of this cultural metamorphosis of vision in Europe, citing "the revolution in painting in the fifteenth century . . . and the invention of perspective; the cartographic encyclopedism of knowledge; the role of optics in modern scientificity. . . . It was a real modification of man's experience: vision slowly invaded the previous domain of touch or of hearing." *The Mystic Fable* (Chicago: University of Chicago Press, 1992), 89.

12. One should also read, in this connection, the course notes prepared by Merleau-Ponty's students at the Sorbonne and approved by him (courses on child psychology given from 1949 to 1952: *Maurice Merleau-Ponty à la Sorbonne, Bulletin de Psychologie* 236, Tome 18, 3–6 [November 1964]). Henri Wallon's notion of "ultra-things" (which reappears in "Indirect Language and the Voices of Silence" [S, 49]), those singular beings that cannot be encompassed by our gaze, and toward which it is impossible to vary our perspective (e.g., the sky, the earth, the sun) is used to explain the "distortions" present in children's drawings. Similarly, parents, or a field, are "as big as a house" for the child. The adult reduces the number of these absolute magnitudes (which is the psychological significance of

the Copernican revolution) but never succeeds in eliminating them al-together. We are always situated in the same way with respect to our bod-ies, and it is impossible, even for adult consciousness, to truly conceive of one's own death. The belief that we are coextensive with being would seem to be inherent in subjectivity.

13. Jean-Paul Sartre, "Merleau-Ponty Vivant," *Les Temps Modernes* 184–85 (1961), 372.

14. In "Metaphysics and the Novel," Merleau-Ponty finds that Stendhal, Bal-zac, and Proust had "difficulty in recognizing their [philosophical] affini-ties" (S, 26).

15. It was Emile Bréhier who accused Merleau-Ponty of "betraying immediate experience." He went on to suggest: "I see your idea as being better ex-pressed in literature and in painting than in philosophy. Your philosophy results in a novel. This is not a defect" (PrP, 30). Merleau-Ponty counters the first charge by explaining that the unreflected exists for us only through reflection; to the second he does not deign to reply.

Chapter 10
Marjorie Grene, The Aesthetic Dialogue of Sartre and Merleau-Ponty

1. This essay was originally written for the Fine Arts Festival of the Univer-sity of Wisconsin, Milwaukee.

2. Maurice Merleau-Ponty, *Les aventures de la dialectique* (Paris: Gallimard, 1955), 131ff.

3. Ibid., 253. In what follows I have relied heavily on a number of Merleau-Ponty's discussions of Sartre, including some of the working notes in his posthumous and incompleted work *Le visible et l'invisible*, but in order not to pepper my argument with references, I have not stopped to mention at each stage the Merleau-Pontian text which supports my own reasoning. This work, like most of those referred to, is now available in translation in the phenomenological series of Northwestern University Press.

4. Published in *Critique de la raison dialectique*, vol. 1 (Paris: Gallimard, 1960), and translated by Hazel Barnes as *Search for a Method* (New York: Knopf, 1963).

5. Introduction to Jean Genet, *Our Lady of the Flowers* (London: Blond, 1964), 47.

6. Ibid., 53.

7. See Jean-Paul Sartre, *L'imaginaire* (Paris: Alcan, 1940), translated as *The Psychology of the Imagination* (New York: Rider, 1950).

8. See Jean-Paul Sartre, *The Transcendence of the Ego* (New York: Noonday Press, 1957). First published in *Recherches Philosophiques* (1936).

9. Jean-Paul Sartre, *Situations* (New York: Fawcett World Library, 1966), 126. Cf., on the same page: "Giacometti is a sculptor because he carries his vacuum along with him, as a snail its shell." But compare also the

treatment of Giacometti as a graphic artist in a contrary sense in Merleau-Ponty's "L'oeil et l'espirit" (Paris: Gallimard, 1964), 24.

10. I have argued this in detail elsewhere: cf. my "Tacit Knowing and the Pre-Reflexive Cogito," in *Intellect and Hope* (Durham: Duke University Press, 1968), or my review of Manser's *Sartre* in *Mind* 78 (1969), 141–52.

11. Cf. *Les aventures de la dialectique,* 271.

12. Ibid.

13. Maurice Merleau-Ponty, *Le visible et l'invisible,* (Paris: Gallimard, 1964), 290.

14. Maurice Merleau-Ponty, *La structure du comportment,* 5th ed. (Paris: Presses Universitaires de France, 1963).

15. Maurice Merleau-Ponty, "Le doute de Cézanne," in *Sens et non-sens* (Paris: Nagel, 1948), 15–44, 19–21.

16. Merleau-Ponty, "L'oeil et l'espirit," 29–30. Merleau-Ponty's account here comes close to Polanyi's theory of tacit knowing; my use of "from-to" in particular is borrowed from him. See, e.g., Polanyi, *The Tacit Dimension* (New York: Doubleday, 1966), or *Knowing and Being* (London: Routledge, 1969), and my introduction to the latter.

17. Merleau-Ponty, "L'oeil et l'esprit," 26–27.

18. Ibid., 31.

19. Ibid.

20. Ibid., 67–68.

21. Ibid.

22. Ibid., 68–69.

23. Ibid., 35.

24. Jean-Paul Sartre, *Situations,* vol. 2, quoted in Maurice Merleau-Ponty, "Le langage indirect et les voix du silence," in *Signes* (Paris: Gallimard, 1960), 49ff., 69.

25. Merleau-Ponty, *Signes,* 49ff.

26. Ibid., 69.

27. Ibid., 70.

28. Merleau-Ponty, "L'oeil et l'espirit," 86–87.

29. Ibid., 87.

30. See A. Portmann, "Die Zeit im Leben des Organismus," reprinted from *Eranos Jahrbuch* in *Biologie und Giest* (Frieburg: Herder, 1963), 123ff.

31. Merleau-Ponty, *La structure du comportment.*

32. Merleau-Ponty, "L'oeil et l'esprit," 19.

33. Ibid., 21–22.

34. Merleau-Ponty, *Sens et non-sens,* 34–35.

35. Merleau-Ponty, *Signes,* 99.

36. Ibid., 87.

37. Ibid., 95.

38. Ibid., 71.

39. Merleau-Ponty, *Sens et non-sens,* 35.

40. Ibid., 44.

41. Merleau-Ponty, "L'oeil et l'espirit," 92–93.

42. Ibid.

43. Ibid.

44. In particular, for example, Polanyi, Portmann, Plessner, perhaps also David Bohn. See my *Knower and the Known* (New York: Basic Books, 1966), and *Approaches to a Philosophical Biology* (New York: Basic Books, 1969). On the side of experimental psychology, J. J. Gibson's *The Senses Considered as Perceptual Systems* (Ithaca: Cornell University Press, 1966), seems to me also to show a striking convergence with this philosophical tendency.

Chapter 11
Linda Singer, Merleau-Ponty on the Concept of Style

1. Maurice Merleau-Ponty, "Indirect Language and the Voices of Silence," in *Signs*, trans. R. McCleary (Evanston: Northwestern University Press, 1964), 52; ILVS, 89.

2. Maurice Merleau-Ponty, *Sense and Non-Sense*, trans. Hubert and Patricia Dreyfus (Evanston: Northwestern University Press, 1964), 3.

3. Merleau-Ponty, "Cézanne's Doubt," in *Sense and Non-Sense*, 19; CD, 69.

4. S, 54–57; ILVS, 91–94.

5. Ibid., 45; 82–83.

6. Ibid., 74; 54–55; 91–92.

7. Ibid., 69; 105.

8. Maurice Merleau-Ponty, *Phenomenology of Perception*, trans. Colin Smith (London: Routledge, 1962), 450.

9. Ibid., 455.

10. S, 455; ILVS, 91.

11. Maurice Merleau-Ponty, *The Visible and the Invisible*, trans. Alphonso Lingis (Evanston: Northwestern University Press, 1968), 237.

12. *Phenomenology of Perception*, viii.

Chapter 12
Olivier Mongin, Since Lascaux

1. Michel Lefeuvre, *Merleau-Ponty au-delà de la phénomélogie* (Paris: Klincksieck, 1976), 353.

2. Claude Lefort, *Sur une colonne absente* (Paris: Gallimard, 1978).

3. From a letter addressed to Martial Guéroult, quoted by Claude Lefort in his editor's preface to *The Prose of the World* (PW, xiii). [The entire letter is available in English (see "An Unpublished Text," PrP, 3–11).—*Trans.*]

4. A. A. Brill, trans. (New York, 1947).—*Trans.*

5. PW, 76. [This and other quotations from O'Neill's translation have been slightly modified.—*Trans.*]

6. In *Discours, figure* (Paris: Klincksieck, 1971), J.-F. Lyotard also relates painting to the event. But there it is no longer perception that constitutes

an event; the event is undecidable, arising in the image of the death drive. Note should be taken of Lyotard's references to Paul Klee, a painter who is present in several passages of "Eye and Mind," a posthumous work of Merleau-Ponty.

7. See, e.g., Maurice Blanchot's "Le musée, l'art et le temps," in *Critique* (Dec. 1950).

8. Here the text is not always homogeneous. Painting may be considered as language; from another perspective, it can be considered in the context of a double historicity. . . .

9. It is difficult here not to recall the reference to Charles Péguy, to the Péguian theme of historical inscription (see VI, 173, 196). It is hardly surprising that Péguy should also be referred to by Walter Benjamin, who also expected a Revelation from the event: not a Revelation of neuter Being, as in Heidegger, but a Revelation of humanity. For Benjamin's references to Péguy, see W. Benjamin, *Correspondance, 1929–1940*, vol. 2 (Aubier, 1979), 372.

10. This is a reflection Louis Dumont pursued energetically, showing that if the universal is synonymous with humanity as a whole, it is not perceptible to all human beings. See *L'homme* (July–Dec. 1978).

11. According to the structuralist linguist André Martinet, a given domain of expression (language, painting, music . . .) is only to be considered a language if it reflects the law of double articulation.

> The notion of choice governs . . . the theory of double articulation. To describe a language means to describe the manifold of choices the speaker can make, and that can be recognized by a person who understands the language. These choices are of two kinds: (a) Those of the first articulation have a signifying value, i.e., they concern units that have meaning. E.g., in the statement: "John began after Bill," the choice of "Bill" rather than "Jill," "him," "the war," etc. To say that these choices constitute one articulation is to make a two-fold hypothesis. First, that there are minimal choices (choices of elementary units of meaning, or monemes, such as "Bill"), and secondly that larger choices (such as the choice of "after you") can be understood on the basis of the choice of monemes (thus the very strong hypothesis is made that the difference between "began after Bill" and "began after the war" can be explained by the difference between "Bill" and "the war").— (b) The choices of the second articulation between units that are merely distinguishable—phonemes—whose sole function is to make possible the distinction between monemes. Thus the choice of the "b" of "Bill" is not directly based on the will to signify, but only indirectly, to the extent that it is necessitated by the choice of the moneme "Bill," which it distinguishes, e.g., from "Jill." Here again Martinet makes the hypothesis that there is articulation, i.e., that there are minimal choices (choices of phonemes such as "b") and that they are at the basis of the choice of higher segments. (Ducrot-Todorov, *Dictionnaire encyclopédique des sciences du language* [Paris: Seuil, 1972]).

12. Other answers have been given to this debate. See Mikel Dufrenne, *Esthétique et philosophie*, vol. 2 (Paris: Klinksieck, 1976), 73–112. In Dufrenne's view, painting is not a language, because the constitutive elements of the discourse of imagery do not possess a value independently from the concatenation in which they appear.

13. *The Raw and the Cooked* (Chicago: The University of Chicago Press, 1983), 22. Translation of *Le cru et le cuit* (Paris: Plon, 1964).—*Trans.*

14. Claude Lévi-Strauss, *Savage Mind* (Chicago: The University of Chicago Press, 1968).—*Trans.*

15. See Pierre Livet, "Pensée du temps et recherche éthique," in which ethics is inseparable from a reflection on temporality. *Esprit* 66 (June 1982), 78–88.

16. What follows is from Claude Lévi-Strauss, "De quelques rencontres," *l'Arc* 46 (1971), 45–47.—*Trans.*

17. See EM, 123.—*Trans.*

Chapter 13
Mikel Dufrenne, Eye and Mind

1. See *Les Temps Modernes* 184–85 (Oct. 1961), 372.

2. Maurice Merleau-Ponty, *The Visible and the Invisible*, trans. Alphonso Lingis (Evanston: Northwestern University Press, 1968), 38.

3. Maurice Merleau-Ponty, "Eye and Mind," in the *The Primacy of Perception*, ed. James M. Edie (Evanston: Northwestern University Press, 1964), 175; EM, 135–36.

4. Jean-François Lyotard, *Discours, figure* (Paris: Klincksieck, 1971), 22.

5. Merleau-Ponty, *The Visible and the Invisible*, 46.

6. Merleau-Ponty, "Eye and Mind," 181; EM, 141.

7. Ibid., 182; EM 142.

8. Ibid., 161; EM, 123.

9. Ibid., 166; EM, 127.

Chapter 14
Hugh J. Silverman, Cézanne's Mirror Stage

1. References to Merleau-Ponty's text are included within the body of the article. Pages following *OE* are to the French edition of "L'oeil et l'esprit" (Paris: Gallimard, 1964). Though the translations of passages are mine, an English version by Carleton Dallery entitled "Eye and Mind" is included in *The Primacy of Perception*, ed. James M. Edie (Evanston: Northwestern University Press, 1964).

2. Among these commentaries on Merleau-Ponty's account of painting, none of the following say anything about self-portraiture: Gary Brent Madison, "La peinture," *La Phénoménologie de Merleau-Ponty* (Paris, 1973),

89–124; Michel Lefeuvre, "Les arts," *Merleau-Ponty au délà de la phénomé-nologie* (Paris, 1976), 353–64; James Gordon Place, "The Painting and the Natural Thing in the Philosophy of Merleau-Ponty," *Cultural Hermeneutics* 4 (1976), 75–91; Mikel Dufrenne, "Eye and Mind," *Research in Phenomenology* 10 (1980), 167–73; and Véronique M. Fóti, "Painting and the Re-Orientation of Philosophical Thought in Merleau-Ponty," *Philosophy Today* 24, no. 2 (Summer 1980), 114–20. The only mention and discussion of self-portraits is in Marjorie Grene, "The Sense of Things," *Journal of Aesthetics and Art Criticism* 38, no. 4 (Summer 1980), 377–89. She cites the case of Courbet rather than Cézanne but only mentions mirroring in passing. When commenting on Grene's essay, Harrison Hall, in "Painting and Perceiving," *Journal of Aesthetics and Art Criticism* 39, no. 3 (Spring 1981), 291–95, misses the issue of self-portraiture altogether.

3. "Cézanne's Doubt" was collected in *Sens et non-sens* (Nagel, Paris: 1948) as "Le doute de Cézanne." References to the text are abbreviated as *Doute*. An English translation by Hubert L. Dreyfus and Patricia A. Dreyfus is included in *Sense and Non-Sense* (Evanston: Northwestern University Press, 1964), 9–25, and as chap. 4 in this volume.

4. Jacques Lacan, *Ecrits* (Paris, 1966), 95.

5. Michel de Montaigne, "Au lecteur," *Essais* (Paris, 1962), 1. The French passage reads: "Je veus qu'on m'y voie en ma façon simple, naturelle et ordinaire, sans contantion et artifice: car c'est moy que je peins." The standard English translation is by Donald M. Frame in *The Complete Essays of Montaigne* (Palo Alto: Stanford University Press, 1958), 2.

6. Jean-Jacques Rousseau, *Les Confessions,* in *Oeuvres Complètes,* vol. 1 (Paris, 1959), 3.

7. For further details concerning the status of autobiographical textuality, see: "The Autobiographical Space and its Limits," *Eros: A Journal of Philosophy and Literary Arts* 8, no. 1 (June 1981), 95–115 (a French version appeared in *Le Deux* [Paris, 10–18, 1980], 279–301 under the title *"Un egale deux ou l'espace autobiographique et ses limites"*); "The Autobiographical Textuality of Nietzsche's *Ecce Homo,"* *Boundary 2* 8, no. 2 (Winter 1981); and "The Time of Autobiography" in *Time and Metaphysics,* ed. D. C. Wood and R. Bernasconi (Conventry, England, 1982).

8. A celebrated M. C. Escher lithograph entitled "Drawing Hands" shows two hands drawing (or writing) each other. Each hand has an artist's pencil in its grasp and they simultaneously give rise to each other. Escher demonstrates what it would mean to achieve the paradoxical condition of making the hand that writes itself visible. But these hands are not writing a life as autobiography. Their visibility lies more in the establishment of their existence than in the articulation of their identity.

9. For an account of the textuality produced in photography, see "The Philosopher's Body and the Body of the Photograph," *Journal of the British Society for Phenomenology* 8 (1982). In that essay, stress is placed on the body of the Other, particularly Sartre and Heidegger, in terms of what is characterized as "photobiographical textuality."

10. This essay was presented at the sixth annual Merleau-Ponty Circle meeting at Colgate University in October 1981. In its formative stages, it constituted the core of lectures given at the Centre International d'Etudes Françaises of the Université de Nice (France) in August 1980 and at the Collegium Phaenomenologicum (Perugia, Italy) in July 1981. The current version benefitted from discussions with colleagues and students on these three occasions and from extended conversations about the topic with Patricia Athay at SUNY, Stony Brook.

Chapter 15
Jacques Taminiaux, The Thinker and the Painter

1. Maurice Merleau-Ponty, "L'oeil et l'esprit" (Paris: Gallimard, 1964), 16; henceforth cited as OE. "Eye and Mind," trans. Carleton Dallery, in *The Primacy of Perception*, ed. James M. Edie (Evanston: Northwestern University Press, 1964), 162; henceforth cited as PrP. Reprinted in this volume, 121–49; henceforth cited as EM.
2. Maurice Merleau-Ponty, *Signes* (Paris: Gallimard, 1960). *Signs*, trans. Richard C. McCleary (Evanston: Northwestern University Press, 1964).
3. *"corps de l'esprit."*
4. In *Signes*, 49–104; *Signs*, 39–83.
5. Quoted by Merleau-Ponty (PrP, 164; OE, 22; EM, 125).
6. "Cet équivalent interne, cette formule charnelle de leur présence que les choses suscitent en moi, pourquoi à leur tour ne susciteraient-ils pas un tracé, visible encore, où tout autre regard retrouvera les motifs qui soutiennent son inspection du monde?"
7. Par le fait même l'unité de la peinture semble être, pour Malraux, transhistorique et dans l'histoire effective il ne voit guère que morcellement, lutte de chaque peintre contre tous les autres, oubli, méconnaissance.
8. Empiétements tels que ni l'acquis ni le nouveau ne le sont jamais tout à fait et que "l'idée . . . d'une totalisation de la peinture . . . est dépourvue de sens."

Chapter 16
Véronique M. Fóti, The Dimension of Color

1. I wish to thank the Fulbright Foundation for awarding me a lectureship in India in 1987. Without it, I would have remained a stranger to the extraordinary colors of Rajasthan.
2. Maurice Merleau-Ponty, *Signs*, trans. Richard McCleary (Evanston: Northwestern University Press, 1964), 22.

3. Maurice Merleau-Ponty, "L'oeil et l'esprit" (Paris: Gallimard, 1964). English translation by Carleton Dallery, "Eye and Mind," in *The Primacy of Perception*, ed. James M. Edie (Evanston: Northwestern University Press, 1964), 159–90; reprinted in this volume, 121–49. These works are cited as *OE*, PrP, and EM, respectively.

4. René Descartes, *Optics*, partial English translation of *La dioptrique* by John Cottingham, Robert Stoothoff, and Dugald Murdoch, in *The Philosophical Works of Descartes*, 2 vols. (Cambridge: Cambridge University Press, 1985), vol. 1, 151–75. This work is referred to as *CMS*, with cross-references given to *Oeuvres de Descartes*, rev. ed., 12 vols., ed. Charles Adam and P. Tannery (Paris: Vrin/C. N. R. S., 1964–76), cited as *AT*.

5. I am referring to the third dream, as narrated by Baillet on the basis of a lost Cartesian text, AT X, 182–85. An English translation appears in John Cottingham, *Descartes* (London: Blackwell, 1986), 161–64. The engravings constitute a surd in the dream which Descartes cannot interpret; but "he ceased to look for an explanation after receiving a visit from an Italian painter the following day" (164).

6. The doctrine derives chiefly from Thomas Aquinas. Cf., for instance, his *Treatise on Man*, questions LXXVIII, LXXXIV, LXXXV, and the *Commentary on Aristotle's De Anima*, lecture 12.

7. Maurice Merleau-Ponty, *Le visible et l'invisible* (Paris: Gallimard, 1964), 223. English translation by Alphonso Lingis, *The Visible and the Invisible* (Evanston: Northwestern University Press, 1964), 170. These texts will be referred to as *VI* and VI, respectively.

8. Ludwig Wittgenstein, *Bemerkungen über die Farbe/Remarks on Colour*, ed. G. E. M. Anscombe, trans. L. McAlister and M. Schättle (Berkeley: University of California Press, 1977), 16.

9. Cf. René Descartes, *Principles of Philosophy*, vol. 2, 2, 4; *CMS*, 222, 224; *AT* VIII, 42, 46. See also Cottingham's discussion, *Descartes*, chapter 4.

10. Descartes, *Principles*, vol. 1, 70; *CMS*, 218; *AT* VIII, 34.

11. Descartes, "Les météores," Discourse 8, Descartes, *Oeuvres et Lettres*, ed. André Bridoux (Paris: Gallimard, 1953), 230–46; cf. 234f.; *AT* VI, 235–344.

12. Descartes, "Description of the Human Body," *CMS*, 323; *AT* XI, 255.

13. In simultaneous and successive contrast, the eye posits the complementary of a given color either by modifying adjacent colors or as an after-image. In contrast reversal, the after-image transfers the (uniform) color of a pattern of shapes to the negative spaces of the ground.

14. Descartes, "The World, or Treatise on Light," *CMS*, 81; *AT* XI, 3.

15. David Michael Levin, *The Opening of Vision: Nihilism and the Postmodern Situation* (New York: Routledge, 1988), 214.

16. For a discussion see Joseph C. Allard, "Mechanism, Music, and Painting in 17th Century France," *The Journal of Aesthetics and Art Criticism* 40 (Spring 1982), 269–79.

17. Johannes Itten, *The Elements of Color*, ed. Faber Birren, trans. Ernst von Hagen (New York: Van Nostrand, 1970), 34.

18. K. Müller-Boré, *Stilistische Untersuchungen zum Farbwort und zur Verwendung der Farbe in der älteren griechischen Poesie* (Berlin, 1922); and W. E. Gladstone, *Studies on Homer and the Homeric Age*, vol. 3 (Oxford, 1958), as cited by Christopher Rowe in "Conceptions of Color and Color Symbolism in the Ancient World," *Eranos* 41 (1972), 327–63.

19. Alice E. Kober, *The Use of Color Terms in the Greek Poets* (Geneva, N.Y.: The W. F. Humphreys Press, 1932), 116.

20. Cf. G. S. Kirk, J. E. Raven, and M. Schofield, *The Presocratic Philosophers*, 2d ed. (Cambridge: Cambridge University Press, 1983), 384.

21. See Eva C. Keuls, *Plato and Greek Painting* (Leiden: Brill, 1978), chapter 8.

22. Hans-Georg Gadamer, "Idea and Reality in Plato's *Timaeus*," *Dialogue and Dialectic: Eight Hermeneutical Studies on Plato*, trans. P. Christopher Smith (New Haven: Yale University Press, 1980), 156–93 (citation on 160).

23. Levin, *The Opening of Vision*, n. 105, and "Appendi," n. 9, 531, 533.

24. Cf. Eva C. Keul's discussion in *Plato and Greek Painting*, chapter 4.

25. I cite by memory from selections from Gauguin's writings which formed part of the exhibition *The Art of Paul Gauguin*, National Gallery of Art, Washington, D.C., 1988.

26. Arthur Schopenhauer, "Über das Sehn und die Farbe," and "Theoria colorum physiologica," in *Sämtliche Werke*, 2d ed., ed. Arthur Hübscher (Wiesbaden: Brockhaus, 1950), 149–64; 165–97. G. W. F. Hegel, *Enzyklopädie der philosophischen Wissenschaften*, in *Sämtliche Werke*, ed. C. L. Michelet (Berlin, 1942), 277–335.

27. M. Merleau-Ponty, *Phénoménologie de la perception* (Paris: Gallimard, 1945). English translation by Colin Smith, *Phenomenology of Perception* (New York: Humanities Press, 1962). To be cited as *PP* and PhP, respectively.

28. For a discussion, see Rodolphe Gasché, "Reading Chiasms," introduction to Andrzej Warminski, *Readings in Interpretation: Hölderlin, Hegel, Heidegger* (Minneapolis: University of Minnesota Press, 1987), ix–xxvi.

29. Cf. Frederick Burwick, *The Damnation of Newton: Goethe's Color Theory and Romantic Perception* (Berlin: de Gruyter, 1986).

30. Cf. Edwin H. Land, "Experiments in Color Vision," *Scientific American* (May 1959), 84–99, and "The Retinex Theory of Color Vision," *Scientific American* (Dec. 1977), 108–30.

31. Maurice Merleau-Ponty, "Cézanne's Doubt," in *Sense and Non-Sense*, trans. Hubert L. Dreyfus and Patricia A. Dreyfus (Evanston: Northwestern University Press, 1964), 13f. To be referred to as SNS. Reprinted in this volume, 59–75, to be referred to as CD.

32. John Rewald, *Cézanne: a Biography* (New York: Harry N. Abrams, Inc., 1986), 237.

33. Josef Albers, *Interaction of Color* (New Haven: Yale University Press, 1963), 32.

Chapter 17
Jean-François Lyotard, from *Discours, figure*

1. Emmanuel Levinas, "Humanism and An-Archy," in *E. Levinas: Collected Philosophical Papers*, trans. Alphonso Lingis (Dordrecht: Martinus Nijhoff, 1987), 128.
2. VI, 175–76, 200.
3. And when he was going to give up the elements of a philosophy of the cogito in the *Phenomenology of Perception*, he even set about maintaining a unitary philosophy by replacing the "I" with Being.
4. Although I have chosen to translate the "Ça" as "That," in order to convey its essentially third-person quality, it is clear from what follows that Lyotard co-intends the Freudian sense of the term, the Id, or Desire.—*Trans.*
5. The French *en sens* appears to be used ambiguously here to mean at once signification and the senses.—*Trans.*
6. Pierre Kaufmann shows this clearly at the end of the first chapter of *L'expérience émotionnelle de l'espace* (Paris: Vrin, 1967).
7. See especially Levinas, "Humanism and An-Archy."
8. Merleau-Ponty:

> [W]e are catching sight of the necessity of another operation besides the conversion to reflection, more fundamental than it, of a sort of *hyperreflection* [*sur-réflexion*] that would also take itself and the changes it introduces into the spectacle into account. It accordingly would not lose sight of the brute thing and the brute perception and would not finally efface them, would not cut the organic bonds between the perception and the thing perceived with a hypothesis of inexistence. On the contrary, it would set itself the task of thinking about them, of reflecting on the transcendence of the world as transcendence, speaking of it not according to the law of the word-meanings inherent in the given language, but with a perhaps difficult effort that uses the significations of words to express, beyond themselves, our mute contact with the things, when they are not yet things said. (VI, 38)

As for certain beings that do not admit of fixation in the form of eidetic invariants, such as time, first and foremost, hyperreflection would become "not a superior degree at the ultimate level of philosophy, but philosophy itself" (VI, 46).

9. Ibid., 102.
10. Ibid. The "Pages d'introduction à la prose du monde," published by Claude Lefort in *Revue de Métaphysique et de Morale* 2, 139ff. are a description of the experience of language built entirely on the opposition between the closed and the open.
11. VI, 102–3
12. Ibid., 118; italicized in the original.
13. Ibid., 119.

14. Ibid., 125.
15. For example in "Indirect Language and the Voices of Silence" (chap. 5 in this volume). See also my *Discours, figure* (Paris: Klincksieck, 1985), 92–93, n. 5.
16. Lyotard uses *forclusion*, the standard French translation of Freud's term (German *Verwerfung*, rejection). I have followed Alan Sheridan's usage ("foreclosure") in his translation of Jacques Lacan's work (see *Ecrits* [New York: Norton, 1977]). Foreclosure differs from repression in that it rejects unbearable representations even before they are allowed to enter the unconscious.—*Trans.*
17. Including his discourse on discourse. "Linguistics is nothing but a methodical and mediate way of shedding light, by all the other factual observations on language, on *that speech that speaks within us*, and to which we remain *attached as if by an umbilical chord*, even when we are engaged in our scientific work. We would like to free ourselves from that bond. It would be good to be rid at last of that confused and irritating situation of a *being who is that of which he or she speaks*" ("Pages d'introduction," 148; my emphasis). But we do not succeed: thank God, says the phenomenologist.

Chapter 18
Jean-François Lyotard, Philosophy and Painting in the Age of Their Experimentation: Contribution to an Idea of Postmodernity

1. Denis Diderot, *Salon de 1767*, in *Oeuvres complètes*, 15 vols. (Paris: Club Français du Livre, 1970), vol. 7, 140.
2. Presentation by Catherine Millet at the symposium *Critica 0*, Montecatini, May 1978.
3. Diderot, VII, 165.
4. Friedrich Nietzsche, *Thoughts Out of Season; On the Future of Our Educational Institutions.*
5. Walter Benjamin, "One Some Motifs in Baudelaire" (1939), in *Illuminations*, trans. Harry Zorn (New York: Harcourt, Brace and World, 1968), 157–202.
6. Benjamin, 189.
7. Diderot, *Oeuvres*, vol. 7, 163.
8. Georges Bataille, "La destruction du sujet," in *Manet* (Geneva: Skira, 1955).
9. Gérard Genette, *Figures III* (Paris: Seuil, 1972).
10. Diderot, *Oeuvres*, vol. 7, 146–47.
11. Friedrich Schlegel, *Fragments* (*Athenaeum*, 1978), French translation by P. Lacoue-Labarthe and J.-L. Nancy in *L'absolu littéraire* (Paris: Seuil, 1979), frags. 189 and 201, pp. 123 and 125–26.
12. This is the Latin sense of a saturation of genres in the same work. The magical power of the imprecation which has been attributed from the be-

ginning to Archilochus is not unrelated, in my view, to the permutations of words in pragmatic instances. See Robert C. Elliot, *The Power of Satire: Magic, Ritual, and Art*, 3d ed. (Princeton: Princeton University Press, 1972).

13. Schlegel, *L'absolu*, frag. 201, p. 126.

14. Diderot, *Essai sur la peinture*, in *Oeuvres*, vol. 6, 284–85.

15. Alexandre Kojève, "Pourquoi concret" (1936), in Vasili Kandinsky, *Ecrits complets* (Paris: Denoël, 1970), vol. 2, 395–400. See the discussion of Kandinsky's "concrete period" by Michel Conil Lacoste, *Kandinsky* (Paris: Flammarion, 1979), 81–91.

16. *Untitled—First abstraction*, in the Grohmann catalog. The work is at the Musée National d' Art Moderne (Beaubourg). The question of its date is analyzed by Lacoste, *Kandinsky*, 46–51.

17. Diderot, *Oeuvres*, vol. 7, 105.

18. The sense of figural here is that of its use in Jean-François Lyotard, *Discours, figure* (Paris: Klincksieck, 1971).

19. Diderot, *Oeuvres*, vol. 7, 105ff.

20. Maurice Merleau-Ponty, *The Visible and the Invisible*, trans. Alphonso Lingis (Evanston: Northwestern University Press, 1968), 144.

21. Ibid., 154.

22. "Eye and Mind," in *The Primacy of Perception* (Evanston: Northwestern University Press), 185; EM, 144.

23. Reproduced in Man Ray, *Photographs (1920–1934)* (New York: East River Press, 1975), 42.

24. Especially Benjamin's "On Some Motifs," 188–89 (more so than in the "Petite histoire de la photographie," which was written earlier); and Merleau-Ponty, "Eye and Mind," 185–88; EM, 144–48.

25. This is Vincent Descombe's argument in *Le même et l'autre: Quarante-cinq ans de philosophie française (1933–1978)* (Paris: Minuit, 1979), 219–21.

26. On the heretofore unfulfilled request for universality in aesthetics, see Theodor W. Adorno, *Frühe Einleitung* (1970), French translation by Marc Jimenez and Eliane Kaufholz, *Autour de la théorie esthétique: Paralipomena, introduction première* (Paris: Klincksieck, 1976), 109–45. The situation can be summarized in two sentences: "No theory, not even aesthetic theory, can do without elements of universality" (119); and "The universal is the scandal of art" (134).

27. Benjamin, "One Some Motifs," 161.

28. Ibid.

29. Adorno, *Aesthetische Theorie* (1970), French translation by Marc Jimenez, *Théorie esthétique* (Paris: Klincksieck, 1974), 58.

30. Raymond Federman, "Voices within Voices," in Michel Benamou and C. Caramello, eds., *Performance in Postmodern Culture* (Milwaukee and Madison: Center for Twentieth-Century Studies and Coda Press, 1977), 159–98.

31. Adorno, *Introduction première*, 143; *Negative Dialectics* (1966), trans. E. B. Ashton (New York: Seabury Press, 1973).

32. "This," wrote Benjamin, "would be a peak achievement of the intellect. It would turn the incident into a moment that has been lived [*Erlebnis*]." "On Some Motifs," 165.
33. Paul Cézanne, *Correspondence*, ed. J. Rewald (Paris: Grasset, 1937), 283 (letter to his son, 12 August 1906). The word "*relations*" should be understood in the sense of forms of support by powerful persons.

Chapter 20
Wayne J. Froman, Action Painting and the World-as-Picture

1. H. W. Petzet, "Preetorius und Heidegger über abstrakte Kunst," *Universitas* 8 Jg. (Stuttgart, 1953), cited by Otto Pöggeler in "Heidegger Today," in *Martin Heidegger: On Europe and America*, ed. E. G. Ballard and C. E. Scott.
2. Martin Heidegger, "The Age of the World Picture," trans. William Lovitt, in *The Question Concerning Technology and Other Essays* (New York: Harper and Row, 1977), 124.
3. Ibid., 119.
4. Maurice Merleau-Ponty, "Eye and Mind," trans. Carleton Dallery, in *The Primacy of Perception*, ed. James M. Edie (Evanston: Northwestern University Press, 1964), 174; reprinted in this volume, 121–49.
5. PrP, 176; EM, 136.
6. PrP, 177; EM, 137.
7. Heidegger, "Poetically Man Dwells," in *Poetry, Language, Thought*, trans. Albert Hofstadter (New York: Harper and Row, 1971), 218.
8. PrP, 184; EM, 143.
9. PrP, 184; EM, 143; emphasis mine.
10. For an extended discussion of "reversibility," see my *Merleau-Ponty: Language and the Act of Speech* (Bucknell University Press, 1982).
11. Harold Rosenberg, "The Concept of Action," in *Artworks and Packages* (New York: Dell, 1969), 226.
12. Ibid., 217.
13. " 'Only a God Can Save Us Now': An Interview with Martin Heidegger," trans. David Schendler, *Graduate Faculty Philosophy Journal* 6, no. 1, 26.

Chapter 21
Robert Burch, On the Topic of Art and Truth: Merleau-Ponty, Heidegger, and the Transcendental Turn

1. This paper was first presented to a meeting of the Merleau-Ponty Circle, 28 Sept. 1985, at Southern Illinois University, Carbondale, Illinois, under the title "A Reflection on Art and Truth: Merleau-Ponty and Heidegger." It appears here with only slight revisions and additions.

2. Martin Heidegger, "Brief über den Humanismus," in *Wegmarken* (Frankfurt: Klostermann, 1967), 167.

3. A rationale for this equation of philosophical and ontological truth is provided passim in the discussion to follow. Suffice it for now to note that the formulation is explicitly Heideggerian. "We now claim: Being is the genuine and singular theme of philosophy. . . . Philosophy . . . is ontology" (*Grundprobleme der Phänomenologie*, [Frankfurt: Klostermann, 1975], 15). In one of his later "working notes," Merleau-Ponty writes: "Philosophy is the study of the *Vorhabe* of Being" to be understood as "Being speaking in us" (*Le visible et l'invisible*, ed. Claude Lefort, [Paris: Gallimard, 1964], 257, 250).

4. Immanuel Kant, *Kritik der reinen Vernunft*, ed. R. Schmidt (Hamburg: Felix Meiner, 1956), 19–20; B xvi.

5. "Transcendental philosophy," insofar as it "treats of the understanding and of reason itself in a system of all concepts and fundamental principles which relate to objects in general" is itself *"Ontologia"* (Kant, *Kritik der reinen Vernunft*, 758; B 873).

6. Immanuel Kant, *Gesammelte Schriften*, Preussische Akademie hrsg. (Berlin, 1902–38), vol. 4, 467, n. 1.

7. Kant, *Kritik der reinen Vernunft*, 12; A xx.

8. Ibid., 374; B 404.

9. Ibid., 176b; B 158.

10. Ibid., 18; B xiii.

11. Ibid., 18; B xiv.

12. Ibid., 12; A xx.

13. Kant, *Gesammelte Schriften*, vol. 4, 451.

14. Kant, *Kritik der reinen Vernunft*, 272ff.; B 274ff.

15. F. W. J. von Schelling, *Ausgewählte Werke* (Stuttgart und Augsburg: Cotta, 1856–61), vol. 1, part 3, 627.

16. Ibid., 619.

17. Ibid., 624.

18. Ibid., 618.

19. Ibid., 629.

20. Ibid., 349.

21. Ibid., 627.

22. See the posthumously published Jena lectures, *Philosophie der Kunst* (1802–4) in F. W. J. von Schelling, *Ausgewählte Werke*, vol. 1, part 5.

23. G. W. F. Hegel, *Phänomenologie des Geistes*, ed. J. Hoffmeister, 6 Aufl. (Hamburg: Felix Meiner, 1952), 26.

24. Ibid., 19.

25. G. W. F. Hegel, *Vorlesungen über die Ästhetik* (Frankfurt: Suhrkamp, 1970), vol. 1, 151.

26. Ibid., 139.

27. Ibid., 141.

28. Ibid., 144.

29. Ibid., 141.

30. G. W. F. Hegel, *Wissenschaft der Logik* (Hamburg: Felix Meiner, 1963), vol. 1, 94.

31. G. W. F. Hegel, *Enzyklopädie der philosophischen Wissenschaften* (Frankfurt: Suhrkamp, 1970), vol. 1, 339, section 187, zus.

32. Ibid., vol. 2, 34–35, section 250.

33. Ibid., vol. 2, 28, section 248.

34. Ibid., vol. 1, 372–73, section 215.

35. Maurice Merleau-Ponty, "Un inédit de Maurice Merleau-Ponty," *Revue de Métaphysique et de Morale* 4 (1962), 404–5.

36. Maurice Merleau-Ponty, "L'oeil et l'esprit" (Paris: Gallimard, 1964), 12.

37. Maurice Merleau-Ponty, *Phénoménologie de la perception* (Paris: Gallimard, 1945), i.

38. Maurice Merleau-Ponty, *Le visible et l'invisible* (Paris: Gallimard, 1964), 173.

39. Ibid., 228–29.

40. Ibid., 253.

41. Ibid., 261.

42. Merleau-Ponty, "L'oeil et l'esprit," 19.

43. Merleau-Ponty, *Le visible et l'invisible*, 173.

44. Ibid., 179.

45. Ibid.

46. Ibid., 224.

47. Ibid., 171.

48. Ibid., 251.

49. Ibid., 328.

50. Ibid., 257.

51. Ibid., 250–51.

52. Ibid., 224.

53. Merleau-Ponty, "L'oeil et l'esprit," 13.

54. Ibid., 91.

55. Ibid., 14.

56. Merleau-Ponty, *Le visible et l'invisible*, 251.

57. Maurice Merleau-Ponty, *La prose du monde*, ed. Claude Lefort (Paris: Gallimard, 1969), 92.

58. Merleau-Ponty, "L'oeil et l'esprit," 88, 24.

59. Ibid., 87.

60. Ibid., 59.

61. Merleau-Ponty, *La prose du monde*, 71.

62. Ibid., 66.

63. Merleau-Ponty, "L'oeil et l'esprit," 22.

64. Ibid., 88.

65. Ibid., 81.

66. Maurice Merleau-Ponty, "Le primat de la perception et ses conséquences philosophiques," *Bulletin de la Société Française de Philosophie* 49 (1947), 144.

67. Merleau-Ponty, "L'oeil et l'esprit," 90.

68. Ibid.
69. Ibid., 91.
70. Merleau-Ponty, *La prose du monde*, 68.
71. Merleau-Ponty, "L'oeil et l'esprit," 91.
72. Merleau-Ponty, *Le visible et l'invisible*, 320.
73. Ibid., 312.
74. Ibid., 318, 321.
75. Ibid., 319.
76. Ibid., 312.
77. Ibid., 319.
78. Ibid., 223.
79. Martin Heidegger, *Holzwege*, 5 Aufl. (Frankfurt: Klostermann, 1972), 59.
80. Merleau-Ponty, *Le visible et l'invisible*, 319.
81. Martin Heidegger, *Sein und Zeit*, 12 Aufl. (Tübingen: Niemeyer, 1972), 38.
82. Merleau-Ponty, *Le visible et l'invisible*, 277.
83. G. W. F. Hegel, *Enzyklopädie der philosophischen Wissenschaften*, vol. 1, 203, section 95. Cf. Schelling, *Ausgewählte Werke*, vol. 1, part 2, 67.
84. Schelling, *Ausgewählte Werke*, vol. 1, part 5, 369.
85. Merleau-Ponty, *Le visible et l'invisible*, 319.
86. Ibid., 306–7.
87. Martin Heidegger, *Metaphysiche Anfangsgründe der Logik* (Frankfurt: Klostermann, 1978), 194–95. Cf. *Sein und Zeit*, 183.
88. This recalls an issue that was deferred at the outset (sup., n. 1). To those whose interest in the art/truth relation begins not from philosophy but with a concrete involvement with works, the *philosophical* valorization of particular sorts of works might well be seen to close off genuine consideration of the actual experience of works. Both Merleau-Ponty and Heidegger suggest a distinction between "beginnings" and "origins" and locate the truth of the former in the latter (see, e.g., Martin Heidegger, *Hölderlins Hymen "Germanien" und "der Rhein"* [Frankfurt: Klostermann, 1980], 3–4, and Merleau-Ponty, *Le visible et l'invisible*, passim, esp. 219, 320–21). With this strategy, each in his own way presumes to disclose an original "truth" that pertains at once both to the work of art and to the essence of experience. Accordingly, whatever in general might count as a "work" or in particular count as a work having special "aesthetic" significance, or whatever aesthetic concepts, definitions and analyses in the narrower sense might be brought into play in a theory of art, is in principle decided in advance from the perspective of the ontological *Ursprungsklärung*. It is in these terms that the force, affective or otherwise, with which a work may strike us is in principle to be understood. Being consecrated in the name of truth, the work of art may gain thereby in cultural value; but in the event it may well lose a voice of its own. In this regard, artistic souls may discover too late that, as the saying goes, they can walk with the philosophical devil only to the first bridge.
89. Heidegger, *Holzwege*, 60.

90. Heidegger, "Zur Seinsfrage," in *Wegmarken*, 235.

91. Cf. Martin Heidegger, *Kant und das Problem der Metaphysik*, 4 Aufl. (Frankfurt: Klostermann, 1973), 25.

92. Martin Heidegger, *Zur Sache des Denkens* (Tübingen: Niemeyer, 1969), 28.

93. Heidegger, *Sein und Zeit*, 183. Cf. *Metaphysiche Anfangsgründe der Logik*, 194–95.

94. Heidegger, *Sein und Zeit*, 25.

95. Thus, for example, Heidegger's invocation of Klee's *Heilige aus einem Fenster* and *Tod und Feuer* at the outset of this meditation does not serve, as it might have for Merleau-Ponty, to bring those carnal origins into view, but serves, at least as Merleau-Ponty might see it, to legitimate a thinking that abstracts from them further.

96. Martin Heidegger, "Vom Wesen der Wahrheit," in *Wegmarken*, 89.

97. H.-G. Gadamer, *Kleine Schriften* (Tübingen: J. C. B. Mohr, 1967), 74.

98. Martin Heidegger, "Brief über den 'Humanismus,' " in *Wegmarken*, 168.

99. Heidegger, "Zur Seinsfrage," in *Wegmarken*, 235.

100. Kant, *Gesammelte Schriften*, vol. 4, 367.

Selected Bibliography

Adriani, Gotz. *Cézanne Watercolors*. Trans. Russell M. Stockman. New York: Harry N. Abrams, Inc., 1983.

Barr, Alfred H. *Matisse: His Art and His Public*. New York: The Museum of Modern Art, 1951.

Bate, Michele. "The Phenomenologist as Art Critic: Merleau-Ponty and Cézanne." *The British Journal of Aesthetics* 14 (Autumn 1974), 344–50.

Behnke, Elizabeth A. "At the Service of the Sonata: Music Lessons with Merleau-Ponty." *Somatics* 4, no. 2 (1983), 32–34. Reprinted in *Merleau-Ponty: Critical Essays*. Ed. Henry Pietersma. Washington, D.C.: The University Press of America, 1990. 23–29.

Blanchot, Maurice. "Le musée, l'art et le temps." *Critique* 34 (December 1950), 195–208.

Boschetti, Anna. *The Intellectual Enterprise: Sartre and "Les Temps Modernes."* Trans. Richard C. McCleary. Evanston: Northwestern University Press, 1988.

Bree, Germaine. *Camus and Sartre: Crisis and Commitment*. New York: Dell Publishing, 1972.

Capalbo, Creusa. "L'historicité chez Merleau-Ponty." *Revue Philosophique de Louvain* 73 (August 1975), 511–35.

Casey, Edward S. "Sartre on Imagination." *The Philosophy of Jean-Paul Sartre*. Ed. Paul Arthur Schlipp. The Library of Living Philosophers. Vol. 16. La Salle: Open Court, 1981. 139–66.

Certeau, Michel de. "The Madness of Vision." Trans. Michael B. Smith. *Enclitic* 7, no. 1 (University of Minnesota) (Spring 1983), 24. Cf. "La folie de la vision." *Esprit* 66 (June 1982), 89.

Charlesworth, James H. "Reflections on Merleau-Ponty's Phenomenological Description of 'Word.'" *Philosophy and Phenomenological Research* 30 (June 1970), 609–13.

Charron, Ghyslain. "Du langage: La linguistique de Martinet et la phénoménologie de Merleau-Ponty." *Revue de l'Université d'Ottawa* 40 (April–June 1970), 260–84.

Claudel, Paul. *Art poétique. Oeuvre poétique*. Paris: Gallimard, 1957.

Cowley, Fraser. "L'expression et la parole d'après Merleau-Ponty." *Dialogue* 5, no. 3 (December 1966), 360–72.

Crowther, Paul. "Merleau-Ponty: Perception into Art." *The British Journal of Aesthetics* 22 (Spring 1982), 138–49.

Cruikskank, John. "Philosophie et littérature." *Philosophie et Litérature*. Deuxième colloque de la Société Britannique de Philosophie de langue française. Hull: Fretwells Ltd., 1963.

Dallery, Robert Carleton. "Philosophy as Integrative Speech. Studies in Plato and Merleau-Ponty, with an Appendix: A Translation of Merleau-Ponty's *L'oeil et l'esprit*." Doctoral Dissertation, Yale University, 1968. *Dissertation Abstracts* 30, Sept.–Oct. 1969.

Daly, James. "Merleau-Ponty's Concept of Phenomenology of Language." *St. Louis Quarterly* 4 (1966), 325–42.

Derrida, Jacques. "The Time of a Thesis: Punctuations." *Philosophy in France Today*. Ed. Alan Montefiore. Cambridge: Cambridge University Press, 1983. 34–50.

Dillon, Martin. "*Eye and Mind*: The Intertwining of Vision and Thought." *Man and World* 13 (1980), 155–71.

———. *Merleau-Ponty's Ontology*. Bloomington: Indiana University Press, 1988.

Dolgov, K. M. "The Philosophy and Aesthetics of Maurice Merleau-Ponty." *Soviet Studies in Philosophy* 14 (Winter 1975–76), 67–92.

Dufrenne, Mikel. *The Phenomenology of Aesthetic Experience*. Trans. Edward S. Casey. Evanston: Northwestern University Press, 1973.

———. "Eye and Mind." *In the Presence of the Sensuous*. Ed. Mark Roberts and Dennis Gallagher. Humanities Press, 1987. 69–74.

Dupriez, B. *L'étude des styles ou la commutation en littérature*. Paris-Montreal-Bruxelles: Didier, 1969.

Edie, James M. "Expression and Metaphor." *Philosophy and Phenomenological Research* 23, no. 4 (June 1963), 538–61.

Ehrmann, Jacques Etienne, ed. *Structuralism*. New York: Doubleday, 1970.

Fabre-Luce, Anne. "Le devenir des signes." *La Quinzaine Littéraire* 85 (15–31 Dec. 1969), 22–24 (apropos of *La prose du monde*).

Faye, Jean-Pierre. "Interphones et entrelacs." *Tel Quel* 20 (Winter 1965), 84–90.

Flynn, Bernard Charles. "Textuality and the Flesh: Derrida and Merleau-Ponty." *Journal of the British Society for Phenomenology* 15, no. 2 (May 1984), 164–77.

Fóti, Véronique M. "Painting and the Re-Organization of Philosophical Thought in Merleau-Ponty." *Philosophy Today* 24 (Summer 1980), 114–20.

———. "The Dimension of Color." *International Studies in Philosophy* 22, no. 3 (1990), 13–28.

Foucault, Michel. "Las Meninas." *The Order of Things: An Archaeology of the Human Sciences*. Translation of *Les mots et les choses*. New York: Random House, 1970. 3–16.

———. "The Prose of the World." *Diogenes* 53 (Spring 1966), 17–37.

———. *This is Not a Pipe: With Illustrations and Letters by René Magritte*. Trans. and ed. James Harkness. Berkeley: University of California Press, 1983.

Froman, Wayne. "Action Painting and the World as Picture." *Journal of Aesthetics and Art Criticism* 46 (Summer 1988), 469–75.

Fry, Roger. *Cézanne: A Study of His Development*. New York: Macmillan, 1927.

Gasche, Rodolphe. "Deconstruction as Criticism." *Glyph* 6. Baltimore: The Johns Hopkins University Press, 1979. 177–215.

Geraets, Theodore F. *Vers une nouvelle philosophie transcendentale: La genèse de la philosophie de Maurice Merleau-Ponty jusqu'à la "Phénoménologie de la Perception."* The Hague: Martinus Nijhoff, 1971.

Gillan, Garth. "In the Folds of the Flesh: Structure and Meaning." *The Horizons of the Flesh: Critical Perspectives on the Thought of Merleau-Ponty.* Ed. Garth Gillan. Carbondale: Southern Illinois University Press, 1972.

Gombrich, E. H. "Malraux's Philosophy of Art in Historical Perspective." *Malraux: Life and Work.* Ed. Martine de Courcel. New York: Harcourt, Brace, Jovanovich, 1976.

Green, André. "Du comportement à la chair: Itinéraire de Merleau-Ponty." *Critique* 211 (December 1964), 1017–42. (Special number devoted to Merleau-Ponty entitled, "Presence de Merleau-Ponty.")

Grene, Marjorie. "The Aesthetic Dialogue of Sartre and Merleau-Ponty." *Journal of the British Society for Phenomenology* 1 (May 1970), 59–72.

———. "The Sense of Things." *The Journal of Aesthetics and Art Criticism* 38 (Summer 1980), 377-90.

Hall, Harrison. "Painting and Perceiving." *The Journal of Aesthetics and Art Criticism* 39 (Spring 1981), 291–95.

Heidegger, Martin. "Letter on Humanism." *Martin Heidegger: Basic Writings.* Ed. David Farrell Krell. New York: Harper and Row, 1977. 193–242.

———. "The Origin of the Work of Art." *Martin Heideger: Basic Writings.* Ed. David Farrell Krell. New York: Harper and Row, 1977. 149–92.

Ihde, Don. "Language and Two Phenomenologies." *Southern Journal of Philosophy* 8 (Winter 1970), 399–408.

Ingarden, Roman. *The Cognition of the Literary Work of Art.* Trans. R. A. Crowley and K. R. Olson. Evanston: Northwestern University Press, 1973.

Johnson, Galen A. "Merleau-Ponty's Early Aesthetics of Historical Being: The Case of Cézanne." *Research in Phenomenology* 17 (October 1987), 211–25.

———. "The Colors of Fire: Depth and Desire in Merleau-Ponty's *Eye and Mind.*" *The Journal of the British Society for Phenomenology.* Forthcoming, 1993.

———. "Desire and Invisibility in the Ontology of *Eye and Mind*: Some Remarks on Merleau-Ponty's Spirituality." *Phaenomenologica.* Kluwer Academic Publishers. *Merleau-Ponty in Contemporary Perspective.* Ed. P. Burke and J. Van der Veken. 1993. 85–96.

———. "Generosity and Forgetting in the History of Being: Merleau-Ponty and Nietzsche." *Continental Philosophy.* Vol. 5, *Questioning Foundations.* Ed. Hugh J. Silverman. New York: Routledge, 1993. 196–212.

———. "Husserl and Merleau-Ponty: History, Language and Truth." *Merleau-Ponty: Critical Essays.* Ed. Henry Pietersma. Washington, D.C.: University Press of America, 1990. 197–217.

———. "Painting, Nostalgia, and Metaphysics." *Bulletin de la Société Américaine de Philosophie de Langue Française* 5, no. 1 (Spring 1993), 55–70.

Johnson, Galen A. and Smith, Michael B., eds. *Ontology and Alterity in Merleau-Ponty*. Evanston: Northwestern University Press, 1990.

Jones, Edwin. *Reading the Book of Nature: A Phenomenological Study of Creative Expression in Science and Painting*. Athens: Ohio University Press, 1989.

Kaelin, Eugene. *An Existentialist Aesthetics: The Theories of Sartre and Merleau-Ponty*. Madison: The University of Wisconsin Press, 1962.

――――. *Art and Existence: A Phenomenological Aesthetics*. Lewisburg: Bucknell University Press, 1970.

Kagan, Andrew. *Paul Klee/Art and Music*. Ithaca: Cornell University Press, 1983.

Kaufmann, Pierre. "De la vision picturale au désir de peindre." *Critique* 211 (December 1964), 1047–64. (Special issue devoted to Merleau-Ponty.)

Klee, Paul. *The Thinking Eye*. Vol. 1 of *Klee's Journals*. New York: George Wittenborn, 1961.

――――. "1924 Lecture at Jena." *Paul Klee: His Life and Work in Documents*. Ed. Felix Klee. New York: George Braziller, 1962. 176–77.

Klein, Robert. "Peinture moderne et et phénoménologie: A propos de *L'oeil et l'esprit*." *Critique* 191 (April 1963), 336ff.

Kwant, Remy C. *From Phenomenology to Metaphysics. The Later Work of Merleau-Ponty*. Pittsburgh: Duquesne University Press, 1966.

――――. *The Phenomenology of Expression*. Pittsburgh: Duquesne University Press, 1970.

Lagueux, Maurice. "Merleau-Ponty et la linguistique de Saussure." *Dialogue* 4, no. 3 (December 1965), 351–64.

Lanigan, Richard L. "Rhetorical Criticism: An Interpretation of Maurice Merleau-Ponty." *Philosophy and Rhetoric* 2, no. 2 (Spring 1969), 61–71.

――――. "Merleau-Ponty's Phenomenology of Communication." *Philosophy Today* 14, no. 2 (Summer 1970), 79–88.

Lapointe, François H. "Selected Bibliography on Art and Aesthetics in Merleau-Ponty." *Philosophy Today* 17 (Winter 1973), 292–96.

Lefeuvre, Michel. "Musique et peinture ou Lévi-Strauss et Merleau-Ponty." *Etudes* 140 (May 1974), 727–35.

Lefort, Claude. "Bitran ou la question de l'oeil." *Sur une colonne absente: Ecrits autour de Merleau-Ponty*. Paris: Gallimard, 1978. 176–213.

――――. "L'idée d'être brut et d'esprit sauvage." *Les Temps Modernes* 17, nos. 184–85 (October 1961), 255–86.

――――. "Introduction." *La prose du monde*. Paris: Gallimard, 1969. i–xiv.

Lévi-Strauss, Claude. "De quelques rencontres." *L'Arc* (Aix-en-Provence) 46 (1971), 43–47.

Levine, Stephen K. "Merleau-Ponty's Philosophy of Art." *Man and World* 2, no. 3 (August 1969), 438–52.

Lewis, Phillip E. "Merleau-Ponty and the Phenomenology of Language." *Yale French Studies* 36–37 (1964–65), 19–40.

Lyotard, Jean-François. *Discours, figure*. 4th ed. Paris: Klincksieck, 1985.

――――. *Phenomenology*. Trans. Brian Beakley. Albany: SUNY Press, 1991.

――――. "Philosophy and Painting in the Age of Experimentation." Trans. M. Brewer and D. Brewer. *Camera Obscura* 12 (1984), 110–25.

————. *The Postmodern Condition*. Trans. G. Bennington and B. Massumi. Manchester: Manchester University Press, 1984.

Madison, Gary. *The Phenomenology of Merleau-Ponty: A Search for the Limits of Consciousness*. Athens: Ohio University Press, 1981.

————. "Merleau-Ponty and Postmodernity." *The Hermeneutics of Postmodernity: Figures and Themes*. Bloomington: Indiana University Press, 1988.

Magritte, Rene. "Letter to Alphonse de Waehlens (28 April 1962)." *Magritte: Ideas and Images*. Ed. Harry Torczyner. Trans. Richard Miller. Harry N. Abrams, Inc., 1977. 55.

Major, Jean-Louis. "Pensée concrète, art abstrait." *Dialogue* 1, no. 2 (1962), 188–201.

————. "Le philosophe comme critique littéraire." *Dialogue* 4, no. 2 (September 1965), 230–42.

Malraux, Andre. *The Voices of Silence*. Trans. Stuart Gilbert. Princeton: Princeton University Press, 1978. *Les Voix du Silence*. Paris: Pléiade, 1951.

Mallin, Samuel B. "Chiasm, Line and Art." *Merleau-Ponty: Critical Essays*. Ed. Henry Pietersma. Washington, D.C.: The University Press of America, 1990. 219–51.

Mazis, Glen A. "*La chair et l'imaginaire*: The Developing Role of Imagination in Merleau-Ponty's Philosophy." *Philosophy Today* 32, no. 4 (Spring 1988), 30–42.

McCleary, Richard Calverton. "Translator's Preface." *Signs*. Evanston: Northwestern University Press, 1964. ix–xxxii.

Merleau-Ponty, Maurice. "L'imagination." *Journal de Psychologie Normale et Pathologique* 33, nos. 9–10 (Nov.–Dec. 1936), 756–61. Trans. Michael B. Smith in *Texts and Dialogues: Merleau-Ponty*. 108–14.

————. *Les philosophes célèbres*. Paris: Editions d'Art, Lucien Mazenod, 1956.

————. "Philosophy and Non-Philosophy Since Hegel." Ed. Claude Lefort. *Textures*, nos. 8 and 9 (1984) and nos. 10 and 11 (1975). Trans. Hugh Silverman in *Telos* 29 (1976), 43–105.

————. "The Experience of Others (1951–42)." Trans. Fred Evans and Hugh J. Silverman. *Review of Existential Psychology and Psychiatry* 18, nos. 1, 2, and 3: "Merleau-Ponty and Psychology" (1982–83), 33–63.

————. *Texts and Dialogues*. Ed. Hugh J. Silverman and James Barry, Jr. Atlantic Highlands: Humanities Press, 1991.

For additional writings by Merleau-Ponty, consult the list of abbreviations in the prefatory materials.

Michaux, Henri. "Aventures de lignes." Preface to the French translation of Will Grohmann, *Paul Klee*. Trans. Jean Descoullayes and Jean Philippon. Paris: Flinker, 1954. 5–8.

Mohanty, J. N. "Husserl's Theory of Meaning." *Husserl: Expositions and Appraisals*. Ed. Frederick Elliston and Peter McCormick. Notre Dame: University of Notre Dame Press, 1977.

Mongin, Olivier. "Depuis Lascaux." *Esprit*, no. 66 (June 1982), 67–76.

Munchow, Michael. "Painting and Invisibility—Merleau-Ponty's Line." *Journal of the British Society for Phenomenology*. Forthcoming, 1993.

Olkowski, Dorothea. "Merleau-Ponty's Freudianism: From the Body of Consciousness to the Body of Flesh." *Review of Existential Psychology and Psychiatry* 18, nos. 1, 2, and 3: "Merleau-Ponty and Psychology" (1982–83), 97–116.

Place, James Gordon. "Merleau-Ponty and the Spirit of Painting." *Philosophy Today* 17 (Winter 1973), 280–90.

———. "The Painting and the Natural Thing in the Philosophy of Merleau-Ponty." *Cultural Hermeneutics* 4 (November 1976), 75–92.

Poole, Roger C. "Indirect Communications. 2. Merleau-Ponty and Lévi-Strauss." *New Blackfriars* 47, no. 555 (1966), 594–604.

Raymond, Marcel. "Culture ouverte et langage poétique." *Travaux de linguistique et de littérature* 11, no. 2. Centre de philologie et de littérature romanes de l'Université de Strasbourg. Strasbourg, 1964.

Reboul, Oliver. "Imaginer et percevoir: Alain, la gestalttheorie et Merleau-Ponty." *L'homme et ses passions d'après Alain*. Paris: Presses Universitaires de France, 1968. 106–14.

Rewald, John. "Preface" to *Joachim Gasquet's Cézanne*. Trans. Christopher Pemberton. London: Thames and Hudson, 1991. 7–13.

Rey, Dominique. *La perception du peintre et le problème de l'être: Essai sur l'esthétique et l'ontologie de Maurice Merleau-Ponty*. Thèse presentée à la Faculté des Lettres de l'Université de Fribourg/Suisse pour obtenir le grade de docteur (1978).

Ricoeur, Paul. "Hommage à Merleau-Ponty." *Esprit*, no. 296 (1961), 1115–20.

———. "New Developments in Phenomenology in France: The Phenomenology of Language." *Social Research* 34, no. 1 (1967), 1–30.

Robinet, André. *Merleau-Ponty, sa vie, son oeuvre, avec un exposé de sa philosophie.* (Collection "Philosophes.") Paris: Presses Universitaires de France, 1963. 2d ed. revised and updated, 1970.

Said, Edward K. "Labyrinth of Incarnation: The Essays of Maurice Merleau-Ponty." *Kenyon Review* 29, no. 1 (January 1967), 54–68.

Sartre, Jean-Paul. *The Psychology of Imagination*. Trans. Bernard Frechtman. New York: Philosophical Library, 1948.

———. "Merleau-Ponty." *Situations*. Trans. Benita Eisler. Greenwich: Fawcett Publications, 1965.

———. *Literature and Existentialism*. Trans. Bernard Frechtman. Secaucus: The Citadel Press, 1980.

Schmidt, James. *Maurice Merleau-Ponty: Between Phenomenology and Structuralism.* New York: St. Martin's Press, 1985.

Shapiro, Meyer. *Paul Cézanne*. New York: Harry N. Abrams, Inc., 1952.

Silverman, Hugh J. "Cézanne's Mirror Stage." *Journal of Aesthetics and Art Criticism* 40, no. 4 (Summer 1982), 369–79.

———. "Merleau-Ponty and Derrida: Writing on Writing." *Ontology and Alterity in Merleau-Ponty*. Ed. Galen A. Johnson and Michael B. Smith. Evanston: Northwestern University Press, 1990. 130–41.

Singer, Linda. "Merleau-Ponty on the Concept of Style." *Man and World* 14 (1981), 153–63.

————. *The Mystery of Vision and the Miracle of Painting: A Critical Examination of Merleau-Ponty's Philosophy of the Visual Arts.* Doctoral Dissertation, State University of New York, Binghamton, 1991.

Slaughter, Jr., Thomas F. "Some Remarks on Merleau-Ponty's Essay 'Cézanne's Doubt.'" *Man and World* 12 (1979), 61–69.

Smith, Colin. "Merleau-Ponty and Structuralism." *Journal of the British Society for Phenomenology* 3 (October 1971), 46–52.

Smith, Michael. "L'esthétique de Merleau-Ponty." *Les Etudes Philosophiques* 1 (1988), 73–98.

Taminiaux, Jacques. "The Thinker and the Painter." *Merleau-Ponty Vivant.* Ed. M. C. Dillon. Albany: SUNY Press, 1991. 195–212.

Tillette, Xavier. *Maurice Merleau-Ponty ou la mesure de l'homme.* Paris: Seghers, 1970. Collection "Philosophes de tous les temps," no. 64.

Van Haecht, Louis. "Beauté visible et métaphysique." *Revue Philosophique de Louvain* (February 1962), 100–117.

Vollard, Ambroise. *Cézanne.* New York: Dover Publications, 1984.

Waelhens, Alphonse de. *Une philosophie de l'ambiguïté. L'existentialisme de Maurice Merleau-Ponty.* Louvain: Publications Universitaires de Louvain, 1st ed. 1951; 3d rev. ed. 1968.

————. "Merleau-Ponty philosophe de la peinture." *Revue de Métaphysique et de Morale* 67, no. 4 (Oct.–Dec. 1962), 431–49.

Watson, Stephen. "Merleau-Ponty and Foucault: De-aestheticization of the Work of Art." *Philosophy Today* 28 (Summer 1984), 148–67.

————. "Merleau-Ponty's Involvement with Saussure." *Continental Philosophy in America.* Ed. Hugh J. Silverman. Pittsburgh: Duquesne University Press, 1983.

Wechsler, Judith. *Cézanne in Perspective.* Englewood Cliffs: Prentice Hall, 1975.

Williams, Forrest. "Cézanne and French Phenomenology." *The Journal of Aesthetics and Art Criticism* 12 (June 1954), 481–92.